JOU

D0774897

ROBYN DAVIDSON was born in 1950 in a small Queensland country town. She is the author of *Tracks*, the account of her epic journey across the Australian desert with four camels, which won the 1980 Thomas Cook Travel Book Award; a collection of essays, *Travelling Light*; a novel, *Ancestors*, which was published in 1989 and was shortlisted for the Premier's Award in Australia; and *Desert Places*, the story of her travels with an Indian nomad, which was published in 1996 and was shortlisted for the Thomas Cook Travel Book Award. She has travelled extensively throughout the world and currently lives in Australia, London and India.

★   ★   ★

'Undoubtedly a collection of extraordinarily fresh and exciting writing
. . . just goes to show how splendid travel writing can be'
Oldie

'As Robyn Davidson's robust anthology reveals, travel writing
is a protean and remarkably resilient form that lurks behind many
disguises . . . You'd have to have a heart of stone not to enjoy *Journeys*.
From the familiar (Auden in Iceland and Hunter S. Thompson in the
Nevada desert with his stoned lawyer) to the exotic (the angular
staccato of Senwosret I, writing two millennia ago), the collection
is a delight. Some of the pieces approach the sublime.'
Spectator

'In *Journeys* [Robyn Davidson] gives house room to "all kinds of
characters you would never think of as travel writers" . . .
This is travel as state of mind.'
Daily Telegraph

'Her selection is invigorating: it succeeds absolutely'
The Times

'It makes a refreshing change to pick up some of the most memorable travel writing of past centuries and picture the impression writers such as Livingstone or James Cook must have made on readers who could barely imagine the existence of far-flung places.'
Observer

'The links and juxtapositions are wonderful'
Guardian

'It amounts to a who's who of travel writing since the genre was invented, including Hemingway, Auden, Chatwin, Lessing, Katherine Mansfield, a cast of almost 100, the predictable and the astounding, the execrable and the exquisite. You will be reading it forever.'
Glasgow Herald

'Instead of travellers disconnectedly traversing landscapes we get all sorts of people in all sorts of situations, and emotional states, truly engaged in inner as well as outer explorations . . . [A] wonderful, constantly surprising book which, while it travels across continents and timelines, is never afraid to arrive at the truth.'
Sunday Tribune

'An enthralling off-the-beaten-tracks anthology . . . I recommend Robyn Davidson's *Journeys* as an anthology of literary excellence.'
Irish Times

JOURNEYS

An Anthology

EDITED BY ROBYN DAVIDSON

PICADOR

First published 2001 by Picador as *The Picador Book of Journeys*

This edition published 2002 by Picador
an imprint of Pan Macmillan Ltd
Pan Macmillan, 20 New Wharf Road, London N1 9RR
Basingstoke and Oxford
Associated companies throughout the world
www.panmacmillan.com

ISBN 0 330 36863 X

3 5 7 9 8 6 4 2

A CIP catalogue record for this book is available from
the British Library.

Typeset by Intype London Ltd
Printed and bound in Great Britain by
Mackays of Chatham plc, Chatham, Kent

Contents

Acknowledgements

Thank you to those genuine men of literature, Pankaj Mishra and Murray Bail, for the reading lists they've given me over the years, and for cheering me up. Both have provided useful suggestions for this anthology. Thanks to David A. for the Wallace extract; Pat K. for the *Kabloona* extract; Julie C. for the Antelme. Most of all, I'd like to express my gratitude to my editor Mary Mount for effort and tolerance beyond the call of duty.

EDITOR'S NOTE

To prevent this book from being too unwieldy, I have, where I thought appropriate, edited the text.

Introduction

Shortly after its publication in 1980 I was surprised to learn that I had written a travel book. I knew nothing about literary genres then, but felt an instinctive recoil, as if my intentions had been misunderstood. I had indeed walked alone through the deserts of my country, and I had used camels to carry my gear – pragmatic solution to lack of cash. But the geographical distances and the means by which I covered them were not, I thought, the important thing.

The book's success had bizarre and unexpected consequences. Firstly, magazine editors and tour companies offered to send me to holiday destinations in order to describe them to people 'back home' who might wish to vacation there but who, it seemed, wished to experience my experience before they felt confident enough to experience their own.

Secondly, publishers pressed me to produce another book, as similar as possible to the first. But the journey had been the unique outcome of singular causes – that was the *point*. To seek to repeat it would be to render my own life kitsch.

But once the world sticks a label on you, it takes great effort to resist conforming to it. Reality takes on the shape of a fish trap and if you are not constantly vigilant, down the funnel you go. Ten years after *Tracks* was published, I yielded. I went to India and lived with nomads. My intention was genuine enough – I was interested in transhumance and I did want to write something resembling ethnography. I would select one group, live with them over a long period of time and study them in isolation from their wider context. When it came time to write it all up, I would edit myself out of the account.

That intention was rendered ludicrous from the word go. There is no such thing as a disinterested observer (I carried my concepts with me, through which I interpreted what I saw), just as there is no such thing as a community isolated, spatially or temporally, from the greater society in which it is embedded. I also carried my own time with me – post-industrial time. I could get into a jeep and in a few hours be at a telephone booth, or in a large city – a journey which would take my companions weeks, and involve them in many physical hardships. It was not possible for me to live with them in the way I had envisaged, because I embodied that other version of time.

Both the experience and the attempt to describe it honestly, confirmed my view that the accepted models of travel writing were compromised to such a degree, that the best one could do was subvert a decadent genre.

But commerce has its own laws. If *Desert Places* didn't fit its category, *Desert Places* would have to be retailored. The book was packaged according to the exigencies of the market – exotic travel: subsection, female. (But I shall return to the assets and liabilities of sex in the field of literature a little later.)

I found I could not pass that section of bookshops without feeling obscure irritation towards the browsers I saw there, and sorry for various books I knew were stranded in the stacks, like guests fetched up at the wrong party and forbidden to leave. Nor was I alone in my aversion. There were grumblings of denial from writers you would think represented the very epicentre of the genre – Bruce Chatwin for example, or Paul Theroux. Even Claude Levi-Strauss, in his arresting introduction to *Tristes Tropiques*, confessed to hating travel books, before writing one that is literature of the highest order. To the best of my knowledge, no other genre suffered this weird allergy to itself.

And yet, the vast piles of books written by people who leave home, that I have devoured during forty years of literate life, have given me, for the most part, deep pleasure – a seeming contradiction which begs the questions: what *is* travel writing, and who gets to say so?

All taxonomies are fuzzy sets. That is, boundaries imposed on something that is really a continuum – and in these post-modern days of genre bending they are getting even fuzzier. Literary borders are permeable; books migrate. But this tendency to escape standard classification is countered by a more powerful restraining force, as if ambivalence – the space in which we can make up our own minds – is antithetical to the laws of the marketplace. Readers (or rather, buyers) are encouraged to use the travel section much as tourists are encouraged to experience holiday destinations – herded along the usual routes, all wayward peregrinations discouraged.

Take a spin around that section and you could be forgiven for thinking that the genre is so capacious as to lack meaning. Maps, tourist guides, yachting almanacs, photo essays, rock-climbing manuals, a few hoary classics and shelf upon shelf – a staggering plenitude – of contemporary travelogues, all commissioned, published and usually written with the intention of satisfying a market. It's not that such books don't deserve a place here, nor that they may not be well written and entertaining, it's that they have come to represent the genre as it is generally conceived – that is, a literature to accommodate a longing for the exotic, in an increasingly homogenized and trivialized world.

But the literature of movement covers a vastly more rich and complex range of experiences, and far from being capacious, that section of a bookshop is impoverished by omission. Out in the genre's fuzziest borders, away from its predictable destinations, you can come across all kinds of characters you would never think of as travel writers. Berlioz setting off in a stagecoach with his pistols in his lap, for example, or Nadezhda Mandelstam facing Siberian exile. Clara Schumann sledding her way through Russian snows to perform her husband's music; Kafka made queasy by the sight of naked men playing leapfrog in a nudist colony. Rousseau crossing the Alps; Gautama setting out for that most elusive destination of all – this moment, here, now. And what about the less fortunate travellers, tugged around the world by circumstances over which they have no control – slaves, soldiers and the victims of war? You would not catch them at a travel writers' party, yet their stories all fit an acceptable definition of travel writing (it is the one I have used for this collection): a non-fiction work in which the author goes from point a to point b and tells us something about it.

What makes them different from the commissioned traveloguers, is that they set out because of an inner compulsion to do so, or are driven by some form of necessity, and their tales, therefore, have the power to reconnect us with the essential. Virginia Woolf said that the art of writing 'has for backbone some fierce attachment to an idea . . . something believed in with conviction or seen with precision and thus compelling words to its shape . . .' If we accept that view, then it has to be said that the bulk of contemporary travel writing is pretty spineless.

Describing what lies beyond must be one of the oldest compulsions to story telling. Certainly it was already there at the inception of writing, and the prototype must have existed since human self-consciousness began. The metaphor of the journey is embedded in the very way in which we conceive of life – a movement from birth to death, from this world to the next, from ignorance to wisdom. In Aboriginal philosophy, its metaphorical possibilities extended to include the earth itself – Australia *is* a travel narrative. The desire or necessity to move on, has given and continues to give our world its shape.

Each epoch has reinvented its means of and reasons for travelling, and each has its own distinctive way of speaking about it. From pilgrimage to package tour; holy days to holidays. From the eighteenth-century grand tour, available only to the upper classes, to Thomas Cook and Baedeker – caterers to the masses. From the Homeric mixture of fact and fantasy, to the Enlightenment's project to collect rigorously accurate information about the new world – all have created characteristic accounts of Elsewhere.

But whatever its varying motivations and styles, the value of the literature of restlessness is located as much in the sociological – the unique insights it affords into the disruptive, restructuring activity that is history – as in the literary. This perhaps goes some way to explaining why even its best representatives seem to lack the canonical weight afforded to the classics of other genres. (Flaubert thought it a 'low form of literature' and 'the same as news items'.) But to compare *The Worst Journey in the World* with *Madame Bovary* is a fairly meaningless exercise. Each aims for a different kind of truth, and achieves a different greatness.

The genre's most recent apogee – its great age, if you like – was the nineteenth and early twentieth century, the high moment of Western imperialism. Classics occupy the centre ground of a genre, and writers like Apsley Cherry-Garrard, Mary Kingsley, Euclides da Cunha, threw a long shadow across their territory. These days, things look pretty slumped and irrelevant there at the core. Bill Buford in his introduction to the first of Granta's travel editions, said that recent travel writing reflects a 'wonderful ambiguity, somewhere between fiction and fact' – a sad reflection of the confusion of our times, in which veracity is less important than the need to show-off. Bruce Chatwin is often cited as exemplifying this new trend towards fibbing in the traveller's tale, which seems a little unfair, given that he insisted on calling *Songlines* a novel. But whereas Chatwin could fib with charm, erudition and elegance (he was a born fabulist), lesser writers just fib. Nothing happening out there in travel land? Make it up! What could be more post-modern.

There are exceptions of course. (V. S. Naipaul refers to his travel writing as 'the writing of enquiry', and he so dwarfs even the best of his peers that he could almost be placed in a category of his own.) But the exceptions are prominent because of the lowlands surrounding them.

There are manifold and complex reasons for this decay.

The slaughter of the First World War shattered confidence in Western civilization. Cherry-Garrard's chronicle of Scott's Antarctic expedition is profoundly moving, not because of his descriptions of the sufferings he and his companions endured, but because of what he reveals to us of pre-Great War minds – a species lost to time. *The Worst Journey in the World* was the last great work arising out of the heroic ideal, and it marked the beginning of the decline in the classic travel book form.

A more uneasy traveller emerges after that. Anxious, self-reflective. One begins to hear a tone of lament, for lost places, lost times. Ways of life that were thought primitive by the Victorians, were now seen to possess their own validity, might even be sources of moral or spiritual regeneration. But they were being threatened by the corruptions of the twentieth century, and there was an urgent need to record and preserve them before they all went down the drain of modernity. The empire was fraying, scientific rationalism was being questioned and there was a gathering awareness of the political implications of who gets to describe 'Other'.

To quote Levi-Strauss again: 'The first thing we see as we travel round the world is our own filth, thrown into the face of mankind.' He wrote that when ideas of here and elsewhere, self and other were less fraught with anxiety. Now, in a world in which African nomadic camel herders use mobile phones, we can no longer pretend that our time hasn't penetrated every chink of previousness.

The blame is often laid at the foot of tourism (masses obliterating classes), but it seems to me that tourism is a symptom, not the disease. The word itself dates from the late eighteenth century when people headed for the Lake District, following in the footsteps of the Romantic poets. But it wasn't until the Second World War blew the old orders asunder, that the democratization of travel really began

– one of the most significant episodes in post-war life. It is an irony that just when the ability to both travel and publish has penetrated the boundaries of class, race and sex, there should be nowhere left to 'discover'.

Today's tourism is likely to take the form of a transferral of 'here' to 'there' – chunks of home chopped off and deposited somewhere under a foreign sun, yet happily divested of foreigners.

Meanwhile 'abroad' is now situated at the very core of the familiar. Why go all the way to Egypt to see a souk when there is a perfectly good souk just down a London high street? The people in the London souk will be polyglot – immigrant citizens of the new city, as well as its older residents. In this souk, it is no longer the white man looking at (and describing) Other. Here, the Other looks defiantly back.

Yet all that social upheaval, the mixing and moving, crossing and re-crossing, has been little reflected in travel writing. It's as if the genre has not caught up with the post-colonial reality from which it springs. One would think it should collapse under the weight of its paradoxes, but quite the opposite is happening. There is a passion for travel books harking back to a previous sensibility when home and abroad, occident and orient, centre and periphery were unproblematically defined. Perhaps they are popular for the very reason that they are so deceptive. They create the illusion that there is still an uncontaminated Elsewhere to discover, a place that no longer exists, located, indeed, somewhere between 'fiction and fact'.

The nineteenth century also saw the entry of women into the genre, who co-opted it for their own purposes – usually an exultation in a new-found freedom. Before that, there were few women who could move about as they liked, even fewer who had the education to write about what happened when they did. The new conditions of the Victorian era allowed their numbers to increase exponentially, like mammals at the end of the dinosaur age. They set the tone for what came to be seen as a strongly bounded sub-genre, raising the still contentious question: is women's travel writing different from men's?

A woman sets out into a world whose public domain is organized by and for men. How far can she claim a freedom of action taken for granted by her male counterparts, knowing that she is always, and everywhere, potentially prey? Isabelle Eberhardt solved the problem by dressing as a man. Others waited to reach an age when their sex was no longer so desirable, when they could become, as it were, honorary men. Some took companions or servants with them. Most just took their chances. But it is internalized fear that is most crippling to spontaneity – the necessary reining-in, the ceaseless attention to modesty, to the body and, therefore, to the self. It is perhaps because of this self-consciousness that women's travel writing is often concerned as much with inner states as with outer objects. At its best, it can create a richness and intimacy lacking in the more so-called objective texts. But there are far too many exceptions to prove any rule. Plenty of women have written in the objective mode, just as plenty of men have used the subjective. An individual's sex will be just one factor among many in the uniqueness of his or her perceptions. Certainly as anthropologists, ethnographers and travellers women have helped to reveal the hitherto hidden half of human consciousness, but they have not been able radically to transform the genre, or to revivify it.

Travel literature was always predicated on privilege; it may always have had at least one of its roots in a desire to escape the real world rather than apprehend it better, and it has always reflected the movement of world history as seen from the perspective of the centre. But surely never before has it risked floating free of its own ground.

At the moment the 'travel' section of our bookshops is swamped by books written by a Centre describing its Antipodes. However, already that Periphery is beginning to describe itself to itself without reference to the Centre, and it will eventually journey to what was once the hub and describe that too. This about-face of the 'Other' may well be the one social phenomenon powerful enough to revitalize a clapped-out genre.

But whether it survives as a coherent category or not, as long as we are all travellers in 'this wilderness of the world', we will need to find authentic ways of telling each other what we discover there.

PROLOGUE

BHIKKHU NANAMOLI (translator)

from *'The Life of the Buddha'*, as it appears in the Pali Canon

Before my enlightenment, while I was still only an unenlightened Bodhisatta, I thought: House life is crowded and dusty; life gone forth is wide open. It is not easy, living in a household, to lead a Holy Life as utterly perfect and pure as a polished shell. Suppose I shaved off my hair and beard, put on the yellow cloth, and went forth from the house life into homelessness?

ENGLAND

Samuel Butler (1835–1902)

'Ramblings in Cheapside'

Walking the other day in Cheapside I saw some turtles in Mr Sweeting's window, and was tempted to stay and look at them. As I did so, I was struck not more by the defences with which they were hedged about, than by the fatuousness of trying to hedge that in at all which, if hedged thoroughly, must die of its own defencefulness. The holes for the head and feet through which the turtle leaks out, as it were, on to the exterior world, and through which it again absorbs the exterior world into itself – 'catching on' through them to things that are thus both turtle and not turtle at one and the same time – these holes stultify the armour and show it to have been designed by a creature with more of faithfulness to a fixed idea, and hence onesidedness, than of that quick sense of relative importances and their changes, which is the main factor of good living.

The turtle obviously had no sense of proportion; it differed so widely from myself that I could not comprehend it; and as this word occurred to me, it occurred also that until my body comprehended its body in a physical material sense, neither would my mind be able to comprehend its mind with any thoroughness. For unity of mind can only be consummated by unity of body; everything, therefore, must be in some respects both knave and fool to all that which has not eaten it, or by which it has not been eaten. As long as the turtle was in the window and I was in the street outside, there was no chance of our comprehending one another.

Nevertheless, I knew that I could get it to agree with me if I could so effectually buttonhole and fasten on to it as to eat it. Most men have an easy method with turtle soup, and I had no misgiving but that if I could bring my first premise to bear I should prove the better reasoner. My difficulty lay in this initial process, for I had not with me the argument that would alone compel Mr Sweeting to think that I ought to be allowed to convert the turtles – I mean I had no money in my pocket. No missionary enterprise can be carried on without any money at all, but even so small a sum as half a crown would, I suppose, have enabled me to bring the turtle partly round, and with many half-crowns I could in time no doubt convert the lot, for the turtle needs must go where the money drives. If, as is alleged, the world stands on a turtle, the turtle stands on money. No money, no turtle. As for money, that stands on opinion, credit, trust, faith – things that, though highly material in connection with money, are still of immaterial essence.

The steps are perfectly plain. The men who caught the turtles brought a fairly strong and definite opinion to bear upon them, that passed into action, and later on into money. They thought the turtles would come that way, and verified their opinion; on this, will and action were generated, with the result that the men turned the turtles on their backs and carried them off. Mr Sweeting touched these men with money, which is the outward and visible sign of verified opinion. The customer touches Mr Sweeting with money, Mr Sweeting touches the waiter and the cook with money. They touch the turtle with skill and verified opinion. Finally, the customer applies the clinching argument that brushes all sophisms aside, and bids the turtle stand protoplasm to protoplasm with himself, to know even as it is known.

But it must be all touch, touch, touch; skill, opinion, power, and money, passing in and out with one another in any order we like, but still link to link and touch to touch. If there is failure anywhere in respect of opinion, skill, power, or money either as regards quantity or quality, the chain can be no stronger than its weakest link, and the turtle and the clinching argument will fly asunder. Of course, if there is an initial failure in connection, through defect in any member of the chain, or of connection between the links, it will no more be attempted to bring the turtle and the clinching argument together, than it will to chain up a dog with two pieces of broken chain that are disconnected. The contact throughout must be conceived as absolute; and yet perfect contact is inconceivable by us, for on becoming perfect it ceases to be contact, and becomes essential, once for all inseverable, identity. The most absolute contact short of this is still contact by courtesy only. So here, as everywhere else, Eurydice glides off as we are about to grasp her. We can see nothing face to face; our utmost seeing is but a fumbling of blind finger-ends in an overcrowded pocket.

Presently my own blind finger-ends fished up the conclusion, that as I had neither time nor money to spend on perfecting the chain that would put me in full spiritual contact with Mr Sweeting's turtles, I had better leave them to complete their education at someone else's expense rather than mine, so I walked on towards the Bank. As I did so it struck me how continually we are met by this melting of one existence into another. The limits of the body seem well defined enough as definitions go, but definitions seldom go far. What, for example, can seem more distinct from a man than his banker or his solicitor? Yet these are commonly so much parts of him that he can no more cut them off and grow new ones, than he can grow new legs or arms; neither must he wound his solicitor; a wound in the solicitor is a very serious thing. As for his bank – failure of his bank's action may be as fatal to a man as failure of his heart. I have said nothing about the medical or spiritual adviser, but most men grow into the society that surrounds them by the help of these four main tap-roots, and not only into the world of humanity, but into the universe at large. We can, indeed, grow butchers, bakers, and greengrocers, almost *ad libitum*, but these are low developments, and correspond to skin, hair, or finger-nails. Those of us again who are not highly enough organized to have grown a solicitor or banker can generally repair the loss of whatever social organization they may possess as freely as lizards are said to grow new tails; but this with the higher social, as well as organic, developments is only possible to a very limited extent.

The doctrine of metempsychosis, or transmigration of souls – a doctrine to which the foregoing considerations are for the most part easy corollaries – crops up no matter in what direction we allow our thoughts to wander. And we meet instances of transmigration of body as well as of soul. I do not mean that both body and soul have transmigrated together, far from it; but that, as we can often recognize a transmigrated mind in an alien body, so we not less often see a body that is clearly only a transmigration, linked on to someone else's new and alien soul. We meet people every day whose bodies are evidently those of men and women long dead, but whose appearance we know through their portraits. We see them going about in omnibuses, railway carriages, and in all public places. The cards have been shuffled, and they have drawn fresh lots in life and nationalities, but anyone fairly well up in medieval and last-century portraiture knows them at a glance.

Going down once towards Italy I saw a young man in the train whom I recognized, only he seemed to have got younger. He was with a friend, and his face was in continual play, but for some little time I puzzled in vain to recollect where it was that I had seen him before. All of a sudden I remembered he was King Francis I of France. I had hitherto thought the face of this king impossible, but when I saw it in play I understood it. His great contemporary Henry VIII keeps a restaurant in Oxford Street. Falstaff drove one of the St Gothard diligences for many years, and only retired when the railway was opened. Titian once made me a pair of boots at Vicenza, and not very good ones. At Modena I had my hair cut by a young man whom I perceived to be Raffaello. The model who sat to him for his celebrated Madonnas is first lady in a confectionery establishment at Montreal. She has a little motherly pimple on the left side of her nose that is misleading at first, but on examination she is readily recognized; probably Raffaello's model had the pimple too, but Raffaello left it out – as he would.

Handel, of course, is Madame Patey. Give Madame Patey Handel's wig and clothes, and there would be no telling her from Handel. It is not only that the features and the shape of the head are the same, but there is a certain imperiousness of expression and attitude about Handel which he hardly attempts to conceal in Madame Patey. It is a curious coincidence that he should continue to be such an incomparable renderer of his own music. Pope Julius II was the late Mr Darwin. Rameses II is a blind woman now, and stands in Holborn, holding a tin mug. I never could understand why I always found myself humming 'They oppressed them with burthens' when I passed her, till one day I was looking in Mr Spooner's window in the Strand, and saw a photograph of Rameses II. Mary Queen of Scots wears surgical boots and is subject to fits, near the Horse Shoe in Tottenham Court Road.

Michelangelo is a commissionaire; I saw him on board the *Glen Rosa*, which used to run every day from London to Clacton-on-Sea and back. It gave me quite a turn when I saw him coming down the stairs from the upper deck, with his bronzed face, flattened nose, and with the familiar bar upon his forehead. I never liked

Michelangelo, and never shall, but I am afraid of him, and was near trying to hide when I saw him coming towards me. He had not got his commissionnaire's uniform on, and I did not know he was one till I met him a month or so later in the Strand. When we got to Blackwall the music struck up and people began to dance. I never saw a man dance so much in my life. He did not miss a dance all the way to Clacton, nor all the way back again, and when not dancing he was flirting and cracking jokes. I could hardly believe my eyes when I reflected that this man had painted the famous *Last Judgement* and had made all those statues.

I met Socrates once. He was my muleteer on an excursion which I will not name, for fear it should identify the man. The moment I saw my guide I knew he was somebody, but for the life of me I could not remember who. All of a sudden it flashed across me that he was Socrates. He talked enough for six, but it was all in *dialetto*, so I could not understand him, nor, when I had discovered who he was, did I much try to do so. He was a good creature, a trifle given to stealing fruit and vegetables, but an amiable man enough. He had had a long day with his mule and me, and he only asked me five francs. I gave him ten, for I pitied his poor old patched boots, and there was a meekness about him that touched me. 'And now, Socrates,' said I at parting, 'we go on our several ways, you to steal tomatoes, I to filch ideas from other people; for the rest – which of those two roads will be the better going, Our Father which is in Heaven knows, but we know not.'

I have never seen Mendelssohn, but there is a fresco of him on the terrace, or open-air dining-room, of an inn at Chiavenna. He is not called Mendelssohn, but I knew him by his legs. He is in the costume of a dandy of some five-and-forty years ago, is smoking a cigar, and appears to be making an offer of marriage to his cook. Beethoven both my friend Mr H. Festing Jones and I have had the good fortune to meet; he is an engineer now, and does not know one note from another; he has quite lost his deafness, is married, and is, of course, a little squat man with the same refractory hair that he always had. It was very interesting to watch him, and Jones remarked that before the end of dinner he had become positively posthumous. One morning I was told the Beethovens were going away, and before long I met their two heavy boxes being carried down the stairs. The boxes were so squat and like their owners that I half thought for a moment that they were inside, and should hardly have been surprised to see them spring up like a couple of Jacks-in-the-box. '*Sono indentro?*' said I, with a frown of wonder, pointing to the boxes. The porters knew what I meant, and laughed. But there is no end to the list of people whom I have been able to recognize, and before I had got through it myself, I found I had walked some distance, and had involuntarily paused in front of a second-hand bookstall.

I do not like books. I believe I have the smallest library of any literary man in London, and I have no wish to increase it. I keep my books at the British Museum and at Mudie's, and it makes me very angry if anyone gives me one for my private library. I once heard two ladies disputing in a railway carriage as to whether one of them had or had not been wasting money. 'I spent it in books,' said the accused, 'and it's not wasting money to buy books.' 'Indeed, my dear, I think it is,' was the rejoinder, and in practice I agree with it. *Webster's Dictionary, Whitaker's Almanack*, and *Bradshaw's Railway* guide should be sufficient for any ordinary library; it will be time enough to go beyond these when the mass of useful and entertaining matter which they provide has been mastered. Nevertheless, I admit that sometimes, if not particularly busy, I stop at a second-hand bookstall and turn over a book or two from mere force of habit.

I know not what made me pick up a copy of Aeschylus – of course in an English version – or rather I know not what made Aeschylus take up with me, for he took me rather than I him; but no sooner had he got me than he began puzzling me, as he has done any time this forty years, to know wherein his transcendent merit can be supposed to lie. To me he is, like the greater number of classics in all ages and countries, a literary Struldbrug, rather than a true ambrosia-fed immortal. There are true immortals, but they are few and far between; most classics are as great impostors dead as they were when living, and while posing as gods are, five-sevenths of them, only Struldbrugs. It comforts me to remember that Aristophanes liked Aeschylus no better than I do. True, he praises him by comparison with Sophocles and Euripides, but he only does so that he may run down these last more effectively. Aristophanes is a safe man to follow, nor do I see why it should not be as correct to laugh with him as to pull a long face with the Greek professors; but this is neither here nor there, for no one really cares about Aeschylus; the more interesting question is how he contrived to make so many people for so many years pretend to care about him.

Perhaps he married somebody's daughter. If a man would get hold of the public ear, he must pay, marry, or fight. I have never understood that Aeschylus was a man of means, and the fighters do not write poetry, so I suppose he must have married a theatrical manager's daughter, and got his plays brought out that way. The ear of any age or country is like its land, air, and water; it seems limitless, but is really limited, and is already in the keeping of those who naturally enough will have no squatting on such valuable property. It is written and talked up to as closely as the means of subsistence are bred up to by a teeming population. There is not a square inch of it but is in private hands, and he who would freehold any part of it must do so by purchase, marriage, or fighting, in the usual way – and fighting gives the longest, safest tenure. The public itself has hardly more voice in the question who shall have its ear, than the land has in choosing its owners. It is farmed as those who own it think most profitable to themselves, and small blame to them; nevertheless, it has a residuum of mulishness which the land has not, and does sometimes dispossess its tenants. It is in this residuum that those who fight place their hope and trust.

Or perhaps Aeschylus squared the leading critics of his time. When one comes to think of it, he must have done so, for how is it conceivable that such plays should have had such runs if he had not? I met a lady one year in Switzerland who had some parrots that always travelled with her and were the idols of her life. These parrots would not let anyone read aloud in their presence, unless they heard their own names introduced from time to time. If these were freely interpolated into the text they would remain as still as stones, for they thought the reading was about themselves. If it was not about them it could not be allowed. The leaders of literature are like these parrots; they do not look at what a man writes, nor if they did would they understand it much better than the parrots do; but they like the sound of their own names, and if these are freely interpolated in a tone they take as friendly, they may even give ear to an outsider. Otherwise they will scream him off if they can.

I should not advise anyone with ordinary independence of mind to attempt the public ear unless he is confident that he can out-lung and out-last his own generation; for if he has any force, people will and ought to be on their guard against him, inasmuch as there is no knowing where he may not take them. Besides, they have staked their money on the wrong men so often without suspecting it, that when there comes one whom they do suspect it would be madness not to bet against him. True, he may die before he has out-screamed his opponents, but that has nothing to do with it. If his scream was well pitched, it will sound clearer when he is dead. We do not know what death is. If we know so little about life which we have experienced, how shall we know about death which we have not – and in the nature of things never can? Everyone, as I said years ago in *Alps and Sanctuaries*, is an immortal to himself, for he cannot know that he is dead until he is dead, and when dead how can he know anything about anything? All we know is, that even the humblest dead may live long after all trace of the body has disappeared; we see them doing it in the bodies and memories of those that come after them; and not a few live so much longer and more effectually than is desirable, that it has been necessary to get rid of them by Act of Parliament. It is love that alone gives life, and the truest life is that which we live not in ourselves but vicariously in others, and with which we have no concern. Our concern is so to order ourselves that we may be of the number of them that enter into life – although we know it not.

Aeschylus did so order himself; but his life is not of that inspiriting kind that can be won through fighting the good fight only – or being believed to have fought it. His voice is the echo of a drone, drone-begotten and drone-sustained. It is not a tone that a man must utter or die – nay, even though he die; and likely enough half the allusions and hard passages in Aeschylus of which we can make neither head nor tail are in reality only puffs of some of the literary leaders of his time.

The lady above referred to told me more about her parrots. She was like a Nasmyth hammer going slow – very gentle, but irresistible. She always read the newspaper to them. What was the use of having a newspaper if one did not read it to one's parrots?

'And have you divined', I asked, 'to which side they incline in politics?'

'They do not like Mr Gladstone,' was the somewhat freezing answer; 'this is the only point on which we disagree, for I adore him. Don't ask more about this, it is a great grief to me. I tell them everything,' she continued, 'and hide no secret from them.'

'But can any parrot be trusted to keep a secret?'

'Mine can.'

'And on Sundays do you give them the same course of reading as on a weekday, or do you make a difference?'

'On Sundays I always read them a genealogical chapter from the Old or New Testament, for I can thus introduce their names without profanity. I always keep tea by me in case they should ask for it in the night, and I have an Etna to warm it for them; they take milk and sugar. The old white-headed clergyman came to see them last night; it was very painful, for Jocko reminded him so strongly of his late . . .'

I thought she was going to say 'wife', but it proved to have been only of a parrot that he had once known and loved.

I heard of the parrots a year or two later as giving lessons in Italian to an English maid. I do not know what their terms were. Alas! since then both they and their mistress have joined the majority. When the poor lady felt her end was near she desired (and the responsibility for this must rest with her, not me) that the birds might be destroyed, as fearing they might come to be neglected, and knowing that they could never be loved again as she had loved them. On being told that all was over, she said 'Thank you', and immediately expired.

Reflecting in such random fashion, and strolling with no greater method, I worked my way back through Cheapside and found myself once more in front of Sweeting's window. Again the turtles attracted me. They were alive, and so far at any rate they agreed with me. Nay, they had eyes, mouths, legs, if not arms, and feet, so there was much in which we were both of a mind, but surely they must be mistaken in arming themselves so very heavily. Any creature on getting what the turtle aimed at would overreach itself and be landed not in safety but annihilation. It should have no communion with the outside world at all, for death could creep in wherever the creature could creep out; and it must creep out somewhere if it was to hook on to outside things. What death can be more absolute than such absolute isolation? Perfect death, indeed, if it were attainable (which it is not), is as near perfect security as we can reach, but it is not the kind of security aimed at by any animal that is at the pains of defending itself. For such want to have things both ways, desiring the livingness of life without its perils, and the safety of death without its deadness, and some of us do actually get this for a considerable time, but we do not get it by plating ourselves with armour as the turtle does. We tried this in the Middle Ages, and no longer mock ourselves with the weight of armour that our forefathers carried in battle. Indeed the more deadly the weapons of attack become the more we go into the fight slug-wise.

Slugs have ridden their contempt for defensive armour as much to death as the turtles their pursuit of it. They have hardly more than skin enough to hold themselves together; they court death every time they cross the road. Yet death comes not to them more than to the turtle, whose defences are so great that there is little left inside to be defended. Moreover, the slugs fare best in the long run, for turtles are dying out, while slugs are not, and there must be millions of slugs all the world over for every single turtle. Of the two vanities, therefore, that of the slug seems most substantial.

In either case the creature thinks itself safe, but is sure to be found out sooner or later; nor is it easy to explain this mockery save by reflecting that everything must have its meat in due season, and that meat can only be found for such a multitude of mouths by giving everything as meat in due season to something else. This is like the Kilkenny cats, or robbing Peter to pay Paul; but it is the way of the world, and as every animal must contribute in kind to the picnic of the universe, one does not see what better arrangement could be made than the providing each race with a hereditary fallacy, which shall in the end get it into a scrape, but which shall generally stand the wear and tear of life for some time. 'Do ut des' is the writing on all flesh to him that eats it; and no creature is dearer to itself than it is to some other that would devour it.

Nor is there any statement or proposition more invulnerable than living forms are. Propositions prey upon and are grounded upon one another just like living forms. They support one another as plants and animals do; they are based ultimately on credit, or faith, rather than the cash of irrefragable conviction. The whole universe is carried on on the credit system, and if the mutual confidence on which it is based were to collapse, it must itself collapse immediately. Just or unjust, it lives by faith; it is based on vague and impalpable opinion that by some inscrutable process passes into will and action, and is made manifest in matter and in flesh: it is meteoric – suspended in mid-air; it is the baseless fabric of a vision so vast, so vivid, and so gorgeous that no base can seem more broad than such stupendous baselessness, and yet any man can bring it about his ears by being over-curious; when faith fails, a system based on faith fails also.

Whether the universe is really a paying concern, or whether it is an inflated bubble that must burst sooner or later, this is another matter. If people were to demand cash payment in irrefragable certainty for everything that they have taken hitherto as paper money on the credit of the bank of public opinion, is there money enough behind it all to stand so great a drain even on so great a reserve? Probably there is not, but happily there can be no such panic, for even though the cultured classes may do so, the uncultured are too dull to have brains enough to commit such stupendous folly. It takes a long course of academic training to educate a man up to the standard which he must reach before he can entertain such questions seriously, and by a merciful dispensation of Providence university training is almost as costly as it is unprofitable. The majority will thus be always unable to afford it, and will base their opinions on mother wit and current opinion rather than on demonstration.

So I turned my steps homewards; I saw a good many more things on my way home, but I was told that I was not to see more this time than I could get into twelve pages of the *Universal Review*; I must therefore reserve any remark which I think might perhaps entertain the reader for another occasion.

* * *

EDMUND WILSON (1895–1972)

'Notes on London at the End of the War'

I have never before fully grasped what was meant by 'British rudeness'. The point about it is that what we consider rudeness is their form of good manners. In other countries, manners are intended to diminish social friction, to show people consideration and to make them feel at ease. In England it is the other way: good breeding is something you exhibit by snubbing and scoring off people. This is of course closely connected with their class system, and it is partly a question of accent, vocabulary and general style, which your inferior cannot acquire. I have been told that, when a way of talking begins to pass into common use, the higher people evolve something new which will again fence them off from the lower. Certainly I heard interchanges in London of which I could hardly understand a word.

But their competitiveness is also involved: it is a game to put your opponent at a disadvantage, and if you succeed in saying something blighting in a way which makes it impossible for him to retaliate without a loss of dignity more serious than that which he incurs by accepting it, you are considered to have won the encounter. You have the status of King of the Castle till somebody else comes to pull you down. Nothing in this respect seems to have changed since the days of which Henry Adams wrote in his *Education*, when what he had heard described as 'the perfection of human society' required that a man should be able to 'enter a drawing room where he was a total stranger, and place himself on the hearth-rug, his back to the fire, with an air of expectant benevolence, without curiosity, much as though he had dropped in at a charity concert, kindly disposed to applaud the performers and to overlook mistakes'.

For all that with other peoples is understood by politeness or courtesy they have a special word, *civility*, which is spoken of as something exceptional and rather unimportant. To say that a person is *civil* is usually patronizing; to complain of someone's *incivility*, usually means that a vulgar person has made himself offensive by breaking the rules of the game and not accepting the inferior position to which you have tried to assign him. They have also as a part of their rudeness what may be called mock considerateness, which may well be described in the words of a distinguished Russian artist with whom I once had a talk about the English. 'They're at their worst,' he said, 'when they're being kind! They scratch you and scratch you and scratch you – and then they take out a little bandage and graciously bind you up – and then they begin to scratch again.'

* * *

HEINRICH HEINE (1797–1856)

'London'

I have seen the greatest wonder which the world can show to the astonished mind. I have seen it, and am more astonished than ever. Still vivid in my memory remains the stone forest of houses, and amid them the rushing stream of living human faces, with all their motley passions and all their terrible and restless impulses of love, of hunger, of hatred.

I am speaking of London.

Send a philosopher to London, but, not on your life, a poet! Send a philosopher there and stand him at a corner of Cheapside, and he will learn more there than from all the books of the last Leipzig fair. As the human waves roar around him, a sea of new thoughts will rise before him, and the Eternal Spirit which hovers upon its waters will breathe upon him. The most hidden secrets of the social order will suddenly be revealed to him.

But send no poet to London! This downright earnestness in all things, this colossal uniformity, this machine-like movement, this moroseness even in pleasure, this exaggerated London – smothers the imagination and rends the heart. And should you ever send a German poet there, a dreamer, who stands staring at every single thing – say, a ragged beggar-woman, or a resplendent goldsmith's shop – why then, things will go badly with him, and he will be jostled on all sides, and even knocked down with a mild 'God damn!' God damn! that damned pushing! I soon perceived that these Londoners have much to do. They live on a grand scale, and though food and clothing are dearer there than with us, they must still be better fed and clothed than we are. As behooves gentility, they also have enormous debts, yet sometimes in a boastful mood, they squander their guineas, pay other nations to fight for their pleasure, whose respective kings they give a handsome *douceur* into the bargain. Therefore, John Bull must work day and night to obtain money for such expenses; day and night he must tax his brain to invent new machines, and he sits and reckons in the sweat of his brow, and rushes and scurries without looking about him, from the docks to the Exchange, and from the Exchange to the Strand. Hence it is quite understandable, when a poor German poet stands in his way at the corner of Cheapside gazing into an art-dealer's window he should knock him aside somewhat unceremoniously. 'God damn!'

The picture at which I was gaping at the corner of Cheapside was that of the crossing of the Beresina by the French.

When, jolted out of my preoccupation, I looked again on the roaring street, where a motley throng of men, women, children, horses, stagecoaches, and with them a funeral procession, whirled, groaned, and creaked along, it seemed to me as though all of London were a Beresina Bridge, where everyone presses on in mad haste to save his little scrap of life, where the arrogant rider tramples down the poor pedestrian; where he who falls to the ground is lost for ever; where even the best friends rush by, indifferently, over the corpses of their comrades; and thousands of exhausted and bleeding creatures clutch in vain at the planks of the bridge, and plunge into the icy pit of death.

How much more cheerful and homelike it is in our dear Germany! With what dreamy cosiness, with what Sabbatical quiet things glide along here! Calmly the watch is changed; uniforms and houses gleam in the quiet sunshine, swallows flit over the flag-stones, fat court-councillors' wives smile from the windows, while in the echoing streets there is room enough for the dogs to sniff at one another properly, and for men to stand at ease and discourse on the theatre, and bow low – very, very low! – when some little aristocratic scoundrel or vice-scoundrel, with coloured little ribbons on his shabby little coat, or some court-marshal-lowbrain, powdered and gilded, prances by, graciously returning the greeting.

I had made up my mind in advance not to be astonished at that hugeness of London of which I had heard so much. But I had as little success as the poor schoolboy who had made up his mind not to feel the whipping he was about to receive. The fact was that he expected to receive the usual blows with the usual cane in the usual way on the back; whereas he received a most unusually severe thrashing in an unusual place with a slender switch. I anticipated great palaces, and saw nothing but small houses. But their very uniformity and their infinite number are wonderfully impressive.

*

The stranger who wanders through the great streets of London and does not chance right into the quarters in which the common people live, sees little or nothing of the dire misery there. Only here and there, at the entrance of some dark alley, a ragged woman stands mutely with a suckling babe at her exhausted breast, and begs with her eyes. Perhaps if those eyes are still beautiful, one glances into them and shrinks back at the world of wretchedness to be found here. The common beggars are all old people, generally blackamoors, who stand at the corners of the streets clearing pathways – a very necessary thing in muddy London – and ask for coppers in return. It is only in the dark night that Poverty, with her fellows, Vice and Crime, glides from her lair. She shuns the daylight all the more carefully, since her wretchedness contrasts so glaringly with the pride of wealth which struts about everywhere. Only hunger drives her sometimes from her dark alley at midday, and then she stares with eloquent, mute, beseeching eyes at the rich merchant who hurries past, busy, jingling his coins, or at the idle lord, who, like a surfeited god, rides by on his high horse, now and then glancing with an aristocratically blasé air at the crowds below – as if they were a swarm of ants, or a herd of baser creatures whose joys and sorrows had nothing in common with his feelings. For above this mass of humanity which clings close to the earth, England's nobility soars, like beings of higher order, and regards its little island as a temporary lodging, Italy as its summer garden, Paris as its social salon, and the whole wide world as its property. These nobles sweep along, without cark or care, and their gold is a talisman which makes their wildest wishes come true.

Poor poverty! How agonizing must your hunger be, when others wallow in arrogant surfeit! And when a man, with indifferent hand, throws a crust into your lap, how bitter must be the tears with which you wet it! You drink poison with your own tears. You are surely right when you ally yourself with Vice and Crime. Outlawed criminals often have more humanity in their hearts than those cold, irreproach-able citizens of virtue, in whose bloodless hearts the power of doing evil is quenched – as well as the power of doing good. And even Vice is not always Vice. I have seen women on whose cheeks red vice was painted, but in whose hearts dwelt heavenly purity. I have seen women – would I saw them again!

★   ★   ★

S. D. MAHOMED (1749–?)

from *Shampooing; or, Benefits Resulting from the Use of the Indian Medicated Vapour Bath*

The humble author of these sheets, is a native of India; and was born in the year 1749, at Patna, the capital of Bahar, in Hindoostan, about 290 miles NW of Calcutta. He was educated to the profession of, and served in the Company's service as a Surgeon, which capacity he afterwards relinquished, and acted in a military character, exclusively, for nearly twenty years. In the year 1780, he was appointed to a company under General, then Major Popham; and at the commencement of the year 1784, he left the service and came to England, where he has resided ever since.

The time and attention which he devoted during the early period of his life, to the peculiar modes of Bathing, followed medicinally and as luxuries in the eastern part of the world, induced him to think seriously of introducing into England, that description of Bath, more particularly adapted to the constitution of Europeans; for this purpose, he sedulously applied himself, when he arrived here, in trying such preliminary experiments, as from their complete success, induced him to turn the whole of his attention to this branch of medicinal science. The astonishing effects which this mode of treatment produced in most cases of bodily infirmity, convinced him of the certainty of the hypothesis which he had formed, as to the general benefits on the English constitution; and as that process, which in India is used as a restorative luxury, operated in this country as a most surprising and powerful remedy for many cases of disease, he felt justified in publishing to the world, the discovery which he had made, a discovery not unsupported by proof – proof the most flattering and convincing, as will be shewn in the course of this work.

On Mr Mahomed's arrival in Brighton, from adverse circumstances, he was not immediately enabled to promulgate the decided advantages which his method had over the common warm bathing; he was fortunate, however, in several gratuitous cures, after every other attempt had been made and failed – cures which soon gained circulation among those who were ignorant of the virtues of his Bath, and adducing the most positive and convincing evidence of the great superiority of Shampooing over every other description of treatment, in peculiar cases.

It is the lot of most men, who step out of the common rank of received opinions, to meet with difficulties, and to have to contend with worldly caprice and uncharitableness. It is not in the power of any individual, to give unqualified satisfaction, or to attempt to establish a new opinion without the risk of incurring the ridicule, as well as censure, of some portion of mankind. So it was with him, he, in the face of indisputable evidence, had to struggle with doubts and objections raised and circulated against his Bath, which, but for the repeated and numerous cures effected by it, would long since have shared the common fate of most innovations in science.

Fortunately, however, he has lived to see his Bath survive the vituperations of the weak and the aspersions of the credulous. Its virtues are now well known and established; it has reared itself and stands upon its own merits. It needs little to be said for it, it can speak for itself, we have only to refer to the cases and a conviction of its benefits will stare us in the face. Much more might be said, but the season and the time would be badly selected to pay a tribute beyond the production of the instances which will so shortly be made to appear.

S. D. Mahomed cannot but repeat the hope, that the following sheets may be received with that kindness and indulgence, which has ever been the distinguished characteristic of an English public, whose acceptance of them, will fully recompense the author for his exertions, and afford him a pleasing return for his humble, though grateful endeavours.

FRANCE

VINCENT VAN GOGH (1853–1890)

from *The Poetry and Prose of a Post-Impressionist*

At last I have seen the Mediterranean Sea and have spent a week in Saintes-Maries. I went there in the diligence, via la Camargue, through vineyards and meadows, and across plains, like those in Holland. In Saintes-Maries I saw some little girls who reminded me of Cimabue and Giotto – very much so, in fact; they were thin, rather sad, and mystic. On the beach, which is quite flat and sandy, I saw a number of green, red and blue boats, which were so delightful both in form and colour, that they made me think of flowers. One man alone can navigate a boat of this sort, but they do not go far out. They only venture into deep water when the wind is low and they return as soon as it rises.

I should also very much like to see Africa. But I will not make any definite plans for the future. Everything will depend upon circumstances. What I wanted to experience was the effect of a deep blue sky. Fromentin and Gérôme see no colour in the South, and a number of others are like them. But good Heavens! – if you take a little dry sand up in your hand and hold it close to your eyes, of course it is colourless, just as water and air would be. There is no blue without yellow and orange, and when you paint blue, paint yellow and orange as well – am I not right? . . .

*

This month will be hard for you and me; and yet if we can only see our way to doing so, it would be to our advantage to paint as many blossoming orchards as possible. I am now in full swing, and I believe I shall have to paint the same subject ten times over. I also have a tremendous amount of drawing to do; for I should like to make drawings after the manner of Japanese crape prints. For I must strike the iron while it is hot, and after the orchards I shall be completely exhausted, for the sizes of the canvases are, 32 in. by 24½ in., 36 in. by 27½ in., and 29 in. by 22½ in. We should not have too many with twice the number; for I have an idea that these might break the ice in Holland.

Mauve's death was a hard blow to me, and you will notice that the pink peach trees were painted with some agitation.

I must also paint a starry night, with cypresses, or, perhaps, over a field of ripe corn. We get wonderful nights here. I am possessed by an insatiable lust for work. I shall be glad to see the result at the end of the year. I trust that by that time I shall be less tormented by a certain feeling of ill-ease that is troubling me now. On some days I suffer terribly! but I am not greatly concerned about it, for it is simply the reaction of the past winter, which was certainly not normal. My blood renews itself, and that is the most important thing of all.

* * *

WALTER BENJAMIN (1892–1940)

'Marseilles'

Marseilles – the yellow-studded maw of a seal with salt water running out between the teeth. When this gullet opens to catch the black and brown proletarian bodies thrown to it by ships' companies according to their timetables, it exhales a stink of oil, urine, and printer's ink. This comes from the tartar baking hard on the massive jaws: newspaper kiosks, lavatories, and oyster stalls. The harbour people are a bacillus culture, the porters and whores products of decomposition with a resemblance to human beings. But the palate itself is pink, which is the colour of shame here, of poverty. Hunchbacks wear it, and beggarwomen. And the discoloured women of rue Bouterie are given their only tint by the sole pieces of clothing they wear: pink shifts.

Les bricks, the red-light district is called, after the barges moored a hundred paces away at the jetty of the old harbour. A vast agglomeration of steps, arches, bridges, turrets, and cellars. It seems to be still awaiting its designated use, but it already has it. For this depot of worn-out alleyways is the prostitutes' quarter. Invisible lines divide the area up into sharp, angular territories like African colonies. The whores are strategically placed, ready at a sign to encircle hesitant visitors, and to bounce the reluctant guest like a ball from one side of the street to the other. If he forfeits nothing else in this game, it is his hat. Has anyone yet probed deeply enough into this refuse heap of houses to reach the innermost place in the gynaeceum, the chamber where the trophies of manhood – boaters, bowlers, hunting hats, trilbies, jockey caps – hang in rows on consoles or in layers on racks? From the interiors of taverns the eye meets the sea. Thus the alleyway passes between rows of innocent houses as if shielded by a bashful hand from the harbour. On this bashful, dripping hand, however, shines a signet ring on a fishwife's hard finger, the old Hôtel de Ville. Here, two hundred years ago, stood patricians' houses. The high-breasted nymphs, the snake-ringed Medusa's heads over their weather-beaten doorframes have only now become unambiguously the signs of a professional guild. Unless, that is, signboards were hung over them as the midwife Bianchamori has hung hers, on which, leaning against a pillar, she turns a defiant face to all the brothel keepers of the quarter, and points unruffled to a sturdy baby in the act of emerging from an egg.

Noises. High in the empty streets of the harbour district they are as densely and loosely clustered as butterflies on a hot flower bed. Every step stirs a song, a quarrel, a flapping of wet linen, a rattling of boards, a baby's bawling, a clatter of buckets. Only you have to have strayed up here alone, if you are to pursue them with a net as they flutter away unsteadily into the stillness. For in these deserted corners all sounds and things still have their own silences, just as, at midday in the mountains, there is a silence of hens, of the axe of the cicadas. But the chase is dangerous, and the net is finally torn when, like a gigantic hornet, a grindstone impales it from behind with its whizzing sting.

Cathedral. On the least frequented, sunniest square stands the cathedral. This place is deserted, despite the proximity at its feet of La Joliette, the harbour, to the south, and a proletarian district to the north. As a reloading point for intangible, unfathomable goods, the bleak building stands between quay and warehouse. Nearly forty years were spent on it. But when all was complete, in 1893, place and time had conspired victoriously in this monument against its architects and sponsors, and the wealth of the clergy had given rise to a gigantic railway station that could never be opened to traffic. The façade gives an indication of the waiting rooms within, where passengers of the first to fourth classes (though before God they are all equal), wedged among their spiritual possessions as between cases, sit reading hymn-books that, with their concordances and cross-references, look very much like international timetables. Extracts from the railway traffic regulations in the form of pastoral letters hang on the walls, tariffs for the discount on special trips in Satan's luxury train are consulted, and cabinets where the long-distance traveller can discreetly wash are kept in readiness as confessionals. This is the Marseilles religion station. Sleeping cars to eternity depart from here at Mass times.

The light from greengroceries that is in the paintings of Monticelli comes from the inner streets of his city, the monotonous residential quarters of the long-standing inhabitants, who know something of the sadness of Marseilles. For childhood is the divining rod of melancholy, and to know the mourning of such radiant, glorious cities one must have been a child in them. The grey houses of the Boulevard de Longchamps, the barred windows of the Cours Puget, and the trees of the Allée de Meilhan give nothing away to the traveller if chance does not lead him to the cubiculum of the city, the Passage de Lorette, the narrow yard where, in the sleepy presence of a few women and men, the whole world shrinks to a single Sunday afternoon. A real-estate company has carved its name on the gateway. Does not this interior correspond exactly to the white mystery ship moored in the harbour, *Nautique*, which never puts to sea, but daily feeds foreigners at white tables with dishes that are much too clean and as if surgically rinsed?

Shellfish and oyster stalls. Unfathomable wetness that swills from the upper tier, in a dirty, cleansing flood over dirty planks and warty mountains of pink shellfish, bubbles between the thighs and bellies of glazed Buddhas, past yellow domes of lemons, into the marshland of cresses and through the woods of French pennants, finally to irrigate the palate as the best sauce for the quivering creatures. *Oursins de l'Estaque, Portugaises, Maremmes, Clovisses, Moules marinières* – all this is incessantly sieved, grouped, counted, cracked open, thrown away, prepared, tasted. And the slow, stupid agent of inland trade, paper, has no place in the unfettered element, the breakers of foaming lips that forever surge against the streaming steps. But over there, on the other quay, stretches the mountain range of 'souvenirs', the mineral hereafter of sea shells. Seismic forces have thrown up this massif of paste jewellery, shell limestone, and enamel, where inkpots, steamers, anchors, mercury columns, and sirens commingle. The pressure of a thousand atmospheres under which this world of imagery writhes, rears, piles up, is the same force that is tested in the hard hands of seamen, after long voyages, on the thighs and breasts of women, and the lust that, on the shell-covered caskets, presses from the mineral world a red or blue velvet heart to be pierced with needles and brooches, is the same that sends tremors through these streets on paydays.

Walls. Admirable, the discipline to which they are subject in this city. The better ones, in the centre, wear livery and are in the pay of the ruling class. They are covered with gaudy patterns and have sold their whole length many hundreds of times to the latest brand of apéritif, to department stores, to the 'Chocolat Menier', or Dolores del Rio. In the poorer quarters they are politically mobilized and post their spacious red letters as the forerunners of red guards in front of dockyards and arsenals.

The down-and-out who, after nightfall, sells his books on the corner of rue de la République and the Vieux Port, awakens bad instincts in the passers-by. They feel tempted to make use of so much fresh misery. And they long to learn more about such nameless misfortune than the mere image of catastrophe that it presents to us. For what extremity must have brought a man to tip such books as he has left on the asphalt before him, and to hope that a passer-by will be seized at this late hour by a desire to read? Or is it all quite different? And does a poor soul here keep vigil, mutely beseeching us to lift the treasure from the ruins? We hasten by. But we shall falter again at every corner, for everywhere the Southern peddler has so pulled his beggar's coat around him that fate looks at us from it with a thousand eyes. How far we are from the sad dignity of our poor, the war-disabled of competition, on whom tags and tins of boot blacking hang like braid and medals.

Suburbs. The farther we emerge from the inner city, the more political the atmosphere becomes. We reach the docks, the inland harbours, the warehouses, the quarters of poverty, the scattered refugees of wretchedness: the outskirts. Outskirts are the state of emergency of a city, the terrain on which incessantly rages the great decisive battle between town and country. It is nowhere more bitter than between Marseilles and the Provençal landscape. It is the hand-to-hand fight of telegraph poles against Agaves, barbed wire against thorny palms, the miasmas of stinking corridors against the damp gloom under the plane trees in brooding squares, short-winded outside staircases against the mighty hills. The long Rue de Lyon is the powder conduit that Marseilles has dug in the landscape in order, in Saint-Lazare, Saint-Antoine, Arenc, Septèmes, to blow it up, burying it in the shell splinters of every national and commercial language. Alimentation Moderne, rue de Jamaïque, Comptoir de la Limite, Savon Abat-Jour, Minoterie de la Campagne, Bar du Gaz, Bar Facultatif – and over all this the dust that here conglomerates out of sea salt, chalk, and mica, and whose bitterness persists longer in the mouths of those who have pitted themselves against the city than the splendour of sun and sea in the eyes of its admirers.

* * *

WILLLIAM MAKEPEACE THACKERAY (1811–1863)

from *Early Travel Writings*

The French milliner, who occupies one of the corners, begins to remove the greasy pieces of paper which have enveloped her locks during the journey. She withdraws the 'Madras' of dubious hue which has bound her head for the last five-and-twenty hours, and replaces it by the black velvet bonnet, which, bobbing against your nose, has hung from the Diligence roof since your departure from Boulogne. The old lady in the opposite corner, who has been sucking bonbons, and smells dreadfully of anisette, arranges her little parcels in that immense basket of abominations which all old women carry in their laps. She rubs her mouth and eyes with her dusty cambric handkerchief, she ties up her nightcap into a little bundle, and replaces it by a more becoming headpiece, covered with withered artificial flowers and crumpled tags of ribbon; she looks wistfully at the company for an instant, and then places her handkerchief before her mouth – her eyes roll strangely about for an instant, and you hear a faint clattering noise: the old lady has been getting ready her teeth, which had lain in her basket among the bonbons, pins, oranges, pomatum, bits of cake, lozenges, prayer-books, peppermint-water, copper-money, and false hair – stowed away there during the voyage. The Jewish gentleman, who has been so attentive to the milliner during the journey, and is a traveller and bagman by profession, gathers together his various goods. The sallow-faced English lad, who has been drunk ever since we left Boulogne yesterday, and is coming to Paris to pursue the study of medicine, swears that he rejoices to leave the cursed Diligence, is sick of the infernal journey, and d——d glad that the d——d voyage is so nearly over. '*Enfin!*' says your neighbour, yawning, and inserting an elbow into the mouth of his right and left-hand companion, '*nous voilà*.'

Nous Voilà! We are at Paris! This must account for the removal of the milliner's curl-papers, and the fixing of the old lady's teeth. – Since the last *relais*, the Diligence has been travelling with extraordinary speed. The postilion cracks his terrible whip, and screams shrilly. The conductor blows incessantly on his horn, the bells of the harness, the bumping and ringing of the wheels and chains, and the clatter of the great hoofs of the heavy snorting Norman stallions, have wondrously increased within this last ten minutes; and the Diligence, which has been proceeding hitherto at the rate of a league in an hour, now dashes gallantly forward, as if it would traverse at least six miles in the same space of time. Thus it is, when Sir Robert maketh a speech at St Stephen's – he useth his strength at the beginning, only, and the end. He gallopeth at the commencement; in the middle he lingers; at the close, again, he rouses the House, which has fallen asleep; he cracketh the whip of his satire; he shouts the shout of his patriotism; and, urging his eloquence to its roughest

canter, awakens the sleepers, and inspires the weary, until men say,
What a wondrous orator! What a capital coach! We will ride hence-
forth in it, and in no other!

But, behold us at Paris! The Diligence has reached a rude-looking
gate, or *grille*, flanked by two lodges; the French Kings of old made
their entry by this gate; some of the hottest battles of the late
revolution were fought before it. At present, it is blocked by carts
and peasants, and a busy crowd of men, in green, examining the
packages before they enter, probing the straw with long needles. It
is the Barrier of St Denis, and the green men are the customs-men
of the city of Paris. If you are a countryman, who would introduce
a cow into the metropolis, the city demands twenty-four francs for
such a privilege: if you have a hundredweight of tallow candles, you
must, previously, disburse three francs: if a drove of hogs, nine francs
per whole hog: but upon these subjects Mr Bulwer, Mrs Trollope,
and other writers, have already enlightened the public. In the present
instance, after a momentary pause, one of the men in green mounts
by the side of the conductor, and the ponderous vehicle pursues its
journey.

The street which we enter, that of the Faubourg St Denis, presents
a strange contrast to the dark uniformity of a London street, where
everything, in the dingy and smoky atmosphere, looks as though it
were painted in India-ink – black houses, black passengers, and black
sky. Here, on the contrary, is a thousand times more life and colour.
Before you, shining in the sun, is a long glistening line of *gutter* –
not a very pleasing object in a city, but in a picture invaluable. On
each side are houses of all dimensions and hues; some but of one
storey; some as high as the Tower of Babel. From these the haber-
dashers (and this is their favourite street) flaunt long strips of gaudy
calicoes, which give a strange air of rude gaiety to the street. Milk-
women, with a little crowd of gossips round each, are, at this early
hour of morning, selling the chief material of the Parisian *café-au-
lait*. Gay wine-shops, painted red, and smartly decorated with vines
and gilded railings, are filled with workmen taking their morning's
draught. That gloomy-looking prison on your right is a prison for
women; once it was a convent for Lazarists: a thousand unfortunate
individuals of the softer sex now occupy that mansion: they bake, as
we find in the guide-books, the bread of all the other prisons; they
mend and wash the shirts and stockings of all the other prisoners;

they make hooks-and-eyes and phosphorus-boxes, and they attend chapel every Sunday – if occupation can help them, sure they have enough of it. Was it not a great stroke of the legislature to super-intend the morals and linen at once, and thus keep these poor creatures continually mending? – But we have passed the prison long ago, and are at the Porte St Denis itself.

There is only time to take a hasty glance as we pass: it commemo-rates some of the wonderful feats of arms of Ludovicus Magnus, and abounds in ponderous allegories – nymphs, and river-gods, and pyramids crowned with fleurs-de-lis; Louis passing over the Rhine in triumph, and the Dutch Lion giving up the ghost, in the year of our Lord 1672. The Dutch Lion revived, and overcame the man some years afterwards; but of this fact, singularly enough, the inscriptions make no mention. Passing, then, *round* the gate, and not under it (after the general custom, in respect of triumphal arches), you cross the Boulevard, which gives a glimpse of trees and sunshine, and gleaming white buildings; then, dashing down the Rue de Bourbon Villeneuve, a dirty street, which seems interminable, and the Rue St Eustache, the conductor gives a last blast on his horn, and the great vehicle clatters into the courtyard, where its journey is destined to conclude.

If there was a noise before of screaming postilions and cracked horns, it was nothing to the Babel-like clatter which greets us now. We are in a great court, which Hajji Baba would call the father of Diligences. Half-a-dozen other coaches arrive at the same minute – no light affairs, like your English vehicles, but ponderous machines, containing fifteen passengers inside, more in the cabriolet, and vast towers of luggage on the roof: others are loading: the yard is filled with passengers coming or departing – bustling porters and screaming commissionaires. These latter seize you as you descend from your place, twenty cards are thrust into your hand, and as many voices, jabbering with inconceivable swiftness, shriek into your ear, 'Dis way, sare; are you for ze 'Otel of Rhin? Hôtel de l'Amirauté! – Hôtel Bristol, sare? Monsieur, l'Hôtel de Lille? *Sacr-rrré nom de Dieu, laissez passer ce petit Monsieur!* Ow mosh loggish 'ave you, sare?'

*   *   *

LAURENCE STERNE (1713–1768)

'The Temptation'

[Paris]

When I alighted at the hotel, the porter told me a young woman with a band-box had been that moment inquiring for me. 'I do not know,' said the porter, 'whether she is gone away or no.' I took the key of my chamber of him, and went up stairs; and when I had got within ten steps of the top of the landing before my door, I met her coming slowly down.

It was the fair *fille-de-chambre* I had walked along the Quai de Conti with: Madame de R— had sent her upon some commissions to a *marchande des modes*, within a step or two of the hotel de Modène; and as I had failed in waiting upon her, had bid her inquire if I had left Paris; and, if so, whether I had not left a letter addressed to her.

As the fair *fille-de-chambre* was so near my door, she turned back, and went into the room with me for a moment or two whilst I wrote a card.

It was a fine still evening in the latter end of the month of May – the crimson window-curtains (which were of the same colour as those of the bed) were drawn close – the sun was setting, and reflected through them so warm a tint into the fair *fille-de-chambre*'s face, I thought she blushed; the idea of it made me blush myself. We were quite alone: and that superinduced a second blush before the first could get off.

There is a sort of a pleasing half-guilty blush, where the blood is more in fault than the man; 'tis sent impetuous from the heart, and Virtue flies after it – not to call it back, but to make the sensation of it more delicious to the nerves – 'tis associated.

But I'll not describe it. I felt something at first within me which was not in strict unison with the lesson of virtue I had given her the night before: I sought five minutes for a card – I knew I had not one – I took up a pen – I laid it down again – my hand trembled – the devil was in me.

I know as well as any one he is an adversary, who, if we resist, will fly from us; but I seldom resist him at all, from a terror that, though I may conquer, I may still get a hurt in the combat; so I give up the triumph, for security; and instead of thinking to make him fly, I generally fly myself.

The fair *fille-de-chambre* came close up to the bureau where I was looking for a card – took up first the pen I cast down, then offered to hold me the ink. She offered it so sweetly, I was going to accept it; but I durst not: 'I have nothing, my dear,' said I, 'to write upon.' 'Write it,' said she, simply, 'upon anything.'

I was just going to cry out, Then I will write it, fair girl! upon thy lips.

If I do, said I, I shall perish – so I took her by the hand, and led her to the door, and begged she would not forget the lesson I had given her. She said indeed she would not; and as she uttered it with some earnestness, she turned about, and gave me both her hands, closed together into mine. It was impossible not to compress them in that situation; I wished to let them go; and all the time I held them, I kept arguing within myself against it – and still I held them on. In two minutes I found I had all the battle to fight over again – and I felt my legs and every limb about me tremble at the idea.

The foot of the bed was within a yard-and-a-half of the place where we were standing; I had still hold of her hands; and how it happened I can give no account, but I neither asked her, nor drew her, nor did I think of the bed – but so it did happen, we both sat down.

'I'll just show you,' said the fair *fille-de-chambre*, 'the little purse I have been making today to hold your crown.' So she put her hand into her right pocket, which was next me, and felt for it for some time – then into the left – 'She had lost it.' I never bore expectation more quietly; it was in her right pocket at last – she pulled it out; it was of green taffeta, lined with a little bit of white quilted satin, and just big enough to hold the crown. She put it into my hand – it was pretty; and I held it ten minutes with the back of my hand resting upon her lap – looking sometimes at the purse, sometimes on one side of it.

A stitch or two had broke out in the gathers of my stock; the fair *fille-de-chambre*, without saying a word, took out her little hussive, threaded a small needle, and sewed it up. I foresaw it would hazard the glory of the day; and, as she passed her hand in silence across and across my neck in the manœuvre, I felt the laurels shake which Fancy had wreathed about my head.

A strap had given way in her walk, and the buckle of her shoe was just falling off. 'See,' said the *fille-de-chambre*, holding up her foot. I could not for my soul but fasten the buckle in return; and, putting in the strap, and lifting up the other foot with it when I had done, to see both were right, in doing it too suddenly, it unavoidably threw the fair *fille-de-chambre* off her centre – and then—

YES – and then – Ye whose clay-cold heads and luke-warm hearts can argue down or mask your passions – tell me what trespass is it that man should have them? or how his spirit stands answerable, to the father of spirits, but for his conduct under them?

If nature has so wove her web of kindness, that some threads of love and desire are entangled with the piece — must the whole web be rent in drawing them out? – Whip me such stoics, great governor of nature! said I to myself – Wherever thy providence shall place me for the trials of my virtue – whatever is my danger – whatever is my situation – let me feel the movements which rise out of it, and which belong to me as a man – and if I govern them as a good one — I will trust the issues to thy justice, for thou hast made us – and not we ourselves.

As I finish'd my address, I raised the fair *fille de chambre* up by the hand, and led her out of the room — she stood by me till I lock'd the door and put the key in my pocket – *and then* – the victory being quite decisive – and not till then, I press'd my lips to her cheek, and, taking her by the hand again, led her safe to the gate of the hotel.

* * *

ELIZABETH DAVID (1913–1992)

Introduction to *Mediterranean Food*

A certain amount of nonsense is talked about the richness of the food to be found in all French homes. It is true that the standard is much higher than that of most English households, but it will not, I hope, be taken as an ungracious criticism to say that the chances are that a food-conscious foreigner staying for any length of time with a French middle-class family would find the proportion of rather tough *entrecôtes*, rolled and stuffed roast veal, and *sautéd* chicken exasperatingly high. For parties and festivals there would be more elaborately cooked fish and poultry, separate vegetable courses and wonderful open fruit tarts; but he would not find many dishes were cooked in cream, wine and garlic – it is bad for the *foie*, he would very likely be told. Those who care to look for it, however, will find the justification of France's culinary reputation in the provinces, at the riverside inns, in unknown cafés along the banks of the Burgundy canal, patronized by the men who sail the great petrol and timber barges to and from Marseilles, great eaters and drinkers most of them, in the hospitable farmhouses of the Loire and the Dordogne, of Normandy and the Auvergne, in sea-port bistros frequented by fishermen, sailors, ship-chandlers and port officials; and occasionally also in *cafés routiers*, the lorry drivers' restaurants.

In such places the most interesting food in France is to be found, naturally, because the shopkeepers, the lawyer, the doctor, the *curé*, the gendarme and even those stony-faced post-office officials are exceedingly addicted to the pleasures of the table; and, being thrifty as well, you may be sure they know where the cheapest and best of everything is to be obtained. The peasant farmers are prosperous, and not for nothing are they known as the thriftiest people in Europe. Every scrap of food produced is made use of in some way or another, in fact in the best way possible, so it is in the heart of the country that one may become acquainted with the infinite variety of *charcuterie*, the sausages, pickled pork and bacon, smoked hams, *terrines*, preserved goose, *pâtés*, *rillettes*, and *andouillettes*, the cheeses and creams, the fruits preserved in potent local liqueurs, the fresh garden vegetables, pulled up before they are faded and grown old, and served shining with farmhouse butter, the *galettes* and pancakes made from country flour, the mushrooms, *cèpes*, *morilles* and *truffes* gathered in the forest, the mountain hares, pigeons, partridges and roebuck, the *matelotes* of pike, carp and eel and the fried trout straight from the river, the sustaining vegetable soups enriched with wine, garlic, bacon and sausages, the thousand and one shell-fish soups and stews, the *fritures du golfe*, the *risottos aux fruits de mer* of France's lovely prodigal coast, from Brittany to Biarritz and from Spain to Monte Carlo.

*   *   *

MARCEL PROUST (1871–1922)

'In Memory of a Massacre of Churches'

The Churches Saved

Because I had started fairly late in the afternoon, there was no time to be lost if I wanted to reach, before nightfall, the house of my parents which stood half-way between Lisieux and Louviers. To right, to left, and ahead, the car windows, which I kept closed, produced the effect of, as it were, displaying under glass the lovely September day which, even to the gazer in the open air, showed as something seen through a kind of translucent substance. No sooner did the old pot-bellied houses, leaning to one another across the road, see us in the distance, than they rushed to meet us with a proffered gift of scant, fresh-blooming roses, or displayed with pride young hollyhocks which they had tended, only to be out-topped by the stripling blooms. Here and there was one that leaned affectionately upon a growing pear-tree, thinking, in the blind self-deception of old age, to prop that on which it depended for support, pressing the trunk tightly to its stricken heart, in which now, motionless and evermore embedded, was set the tracery of frail, impassioned branches. Soon the road made a bend, and, the bank of grass that was its right-hand verge becoming lower, I saw the plain of Caen, though not the city which, though it lay within the extended view, could not, for distance, yet be seen, nor even its existence guessed. Only the twin bell-towers of St Etienne, rising in isolation from the dead level of the plain, as though lost in the spreading acreage of fields, seemed set to scale the sky. Another moment, and there were three of them, St Peter's having joined the other two. Brought thus together into a cragged, three-cornered peak, they stood out, as often do, in Turner's pictures, the monasteries or manors from which the study is named, though in the vast setting of sky and fields and river, they occupy as little space as, and seem scarcely less episodic and ephemeral than, the rainbow, the late afternoon light, and the little country girl who, in the foreground, trips with a basket in either hand along the road. The minutes passed: our speed increased: but still before us stood those solitary shapes, like birds perched motionless upon the plain, and caught in a gleam of sun. Then, suddenly, as the distance frayed apart like a mist which, melting, reveals, complete in every detail, some object which till then has been invisible, the towers of La Trinité appeared, or rather, one tower only, so precisely did it mask its neighbour. Then it moved aside, the other came forward, and the pair stood new-aligned. Finally, one laggard belfry, with a sudden, daring twist, set itself fair and square before the other two. And now, between this multiplicity of towers – the distant light touching their steep-pitched tiles with smiling radiance – the city, aping at its lower level, their nimbleness, though falling short of their achievement, took sudden form and began to develop in a mounting figure, a complex, clear-cut fugue of roofs.

I had asked my driver to stop for a moment in front of the towers of St Etienne; but, remembering how long we had taken to approach them when, earlier, they had seemed so close, I had just taken my watch from my pocket to see how many minutes would yet remain before we reached our goal, when the car turned a corner and drew up beneath them. For a long time they had been unattainable, resisting every effort of our mechanized advance to break through the separating distance, so that the car had seemed to be sliding fecklessly along the road, while the space between us and them had stayed unchanged. It was only in the last few seconds that we had realized to the full how fast we had been moving. Like giants whelming us with the vastness of their height, they flung themselves so recklessly before us, that we had only just enough time to keep ourselves from crashing into the porch.

We resumed our journey. Already we had left Caen far behind us. For a few seconds the city had borne us company, but then had disappeared, until only the two belfries of St Etienne, and the single tower of St Peter's remained adrift on the horizon, moving in a mute adieu their sun-touched vanes. At moments, one or other effaced itself, that the other two might catch of us a fleeting glimpse. Soon I could see but two. Then, for the last time, they turned and twisted, like hinged and golden emblems, to disappear at last from view. Often, since then, travelling at sunset through the plain of Caen, I have seen them, sometimes far off, so that they seemed no more than painted flowers upon the background of the sky that arched above the low lines of the fields; sometimes at rather closer range, when, joined by St Peter's belfry, they looked like three young maidens of some ancient legend, abandoned in a darkling solitude. And, while I journeyed on, I would see them seek to follow me with fearful steps, only, after a few awkward movements and uncouth stumbles, to draw their noble shapes into a clustered knot, and slip one behind the other, until they were no more than a single mass of shadow, sweet and patient, sinking into the uprush of the night.

I was beginning to give up all hope of arriving at Lisieux in time to be sure of reaching my parents' house, they, fortunately, not having been warned of my arrival, when, about sundown, we found ourselves abruptly on a hill, at the bottom of which, in a basin turned blood-crimson by the sun, to which we raced at speed, I saw Lisieux, which, hastening ahead, had hurriedly set up its crumbling houses and chimneys stained with red. In an instant everything was just where it should be, and when, some few seconds later, we drew up at the corner of the Rue aux Fèvres, the old houses with their fine shafted timbers holding aloft on saints' and demons' heads a flowering wealth of windows seemed not to have changed at all since the fifteenth century. A breakdown kept us in Lisieux until darkness had fallen. I wished to refresh my memory, before leaving, of some of the carved foliage on the exterior of the cathedral which Ruskin mentions, but the dim lamps which served to light the streets of the town were absent from the square, and Notre Dame was barely visible. Still, I walked forward, wishing at least to touch the famous trees of stone with which the porch is planted, and between whose nobly sculptured leaves once moved, perhaps, the nuptial pomp of Henry II of England and Eleanor of Guyenne. But just as I was feeling my way towards them, they became bathed in a sudden radiance. The great vista of pillared trunks strode from the blackness, the broad modelling of their chiselled leaves standing out in bright relief upon the shadowy background. My driver, the resourceful Agostinelli, paying to ancient stones the tribute of the present, whose gift of life served to make easy the reading of old lessons, was focusing upon each section in turn of the porch I wished to see, the bright beams of his headlights.[1] When I got back to the car, I saw a

1. I could not have foreseen, when I wrote these lines, that, seven or eight years later, this young man would ask to be allowed to type one of my books; would learn to fly, under the assumed name of Marcel Swann (thus fondly associating my own baptismal name and that of one of my characters), and would die at twenty-six in an aeroplane crash off Antibes.

little group of children, drawn thither by their curiosity, bending above the lamps their curly heads, which quivered in the unearthly glare, so that they looked like some little Nativity scene of angels, projected, as it were, from the cathedral in a beam of light.

By the time we left Lisieux it was quite dark. My driver had put on a voluminous rubber cloak, and, round his head, a species of hood, which, swathing the fulness of his young and beardless face, gave him the appearance, as we plunged ever more quickly through the night, of some pilgrim, or, rather, of some nun, dedicated to the service of the God of Speed. From time to time – a St Cecilia, improvising ethereal themes – he touched his keyboard, and drew sweet sounds from the instrument concealed in the car, whose gift of music, though continuous, we note only at such moments as the change of tone, which is the change of gear, comes audibly to us: an abstract music, so to speak, all symbol and all number, which sets the mind thinking of that harmony which, so men say, the spheres produce as they spin through space. But for most of the time, he sat there with his hand upon the wheel – the instrument by which he steered, and like enough for comparison to those instruments of martyred consecration borne by the Apostles who stand against the columns of the Saint-Chapelle in Paris, to the emblem carried by St Bénoit, and, in general, to every stylized form of wheel in the art of the Middle Ages. He seemed to use it but rarely, so motionless was his pose, but held it as he might have done some symbolic object with which convention ordained that he should be associated. In just such a way do saints in cathedral porches hold, one an anchor, one a wheel, a harp, a scythe, a gridiron, a hunting horn, a paint brush. But if these attributes were, in general, intended to recall the art which each, in life, had excellently practised, they sometimes served as a memorial of the nature of their final torment. How dearly I wished that the steering-wheel of this, my young mechanic, might forever symbolize his talent, and not prefigure the nature of his passion!

We had to stop in a village where, for the space of a few moments, I figured for its inhabitants as that traveller who ceased to exist when railways became general, and has now been resuscitated by the motor-car, the figure to whom, in Flemish paintings, the maid of the Inn is seen handing a stirrup-cup, the man one sees in the landscapes of Cuyp, stopping to ask his way of some passer-by – though, as Ruskin says, his mere appearance should have warned the traveller that he was incapable of giving any information – the horseman who, in the *Fables* of Lafontaine, gallops in sunlight and in wind, wrapped in a warm cloak when autumn comes, and the 'traveller would be well advised to take precautions' – the 'cavalier' who, today, scarcely exists at all in reality, though sometimes we see him still cantering at low tide along the shore when the sun is low (a ghost of the past, taking momentary form in the oncoming dark), turning the scene of sea and sand to a 'Marine Study' duly dated and signed, a tiny figure added, it would seem, by Lingelbach, Vouvermans or Adrian Van der Velde, to satisfy the taste for anecdote and human interest of those rich merchants of Haarlem who were the patrons of the fine arts, to a seascape by William Van der Velde or Ruysdael. But the most splendid gift bestowed by the automobile on this modern traveller is that of a splendid independence, by virtue of which he can set out at any hour he pleases, and stop when and where he will. Those will understand my meaning to whom a sudden wind brings an irresistible desire to escape upon its back to the ocean, where they may see, not dead village cobbles flagged in vain by the tempest, but great waves in a surge, prepared to give it blow for blow and roar for roar; those, above all, who know what it means at evening, to dread being shut into a room with their misery, realizing that a whole night lies before them. What happiness it is when one has wrestled long hours with agony, and is just on the point of going upstairs, to be able to say, stilling the beatings of one's heart: 'No, I won't go up, but have them saddle my horse, or bring the car round'; and then, all night long, to flee, leaving behind the villages where pain would have been a suffocating incubus, where one notes its presence under each little sleeping roof, while one speeds along the roads, unrecognized by its watching eyes and safe from its attack.

But my car had stopped at the corner of a hollow lane, before a door smothered in roses and fading iris. We had reached my parents' house. The driver sounded his horn to call the gardener to open the gate; that horn whose strident and monotonous note we find displeasing, but which, like all material things, can turn into something beautiful once it has been touched with sentiment. In my parents' hearts it called forth a happy echo, coming to them like some unexpected word . . . 'I rather think I heard . . . it must be he, it can't be anybody else!' They get up, light a candle, sheltering its flame against the draught from the door which, in their impatience, they have already opened, while, at the far end of the park, the horn whose joyous and now almost human sound they can no longer misconstrue, sends out continuously a level, changeless summons that is like the obsession of their happiness to come, urgent and repetitive, like their waxing, anxious hopes. And I thought how, in *Tristan and Isolde* (first in the second act when Isolde waves her scarf for a signal, and then in the third when the ship arrives) it is, in the first instance by means of a strident repetition, indefinite and increasingly rapid, of two notes – the peculiar succession of which is sometimes, in the world of undisciplined noise, the result of mere chance; in the second, through the growing intensity, the insatiable monotony of the thin, reedy tune played by a poor shepherd-boy, that Wagner, by that very abdication of creative power which is sheer genius, has expressed the greatest sense of expectation waiting on happiness that has ever filled the human heart.

ITALY

KATHERINE MANSFIELD (1888–1923)

from *The Letters and Journals of Katherine Mansfield: A Selection*

To J. M. Murry

8 October 1919. It is awfully hot here – as hot as when we came. The insects are *simply awful.* It's a good thing you left before they got really bad. My leg is so swollen I can only hop today. It is maddening because otherwise I feel so well and strong. Curse these confounded countries!! We have double nets, powder, bathe in verbena, oatmeal, milk, salt water, fresh – but nothing cures them. I think they make the idea of a life in this country absolutely insupportable. Enough of them.

I took the revolver into the garden today and practised with it: how to load and unload and fire. It terrifies me, but I feel 'like a new being' now that I really can handle it and understand it. I'll never give it back. They are fascinating things; one is childishly fascinated. I almost understand old Brontë *père.* No more coffee to be had in San Remo. The Government has taken it over as it has the rice. Dear knows when we shall get any more. It doesn't matter really.

Please send me some books to review. I have none for next week.

12 October 1919. I am sitting in the Bastick chair covered with the Jaeger rug, as although the sun is hot the air is chilly (it's about 4.45 p.m.). It has been a marvellous day here; I've not moved except for meals. I've been reading and writing, and after lunch I fell asleep from the general *shipboard* atmosphere. Speaking of ships, such a small jewel of a sailing ship passed the house today, riding close enough in to see the men on board. She had two small sails at the bows, one big one at the stern, and a medium *very* movable one amidships. The sea is my favourite sea, bright, bright blue, but showing a glint of white as far as one can see. That lift of white seen far away, as far as the horizon, moves me terribly. In fact it is *the very thing* I would like to express in writing: it has *the very quality*. Here comes another most interesting little steamboat – a very small trader, she looks, painted black and red, with a most ridiculous amount of smoke coming out of the funnel. [A drawing of the steamer.] No. I can't draw her.

From where I sit, I cannot see any ground below the balustrade. That is threaded through with sea. One would think it was a sheer drop from there into deep water. What a place, eh, Bogey?

I had a nasty jar last night. As there was no water last week, the laundry was put 'out' and it came home exquisite, covered with a white net with a rose on top, carried by the nicest old body on her head, who seemed to take the greatest fancy to me, as I did to her. *Long* conversations. '*Comme vous êtes bien ici*,' etc., etc., etc., etc. And under all this a bill for 37.85!! This, of course, after the old 'un had gone and the rose had been smelled admired and Wig had thought how *much* better, after all, they order these things in Italy. L.M. did not really 'think it very heavy. I don't think you could have expected it to be less, Katie'. This with her overall 4.50 and an immense white petticoat 3.75! As to serviettes at 1 lira apiece, 'Oh well, my dear, that's not quite sixpence if the exchange is still at 41 for £1. It's about . . . let me see . . . hardly fivepence,' and so on and so on and so on. How I should beat her if I were married to her! It's an awful thought. She thinks I'm made of money. That's the worst of it! On her last but one journey to San Remo she bought *one* hecto of coffee for 4.50 from '*such* a funny little shop' and when I protested she thought 'the parcel was small for the money, but the beans felt very tightly packed'. Could you believe it? However – let her go. And I shall never shoot her because the body would be so difficult to dispose of after. One couldn't make it into a neat parcel or put it under a hearth stone, and she would *never* burn.

Every day I love this house more for some new grace, and every day I hold a minute review of the garden, and there is always something fresh and wonderful. Then there is the wild hill, never the same, *satisfying* one's deep love for what is living and ancient in literature. I look at the hill, dearest Bogey, and because I have not had a classical education, it seems to me full of the spirit of those old boys – the wild fig and olive, the low-growing berries and the tufts of sweet roots . . .

This is the place for lovers. (Hullo! there goes a swallow.) Yes, it is made for lovers. You know, don't you, how even now I am preparing it for you. I look at it and think: I shall put net curtains here – and the baskets under the verandah shall be flower-baskets and—It's enough to keep me busy until May, my very own. Another Sunday. That's two gone – now there are only 26.

20 November 1919. It's a very dull day here with wild ragged clouds and a cold halting miserable wind. My black fit is on me – not caused by the day altogether. Christ! to *hate* like I do. It's upon me today. You don't know what hatred is because I know you have never hated anyone – not as you have loved – equally. That's what I do. My deadly deadly enemy has got me today and I'm simply a blind force of hatred. Hate is the *other* passion. It has all the opposite effects of Love. It fills you with death and corruption, it makes you feel hideous, degraded and old, it makes you long to DESTROY. Just as the other is light, so this is darkness. I hate like that – a million times multiplied. It's like being under a curse. When L.M. goes I don't know what I shall do. I can only think of breathing – lying quite still and breathing. Her great fat arms, her tiny blind breasts, her baby mouth, the underlip always wet and a crumb or two or a chocolate stain at the corners – her eyes fixed on me – fixed – waiting for what I may do that she may copy it. Think what you would feel if you had consumption and lived with a deadly enemy! That's one thing I shall grudge Virginia all her days – that she and Leonard were together. We can't be: we've got to wait our six months, but when they are up, I WILL not have L.M. near. I shall rather commit suicide. That is dead earnest. In fact, I have made up my mind that I shall commit suicide if I don't tear her up by the roots then. It would be kinder for us both – for you and for me, of course I mean. We'd have no love otherwise. You'd only slowly grow to think I was first wicked and then mad. You'd be quite right. I'm both with her – mad, really mad, like Lawrence was, only worse. I leaned over the gate today and dreamed she'd died of heart-failure and I heard myself cry out 'Oh, what heaven! what heaven!'

Should I *not* send this? I must. I want you to know so that when the time comes for her to go, you will remember. The worst thing about hate is that it never spends itself – is never exhausted and in this case isn't even shared. So you come up against something which says: 'Hit me, hit me, hate me, hate – feel *strongly* about me – one way or the other, it doesn't matter which way as long as I make you FEEL.' The man who murders from sheer hate is right to murder; he does it in self-defence. Worst of all is that I can't write a book while I live with her – I tried now for two months. It won't go. It's no good.

* * *

DAVID AREUBENI

from *Jewish Travellers in the Middle Ages*

[A Jewish Ambassador's Audience with the Pope, 1524]

I, David, the son of King Solomon, of righteous memory, from the wilderness of Habor, entered the gate of the City of Rome on the 15th day of Adar, 1524, and a Gentile from Venice came to me and spoke with me in Arabic, and I was angry with him. I went to the Pope's palace, riding on horseback, and my servant before me, and the Jews also came with me, and I entered the presence of Cardinal Egidio, and all the Cardinals and Princes came to see me, and with the said Cardinal was R. Joseph Ashkenazi who was his teacher, and the physician Rabbi, Joseph Sarphati; and I spoke to the Cardinal, and my interpreter was the learned man who came with me, and the Jews heard all that I spoke to the Cardinal, and I said to him that to the Pope I would complete my message. I stayed with the Cardinal all day till the eve of Sabbath, and he promised to bring the matter before the Pope to-morrow. I went away with R. Joseph Ashkenazi and with R. Raphael, the old man who lived in the same house, and we took our Sabbath meal and slept till the morning and I went with them to the Synagogue in order to pronounce the blessing of deliverance from peril before the scroll of the Law. Men, women, and children came to meet us all the way until we entered the house of the said R. Raphael, and I fasted on that Sabbath day. All day long men and women, Jews and gentiles came to visit me until evening.

Cardinal Egidio sent for R. Joseph Ashkenazi to tell me that the Pope
was very pleased and wished to see me on Sunday before eleven.
And so in the morning, before prayers, they gave me a horse and I
went to Borghetto Santo Gile to the house of an old man, the
brother-in-law of R. Joseph Sarphati, before morning prayer; and I
prayed there, and many Jews came to me (may God keep them and
multiply them a thousand fold!). At eight o'clock I went to the house
of the Pope and entered Cardinal Egidio's room, and with me were
about twelve old and honoured Jews. As soon as the Cardinal saw
me, he rose from his chair and we went, I and he, to the apartment
of the Pope, and I spoke with him, and he received me graciously
and said, 'The matter is from the Lord;' and I said to him, 'King
Joseph and his elders ordered me to speak to thee that thou shouldst
make peace between the Emperor and the French King, by all means,
for it will be well with thee and them if thou makest this peace, and
write for me a letter to these two Kings, and they will help us and we
will help them; and write also for me to King Prester John (i.e. the
King of Abyssinia). The Pope answered me, 'As to the two kings
between whom thou askest me to make peace, I cannot do it, but
if thou needest help the King of Portugal will assist thee, and I will
write to him and he will do all, and his land is near to thy country
and they are accustomed to travel on the great sea every year, more
than those in the lands of those other Kings;' and I replied to the
Pope, 'Whatever thou wishest I will do, and I will not turn to
the right or left from what thou biddest me, for I have come for
God's service, and not for anything else, and I will pray for thy
welfare and good all the days of my life.' And the Pope asked the
Cardinal, 'Where does the Ambassador lodge?' and he answered,
'The Jews asked him to go with them,' and the honourable Jews
who were with the Pope told him, 'Let the Ambassador stay with
us for we will honour him for the sake of thy honour,' and the Pope
said to them, 'If you will do honour to him I will pay all your
expenses;' and I said to the Pope, 'I wish to come before thee once
every two days, for to see thee is as seeing the face of God,' and the
Pope answered me that he ordered Cardinal Egidio to come with
me every time I came to see him, and I took leave of the Pope and
went from before him, and I went with the Jews and rejoiced and was
glad of heart. I returned to the old man's house by way of Santo
Gile, but Aaron, the warden, was angry that I went to the old
man's house, and told the Cardinal that the wardens and the whole

congregation had prepared a house for the ambassador and provided servants for him, because I could not remain alone; the Cardinal wrote me that I should go with them, and I went with them. They prepared for me a fine dwelling with three big good rooms, and the master of the house was called Joseph, and he had three sons, the eldest Moses, the second Benjamin, and the third Judah; and they all waited on me, and I stayed in their house six weeks, and I went to the Cardinal's house five days consecutively, for the other Cardinals went to his house and they consulted me from morning to evening, and I fasted in that house six days consecutively; and on Friday they boiled some water for me and put in it many herbs. They did all this for the love of me, because they said that it was medicine after the fast, but my soul was weary, and I wished to drink water, and they gave me the boiled water and I drank a stomach full. This water caused me a great and strong pain in the stomach, for I was not accustomed to drink hot water after a fast. I fasted in Jerusalem six times, seven days and nights, and in Venice, six days and nights, and after all these fasts I drank nothing but cold water with much sugar, and that did me no harm, but they only did it for my good, to give me hot water, because they did not know my constitution, may the householders and the warden be blessed. A great sickness came upon me and I said to them, 'Find me a bath of hot water for I wish to go there;' and a man came called Yomtob Halevi, and he prepared me a bath and a good couch to sleep upon, and I entered the bath and slept there, and that day I let much blood, cupping all my limbs, and then I sent for the physician, R. Joseph Sarphati, and said to him, 'Look how I am; if thou wishest to get a great name, let me stay in thy house and remain with me until my sickness leaves me.' He did so, and I stayed in his house three months, and he paid all the expenses and for all I required, may the Lord bless him and his household! He gave me to eat, and gave me various kinds of remedies and boiled wine for me to drink and heated herbs and placed them on my feet, and washed my feet and anointed me, and took olive oil and put it in a big vessel; and I entered and washed in that hot olive oil, and I came out from the hot oil and lay on a good bed, and they changed the sheets each time, and I lay on the bed like a dead man; and they saw that there was gravel in my water, which is a bad sign, and I told them that I would not die from this illness until I had brought Israel to Jerusalem, built the altar, and offered sacrifice; but I got no sleep and was in great pain and lay between life and death, and they said to me, 'Wilt thou make confession, for that will neither bring death near nor keep it away;' and I was angered with them, and said, 'Go in peace, I do not wish to say the confession, for I trust in God, that he will stay with me and save me.' They were astonished at my good constitution and pleased, and God sent a great sweat on me on that day and I was healed from the great sickness.

* * *

JEAN-JACQUES ROUSSEAU (1712–1778)

from *The Confessions*

[In Hannibal's Footsteps Over the Alps]

I walked gaily on my way with my pious guide and his lively companion. No misadventure disturbed my journey. I was as happy physically and mentally as at any time in my life. I was young, vigorous, healthy, fearless, and full of confidence in myself and others. I was enjoying that short but precious moment in life when its overflowing fullness expands, so to speak, one's whole being, and lends all nature, in one's eyes, the charm of one's own existence. I was less uneasy now, for I had an object to hold my wandering thoughts and fix my imagination. I looked on myself as the creature, the pupil, the friend and almost the love of Mme de Warens. The nice things she had said to me, the slight caresses she had bestowed on me, the tender interest she had seemed to take in me, and her friendly glances, which seemed loving glances to me because they inspired me with love – all this was food for my thoughts as I walked on, and gave me delicious imaginings. Not a fear or a doubt for my future troubled my dreams. By sending me to Turin they had, as I saw it, assumed responsibility for my existence there; they would find me a suitable situation. I need have no further care for myself; others had undertaken to look after me. So I walked with a light step, freed of that burden, and my heart was full of young desires, alluring hopes, and brilliant prospects. Every object I saw seemed a guarantee of my future happiness. I saw in my imagination a country feast in every house and wild game in every meadow; bathing in every river and fishing from every bank; delicious fruit on every tree and voluptuous assignations in its shade; bowls of milk and cream on the mountain-sides, everywhere the delights of idleness, and peace and simplicity, and the joy of going one knew not where. In fact nothing struck my eyes without bringing some thrill of pleasure to my heart. The grandeur, the variety, and real beauty of the landscape amply justified my pleasure, and vanity as well had a hand in it. To be travelling to Italy so young, to have seen so many countries already, to be following in Hannibal's footsteps across the mountains, seemed to me a glory beyond my years. Moreover there were good and frequent inns, and I had a fine appetite and enough to eat. For, indeed, I had no reason to stint myself; my dinner was nothing compared to M. Sabran's.

I do not remember ever having had in all my life a spell of time so completely free from care and anxiety as those seven or eight days we spent on the road. For since we had to suit our pace to Mme Sabran's, it was one long stroll. This memory has left me the strongest taste for everything associated with it, for mountains especially and for travelling on foot. I have never travelled so except in my prime, and it has always been a delight to me. Business and duties and luggage to carry soon compelled me to play the gentleman and hire carriages; then carking cares, troubles, and anxiety climbed in with me, and from that moment, instead of feeling on my travels only the pleasures of the road, I was conscious of nothing but the need to arrive at my destination. For a long time I searched Paris for any two men sharing my tastes, each willing to contribute fifty *louis* from his purse and a year of his time for a joint tour of Italy on foot, with no other attendant than a lad to come with us and carry a knapsack. Many people appeared, seemingly delighted with the idea. But really they all took it for a pipe dream, for a plan one enjoys talking about but has no wish to carry out. I remember talking with such passion of the project to Diderot and Grimm that finally I infected them with my enthusiasm. I thought I had it all settled: but soon it reduced itself to a mere journey on paper, in which Grimm had the amusing idea of getting Diderot to commit various impieties and of handing me over to the Inquisition in his stead . . .

Before I go further I must present my reader with an apology, or rather a justification, for the petty details I have just been entering into, and for those I shall enter into later, none of which may appear interesting in his eyes. Since I have undertaken to reveal myself absolutely to the public, nothing about me must remain hidden or obscure. I must remain incessantly beneath his gaze, so that he may follow me in all the extravagances of my heart and into every least corner of my life. Indeed, he must never lose sight of me for a single instant, for if he finds the slightest gap in my story, the smallest hiatus, he may wonder what I was doing at that moment and accuse me of refusing to tell the whole truth. I am laying myself sufficiently open to human malice by telling my story, without rendering myself more vulnerable by any silence.

My little hoard of money was gone. I had chattered, and my companions had been quick to profit by my silliness. Mme Sabran found means to strip me of everything down to a little piece of silver ribbon which Mme de Warens had given me for my small sword. This I regretted more than all the rest. They would even have kept my sword if I had been less obstinate. They had faithfully paid my expenses on the road; but they had left me nothing. I arrived at Turin without clothes or money or linen, and was left with no means but my merit for acquiring the honour and fortune I intended to win.

I presented my letters of introduction and was immediately taken to the hospice for converts, there to be instructed in the faith which was the price of my subsistence. As I entered I saw a great iron-barred door, which was shut and double-locked behind me, once I was in. This seemed a formidable beginning but hardly an agreeable one, and I had already food for thought when they showed me into a room of considerable size. The only furniture I could see in it was a wooden altar with a great crucifix upon it, at the far end, and four or five chairs round the walls, which were wooden also and appeared to have been waxed, though, in fact, they owed their gloss only to use and rubbing. In this assembly-hall were four or five frightful cut-throats, my fellow pupils, who looked more like the devil's bodyguard than men who aspired to become children of God. Two of these scoundrels were Croats who called themselves Jews or Moors, and who spent their lives, as they confessed to me, roaming Spain and Italy, embracing Christianity and having themselves baptized wherever the rewards . . .

*

There is no soul so vile, no heart so barbarous as to be insusceptible to some sort of affection, and one of the two cut-throats who called themselves Moors took a fancy to me. He was fond of coming up to me and gossiping with me in his queer jargon. He did me little services, sometimes giving me some of his food at table, and he frequently kissed me with an ardour which I found most displeasing. But, frightened though I naturally was by his dusky face, which was beautified by a long scar, and by his passionate glances, which seemed to me more savage than affectionate, I put up with his kisses, saying to myself, 'The poor man has conceived a warm friendship for me; it would be wrong to repulse him.' But he passed by degrees to more unseemly conduct, and sometimes made me such strange suggestions that I thought he was wrong in the head. One night he wanted to share my bed, but I objected on the plea that it was too narrow. He then pressed me to come into his. I still refused, however, for the poor devil was so dirty and smelt so strongly of the tobacco he chewed that he made me feel ill.

Next day, very early in the morning, we were alone together in the assembly-hall. He resumed his caresses, but with such violence that I was frightened. Finally he tried to work up to the most revolting liberties and, by guiding my hand, to make me take the same liberties with him. I broke wildly away with a cry and leaped backwards, but without displaying indignation or anger, for I had not the slightest idea what it was all about. But I showed my surprise and disgust to such effect that he then left me alone. But as he gave up the struggle I saw something whitish and sticky shoot towards the fireplace and fall on the ground. My stomach turned over, and I rushed on to the balcony, more upset, more troubled and more frightened as well, than ever I had been in my life. I was almost sick.

I could not understand what was the matter with the poor man. I thought he was having a fit of epilepsy or some other seizure even more terrible. And really I know of no more hideous sight for a man in cold blood than such foul and obscene behaviour, nothing more revolting than a terrifying face on fire with the most brutal lust. I have never seen another man in that state; but if we appear like that to women, they must indeed be fascinated not to find us repulsive.

I could think of nothing better than to go and inform everybody of what had just happened. Our old woman attendant told me to hold my tongue. But I saw that my story had much upset her, for I heard her mutter under her breath: *Can maledet! brutta bestia!* As I could see no reason for holding my tongue, I took no notice of her but went on talking. I talked so much in fact that next day one of the principals came very early and read me a sharp lecture, accusing me of impugning the honour of a sacred establishment and making a lot of fuss about nothing.

In addition to this rebuke he explained to me a number of things I did not know, but which he did not suspect he was telling me for the first time. For he believed that I had known what the man wanted when I defended myself, but had merely been unwilling. He told me gravely that it was a forbidden and immoral act like fornication, but that the desire for it was not an affront to the person who was its object. There was nothing to get so annoyed about in having been found attractive. He told me quite openly that in his youth he had been similarly honoured and, having been surprised in a situation where he could put up no resistance, he had found nothing so brutal about it all. He carried his effrontery so far as to employ frank terminology and, imagining that the reason for my refusal had been fear of pain, assured me that my apprehensions were groundless. There was no reason to be alarmed about nothing.

I listened to the wretch with redoubled astonishment, since he was not speaking for himself but apparently to instruct me for my own good. The whole matter seemed so simple to him that he had not even sought privacy for our conversation. There was an ecclesiastic listening all the while who found the matter no more alarming than he. This natural behaviour so impressed me that I finally believed such things were no doubt general practice in the world, though I had so far not had occasion to learn of them. So I listened without anger though not without disgust. The memory of my experience, and especially of what I had seen, remained so firmly imprinted on my mind that my stomach still rose when I thought of it. Unconsciously my dislike for the business extended to the apologist, and I could not sufficiently control myself for him not to see the ill effect of his lesson. He shot me a far from affectionate glance, and from that time on spared no pains to make my stay at the hospice unpleasant. So well did he succeed that, seeing only one way of escape, I made the same impassioned efforts to take it as hitherto I had taken to avoid it.

This adventure put me on my guard for the future against the attentions of pederasts. And the sight of men with that reputation, by reminding me of the looks and behaviour of my frightful Moor, has always horrified me that I have found it difficult to hide my disgust. Women, on the other hand, acquired a greater value for me, by way of contrast. I seemed to owe them a reparation for the offences of my sex, that could only be paid by the most delicate affection and personal homage. My memories of that self-styled African transformed the plainest of sluts into an object of adoration.

* * *

JOHN COWPER POWYS (1872–1963)

from *Autobiography*

[Venice]

Oh, how well I remember Llewelyn's excitement when I announced to him that I was going to take him to Venice. It was in the potato garden, near the crumbling wall of Ham Hill Stone across which lay Cole's orchard where we used to shoot at cole-tits and marsh-tits with our catapults, and he was lying in his deckchair amid the tangle of nettles and ground-ivy and stone-crop, listening to a thrush breaking a snail's armour upon a stone; and when I told him he positively cried aloud with joy, so that Willy, hidden in the laurel bushes, came out to learn the news. He had grown weary of his long sickness, and the idea of this daring excursion thrilled him through and through.

But I received a very stern letter from A. R. P. on this occasion which brought down by several pegs the pitch of our high spirits. I intended to travel to Venice by that express from Paris that the hero of Proust's book must have taken on the occasion when he felt that famous unevenness in the paving-stones of St Mark's, which, like that mouthful of the Madeleine dipt in camomile tea, gave him one of his immortality-proving ecstasies; but we were going to meet a very spirited and beautiful girl in Venice and we were also to meet there that resplendent *habitué* of historic Europe, our brilliant friend Louis. It was the fact that I was smuggling Llewelyn off to encounter such provocative persons in such a provocative place that troubled

Bertie. He accused me of acting 'as I always did'; of sacrificing others with reckless unscrupulousness to my lust for dramatic excitement.

His psychological if not his moral insight proved, I regret to say, completely justified. John *was* at his old dramatic tricks again. John *was* at his old trade of a cerebral Pandarus. Well! on this occasion John was fairly 'caught on the hop'.

At Milan, on our way home, Llewelyn fell seriously ill, and we had to remain for weeks and weeks in a hotel in this city till he could move on again. But this was afterwards. This was when we had supped full on the forbidden fruit. For that Venetian visit was a unique experience in both our lives. If Llewelyn paid for it at Milan with hæmorrhages and kidney stones he enjoyed it at the time hardly less than I did. It was lucky we had Louis with us, for he, as he always did, kept his head whereas Llewelyn and I worked ourselves up to such a pitch in our jealous contest for the favours of the beautiful girl who was with us that *our* heads were completely turned. She insisted on dressing up as a boy; and we would accompany her in her gondola in this attire to the remotest possible spots where gondolas could be propelled! If Louis had not kept intact his East Anglian sang-froid heaven knows into what wild events Llewelyn and I, in our mounting rivalry, might have been led.

What I call my heart was hit as it has not been often hit. Though this organ does not change its physical position like that one at Clavadel it is by no means what you would call a passionate heart. But whatever kind of a heart it may be it was certainly pierced through and through by one of the arrows in *that* quiver! It was in fact in a state of such wild imaginative elation that all my insanest mystical impulses whirled up to the surface while all my passion for dramatic gestures responded with kindred motions. The feelings that this beautiful girl in boy's clothes excited in me rose like flames that were as many-coloured in their flashing sword-points as those angels I had prayed to in the London Hospital.

There was some small kind of a war going on at that epoch between Italy and some other country; and I dare say our appearance when we escorted this girl about Venice was odd and striking. At any rate we were disembarking from our gondola one day not far from the Bridge of Sighs when we found ourselves surrounded by an imposing band of officials. It was explained to us that we were under arrest. 'This,' they said, indicating our friend, 'is a feminine one; yes? no?'

Llewelyn whispered to me that it was just as if they had caught a hatful of trespassing butterflies and discovered among them, by the markings under her wings, a fine female specimen. This is the only occasion so far in my life when I have been in the hands of the police; and really when we were all led into some upper chamber, and made to stand in a row before a grave personage at a table, I felt as if the chief of the 'Volentia Army' were being treated as he had so often treated our little nurse from Berkshire, in that robber's roof-attic at Rothesay House!

Our Venetian address was carefully taken down – an hotel on the Lido – and then came the question of our home address. Not one of us had a card except Llewelyn, and he had, by some chance, one of my father's. Never had those familiar words: 'Rev. C. F. Powys, Montacute Vicarage, Somerset' sounded so out of place; but the Venetian official chuckled a good deal and handed the card to one of his subordinates. We caught the word *padre* exchanged between them accompanied by what no doubt was a sly commentary on the progenitive capacity of priests in England. An official at once hurried off to the Lido to verify our story, and once again Llewelyn saved us; for, after his fashion, he had so courted, cajoled, caressed, and generally bewitched our landlady, that the woman led the emissary to think that our social position at home, in spite of the *padre*'s card, was a tremendous one, and that we were only behaving in our accustomed manner, like so many Milords Byron.

But my excitement during those wild Venetian days rose to a pitch that I have never known before or since. I remember going alone to Verona one day and being so elated by the thought of Juliet in her tomb, by the vast stone Amphitheatre, and by that gondola-loving boy-girl, that like Faust I could have cried out to the moment, even if it brought the Judgment Day with it 'O stay! Thou art so fair!' There were clouds without water sweeping across the Verona sky; and their ominous appearance, together with an extraordinary revelation of lightning without thunder, had driven everybody out of the Amphitheatre. And as I sat in that vast semi-cirque – but what was its vulgar Roman antiquity really, compared with the mystic stone-circles of my own land? – my whole nature seemed transformed. I cannot recall now whether or not that boy-girl was actually seated by my side. She was certainly enthroned in my insane imagination; but sometimes it comes back to me that she *was* with me under that lightning without thunder, and sometimes that I was alone that day.

Undoubtedly there do come occasions in a person's life when the underlying fatality of his identity gathers itself together and rises up from the fluctuating waves of his nature like a crested sea-serpent from the bottomless silt. At such moments, whatever stains are on his conscience a person feels able to shriek out, like Macbeth: 'Though Birnam Wood *be* come to Dunsinane; and *thou* opposed, being of no woman born; *yet* I will try the last!'

Alone in that Roman circle, under those clouds from which no drop of rain fell, the thaumaturgic element in my nature rose to such a pitch that I felt, as I have only done once or twice since, that I really *was* endowed with some sort of supernatural power. To what end had the gods thus dedicated me? Merely to indulge in 'dithyrambic analysis' before bewildered, puzzled, derisive audiences? I refused to believe it! I refuse to believe it still. What I felt at that moment in the Verona Amphitheatre was the very thing I had been obscurely fumbling my way towards through all my lusts and my obsessions. I felt it again, only five years ago, when I visited Stonehenge with Littleton on our way from Sherborne to Northwold. The feeling that comes over me at such times is one of most formidable power. It makes me conscious that below all the maudlin silliness of my gaping countenance – and I willingly confess that, even more accurately than the word 'zany' or 'punchinello', the word 'maudlin' exactly describes the wool-gathering, absent-minded foolishness in my face – I conceal a demonic formidableness of my own, of which my enemies were well advised to beware! As I have hinted before, no amount of 'manic elation', or 'paranoia', or 'megalomaniac', can explain the fact that I am the most unlucky person in the world to insult or malign. The evidence of this – of my being able, I mean, and quite unconsciously too, to exercise some kind of 'evil eye', on people who have injured me – has so piled up upon me all my life that it has become a habit with me to pray to my gods anxiously and hurriedly for each new enemy!

* * *

HECTOR BERLIOZ (1803–1869)

from *Memoirs*

[Berlioz hastens back to Paris with loaded pistols and on the way composes an overture.]

It took me a long time to get used to this novel kind of existence, and I had something on my mind which prevented me from taking any interest either in surrounding objects or in the society into which I was thus suddenly thrown. I expected to find letters from Paris waiting for me, and for the next three weeks I watched for them with ever-increasing anxiety.[1]

Unable any longer to control my desire to fathom the reason of this mysterious silence, I determined to return to Paris at once, despite M. Horace Vernet's friendly remonstrances, and his warning that he would be obliged to strike my name off the Academy lists if I persisted in my rash resolve. On my way back I was detained for a week in Florence by an attack of quinsy, which confined me to my bed. While there I made the acquaintance of the Danish architect, Schlick, a capital fellow, who is thought very highly of by connoisseurs. During my illness I re-scored the *Scène du Bal*, in my *Symphonie fantastique*, and added the present coda. It was almost finished when I was allowed out for the first time, and I at once proceeded to the post-office for my letters. The packet which was handed to me contained a letter the tenor of which was inconceivably painful to a man of my years and temperament. I was beside myself with passion, and shed tears from sheer rage; but I made up my mind on the spot what to do. My duty was clear. I must at once proceed to Paris, and kill two guilty women and an innocent man. After that, it would of course, be incumbent on me to commit suicide. I arranged all the details on the spot. Knowing me as they did, my reappearance in Paris would be looked for ... A complete

1. It was from Camille that Berlioz was vainly expecting to hear. He was tortured with jealousy.

disguise and the greatest precautions were therefore necessary; and I rushed off to Schlick, to whom I had already confided my story.

'Good God! what is the matter?' he cried, when he saw my white face.

'Look and see,' I said, handing him the letter.

'This is horrible!' he replied, when he had read it. 'What are you going to do?'

I knew that, if I told him my plan, he would try to dissuade me from carrying it out.

'What am I going to do? Why, return to France, of course; but to my father's house instead of to Paris.'

'That is right, my dear fellow; go home, and in time you will recover from the awful condition into which this unexpected blow has thrown you. Come, cheer up.'

'I will, but I must be off at once. I could not answer for myself tomorrow.'

'We can easily get you off tonight, for I have friends among the police and the postal officials. I will have your passport ready in two hours, and will get you a seat in the diligence which starts five hours hence. Go to your hotel and get ready, and I will meet you there.'

Instead of following his advice, I betake myself to one of the quays on the Arno, where I knew there was a French *modiste*. I enter the shop, look at my watch, and say: 'It is now twelve o'clock, madame; I leave by the mail this evening, and I want to know if you can let me have, before five o'clock, a costume such as would be worn by a lady's maid – robe, hat, green veil, and so on? I will pay you whatever you choose to ask.'

After a moment's consideration, it is arranged that I am to have what I want. I deposit part of the price, and return to the Hôtel des Quatre Nations, on the opposite bank of the Arno.

I call the head porter.

'I am going to Paris at six o'clock this evening, Antoine, and I cannot take my trunk, so kindly look after it, and send it after me to my father's house as soon as you can. I have written down the address.'

I then took the score of the *Scène du Bal*, and, as the instrumentation of the coda was not quite completed, I wrote across it: 'I have not time to finish this; but, if the Paris Concert Society should take it into its head to perform this work during the ABSENCE of the author, I request Habeneck to double the passage for flutes in the bass octave, with the clarinets and horns, the last time the theme is introduced, and to write the chords which follow for full orchestra; that will do for the ending.'

I then seal it up, address it to Habeneck, and pack it in a bag with some clothes. I have a pair of double-barrelled pistols, which I load carefully, and two little bottles of laudanum and strychnine, which I examine and put in my pocket. Then, my mind being at rest with regard to my arsenal, I spend the remainder of my time in wandering about the streets of Florence, with the restless, disturbing demeanour of a mad dog.

At five I adjourn to my dressmaker's and try on my costume, which fits to perfection. In paying for it I put down twenty francs more than the price agreed; the girl at the desk tries to point out my mistake, but is deterred by her mistress, who hastily sweeps the gold into a drawer, saying: 'Leave the gentleman alone, you little stupid; don't you see that he is too busy to listen to your chatter? A thousand thanks, sir; I wish you success. You will look your part to perfection.' I smiled ironically, and she bowed me gracefully out of the shop.

At last it strikes six, and I bid farewell to my honest friend Schlick, who looks upon me as a lost sheep returning to the fold. I stow away my feminine apparel in one of the side pockets of the coach, give a parting glance at Cellini's *Perseus*, with the famous inscription, *Si quis te læserit, ego tuus ultor ero*,[2] and we are off.

We leave mile after mile behind us, but not a word passes between me and the courier. I had a great lump in my throat, and sat with my teeth tightly clenched, unable either to sleep or eat. About midnight, however, he said something to me about my pistols, which he prudently uncapped and hid under the cushions. He was afraid we might be attacked, and in that case, said he, it is much better to remain passive, unless you wish to be murdered.

'Just as you please,' I replied. 'I don't want to raise any difficulties, and I bear the brigands no grudge.'

My companion did not know what to make of me, and, as I had taken nothing but a little orange juice since we started, he began to regard me as scarcely human. When we arrived at Genoa I discovered that a fresh misfortune had befallen me, and that I had lost my

2. 'If any offend thee, I will avenge thee.' This celebrated statue stands in the Grand Ducal Square, from which the mails start.

female outfit. We had changed carriages at a village called Pietra
Santa, and I had left my disguise behind. 'Fire and thunder!' I said.
'It looks as if some damned good angel were bent on hindering my
purpose. But we shall see!'

I sent for a courier who could speak both French and Genoese,
and asked him to take me to a dressmaker. It was nearly midday, and
the next coach started at six. I demand a costume: impossible to
finish one in so short a time. We go to another dressmaker, then
to a third, and a fourth, without success. At last we find a woman
who is willing to try; she accomplishes the task, and my disaster is
repaired. Unluckily, however, upon examining my passport, the
Sardinian police take it into their heads that I am a *carbonaro*,
a conspirator, a patriot, or Heaven knows what, refuse to *viser* my
passport for Turin, and advise me to travel via Nice instead.

'Well, then, *viser* it for Nice, in Heaven's name! What do I care
whether I pass through hell, so long as I pass?'

I don't know which of us was the greater fool, the police, who
saw a revolutionist in every Frenchman, or I, who feared to set foot
in Paris except disguised as a woman, lest my purpose should reveal
itself in my face; forgetting, like an idiot, that I could have remained
quietly in an hotel in Paris for a few hours, and sent for any number
of effective disguises at my leisure.

When people are possessed with any single idea they always
fancy, in the drollest way, that everyone else is full of it too, and act
upon the supposition.

Still in a rage, I set out on my way to Nice, rehearsing on the
way every point of the little *comedy* I intended to play in Paris. I
would go to my *friends'* house, about nine o'clock in the evening,
when the family would be assembled for tea, and send in to say that
the Countess M.'s maid is waiting with an urgent message; I am
shown into the drawing-room; I hand over a letter, and, while it is
being read, produce my pistol and blow out the brains, first of
number one, and then of number two; and, seizing number three
by the hair, throw off my disguise, and finish her off in the same
manner, regardless of her shrieks. Then, before this concert of voices
and instruments attracts attention, I hasten to deposit the contents
of the remaining barrel in my own right temple; and if the pistol
misses fire (which has happened before now), I shall at once resort
to my small bottles. A charming comedy! It is really a great pity it
was never put upon the stage.

And yet there were moments when, in spite of my wrath, I could not help feeling sorry that my plans, excellent as they otherwise were, involved my own suicide. It seemed hard to bid farewell to life and art, to go down to posterity merely as a brute who could not get on in the world; to leave my unfinished symphony, and all the other greater works which were seething in my brain . . . Ah! . . . it is . . . And then suddenly my fell purpose gained the upper hand once more . . . No, no, no, no, no, they must all die, they must, and they shall! . . . And the horses trotted on, bearing me nearer and nearer to France.

It was night, and we were travelling along the Corniche road, which is cut out of the steep precipice of rocks overhanging the sea. For more than an hour I had been indulging in bright dreams of what the future might have had in store for me when the postilion stopped the horses to put on the drag, and suddenly, through the stillness, the sound of the roaring breakers dashing against the foot of the precipice broke on my ear. The raging fury of the waves raised a corresponding tempest in my breast, fiercer and deadlier than any I had yet experienced. I sat like a raving lunatic, clutching the seat with both hands, ready to spring out and dash myself over the cliff, and uttered such a wild, fierce yell that the unfortunate conductor started away in horror, evidently regarding me as a devil doomed to wander on the earth with a piece of the true cross in his possession.

It must be admitted that, although I was not yet out of danger, the fever was intermittent. When I became aware of this, I reasoned thus with myself – not altogether foolishly, considering the place and the hour: supposing, in one of these lucid intervals (that is to say, the moments in which life smiled to me; you see I was virtually vanquished), supposing, in one of these lucid intervals, I said, I were to prepare myself for the next attack by tying myself up in some way and having something to cling to . . . I might arrive at some . . . definite . . . conclusion. Let me see.

We were passing through a little Sardinian village on the sea-shore (the sea was much calmer), and when we stopped to change horses I told the conductor to wait while I wrote a letter; I go into a little café and write a letter on a scrap of paper to the director of the Académie de Rome, asking M. Horace Vernet to be so good as not to strike my name off the Academy lists, if he had not already done so, as I had not yet broken through the rules; and I gave him

MY WORD OF HONOUR that I would not cross the Italian frontier until I had received his answer, which I would await at Nice.

Now that I had bound myself by a promise I went on my way most peacefully, feeling that if I were expelled from the Academy and launched penniless on the world, I could still fall back upon my murderous plan; and then . . . I suddenly found out that . . . I was hungry, having eaten nothing since I left Florence. Oh, beneficent nature! I was evidently cured!

The struggle was not quite over, however, when I reached Nice. I waited for several days, and then M. Vernet's answer came. It was a friendly, kindly, paternal letter, and touched me deeply. He did not know the cause of my trouble, but he gave me the most kindly counsel, and pointed out to me that work and art were the two greatest remedies for troubles of the soul. He told me my name was still on the lists, that the minister should not hear of my escapade, and that I should be received with open arms when I returned.

'Well, they are saved,' I said, with a deep sigh. 'And supposing now I were to lead a quiet, happy life, and give myself up entirely to music, would not that be too curious? Let us try.'

And so I drink deep draughts of the sunny, balmy air of Nice, and life and joy return to me, and I dream of music and the future. I spend a whole month in Nice wandering in groves of orange-trees, bathing in the sea, sleeping on the heather on the Villefranche hills, and looking down from those glorious heights on the silent coming and going of the distant ships. I live entirely alone. I write the overture to *King Lear*. I sing. I believe in a God. Convalescence!

These were the three happiest weeks in my life. Oh, Nizza!

Once more my peace was disturbed by the King of Sardinia's police.

I had recently made the acquaintance of two officers of the Piedmontese garrison, whom I used to meet at the café; and one day I played a game of billiards with them, which was quite enough to arouse the suspicions of the chief of police.

'It is quite clear that that young musician has not come here to see *Matilda de Sabran*' (the only piece which was then being played), 'because he never goes to the theatre. He spends his days on the Villefranche rocks evidently waiting for a signal from some revolutionary ship . . . He does not dine at the *table d'hôte* . . . that is to avoid being drawn into conversation by the secret agents. Now he is gradually making the acquaintance of our officers in order to open up the negotiations with which "*Young Italy*" has entrusted him. The conspiracy is as clear as daylight.'

Oh, great man – oh, wily diplomat – thou ravest!

I am summoned to the police office, and formally interrogated.

'What are you doing here?'

'Recovering from a painful illness. I compose and dream, and thank God for the sunshine, the beautiful sea, and the green hills.'

'You are not a painter?'

'No.'

'Yet you are always drawing something in an album. Is it plans?'

'Yes; plans for an overture for *King Lear*. The designs and the instrumentation are ready, and I think the beginning will be somewhat formidable.'

'What do you mean by the beginning? Whom do you mean by *King Lear*?'

'He is a poor old English king.'

'English!'

'Yes. Shakespeare says he lived about eighteen hundred years ago, and he foolishly divided his kingdom between his two wicked elder daughters, who turned him out of doors when he had nothing more to give them. You see there are few kings . . .'

'Never mind the king . . . What do you mean by instrumentation?'

'It is a musical term.'

'Always the same excuse! Now, sir, we are well aware that it is impossible to write music walking silently about the sea-shore, with nothing but an album and a pencil, and no piano. So be good enough to tell us where you want to go, and you shall have your passport. You cannot stay here any longer.'

'Then I will return to Rome, and compose there without a piano, if you have no objection.'

So the following day I left Nice, reluctant, but full of life and happiness. And in this way it came to pass that my loaded pistols missed fire.

All the same, I liked my *little comedy*; and I sometimes think it is a pity that it was never played.

★ ★ ★

A. I. HERZEN (1812–1870)

'The Dream'

Do you remember, friends, how lovely was that winter day, bright and sunny, when six or seven sledges accompanied us to Chërnaya Gryaz, when for the last time we clinked glasses and parted, sobbing?

*

That was the 21st of January, 1847.

Seven years have passed since then, and what years! Among them were 1848 and 1852.

All sorts of things happened in those years, and everything was shattered – public and private: the European revolution and my home, the freedom of the world and my personal happiness.

Of the old life not one stone was left upon another. Then my powers had reached their fullest development; the previous years had given me pledges for the future. I left you boldly, with headlong self-reliance, with haughty confidence in life. I was in haste to tear myself away from the little group of people who were so thoroughly accustomed to each other and had come so close, bound by a deep love and a common grief. I was beckoned to by distance, space, open conflict, and free speech. I was seeking an independent arena, I longed to try my powers in freedom . . .

Now I no longer expect anything: after what I have seen and experienced nothing will move me to any particular wonder or to deep joy; joy and wonder are curbed by memories of the past and fear of the future. Almost everything has become a matter of indifference to me, and I desire as little to die tomorrow as to live long; let the end come as casually and senselessly as the beginning.

And yet I have found all that I sought, even recognition from this old, complacent world – and along with this I found the loss of all my beliefs, all that was precious to me, have met with betrayal, treacherous blows from behind, and in general a moral corruption of which you have no conception.

It is hard for me, very hard, to begin this part of my story; I have avoided it while I wrote the preceding parts, but at last I am face to face with it. But away with weakness: he who could live through it must have the strength to remember.

From the middle of the year 1848 I have nothing to tell of but agonizing experiences, unavenged offences, undeserved blows. My memory holds nothing but melancholy images, my own mistakes and other people's: mistakes of individuals, mistakes of whole peoples. Where there was a possibility of salvation, death crossed the path. . . .

Alarmed by the Paris of 1847, I had opened my eyes to the truth for a moment, but was carried away again by the events that seethed about me. All Italy was 'awakening' before my eyes! I saw the King of Naples tamed and the Pope humbly asking the alms of the people's love – the whirlwind which set everything in movement carried me, too, off my feet; all Europe took up its bed and walked – in a fit of somnambulism which we took for awakening. When I came to myself, it had all vanished; la Sonnambula, frightened by the police, had fallen from the roof; friends were scattered or were furiously slaughtering one another . . . And I found myself alone, utterly alone, among graves and cradles – their guardian, defender, avenger, and I could do nothing because I tried to do more than was usual.

And now I sit in London where chance has flung me – and I stay here because I do not know what to make of myself. An alien race swarms confusedly about me, wrapped in the heavy breath of ocean; a world dissolving into chaos, lost in a fog in which outlines are blurred, in which a lamp gives only murky glimmers of light.

. . . And that other land – washed by the dark-blue sea under the canopy of dark-blue sky . . . it is the one shining region left until the far side of the grave.

O Rome, how I love to return to your deceptions, how eagerly I run over day by day the time when I was intoxicated with you!

. . . A dark night. The Corso is filled with people, and here and there are torches. It is a month since a republic was proclaimed in Paris. News has come from Milan – there they are fighting, the people demand war, there is a rumour that Charles Albert is on the way with troops. The talk of the angry crowd is like the intermittent roar of a wave, which alternately comes noisily up the beach and then pauses to draw breath.

The crowds form into ranks. They go to the Piedmontese ambassador to find out whether war has been declared.

'Fall in, fall in with us,' shout dozens of voices.

'We are foreigners.'

'All the better; *Santo Dio*, you are our guests.'

We joined the ranks.

'The front place for the guests, the front place for the ladies, *le donne forestiere!*'

And with passionate shouts of approval the crowd parted to make way. Ciceruacchio and with him a young Russian poet, a poet of popular songs, pushed their way forward with a flag, the tribune shook hands with the ladies and with them stood at the head of ten or twelve thousand people – and all moved forward in that majestic and harmonious order which is peculiar to the Roman people.

The leaders went into the Palazzo, and a few minutes later the drawing-room doors opened on the balcony. The ambassador came out to appease the people and to confirm the news of the war; his words were received with frantic joy. Ciceruacchio was on the balcony in the glaring light of torches and candelabra, and beside him under the Italian flag stood four young women, all four Russians – was it not strange? I can see them now on that stone platform, and below them the swaying, innumerable multitude, mingling with shouts for war and curses for the Jesuits, loud cries of '*Evviva le donne forestiere!*'

In England they and we should have been greeted with hisses, abuse, and perhaps stones. In France we should have been taken for venal agents. But here the aristocratic proletariat, the descendants of Marius and the ancient tribunes, gave us a warm and genuine welcome. We were received by them into the European struggle . . . and with Italy alone the bond of love, or at least of warm memory, is still unbroken.

And was all that . . . intoxication, delirium? Perhaps – but I do not envy those who were not carried away by that exquisite dream. The sleep could not last long in any case: the inexorable Macbeth of real life had already raised his hand to murder sleep and . . .

My dream was past – it has no further change.

SPAIN

V. S. PRITCHETT (1900–1997)

from *The Spanish Temper*

Castile is a landscape of hidden villages, suddenly come upon, like
crocks of earthenware in the soil, crumbling in the summer heat,
sodden in the torrential rains of the winter; it is a place of sunsets
in the haze of dust and of short twilights when the sky at the last
moment goes green over the sharp violet mountains, which seem to
have been cut out by a knife. The towns have no suburbs, but end
abruptly in a mediæval wall or the long wall of some property.
The landscape of Castile, Unamuno said, is for monotheism, not
pantheism. God is a precise thing like a stone, the Christ is a real
man bleeding, and the blood of His wounds stains the mother's
cheeks as she leans against Him; the Virgin is a real girl. In this
country the cemeteries are lonely, for they lie well out of the towns,
with their enormous memorials, like small palaces. The black cypress
marks the spot. Here if you die, you die. The peasants of these
villages are like dethroned kings, grave in their speech, phlegmatic
in their humour, with an irony as dry as Sancho Panza's, like the
voice of the earth itself:

> And so my master, these honours that your Grace would confer
> upon me as your servant and a follower of knight-errantry –
> which I am, being your Grace's squire – I would have you
> convert, if you will, into other things that will be of more profit
> and advantage to me; for though I hereby acknowledge them
> as duly received, I renounce them from this time forth until
> the end of the world. [Samuel Putnam's translation.]

If one stands on the edge of the *meseta* on the outskirts of some
place like Burgos, the first big town, the night comes down to one's

feet. The loneliness is complete. There is the warm smell of the land
and its pungent scrub, the trilling of the crickets as numerous as the
large stars, which come so low in the plain that one might put out
one's hand to touch them; and, to mark the human isolation, one
hears the sound of some labourer tapping through the dust on his
donkey and singing one of those songs which are made out of
nothing and seem to have half Africa or half India in their melancholy
fall, in those final 'a's' and 'o's' which drag on and break into smaller
and smaller fragments of sound, till they vanish like sand:

'*Era la noche de la fiesta-a-a-a-a.*'

All songs of desire and jealousy, the reminiscences of the casuistical
details of passion. And it is not a night of blackness, but of some
dark and luminous substance: that dark silver one sees hanging like
a body over Goya's *Dos de Mayo*. If El Greco painted out of the day
and the land, Goya paints out of the night.

The hours are long in the sun in Castile. When the table-top hills
fall back, one sees the small rivers in the yellow soil, and the miles
of cornland where the mattock or the primitive, cattle-drawn plough
has granulated the earth. For the steppe is not all desert; parts of it
are wheat-bearing, and, like long, low white redoubts, walled in, as
one would think, for defence, one sees the warehouses of the corn
and the olive-oil companies. As in the Basque countries, the land is
broken up in the northern parts – around Burgos for example – into
small properties which are minutely divided among members of a
family. Sons are what a man wants, though when he dies he may
have to split his ground equally into patches of an acre or two, even
divide one olive tree among all so that they may own no more than
a branch each. In these parts the people are very poor, and one
would expect to find that hatred of the Church and the landlords
which is common in other poor parts. There is no hatred. Their
small property, their mercilessly divided crops, make the peasants
deeply conservative. And at night, in the harvest time, the back
streets of Burgos roar with the shouts and quarrels of the wine-
drinkers – a sound of drunkenness I have heard nowhere else in
Spain, except in Andalusia, where they drink sherry by the dozen
glasses; for outside of Burgos the Castilians are the soberest people
in Europe. Only when one leaves Burgos well behind and when the
average rainfall is even smaller does one meet the peasants who are
hostile to landlord, moneylender, and Church.

And so Castile stretches towards its backbone, the Guadarrama and the Gredos mountains. There will be miles where the soil looks like stripes of red lead or ochre, distances of sulphur and tin, the sharp colours of incineration, as if great areas of the kingdom had been raked out of a furnace. As the train climbs to Santa Teresa's Ávila, there will be miles of wilderness where granite is piled up among the oaks or the short pines, and one sees the red fan of the partridge as it flies and the hunter standing with his horn and his gun. One feels lonely and free in the vast space of Castile, and the few roads suggest long, monotonous journeys. The eye picks up the green of the rare acacias or poplars which mark the metalled roads. On some mule track we mark the figure of some peasant riding away on a mule: miles between that figure and ourselves – who is he? What is the solitary insect thinking? What peasant with skin incised by wind and sun? We become absorbed, in these dawdling hours, in the task of overtaking a man who would greet one openly, talk in a pure, almost Biblical tongue, and who will speak his business straight out and expect to hear all yours.

'Good day. I am going to Santa X with this corn. I am from that village. There I have my family, my so many brothers, my so many sisters. Where do you come from? What country, what village? Where is England? Is that in France? Are you married? How many children have you? If you have, good; if you have not, bad. God has not granted them. What is your employment? How much do you earn? In your country' – the final deciding question – 'is there plenty to eat?' And after that – some string of proverbs, a page of Don Quixote, a page of Sancho Panza. And then that lordly Spanish sentence of farewell and one's impression that one has been talking as a nobleman to a nobleman – as the Aragonese say, 'We are as noble as the King but not as rich.'

The egalitarianism of the Spaniards is not like the citizenship of the French, nor the anonymity of the English or American democracy, where we seek the lowest common denominator and try to hide our distinctions. The Spanish live in castes, but not in classes, and their equality – the only real equality I have met anywhere in the world – is in their sense of nobility or, rather, in the sense of the absolute quality of the person. One will hear this sentence spoken of people living in the lowest wretchedness: 'They are noble people.' These words are not especially a compliment, nor do they convey resignation, pity, or regret; they are meant, almost conventionally, to describe the normal condition of man.

If we were to travel with this man on the mule or donkey, we would not see his village until we were right upon it. It is some ruinous, dusty place, the colour of the soil it stands in, and most houses will be of a single storey. Only the fortress wall of its church will stand out, plainly buttressed high above the hut roofs of the village and built to last till the end of the world. It is the spire, the belfry, or the dome of the church that one sees first in the plain, rising inch by inch like a spear or a helmet, and it will give to the mind a lasting sense of a bare, military country, frugal and hard. In the wars of reconquest against the Moors, some of the churches – and cathedrals like Ávila – were built as forts, and of that time it has been said that the Spaniards did not know which they wanted most – the Kingdom of God or their own land. The centre of the village is a square of tottering stone arcades; the mule carts or the occasional lorry stand there. The inn, if there is one, will not be a hotel, nor even a *fonda* – the Arab word – but perhaps a *posada*: a place one can ride into with mule or donkey, where one can stable an animal and lie down oneself on a sack of straw, the other side of the stall. There are grand *posadas* like the Posada de la Sangre of Cervantes, which still exists in Toledo, places of heavily beamed roofs, and of courtyards upon which one may look down from the interior galleries; if the village is small enough there may only be a *venta* or tavern for the sale of wine and *aguardiente*. But there will be a ewer of water in the corner of the stone floor with a tin dipper in it, and that is what, in this dusty country, you make for. The water is cold and beautiful. Everyone praises its purity, and the man or woman staring at you with that prolonged and total Spanish stare will tell you soberly that this particular water is famous throughout the world as the best water on earth.

At nine o'clock at night they will ask you what you want to eat.

'What have you got?'

'Whatever the *señor* wishes.'

And a Dutch auction begins. Meat, alas there isn't any; chicken, they regret; it comes down in the end to garlic soup and how many 'pairs of eggs' can you eat, with a chunk of garlic sausage thrown in? They have 'wonderful wine, the finest for miles' – but it turns out to be thin, vinegarish, and watered. The oil is rancid, but the stick fire blazes, the smoke fills the room, and there is war in your stomach that night unless you are used to the crude Spanish fry and to garlic as strong as acetylene. The food might turn out better than this of course; there might be *bacalao*, if you can eat dry salted cod; there might be pork off the black pigs; and resinous wine, scraping the top off your tongue, with flavour of the pine cask. They might catch and kill that screeching chicken in the yard or give you goat cheese and the close white bread which has come in again after the years of war and starvation. But good or bad, full or meagre, the meal will not be squalid or sluttish. There will be a piety and honourableness about it, no scrambling round the trough. The woman's hard voice will command the room and one will break one's bread with the dignity of a lean person who speaks of other things. 'We give what we have' – not the 'you eat the official portion which you're given or go without' of our sour democracies. They still – even after the Civil War, in which so much of Spanish custom died – turn to their neighbour before they eat and say: 'Would you like this?' and even lift the plate.

'Please enjoy it yourself,' is the reply.

Being so noble, they could (they convey) do without food altogether; or like the penniless starving lord in the picaresque tale of Lazarillo de Tormes, send in the starving servant to say: 'Thank you, we have eaten already.' Sober, frugal, austere is the Castilian living in these small towns that look like heaps of broken pottery in the plain.

* * *

ERNEST HEMINGWAY (1899–1961)

'Bullfighting'

The bullfight is not a sport in the Anglo-Saxon sense of the word, that is, it is not an equal contest or an attempt at an equal contest between a bull and a man. Rather it is a tragedy; the death of the bull, which is played, more or less well, by the bull and the man involved and in which there is danger for the man but certain death for the animal. This danger to the man can be increased by the bullfighter at will in the measure in which he works close to the bull's horns. Keeping within the rules for bullfighting on foot in a closed ring formulated by years of experience, which, if known and followed, permit a man to perform certain actions with a bull without being caught by the bull's horns, the bullfighter may, by decreasing his distance from the bull's horns, depend more and more on his own reflexes and judgment of that distance to protect him from the points. This danger of goring, which the man creates voluntarily, can be changed to certainty of being caught and tossed by the bull if the man, through ignorance, slowness, torpidness, blind folly or momentary grogginess breaks any of these fundamental rules for the execution of the different *suertes*. Everything that is done by the man in the ring is called a *suerte*. It is the easiest term to use as it is short. It means act, but the word act has, in English, a connotation of the theatre that makes its use confusing.

People seeing their first bullfight say, 'But the bulls are so stupid. They always go for the cape and not for the man.'

The bull only goes for the percale of the cape or for the scarlet serge of the *muleta*[1] if the man makes him and so handles the cloth that the bull sees it rather than the man. Therefore to really start to see bullfights a spectator should go to the *novilladas* or apprentice fights. There the bulls do not always go for the cloth because the bullfighters are learning before your eyes the rules of bullfighting and they do not always remember or know the proper terrain to take and how to keep the bull after the lure and away from the man. It is one thing to know the rules in principle and another to remember them as they are needed when facing an animal that is seeking to kill you, and the spectator who wants to see men tossed and gored rather than judge the manner in which the bulls are dominated should go to a *novillada* before he sees a *corrida de toros* or complete bullfight. It should be a good thing for him to see a *novillada* first anyway if he wants to learn about technique, since the employment of knowledge that we call by that bastard name is always most visible in its imperfection. At a *novillada* the spectator may see the mistakes of the bullfighters, and the penalties that these mistakes carry. He will learn something too about the state of training or lack of training of the men and the effect this has on their courage.

One time in Madrid I remember we went to a *novillada* in the middle of the summer on a very hot Sunday when every one who

1. The small red cloth cape with which the bullfighter makes passes at the bull.

could afford it had left the city for the beaches of the north or the mountains and the bullfight was not advertised to start until six o'clock in the evening, to see six Tovar bulls killed by three aspirant matadors[2] who have all since failed in their profession. We sat in the first row behind the wooden barrier and when the first bull came out it was clear that Domingo Hernandorena, a short, thick-ankled, graceless Basque with a pale face who looked nervous and incompletely fed in a cheap rented suit, if he was to kill this bull would either make a fool of himself or be gored. Hernandorena could not control the nervousness of his feet. He wanted to stand quietly and play the bull with the cape with a slow movement of his arms, but when he tried to stand still as the bull charged his feet jumped away in short, nervous jerks. His feet were obviously not under his personal control and his effort to be statuesque while his feet jittered him away out of danger was very funny to the crowd. It was funny to them because many of them knew that was how their own feet would behave if they saw the horns coming toward them, and as always, they resented any one else being in there in the ring, making money, who had the same physical defects which barred them, the spectators, from that supposedly highly paid way of making a living. In their turn the other two matadors were very fancy with the cape and Hernandorena's nervous jerking was even worse after their performance. He had not been in the ring with a bull for over a year and he was altogether unable to control his nervousness. When the banderillas[3] were in and it was time for him to go out with the red cloth and the sword to prepare the bull for killing and to kill, the crowd which had applauded ironically at every nervous move he had made knew something very funny would happen. Below us, as he took the muleta and the sword and rinsed his mouth out with water I could see the muscles of his cheeks twitching. The bull stood against the barrier watching him. Hernandorena could not trust his legs to carry him slowly toward the bull. He knew there was only one way he could stay in one place in the ring. He ran out toward the bull, and ten yards in front of him dropped to both knees on the

2. A matador is the principal performer – along with the bull – in bullfighting; he is one who works the muletas and kills the bull with a sword thrust between the shoulder blades.
3. Short, barbed sticks planted in the bull's sides by the banderilleros, men on foot who assist the matador.

sand. In that position he was safe from ridicule. He spread the red cloth with his sword and jerked himself forward on his knees toward the bull. The bull was watching the man and the triangle of red cloth, his ears pointed, his eyes fixed, and Hernandorena knee himself a yard closer and shook the cloth. The bull's tail rose, his head lowered and he charged and, as he reached the man, Hernandorena rose solidly from his knees into the air, swung over like a bundle, his legs in all directions now, and then dropped to the ground. The bull looked for him, found a wide-spread moving cape held by another bullfighter instead, charged it, and Hernandorena stood up with sand on his white face and looked for his sword and the cloth. As he stood up I saw the heavy, soiled gray silk of his rented trousers open cleanly and deeply to show the thigh bone from the hip almost to the knee. He saw it too and looked very surprised and put his hand on it while people jumped over the barrier and ran toward him to carry him to the infirmary. The technical error that he had committed was in not keeping the red cloth of the *muleta* between himself and the bull until the charge; then at the moment of jurisdiction as it is called, when the bull's lowered head reaches the cloth, swaying back while he held the cloth, spread by the stick and the sword, far enough forward so that the bull following it would be clear of his body. It was a simple technical error.

That night at the café I heard no word of sympathy for him. He was ignorant, he was torpid, and he was out of training. Why did he insist on being a bullfighter? Why did he go down on both knees? Because he was a coward, they said. The knees are for cowards. If he was a coward why did he insist on being a bullfighter? There was no natural sympathy for uncontrollable nervousness because he was a paid public performer. It was preferable that he be gored rather than run from the bull. To be gored was honorable; they would have sympathized with him had he been caught in one of his nervous uncontrollable jerky retreats, which, although they mocked, they knew were from lack of training, rather than for him to have gone down on his knees. Because the hardest thing when frightened by the bull is to control the feet and let the bull come, and any attempt to control the feet was honorable even though they jeered at it because it looked ridiculous. But when he went on both knees, without the technique to fight from that position; the technique that Marcial Lalanda, the most scientific of living bullfighters, has, and which alone makes that position honorable; then Hernandorena admitted his nervousness. To show his nervousness was not shameful; only to admit it. When, lacking the technique and thereby admitting his inability to control his feet, the matador went down on both knees before the bull the crowd had no more sympathy with him than with a suicide.

For myself, not being a bullfighter, and being much interested in suicides, the problem was one of depiction and waking in the night I tried to remember what it was that seemed just out of my remembering and that was the thing that I had really seen and, finally, remembering all around it, I got it. When he stood up, his face white and dirty and the silk of his breeches opened from waist to knee, it was the dirtiness of the rented breeches, the dirtiness of his slit underwear and the clean, clean, unbearably clean whiteness of the thigh bone that I had seen, and it was that which was important.

* * *

LUIS BUNUEL (1900–1983)

'Earthly Delights'

I can't count the number of delectable hours I've spent in bars, the perfect places for the meditation and contemplation indispensable to life. Sitting in bars is an old habit that's become more pronounced through the years; like Saint Simeon Stylites perched on his pillar talking to God, I've spent long quiet hours daydreaming, nodding at the waiter, sometimes talking to myself, watching the startling sequences of images that pass through my mind's eye. Today I'm as old as the century and rarely go out at all; but all alone, during the sacrosanct cocktail hour, in the small room where my bottles are kept, I still amuse myself by remembering the bars I've loved.

First of all, you must be clear about the difference between a bar and a café. For example, I've never been able to find a decent bar in Paris. On the other hand, the city is filled with superb cafés; from Belleville to Auteuil, no matter where you go, you can always find a table, and a waiter to take your order. Without cafés, without *tabacs*, without those marvellous terraces, Paris is unimaginable. If they suddenly disappeared, it would be like living in a city that had been levelled by an atomic bomb.

There are certain cafés which have a special importance for me. The surrealists, for example, pursued many of their activities at the Café Cyrano on the place Blanche, or at the Select on the Champs-Elysées. I remember being invited to the opening of the famous La Coupole in Montparnasse, where I met with Man Ray and Louis Aragon to plan the preview of *Un Chien andalou*. The list is endless, but the crucial point is that the café is synonymous with bustle, conversation, camaraderie and women.

The bar, on the other hand, is an exercise in solitude. Above all else, it must be quiet, dark, very comfortable – and, contrary to modern mores, no music of any kind, no matter how faint. In sum, there should be no more than a dozen tables, and a clientele that doesn't like to talk.

One of my favourites is the bar at the Plaza Hotel in Madrid. It's ideally situated – in the basement, where you can't be distracted by the view. The head waiter knows me well, and always gives me my favourite table, where my back is to the wall. You can even eat dinner there; the lighting is discreet, but sufficient.

The Chicote in Madrid is also full of precious memories, but somehow it's nicer to go there with friends. There's also the bar in the Paular Hotel, in the northern part of the city, set in the courtyard of a magnificent Gothic monastery. The room is long and lined with tall granite columns; and except on weekends, when the place trembles with tourists and noisy children, it's usually half empty. I can sit there for hours, undisturbed, surrounded by Zurbarán reproductions, only half conscious of the shadow of a silent waiter floating by from time to time, ever respectful of my alcoholic reveries.

I loved the Paular the way I love my closest friends. At the end of a working day, my scriptwriter-collaborator Jean-Claude Carrière would leave me there to meditate. After forty-five minutes, I'd hear his punctual footsteps on the stone floor; he'd sit down opposite me at the table, which was the signal for me to tell him a story that I'd made up during my reverie. (I've always believed that the imagination is a spiritual quality that, like memory, can be trained and developed.) The story might have nothing to do with our scenario, or, then again, it might; it could be a farce or a melodrama, short or long, violent or sublime. The important thing was merely to tell it.

Alone with Zurbarán, my favourite drink, and the granite

columns cut from that marvellous Castilian stone, I'd let my mind wander, beyond time, open to the images that happened to appear. I might be thinking about something prosaic – family business, a new project – when all of a sudden a picture would snap into focus, characters emerge, speak, act out their passions. Sometimes, alone in my corner, I'd find myself laughing aloud. When I thought the scene might fit into our scenario, I'd backtrack and force myself to direct the aimless pictures, to organize them into a coherent sequence.

I also remember a bar at the Plaza Hotel in New York, a busy meeting place which at the time was off-limits to women. Any friend of mine passing through New York knew that if he wanted to find me, he had only to go to the Plaza bar at noon. (Now, unfortunately, that magnificent bar with its superb view of Central Park has become a restaurant, with only a couple of real bar tables left.)

I also have certain special bars in Mexico, like El Parador in Mexico City, although, like the Chicote, it's more congenial to be there with friends. Then there's the bar in the San José Purua Hotel in Michoacán, where for thirty years I used to hibernate to write my scripts. The hotel was situated on the side of a deep canyon overrun with semitropical vegetation, and although views are usually liabilities where bars are concerned, this panorama was spectacular. Luckily, there was a *ziranda* – a tropical tree with curving branches interlaced like a nest of huge snakes – just in front of the window, which screened part of the landscape. My eyes would follow aimlessly along the myriad intersections of the branches; sometimes I'd put an owl on one of them, or a naked woman, or some other incongruous element. And then one day, for no apparent reason, the bar was closed. I can still see my producer Serge Silberman, Jean-Claude, and myself searching desperately through the endless corridors of the hotel in 1980 for a place to work. (These are murderous times – not even bars are spared!)

Talking about bars leads me inevitably to the subject of drinks, about which I can pontificate for hours. In the interests of my readers, I'll try to be concise, but for those who aren't interested – and, unfortunately, I'm sure they're numerous – I'd advise you simply to skip the next few pages.

I'll have to put wine, red wine in particular, at the top of the list. France produces both the best and the worst; in fact, there's nothing more horrendous than the famous *coup de rouge* served up in Parisian bistros, except perhaps for Italian wines, which have never seemed completely authentic to me. I'm also very fond of Spanish Valdepeñas, which should be drunk chilled and preferably our of a goatskin. There's also a white Yepes that comes from the area around Toledo. In America, there are some good California wines, especially Cabernet, and sometimes I drink a Chilean or Mexican wine. Curiously, I never drink wine in a bar, for wine is a purely physical pleasure and does nothing to stimulate the imagination.

To provoke, or sustain, a reverie in a bar, you have to drink English gin, especially in the form of the dry martini. To be frank, given the primordial role played in my life by the dry martini, I think I really ought to give it at least a page. Like all cocktails, the martini, composed essentially of gin and a few drops of Noilly Prat, seems to have been an American invention. Connoisseurs who like their martinis very dry suggest simply allowing a ray of sunlight to shine through a bottle of Noilly Prat before it hits the bottle of gin. At a certain period in America it was said that the making of a dry martini should resemble the Immaculate Conception, for, as Saint Thomas Aquinas once noted, the generative power of the Holy Ghost pierced the Virgin's hymen 'like a ray of sunlight through a window – leaving it unbroken'.

Another crucial recommendation is that the ice be so cold and hard that it won't melt, since nothing's worse than a watery martini. For those who are still with me, let me give you my personal recipe, the fruit of long experimentation and guaranteed to produce perfect results. The day before your guests arrive, put all the ingredients – glasses, gin, and shaker – in the refrigerator. Use a thermometer to make sure the ice is about twenty degrees below zero (centigrade). Don't take anything out until your friends arrive; then pour a few drops of Noilly Prat and half a demitasse spoon of Angostura bitters over the ice. Shake it, then pour it out, keeping only the ice, which retains a faint taste of both. Then pour straight gin over the ice, shake it again, and serve.

(During the 1940s, the director of the Museum of Modern Art in New York taught me a curious variation. Instead of Angostura, he used a dash of Pernod. Frankly, it seemed heretical to me, but apparently it was only a fad.)

After the dry martini comes one of my own modest inventions, the Buñueloni, best drunk before dinner. It's really a takeoff on the famous Negroni, but instead of mixing Campari, gin, and sweet

Cinzano, I substitute Carpano for the Campari. Here again, the gin – in sufficient quantity to ensure its dominance over the other two ingredients – has excellent effects on the imagination. I've no idea how or why; I only know that it works.

I should take this moment to assure you that I'm not an alcoholic. Of course, I've occasionally managed to drink myself into oblivion, but most of the time it's a kind of ritual for me, one that produces a high rather like that induced by a mild drug, a high that helps me live and work. If you were to ask if I'd ever had the bad luck to miss my daily cocktail, I'd have to say that I doubt it; where certain things are concerned, I plan ahead.

I never drank so much in my life as the time I spent five months in the United States during Prohibition. I had a two-fingered bootlegger friend in Los Angeles who taught me that the way to tell real gin from ersatz was to shake the bottle in a certain way. Real gin, he assured me, bubbles. It was a time when you could get your whiskey in the local pharmacy, with a prescription, and your wine in a coffee cup when you went to the right restaurant. There was a good speakeasy in New York where you rapped out a code on the door, stood for inspection at the judas, and slipped inside quickly once the door was opened. It looked like any other bar, and you could get whatever kind of liquor you wanted. (Prohibition was clearly one of the more nonsensical ideas of the century. Americans got fabulously drunk, although with repeal they seem to have learned to drink more intelligently.)

Another of my weaknesses is the French aperitif, like the *picon*-beer-grenadine and the mandarin-curaçao-beer, which made me drunker more quickly and more definitively than the dry martini. Now, these exotic concoctions seem to be becoming extinct; in fact, the decline of the aperitif may well be one of the most depressing phenomena of our time.

I do drink other things, of course – vodka with my caviar, aquavit with smoked salmon. I like Mexican tequila and mezcal, even though they're really only substitutes for the real thing. Whiskey I've never understood; it's one drink that truly doesn't appeal to me.

I remember reading once, in one of those advice columns in a popular French magazine – *Marie-France*, I think – that gin was an excellent tranquillizer, that it allayed the anxiety that often goes with air travel. Since I'd always been profoundly terrified in airplanes, I decided to give it a try. (My fear was constant and irrepressible.

If I saw one of the pilots walking down the aisle with a serious expression on his face, I always assumed zero hour had come. If, on the other hand, he walked by smiling, I knew immediately that we were in big trouble, and that he was only trying to make us believe otherwise.) All my fears magically disappeared the day I decided to take *Marie-France*'s advice. Each time I had to fly, I took a flask of gin wrapped in a newspaper to keep it cool. While I waited in the airport for my flight to be announced, I'd sneak a few swallows and immediately feel completely relaxed, ready to confront the worst turbulence with equanimity.

If I had to list all the benefits derived from alcohol, it would be endless. In 1977, in Madrid, when I was in despair after a tempestuous argument with an actress who'd brought the shooting of *That Obscure Object of Desire* to a halt, the producer, Serge Silberman, decided to abandon the film altogether. The considerable financial loss was depressing us both until one evening, when we were drowning our sorrows in a bar, I suddenly had the idea (after two dry martinis) of using two actresses in the same role, a tactic that had never been tried before. Although I made the suggestion as a joke, Silberman loved it, and the film was saved. Once again, the combination of bar and gin proved unbeatable.

One day in New York, in the 1940s, my good friend Juan Negrín, the son of the former Republican prime minister, and his wife, the actress Rosita Díaz, and I came up with the notion of opening a bar called the Cannonball. It was to be the most expensive bar in the world, and would stock only the most exotic beverages imported from the four corners of the earth. We planned an intimate bar, ten tables maximum, very comfortable and decorated with impeccable taste. An antique cannon at the door, complete with powder and wick, would be fired, night or day, each time a client spent a thousand dollars. Of course, we never managed to realize this seductive and thoroughly undemocratic enterprise, but we thought it amusing to imagine your ordinary wage earner in the neighbouring apartment building, awakened at four in the morning by the boom of a cannon, turning to his wife next to him in bed and saying: 'Another bastard coughing up a thousand bucks!'

To continue this panegyric on earthly delights, let me just say that it's impossible to drink without smoking. I began to smoke when I was sixteen and have never stopped. My limit is a pack a day. I've smoked absolutely everything but am particularly fond of Spanish and French cigarettes (Gitanes and Celtiques especially) because of their black tobacco.

If alcohol is queen, then tobacco is her consort. It's a fond companion for all occasions, a loyal friend through fair weather and foul. People smoke to celebrate a happy moment, or to hide a bitter regret. Whether you're alone or with friends, it's a joy for all the senses. What lovelier sight is there than that double row of white cigarettes, lined up like soldiers on parade and wrapped in silver paper? If I were blindfolded and a lighted cigarette placed between my lips, I'd refuse to smoke it. I love to touch the pack in my pocket, open it, savour the feel of the cigarette between my fingers, the paper on my lips, the taste of tobacco on my tongue. I love to watch the flame spurt up, love to watch it come closer and closer, filling me with its warmth.

I once had a friend from my student days called Dorronsoro, who was from the Basque country and, as a Spanish Republican, was exiled to Mexico. When I visited him in the hospital, he had tubes everywhere, as well as an oxygen mask, which he'd take off from time to time for a quick puff on a cigarette. He smoked until the last hours of his life, ever faithful to the pleasure that killed him.

Finally, dear readers, allow me to end these ramblings on tobacco and alcohol, delicious fathers of abiding friendships and fertile reveries, with some advice: Don't drink and don't smoke. It's bad for your health.

It goes without saying that alcohol and tobacco are excellent accompaniments to lovemaking – the alcohol first, then the cigarettes. No, you're not about to hear any extraordinary erotic secrets. Men of my generation, particularly if they're Spanish, suffer from a hereditary timidity where sex and women are concerned. Our sexual desire has to be seen as the product of centuries of repressive and emasculating Catholicism, whose many taboos – no sexual relations outside of marriage (not to mention within), no pictures or words that might suggest the sexual act, no matter how obliquely – have turned normal desire into something exceptionally violent. As you can imagine, when this desire manages to overcome the obstacles, the gratification is incomparable, since it's always coloured by the sweet secret sense of sin.

With rare exceptions, we Spaniards knew of only two ways to make love – in a brothel or in marriage. When I went to France for the first time in 1925, I was shocked, in fact disgusted, by the men and women I saw kissing in public, or living together without the sanction of marriage. Such customs were unimaginable to me; they seemed obscene. Much of this has changed, of course, over the years; lately, my own sexual desire has waned and finally disappeared, even in dreams. And I'm delighted; it's as if I've finally been relieved of a tyrannical burden. If the devil were to offer me a resurgence of what is commonly called virility, I'd decline. 'Just keep my liver and lungs in good working order,' I'd reply, 'so I can go on drinking and smoking!'

Safe at last from the perversions that lie in wait for old, impotent men, I can think back with equanimity on the whores in Madrid and Paris, the taxi girls in New York. And except for the occasional French *tableau vivant*, I've seen only one pornographic movie in my life – provocatively entitled *Sister Vaseline*. I remember a nun in a convent garden being fucked by the gardener, who was being sodomized by a monk, until finally all three merged into one figure. I can still see the nun's black cotton stockings which ended just above the knee. René Char and I once plotted to sneak into a children's movie matinée, tie up the projectionist, and show *Sister Vaseline* to the young audience. *O tempora! O mores!* The profanation of childhood seemed to us one of the more seductive forms of subversion. (Needless to say, we never got beyond the planning stage.)

Then there were my bungled orgies. When I was young, the idea of an orgy was tremendously exciting. Charlie Chaplin once organized one in Hollywood for me and two Spanish friends, but when the three ravishing young women arrived from Pasadena, they immediately got into a tremendous argument over which one was going to get Chaplin, and in the end all three left in a huff.

There was also the time that my friend Ugarte and I invited Lya Lys (who played in *L'Age d'or*) and a friend of hers to my place in Los Angeles. We'd laid in all the necessities, right down to the flowers and champagne; but the two women simply talked for an hour and then politely said goodbye.

I remember, too, at about the same period, the Russian director (his name escapes me now) who finally received authorization to come to Paris. As soon as he arrived, he asked me to put together a small, 'typically French' orgy for him. I laughed; he couldn't have picked a more unsuitable person for the job. Finally, I asked Aragon what to do.

'Well, *mon cher ami*,' he began delicately, 'the question is, would you prefer to be . . .'

Here he used a word that, even after all this time, I can't bring myself to write. (In fact, the proliferation of gutter words in the works of modern writers disgusts me. They use them gratuitously, in a pretence of liberalism which is no more than a pathetic travesty of liberty.) In any case, I answered with a resounding negative, upon which he advised me to forget orgies altogether. The poor director eventually returned to his homeland, minus that particular experience.

* * *

CAMILO JOSÉ CELA (1916–)

'From The Henares To The Tajuña'

From Guadalajara, the traveller sets forth on foot by the main highway to Zaragoza, along the river. It is noontime and a fierce sunlight falls directly on the road. The traveller walks in the ditch, on the dirt; the asphalt is harsh and hot and hard on the feet. Going out of the city, the traveller passes a lunch bar which has a suggestive name, full of resonance, a bar called The Mysteries of Tangiers. Just before this he had gone into a greengrocer's to buy some tomatoes.

'Can you give me three-quarters of a kilo of tomatoes?'

'Eh?'

The vegetable woman is deaf as a post.

'I said, can you give me three-quarters of a kilo of tomatoes?'

The woman doesn't move; she seems sunk in profound distrust.

'They're green.'

'That's all right; they're to eat raw.'

'Eh?'

'I said, I DON'T CARE!'

The woman considers, probably, that her duty lies in not selling green tomatoes.

'Are you going to Zaragoza for a vow?'

'No, señora.'

'Eh?'

'I said, NO!'

'Because a lot of people used to go to Zaragoza; they used to carry their things on their backs, too.'

'I'm sure they did, señora; now, can you give me three-quarters of a kilo of tomatoes?'

The traveller cannot shout any louder than he is shouting. His throat is dry; he would have paid five pesetas for a tomato. The door of the shop is full of children who are looking at the traveller; children of all sizes, with all colours of hair; children who don't talk or move, who stare fixedly like cats, without blinking.

A red-haired boy with his face covered with freckles tells the traveller, 'She's deaf.'

'So I can see, my boy.'

The boy smiles.

'Are you going to Zaragoza for a vow?'

'No, my cherub; I am not going to Zaragoza. Do you know where I can buy three-quarters of a kilo of tomatoes?'

'Yes, señor; come with me.'

The traveller, followed by twenty or twenty-five children, goes off in search of tomatoes. Some of the children run a few steps so they can get a good look at the traveller and keep up with him. Others get bored and drop behind. From the doorway of a house, a woman asks one of the children in a whisper, 'What does he want?'

And the boy with the shock of red hair answers in a pleased tone, 'Nothing; we're looking for tomatoes.'

The woman isn't satisfied and makes another try.

'Is he going to Zaragoza?'

And the boy turns around and answers drily, almost indignantly, 'No; do you think there's no place to go around here except Zaragoza?'

As he passes in front of the lunch bar, the man who – what a coincidence! – is not going to Zaragoza feels as though he has just been fished out of a pool where he was drowning. The traveller is with his helper; the boy with the saffron hair is beside him. The boy had said, 'Will you permit me to accompany you for a few hectometres?'

And the traveller, who feels limitless admiration for children who speak pedantically, had told him, 'Very well; I will permit you to accompany me for a few hectometres.'

Now that he is on the highway, the traveller stops at a little stream to wash a bit. The water is cool and very clean.

'The water is very crystalline, isn't it?'

'Yes, my child; too crystalline for words.'

The traveller takes off his pack and strips to the waist. The boy sits on a rock and watches him.

'You aren't very hairy.'

'Well . . . no; I suppose not.'

The traveller squats down and begins to bathe his hands.

'Are you going very far?'

'Yeees . . . fairly far. Give me the soap.'

The boy opens the soap dish and brings it to him. He is a very helpful boy.

'I was just thinking, if you're going very far in this heat—'

'Sometimes it's even hotter. Give me the towel.'

The boy gives him the towel.

'Were you born in Madrid?'

The traveller, while he dries himself, decides to take the offensive. 'No, not in Madrid. What's your name?'

'Armando, at your service. Armando Mondéjar Lopez.'

'How old are you?'

'Thirteen.'

'What are you studying for?'

'Technician.'

'What kind of technician?'

'I don't know; just a technician.'

'What does your father do?'

'He works in the provincial government.'

'What's his name?'

'Pío.'

'How many brothers and sisters do you have?'

'There are five of us; four boys and a girl. I'm the oldest.'

'Are you all light-haired?'

'Yes, señor, all of us are red-haired; my father is too.'

In the boy's voice there is a vague tone of sadness. The traveller wishes he hadn't asked so many questions. He thinks for a moment, as he puts away the towel and the soap and takes out the tomatoes, the bread, and a can of *foie gras*, that he has gone too far with his interrogation.

'Shall we have something to eat?'

'All right, if you want to.'

The traveller tries to make himself agreeable, and little by little the boy begins to be happy again, as he was before he said, 'Yes, all of us are red-haired; my father is too.' The traveller tells the boy that he is not going to Zaragoza, that he is going to take a little trip through the Alcarria; he tells him where he was born, what his name is, how many brothers and sisters he has. By the time he tells him about a cousin of his who squints and lives in Malaga and is named Jenaro, the boy is helpless with laughter. Then he tells him about the war and the boy listens attentively, greatly impressed, with his eyes wide open.

'Did you ever get shot?'

The traveller and the boy have become great friends and they keep on, talking all the way, until they get to the road that goes to Iriépal. The boy says goodbye.

'I have to go back; my mother wants me to be home by lunch-time. And anyway she doesn't like to have me go this far – she's always telling me so.'

The traveller puts out his hand, but the boy doesn't take it.

'It's because it's dirty, you know.'

'Come on, don't be silly! What difference does that make?'

The boy looks at the ground.

'It's because I'm always putting my finger in my nose.'

'What of it? I saw you do it. I stick my finger in my nose some-times. It feels good, doesn't it?'

'Yes, señor; it does feel good.'

The traveller starts off and the boy stays by the side of the road looking after him. When he has gone a long way the traveller turns around. The boy is waving goodbye. His hair shines like fire in the sunlight. The boy has beautiful, shining, enchanting hair, even though he believes the contrary.

A little farther on, the traveller sits down to eat in a gully, below an olive grove. Then he has a swallow of wine, unfolds his blanket and lies down to take a nap under a tree. Every now and then a bicycle or an official car goes down the highway. Some distance away, sitting in the shade of an olive tree, a shepherd is singing. The sheep are huddled together motionless, half-dead with the heat. Lying on his blanket, the traveller has a close view of the life of insects as they dash from one place to another and then stop suddenly while they rhythmically wave their long, hair-thin antennae. The fields are green and well cared for, and the wild flowers – red poppies, white daisies blue-flowered thistles, and the little golden buttons of the buttercups – grow along the edges of the highway outside the culti- vated fields.

Some girls who have decorated their broad straw hats with sprigs of cornflower pass by; they are wearing flowered dresses and they walk freely, lightly, as graceful as gazelles. The traveller watches them go by and closes his eyes. He likes to fall asleep with the memory of some last pleasant sensation in his mind; a stork flying past, a child splashing in the backwater of a stream, a bee sucking the flowers on a thorn bush, a young woman walking in the first heat of summer with arms bare and hair loose on her shoulders.

The traveller, back on the road and fresh from his nap, thinks about things he hasn't thought of for many years, and he feels as though some little breeze had made his heart light.

When he gets to Taracena he fills his canteen with white wine. In Taracena there is no red wine – noble as the blood of animals, pungent and ancient as a terrifying family history. There is no inn in Taracena, either. No inn and no lodging of any kind. But there is a cool, clean tavern in Taracena with a freshly sprinkled earthen floor. The woman who keeps the tavern has a very studious little girl; a girl of ten who gets up from her nap without being told and goes back to school.

Taracena is a town of adobe houses, an ashy, light-grey town; a town that seems to be covered with a dust as fine and delicate as the dust on books which have rested for years on the shelf without being touched or disturbed. The traveller recalls Taracena as being uninhabited. He doesn't see a soul. In the heat of four o'clock in the afternoon, there is only a child playing apathetically with some apricot pits. A mule cart, with its long tongue lying on the ground, is baking in the middle of a little plaza. A few hens are scratching in some heaps of dung. On the front of a house, some well-washed shirts, so stiff and rigid that they seem to be made of cardboard, shine like snow.

The traveller chats with the woman of the tavern.

'Is there water in the town, señora?'

'Yes, señor, a great deal of water, and very good, too. We have the same water here as in the capital.'

The traveller sets off again; since it is the first day, his legs are a little tired. The woman comes to the door to say goodbye to him.

'Goodbye, and good luck. Are you going to Zaragoza?'

'Goodbye, señora, many thanks. No, I'm not going to Zaragoza.'

The traveller reflects on the farewells given to men who travel, a little like the farewell one gives to those one will never see again. The 'Goodbye, and good luck' that the country girl or the tavern woman or the washerwoman or the mule driver gives, is a farewell forever, a lifelong farewell, a farewell laden with unrecognized sorrow. Their souls and all their five senses go into that 'Goodbye and good luck.'

★ ★ ★

GEORGE ORWELL (1903–1950)

from *Homage to Catalonia*

The days grew hotter and even the nights grew tolerably warm. On a bullet-chipped tree in front of our parapet thick clusters of cherries were forming. Bathing in the river ceased to be an agony and became almost a pleasure. Wild roses with pink blooms the size of saucers straggled over the shell-holes round Torre Fabian. Behind the line you met peasants wearing wild roses over their ears. In the evenings they used to go out with green nets, hunting quails. You spread the net over the tops of the grasses and then lay down and made a noise like a female quail. Any male quail that was within hearing then came running towards you, and when he was underneath the net you threw a stone to scare him, whereupon he sprang into the air and was entangled in the net. Apparently only male quails were caught, which struck me as unfair.

There was a section of Andalusians next to us in the line now. I do not know quite how they got to this front. The current explanation was that they had run away from Malaga so fast that they had forgotten to stop at Valencia; but this, of course, came from the Catalans, who professed to look down on the Andalusians as a race of semi-savages. Certainly the Andalusians were very ignorant. Few if any of them could read, and they seemed not even to know the one thing that everybody knows in Spain – which political party they belonged to. They thought they were Anarchists, but were not quite certain; perhaps they were Communists. They were gnarled, rustic-looking men, shepherds or labourers from the olive groves, perhaps, with faces deeply stained by the ferocious suns of farther south. They were very useful to us, for they had an extraordinary dexterity at rolling the dried-up Spanish tobacco into cigarettes. The issue of cigarettes had ceased, but in Monflorite it was occasionally possible to buy packets of the cheapest kind of tobacco, which in appearance and texture was very like chopped chaff. Its flavour was not bad, but it was so dry that even when you had succeeded in making a cigarette the tobacco promptly fell out and left an empty cylinder. The Andalusians, however, could roll admirable cigarettes and had a special technique for tucking the ends in.

Two Englishmen were laid low by sunstroke. My salient memories of that time are the heat of the midday sun, and working half-naked with sandbags punishing one's shoulders which were already flayed by the sun; and the lousiness of our clothes and boots, which were literally dropping to pieces; and the struggles with the mule which brought our rations and which did not mind rifle-fire but took to flight when shrapnel burst in the air; and the mosquitoes (just beginning to be active) and the rats, which were a public nuisance and would even devour leather belts and cartridge-pouches. Nothing was happening except an occasional casualty from a sniper's bullet and the sporadic artillery-fire and air-raids on Huesca. Now that the trees were in full leaf we had constructed snipers' platforms, like machans, in the poplar trees that fringed the line. On the other side of Huesca the attacks were petering out. The Anarchists had had heavy losses and had not succeeded in completely cutting the Jaca road. They had managed to establish themselves close enough on either side to bring the road itself under machine-gun fire and make it impassable for traffic; but the gap was a kilometre wide and the Fascists had constructed a sunken road, a sort of enormous trench, along which a certain number of lorries could come and go. Deserters reported that in Huesca there were plenty of munitions and very little food. But the town was evidently not going to fall. Probably it would have been impossible to take it with the fifteen thousand ill-armed men who were available. Later, in June, the Government brought troops from the Madrid front and concentrated thirty thousand men on Huesca, with an enormous quantity of aeroplanes, but still the town did not fall.

When we went on leave I had been a hundred and fifteen days in the line, and at the time this period seemed to me to have been one of the most futile of my whole life. I had joined the militia in order to fight against Fascism, and as yet I had scarcely fought at all, had merely existed as a sort of passive object, doing nothing in return for my rations except to suffer from cold and lack of sleep. Perhaps that is the fate of most soldiers in most wars. But now that I can see this period in perspective I do not altogether regret it. I wish, indeed, that I could have served the Spanish Government a little more effectively; but from a personal point of view – from the point of view of my own development – those first three or four months that I spent in the line were less futile than I then thought. They formed a kind of interregnum in my life, quite different from anything that had gone before and perhaps from anything that is to come, and they taught me things that I could not have learned in any other way.

The essential point is that all this time I had been isolated – for at the front one was almost completely isolated from the outside world: even of what was happening in Barcelona one had only a dim conception – among people who could roughly but not too inaccurately be described as revolutionaries. This was the result of the militia system, which on the Aragon front was not radically altered till about June 1937. The workers' militias, based on the trade unions and each composed of people of approximately the same political opinions, had the effect of canalizing into one place all the most revolutionary sentiment in the country. I had dropped more or less by chance into the only community of any size in Western Europe where political consciousness and disbelief in capitalism were more normal than their opposites. Up here in Aragon one was among tens of thousands of people, mainly though not entirely of working-class origin, all living at the same level and mingling on terms of equality. In theory it was perfect equality, and even in practice it was not far from it. There is a sense in which it would be true to say that one was experiencing a foretaste of Socialism, by which I mean that the prevailing mental atmosphere was that of Socialism. Many of the normal motives of civilized life – snobbishness, money-grubbing, fear of the boss, etc. – had simply ceased to exist. The ordinary class-division of society had disappeared to an extent that is almost unthinkable in the money-tainted air of England; there was no one there except the peasants and ourselves, and no one owned anyone else as his master. Of course such a state of affairs could not last. It was simply a temporary and local phase in an enormous game that is being played over the whole surface of the earth. But it lasted long enough to have its effect upon anyone who experienced it. However much one cursed at the time, one realized afterwards that one had been in contact with something strange and valuable. One had been in a community where hope was more normal than apathy or cynicism, where the word 'comrade' stood for comradeship and not, as in most countries, for humbug. One had breathed the air of equality. I am well aware that it is now the fashion to deny that Socialism has anything to do with equality. In every country in the world a huge tribe of party hacks and sleek little professors are busy 'proving' that Socialism means no more than a planned state-capitalism with the grab-motive left intact. But fortunately there also exists a vision of Socialism quite different from this. The thing that attracts ordinary men to Socialism and makes them willing to risk their skins for it, the 'mystique' of Socialism, is the idea of equality; to the vast majority of people Socialism means a classless society, or it means nothing at all. And it was here that those few months in the militia were valuable to me. For the Spanish militias, while they lasted, were a sort of microcosm of a classless society. In that community where no one was on the make, where there was a shortage of everything but no privilege and no boot-licking, one got, perhaps, a crude forecast of what the opening stages of Socialism might be like. And, after all, instead of disillusioning me it deeply attracted me. The effect was to make my desire to see Socialism established much more actual than it had been before. Partly, perhaps, this was due to the good luck of being among Spaniards, who, with their innate decency and their ever-present Anarchist tinge, would make even the opening stages of Socialism tolerable if they had the chance.

Of course at the time I was hardly conscious of the changes that were occurring in my own mind. Like everyone about me I was chiefly conscious of boredom, heat, cold, dirt, lice, privation, and occasional danger. It is quite different now. This period which then seemed so futile and eventless is now of great importance to me. It is so different from the rest of my life that already it has taken on the magic quality which, as a rule, belongs only to memories that are years old. It was beastly while it was happening, but it is a good patch for my mind to browse upon. I wish I could convey to you the atmosphere of that time. I hope I have done so, a little, in the earlier chapters of this book. It is all bound up in my mind with the winter cold, the ragged uniforms of militiamen, the oval Spanish faces, the Morse-like tapping of machine-guns, the smells of urine and rotting bread, the tinny taste of bean stews wolfed hurriedly out of unclean pannikins.

The whole period stays by me with curious vividness. In my memory I live over incidents that might seem too petty to be worth recalling. I am in the dug-out at Monte Pocero again, on the ledge of limestone that serves as a bed, and young Ramon is snoring with his nose flattened between my shoulder-blades. I am stumbling up the mucky trench, through the mist that swirls round me like cold steam. I am halfway up a crack in the mountainside, struggling to keep my balance and to tug a root of wild rosemary out of the ground. High overhead some meaningless bullets are singing.

I am lying hidden among small fir-trees on the low ground west of Monte Oscuro, with Kopp and Bob Edwards and three Spaniards. Up the naked grey hill to the right of us a string of Fascists are climbing like ants. Close in front a bugle-call rings out from the Fascist lines. Kopp catches my eye and, with a schoolboy gesture, thumbs his nose at the sound.

I am in the mucky yard at La Granja, among the mob of men who are struggling with their tin pannikins round the cauldron of stew. The fat and harassed cook is warding them off with the ladle. At a table nearby a bearded man with a huge automatic pistol strapped to his belt is hewing loaves of bread into five pieces. Behind me a Cockney voice (Bill Chambers, with whom I quarrelled bitterly and who was afterwards killed outside Huesca) is singing:

> There are rats, rats,
> Rats as big as cats,
> In the . . .

A shell comes screaming over. Children of fifteen fling themselves on their faces. The cook dodges behind the cauldron. Everyone rises with a sheepish expression as the shell plunges and booms a hundred yards away.

I am walking up and down the line of sentries, under the dark boughs of the poplars. In the flooded ditch outside the rats are paddling about, making as much noise as otters. As the yellow dawn comes up behind us, the Andalusian sentry, muffled in his cloak, begins singing. Across no man's land, a hundred or two hundred yards away, you can hear the Fascist sentry also singing.

On 25 April, after the usual *mañanas*, another section relieved us and we handed over our rifles, packed our kits and marched back to Monflorite. I was not sorry to leave the line. The lice were multiplying in my trousers far faster than I could massacre them, and for a month past I had had no socks and my boots had very little sole left, so that I was walking more or less barefoot. I wanted a hot bath, clean clothes and a night between sheets more passionately than it is possible to want anything when one has been living a normal civilized life. We slept a few hours in a barn in Monflorite, jumped a lorry in the small hours, caught the five o'clock train at Barbastro and – having the luck to connect with a fast train at Lerida – were in Barcelona by three o'clock in the afternoon of the 26th. And after that the trouble began.

SWEDEN

FRANZ KAFKA (1883–1924)

from *The Diaries of Franz Kafka, 1910–1923*

When I see these stark-naked people moving slowly past among the trees (though they are usually at a distance), I now and then get light, superficial attacks of nausea. Their running doesn't make things any better. A naked man, a complete stranger to me, just now stopped at my door and asked me in a deliberate and friendly way whether I lived here in my house, something there couldn't be much doubt of, after all. They come upon you so silently. Suddenly one of them is standing there, you don't know where he came from. Old men who leap naked over haystacks are no particular delight to me either.

Walked to Stapelburg in the evening. With two people I introduced and recommended to one another. Ruins. Back at ten. Some nudists prowling about among the haystacks on the meadow in front of my cabin, disappeared into the distance. At night, when I walked across the meadow to the toilet, there were three of them sleeping in the grass.

ICELAND

W. H. AUDEN (1907–1973)

from *Letters from Iceland*

AKUREYRI, WEDNESDAY I was right. My throat is much worse, like a lime kiln. I don't know whether this stage is the most unpleasant or the next, when I shall cry for two days. Most disfiguring and embarrassing and I've only got one handkerchief. I suppose my It is really repenting its sins, which it apparently has to do about every six months, but I wish it wouldn't. I caught the nine o'clock bus to Myvatn, full of Nazis who talked incessantly about *Die Schönheit des Islands*, and the Aryan qualities of the stock. '*Die Kinder sind so reizend: schöne blonde Haare und blaue Augen. Ein echt Germanischer Typus.*' I expect this isn't grammatical, but that's what it sounded like. I'm glad to say that as they made this last remark we passed a pair of kids on the road who were as black as night. In the corner was a Danish ornithologist with a pursed little mouth, like a bank clerk who does a little local preaching in his spare time, who answered a Danish girl next to him in explosive monosyllables as if he were unused to talking and couldn't moderate his voice. Two more hikers got in, Austrians this time, and then a German ornithologist with a guide who looked a cross between Freud and Bernard Shaw. For the first time I have struck a dud bus. It developed a choke in the petrol feed and got slower and slower. We got to the Godafoss and I had some coffee while the Germans went to admire. One waterfall is extraordinarily like another. We didn't get to Myvatn till three o'clock and I was hungry and seedy and cross. The lake is surrounded by little craters like candle snuffers and most attractive. Hay was being made everywhere and the haymakers were using aluminium rakes, which I have never seen before. I had to make arrangements for an old German and his beautiful daughter who knew no English or

Icelandic, who wanted to go to Dettifoss but didn't know if they dare. Papa was afraid it was too much for daughter, and daughter that it was too much for Papa, especially the horses. As he can't have weighed a pound under sixteen stone, it is the horses who should worry. Afterwards I lay in the sun watching the hay being made and taking photographs. If I can get them developed in time, and any of them come out, I'll send you some. It's a pity I am so impatient and careless, as any ordinary person could learn all the technique of photography in a week. It is *the* democratic art, i.e. technical skill is practically eliminated – the more fool-proof cameras become with focusing and exposure gadgets the better – and artistic quality depends only on choice of subject. There is no place for the professional still photographer, and his work is always awful. The only decent photographs are scientific ones and amateur snapshots, only you want a lot of the latter to make an effect. A single still is never very interesting by itself. We started back about five, more crowded than ever, and the petrol stoppage much worse. We stopped to fill up and I was very annoyed because I was the wrong side of the bus to take the farmer's girl working the pump, which would have made a beautiful Eisenstein sort of shot. The bus got weaker and weaker and I thought we were going to run backwards down a hill. A lot of passengers got off at a school, thank goodness, and we tottered home, back-firing all the way, with a magnificent sunset over the mountains, and got in about ten. I went to eat and then ran into some drunk Norwegian sailors. An Icelandic acquaintance of theirs passed and greeted one by slapping him on the bottom, which started a furious argument conducted entirely in English, something like this.

— Why did you do that?
— Why shouldn't I?
— Don't you know it's an insult to slap a man on his arse?
— No, it isn't.
— Yes, it is.
— No it isn't. It's an Icelandic custom.
— Oh no, it isn't.
— How do you know?
— How do I know. Everybody knows.
— No, they don't.
— I tell you it's an insult to slap a chap's arse.
— How can you tell me when you don't know about Iceland?

— If you don't know that, you're goddam uneducated.
— How should I know that when I know it isn't.
   (Two officers stroll up and stand by. The crowd begins to disperse.)
— Well, be more careful, next time, Mister, see.
— Same to you.

GERMANY

WERNER HERZOG (1942–)

from *Walking in Ice*

At the end of November 1974, a friend from Paris called and told me that Lotte Eisner was seriously ill and would probably die. I said that this must not be, not at this time, German cinema could not do without her now, we would not permit her death. I took a jacket, a compass and a duffel bag with the necessities. My boots were so solid and new that I had confidence in them. I set off on the most direct route to Paris, in full faith, believing that she would stay alive if I came on foot. Besides, I wanted to be alone with myself . . .

*

Munderkingen. Again my left thigh starts acting up around the groin, making me mad, for otherwise it would be fine. Here is a country fair and cattle market, everywhere farmers in wellingtons, pig transports, cows. I bought myself a cap, a kind of storm hat, a bit too small and utterly repulsive. Then long johns. Just outside town, a small church to one side and an inhabited trailer right next to it. An old man came out, and for a long while he bent over bare severely trimmed rose bushes. I undressed in a corner of the church, while the wind was swirling a solitary tree leaf round my head. In the distance the thunder of cannon and jet fighters, which is how my mother described the outbreak of the War. A few miles further on, a low-flying jet fighter attacked a hedge, the hedge firing back from all barrels; it was nothing but a camouflaged tank that spun about and fired in a flash, while the jet fighter attacked from all angles . . .

*

Beyond Geising the snowfall starts to turn into a squall and I walk more aggressively, for stopping would mean I'd start to freeze at once, as I'm soaked to the skin, so in this way I can at least keep the machine running. Wet, driving snow falls intensely in front, sometimes from the side as well, as I compulsively lean into it, the snow covering me immediately, like a fir tree, on the side exposed to the wind. Oh how I bless my cap. On old brown photos the last Navajos, crouching low on their horses, wrapped in blankets, covered in rugs, move through the snowstorm towards their doom: this image refuses to leave my mind and strengthens my resolve. The road is quickly buried in drifts of snow. In the blizzard a truck gets stuck in the muck of the field with its lights on and cannot move; the farmer standing next to it gives up, not knowing what to do. The two of us, spectres both, don't salute. Oh, it's such a hard march as the wind bearing burning snow blows bitingly into my face, completely horizontal. And most of the time it's all uphill, though downhill everything hurts as well. I am a ski jumper, I support myself on the storm, bent forward, far, far, the spectators surrounding me a forest turned into a pillar of salt, a forest with its mouth open wide. I fly and fly and don't stop. Yes, they scream. Why doesn't he stop? I think, Better keep on flying before they see that my legs are so brittle and stiff that they'll crumble like chalk when I land. Don't quit, don't look, fly on. Then a dwarfish winegrower on a tractor, then my little one listened to my chest to see if my heart was still beating. The watch I gave him is also going, he says it's ticking. I always wanted a postcard from the dam that burst in Fréjus, because of the landscape. And in Vienna, when the old Danube bridge crashed down at dawn, an eyewitness who had wanted to cross said that the bridge had flattened out like an old man going to sleep. All around there are cornfields, which calls for more thinking.

My right ankle has worsened. If it goes on swelling I won't know what to do. I cut across the curves sloping downward to Gammertingen, it's getting so steep and it really hurts. At a sharp turn my left leg suddenly tells me what a meniscus is, as heretofore I'd known it only in theory. I'm so dramatically wet that before entering an inn I hesitate outside for quite a long time. But necessity forces me to overcome my worst fears. Haile Selassie was executed. His corpse was burned together with an executed greyhound, an executed pig, and an executed chicken. The intermingled ashes were scattered over the fields of an English county. How comforting this is.

*

As afterthought just this: I went to Madame Eisner, she was still tired and marked by her illness. Someone must have told her on the phone that I had come on foot, I didn't want to mention it. I was embarrassed and placed my smarting legs up on a second armchair, which she pushed over to me. In the embarrassment a thought passed through my head, and, since the situation was strange anyway, I told it to her. Together, I said, we shall boil fire and stop fish. Then she looked at me and smiled very delicately, and since she knew that I was someone on foot and therefore unprotected, she understood me. For one splendid, fleeting moment something mellow flowed through my deadly tired body. I said to her, open the window, from these last days onward I can fly.

* * *

ROBERT ANTELME (1917–1990)

from *The Human Race*

Escape, 1945

April 4. The cannon thundered all night long.

We had no trouble distinguishing its sound from that of bombs or of anti-aircraft guns. They must have been about forty kilometres away. For several days there'd been talk of evacuation.

I hadn't slept much. When I woke up daylight was visible through the block's shutters. The time for roll call had passed, but that didn't surprise anybody. This was really going to be the last or next-to-last day that we'd spend at Gandersheim. The sleeping room was quiet. A guy pushed a shutter open and daylight flooded in. It was sunny. The sky was clear. The square where roll call was held appeared through the window, empty and quiet. It was a truly lovely spring morning, perhaps the quietest, clearest morning we'd known; and we could even hear the songs of birds as they flew out of the woods.

First of all we heard footsteps outside; then, suddenly, a loud uproar in the entryway. Yelling men burst into the sleeping room, rifles or machine guns slung on their shoulders. We recognized them: they were the kapos. They were all there: Fritz, Ernst, the

Werkkontroll, and the others, wearing *Werkschutz* outfits. Two German prisoners who weren't kapos and the Rumanian, the SS laundryman, were with them; the SS had armed them and put them in uniform.

The day before, those who weren't able to walk had been asked to give their names; they were told that, in the event of evacuation, they would stay at Gandersheim. Some guys had given their names, and the kapos were coming to get them.

Nobody moved. The kapos became riled. They yelled louder and went from bed to bed, thumping the floor with their rifle butts. The two German prisoners among them kept still. Fritz and Ernst were striding up and down the aisle hammering the bedsteads with their rifle butts. Even so, nobody was moving.

Then they went to find the *Stubendienst*, who came with a list; they threatened to clear everybody out. The *Stubendienst* called the guys' names: Pelava, André, two others.

Pelava, the old man from Toulouse who had big carbuncles on his legs, lifted himself up on his pallet and began, with difficulty, to put on his socks. To hurry him up, Fritz walked up to the bed and smacked it with his rifle butt. Ernst was doing the same over where little André was. They kept on yelling, '*Los, los!*'

But old Pelava didn't move any faster.

The two Germans were standing near the door; they weren't used to it yet, and they weren't yelling. The Rumanian was. He was yelling at everybody who was lying down; he was crowing like a rooster. The *Stubendienst* was following the operation in silence.

Fritz, Ernst, and the others no longer had the cross painted on their backs. When they'd arrived from Buchenwald, they were wearing striped outfits; then they were allowed to wear civilian clothes – at first with a little cross and the green triangle on the back, later without either cross or triangle. Now they had a *Werkschutz* uniform and rifles. They'd managed to change sides, and in their uniforms they were bursting with strength. Slow, difficult work. But they'd pulled it off.

The four guys had got down from their beds, and the kapos had grouped themselves around them in the aisle. They were about to set off.

Then, suddenly, the guys who hadn't been called and who up till then hadn't said anything, suspected something, and from their pallets they shouted, 'Don't go! Try to walk! Don't go!'

From the four there was no reply. They had been asked whether they could walk, and they had said no. That was all. But their names were written down. Pelava started to head back to his bed, but the kapos stopped him.

'Don't go! Don't go!' the guys were yelling.

But the kapos were already leading them away. Pelava passed close to my bed. He was dragging himself along, head down. The little redhead was smiling and looking at his friends.

'Don't go! Don't go!'

The kapos were yelling, *'Los!'*

And the four of them proceeded out of the sleeping room.

The guys had been gone for perhaps fifteen minutes. I'd finally got up from my pallet, and I was mechanically putting on my shoes. Others were getting up and slowly getting dressed. The only noise was the rustling and creaking of the pallets. And no sound came from the little room that lodged the block chief and the *Stubendienst*. The shutters were almost all wide open and daylight filled the barracks. It was very bright, and we could see patches of blue sky at the tops of the windows. The square was still empty.

A burst of machine gun fire. Another burst of machine gun fire. A few isolated shots. A final shot.

'They've shot them!'

'You're crazy!'

'I tell you, they've shot them!'

The two guys were sitting on their pallets, their heads craned forward; they were looking at one another, still listening. They were the only ones who had spoken; but all the others, also sitting up and craning forward, were listening too. All these cropped heads, all these wild-eyed faces were listening. There was no further sound.

Pelava, little André, the two others and the guys who were sick – though we didn't as yet know about them – had just been murdered. While we were putting on our shoes. Pelava who had just woken up and who had then pulled on his socks as he did every morning and who had then gone with them because he wasn't in shape for walking and who had gone past me, close to my bed, without saying anything, and who didn't know where they were taking him. He'd gone off like someone who doesn't know, who simply follows. That's how they had left, and they had been made to take a strange path, which got stranger and stranger. They had gone farther and farther from the room, they had climbed towards the woods. They had just got out of bed, and they were made to climb towards the woods, and Fritz hadn't opened his mouth. Nobody had said anything to them. They'd had to figure it out all by themselves. But it was the first time that this had happened here.

We'll never know when they understood that they were going to be killed because they'd said they couldn't walk. The kapos hadn't had anything to say to them. They'd been touchy, in the sleeping room, because they were in a hurry, but they hadn't yelled any more than usual at Pelava or the others, and they hadn't hit them. They'd even been calm when they left the room.

No. When they arrived in the woods with the four guys in line, when the sick arrived there, with the SS sentries, they simply stopped.

They calmly moved off a little to one side. And they fired into the lot of them: pumped shots into the guys with pneumonia, into the guys with tuberculosis; into the guys swollen from edema, into the guys without voices; into the guys with bones for legs, into all those guys who thought they were going to make a left turn, towards the road. That's what they'd been, the burst of gunfire, and the next burst of gunfire, and the silence, and the isolated shots. The bullets were tearing into their bellies while we were sitting on our pallets, eyes staring, listening.

We pieced this together later on. We also learned that Félix had tried to escape into the woods. Fritz had run after him, wounded him first in the shoulder, then blown his head off.

The serving began an hour later. We were to receive three quarter-loaves of bread, because we were going to pull out. Guys were holding enormous pieces of bread in their hands – we'd never had anything so big – and a chunk of margarine. Fritz was watching the serving. He appeared at ease; he was smiling. I held my breath when I passed him, to avoid his odour. He didn't slap, he didn't kick, he was even almost friendly at the serving that morning. We were leaving together. He'd just murdered the guys, and he was in good form. Later on, he'd be alongside the column, keeping it up.

I went back into the room with my bread. I sat down on my bed and cut a slice. Another guy was sitting not far from me and was already eating. A guy came up and asked him, 'You really think they killed them?'

The guy sitting down looked at him contemptuously. 'You stupid ass. Haven't you understood yet?'

They are forty kilometres away, only half an hour by car. We can't hang around here any longer or tomorrow we ourselves will be in the thick of it. It's already pretty close, with planes flying lower. They're almost here. The SS are fleeing, but they're taking us with them.

Roll call. The kapos and the SS look through the barracks. They are empty.

On the square, the ground is very dry, and the sun is warm. A whistle blows, and we set out in order: Poles, Russians, French, Italians. About four hundred and fifty of us.

The woods are a dark green, and the sun pours down on them; the hillside is green and reddish-brown. It happened this morning. I have looked around, verified that none of them are here. They're not here. The others are less than forty kilometres away, and we can still die, and when they come still closer we'll still be able to die, till the end. Those guys had heard the cannon, they died listening to it.

They are up on the hillside. As for us, we won't die here. We will never come back inside this barbed wire. We're being shoved out; the space being yielded has to be cleansed, emptied of people like us. Come what may, we have to be kept, or else killed. Everything is precise, now.

We took the road to the left, in the direction away from the front.

Each step we take works against us, we'd prefer to be taking it in a backward direction, we'd prefer that those with the cannon advance two steps to every one of ours. The war is slow, so long as nobody comes up and taps us on the shoulder we haven't been saved, there are so many twists and turns before the road gets to where we are, and who knows of our existence? Who has seen us? We remain with the SS, and we're fleeing from conquered ground. It's in their eyes that we'll probably follow the battle which is going to free us. They are advancing. A frown, a blow from a rifle butt, we are moving towards the last of those blows from rifle butts.

We go through a hamlet. The unpaved street is muddy. One-storey houses; in front of them, a few women, some small yellow-haired children; a bar, nobody inside it. There aren't any men in this hamlet. The women look at the SS, one of whom goes to get a drink in the bar. Our SS men have it easy. The men from this hamlet must be at the front. The women stand there, see us. It's a bad sign when you see people like us go by. We remember those little villages we went through when we were retreating, behind the Maginot Line. Here, too, everything will stay put; we abandon them to our side. The nearly deserted village, these women's passivity, the column going through: these are signs of defeat, there's no mistaking it. But this hamlet is still within the German space that says *no*. Whether it defends itself or whether it doesn't, it's saying *no*. Photographs of Hitler still hang in the houses. An SS man can still go into a bar and be welcomed there by the owner's wife. We're still nothing. The hamlet will probably be swallowed up, digested in two days' time, though the houses will remain the same. In front of us, over there, are houses, hills where they will still be saying *no* for yet one more day. And they want to make us say *no*; we have to be docile, we have to prefer Germany, we have to stay with those who make their last stand here.

We've got beyond the hamlet. An SS sentry has given me his suitcase to carry; it's heavy. We carry whatever will not fit in the cart. From time to time, I switch hands. My hand is sore. The suitcase pulls at my arm, at my shoulder, at my back; my arm's nothing but a stick with a weight hanging at its end. But if I open my hand, the suitcase will fall, and may break. It's becoming too painful. I switch hands. I am red in the face. How long can I carry it? I still have enough strength to walk; but I'll have to let go of the suitcase. I change hands again. I ought to change every minute; the smarting doesn't have time to subside. I look at the guys. Some are carrying suitcases; they're red, too. The others are grey; they walk slowly, trying to keep away from the guys carrying suitcases, in order not to have to take one.

I put it down and keep going. The guys behind me avoid it and keep walking. Nobody picks it up. The SS man saw me, and he rushes towards me. Blows with the rifle butt. I have to go get it; it's still on the ground, about thirty yards behind the column. I pick it up, with the SS man watching me. I walk rapidly back to my place, taking little steps, leaning to the left. I'm sweating a little, and my glasses slide down my nose; I push them back with my left hand. I change the suitcase from one hand to the other. I'm sinking, I'm fighting for air, all I can do now is make faces. If I stop, I'll get hit.

If I fall, a burst from the machine pistol. It can all happen very fast.
I put the suitcase down again. The SS man didn't see me. I hide on
the right side of the column, and that seems to be that.

I realize now that an effort like that, if it had to be maintained
for some time, would suffice to kill me. I was already floundering.
I could no longer close my mouth, and I couldn't tell one guy from
another. My strength runs out right away. My head can still drive
me, repeat, 'You've got to,' 'You've got to'; but not for long. It too
gets worn out, stops wanting to do anything anymore. I've held on
for nine months; but if they make me carry that suitcase again, I'm
finished.

We went through several hamlets, then entered a wooded area. The
road was straight, running along a forest's edge. The SS whistled for
a halt; the column broke up and we sat down under the trees. I was
with Francis, Riby, Paul, and Cazenave, who was from Paris. We
took out our bread. The sky was full of clouds. The woods were
dark; we had a cool breeze on our backs. We began to eat. The SS
men had us encircled, sitting about twenty yards apart from each
other, their guns beside them, eating. Their bread wasn't the same
sort as ours. They cut bigger pieces than we did, without eyeing it
as we did. My three quarter-loaves supply was shrinking. I'd already
eaten more than one quarter, and this was only the first day of the
march. I cut an even slice and I spread a little margarine on it; I cut
the slice into small cubes with my knife and chewed them for a long
time. This bread turned to mush very quickly in your mouth. You'd
eat with your head down, glancing now at the ground, now at the
bread. The Poles and Russians were quiet, and so were we; the Italians
were talking. Lucien had a wooden box that he carried on his
shoulder with a stick. He opened his box in the woods, and ate meat
with his bread and made coffee; he was fat, he carried his box
without any trouble. Since we'd left, he was being inconspicuous,
walking with the cooks, and not yelling.

Everybody was eating something: Lucien, his meat; the SS men,
sausages and fruit preserves; we, bread and margarine. The SS behaved like soldiers while they ate. We had to pay attention, and
couldn't both eat and talk. My bread was shrinking and I made
myself put it under my jacket, and I put my knife back in my pocket.
The whistle ending the halt hadn't been blown yet, and I lay back
on the cool moss. The war was going to end. There were patches

of white sky between the branches of the trees. In the block there was a guy who would say, 'This will be the most beautiful day of my life, yes, the most beautiful day of my life.' The sky was very near; it was cool and the moss was damp. The bread was still heavy on my chest, and I still had some; I'd cut another slice in a little while, and I'd still be a prisoner when I cut my last slice of it. The last slice of the war. I was still here, and it was true: I was getting ready to live the most beautiful day of my life. The SS men were all around us, to keep that day from coming. Either we or they were going to die. Who would pay? Cazenave wasn't strong and he suffered from rheumatism; and the SS didn't want to die, and didn't want to leave. And it was proceeding: if there were some paratroopers it might come about now, or in fifteen minutes. We'd know who our friends were, we'd run along the road; we'd find the strength, of course we would.

The dampness of the moss was getting to my back. The SS were talking among themselves. Ah, to break into their conversation, to say to them: 'The war's over, you can stop . . . But *we're* leaving.' We weren't able to speak the truth. Never would they believe us, *never*. We couldn't see the same sun. *Der Krieg ist nicht fertig, nein, nein* . . . and then the gun barrel in your belly. They were losing the war, but they were eating.

I was cold and I got up. Paul was eating. He looked at the bread he had left and cut another slice; he didn't hesitate for long. I hesitated; I felt the piece underneath my jacket. The sound of the whistle saved it.

We have walked for several hours. It must be five o'clock in the afternoon. We've left the plain. We start up a steep bit of road that rises along the side of a mountain; we follow the edge of a quarry. No houses. Far off, we hear dogs barking. The column stops for a minute because those pulling the cart are having a hard time keeping up and we have to wait for them. We start again when we see them come around the last bend. The air is very cool, the sky is red, and the clouds soar and glide along. Evening comes. The uphill path is steep, and a comrade in front of me stops and lowers his head. His buddy stops with him.

'Don't stop. Walk. We'll get there. Walk, walk!' says his buddy. He is gasping and doesn't reply. Nobody has fallen yet. The kapos have spotted him. We pass them. He still has a little time. The

Italians are behind us; but he mustn't let the whole column pass by
him. Fritz has stopped; he's ready. I look back. The comrade still
hasn't stirred; he stands motionless on the road, his head hanging.
Finally, his friend takes his arm and places it around his own neck
and pulls him along. We're walking very slowly, and, taking little
steps, he's able to catch up with us. He is crying.

Fritz has started walking again. Once again the comrade stops,
lowers his head, and hugs his stomach; his mouth is contorted. His
friend still has his arm around his neck. The kapos are waiting.
Everybody has seen that the kapos are ready. The friend tugs at him.
'Come on, come on. Walk. Walk. We're getting there.' He's holding
his stomach. He has to start again; his friend tugs him. He takes two
steps, then stops, doubled over. The kapos are still observing him,
awaiting his decision. There's nothing we can do.

He manages to start up again.

The day draws to a close. The dogs' barking gets closer; it comes
from the dark valley ahead of us. We can no longer hear the cannon.
The column stops at a crossroads. A small road leads straight down
on our right. The Poles and the Russians stay on the main road;
with the Italians we take the one that goes down, walking quickly.
The barking gets closer and closer; in the dark, it's the only sound.
The sky is red, and clouds glide by. We hurry down the hill, tripping
over stones; our knees have a hard time supporting us. In the valley
a large wooden house comes into sight; we can see the kennels. The
barking is like that at Buchenwald and Fresnes. SS dogs: SS and dogs
form a couple. Like SS men, these dogs, too, begin by being small
and endearing and playful.

The valley is dark. The dogs' noise and the night weigh crushingly
upon us. The dogs are theirs, the valley and the night are also theirs;
we're in their country. This patch of red sky and these forests weigh
upon us. Who can reach us, here? Our side is winning the war, but
you can't tell that from here; we don't hear the cannon anymore,
just the dogs.

We are almost at the bottom of the valley. The large house is on
the left. We leave the road and take a little path that leads to it.
There's a big yard in front of the house, with little doghouses; in
each one, a dog is barking. We're probably going to sleep here. The
column halts in the yard. They count us, and we go into a room
that looks like a gymnasium. It has a floor, and we form little groups
and sit down.

We're crammed in one on top of the other. It's almost dark in the room. A sentry and a kapo guard the entrance. If we have to shit, we must go outside, and only one at a time. There's already a line. The dogs have quieted down. The kapos sent some guys to fetch some sacks. Those sacks contain dog biscuits. At first, the kapos try handing them out, but we dive into the sacks. It's a free-for-all. We stuff some into our pockets. We pass some to a guy who puts them in his bag. The guys who haven't been able to get close are yelling. The SS arrive with their truncheons, and we retreat from the half-empty sacks. I bite into a biscuit, it's hard, it has ground up bones in it, they have a sour taste.

It is nighttime now, and the SS men would like to to sleep. They have set up in a little room adjoining ours; their door is partially open, and light comes through. The guys attack the sacks again, and again it's a free-for-all. But the sacks are almost empty.

Legs are trampled as guys heading out to shit try to step over guys lying on the floor, and there is a vast rumbling throughout the darkened room. An SS man comes in: '*Ruhe!*' The rumbling subsides for a minute, then swells anew. You can't tell who is making the noise. I'm not making any. I am lying between some Italian's legs. Who's yelling?

'You son of a bitch! You can't watch where you're going?'

'You want me to shit right here?'

'Just get the fuck off me!'

That comes from behind us. Someone's foot steps on my face; I grab the ankle and, since it doesn't resist, I raise it and set it down on the floor between my legs, from where it is gone a moment later. I try to sleep amidst that uproar. But there's still the line at the door. Some guys are yelling that they have diarrhoea and are being prevented from going out. They can't hold it any longer and finally they pull down their pants and squat over beside the wall.

'God damn it, there's someone shitting right in here!'

The guy shitting doesn't reply, he merely goes ahead.

'Kapo! Hey, he's shitting right here!'

A flashlight comes on. The guy is crouching in the beam of light.

'*Scheisse, Scheisse!*' yells the kapo.

The kapo strikes, the guy falls over.

'*Scheisserei,*' the guy moans. 'Diarrhoea.'

'*Was Scheisserei, Schwein!*'

If suddenly the entire room were illuminated you'd see a vast

tangle of striped rags, crooked arms, sharp elbows, purple hands,
huge feet; open mouths aimed at the ceiling, closed eyes in bony faces
covered with blackened skin, deathlike skulls, each shape endlessly
resembling every other, inert and as if laid out in the slime of a
shallow pond. You'd also see lone individuals sitting here and there,
quiet madmen chewing away on dog biscuits in the night, and then
others, doubled over, shifting from one foot to the other in front of
the door.

The valley outside is dark. From it there comes no sound. The dogs
are sleeping a healthy, sated sleep. The trees breathe calmly. The
nocturnal insects feed in the fields. The leaves perspire, and the air
fills with moistures. Dew covers the fields, and in a little while they
will gleam in the sun; they are right there, next to us, and we should
be able to touch them, be able to caress that vast soft pelage. But
what calls for caressing and how does one caress? What is soft
beneath the fingers, what exists only to be touched?
    Never shall we have been so aware of nature's wholesome good-
ness; never so ready to behold as omnipotent the tree that will surely
still be alive tomorrow. We have forgotten about everything that is
dying and rotting in this powerful night, forgotten about sick and
isolated animals. We have banished death from natural things,
because in them we see no spirit working actively against them,
dogging them. We feel as though all possible rottenness has been
sucked up into ourselves. What exists in this room appears to us like
the sickness of sicknesses, and our dying here like the only real death.
To us who look so like animals any animal has taken on qualities of
magnificence; to us who are so similar to any rotting plant, that
plant's destiny seems as luxurious as a destiny that concludes with
dying in bed. We have come to resemble whatever fights simply to
eat, and dies from not eating; come to where we exist on the level
of some other species, which will never be ours and towards which
we are tending. But this other species which at least lives according
to its own authentic law – animals cannot become more animal-like
– appears to us as magnificent as our 'true' species, whose law may
also be to lead us here to where we are. Yet there is no ambiguity:
we're still men, and we shall not end otherwise than as men. The
distance separating us from another species is still intact. It is not
historical. It's an SS fantasy to believe that we have an historical
mission to change species, and as this mutation is occurring too

slowly, they kill. No, this extraordinary sickness is nothing other than a culminating moment in man's history. And that means two things. First, that the solidity and stability of the species is being put to the test. Next, that the variety of the relationships between men, their colour, their customs, the classes they are formed into mask a truth that here, at the boundary of nature, at the point where we approach our limits, appears with absolute clarity: namely, that there are not several human races, there is only one human race. It's because we're men like them that the SS will finally prove powerless before us. It's because they shall have sought to call the unity of this human race into question that they'll finally be crushed. Yet their behaviour, and our situation, are only a magnification, an extreme caricature – in which nobody wants or is perhaps able to recognize himself – of forms of behaviour and of situations that exist in the world, that even make up the existence of that older 'real world' we dream about. For in fact everything happens in that world as though there were a number of human species, or, rather, as though belonging to a single human species wasn't certain, as though you could join the species or leave it, could be halfway in it or belong to it fully, or never belong to it, try though you might for generations, division into races or classes being the canon of the species and sustaining the axiom we're always pepared to use, the ultimate line of defence: 'They aren't people like us.'

And so, seen from here, luxuriousness is the property of the animal, and divineness is the property of trees, and we are unable to become either animals or trees. We are not able to, and the SS cannot make us succeed in it. And it is just when it has taken on the most hideous shape, it is just when it is about to become our own face – that is when the mask falls. And if, at that moment, we believe what, here, is certainly that which requires the most considerable effort to believe, that 'The SS are only men like ourselves'; if, at the moment when the distance between beings is at its greatest, at the moment when the subjugation of some and the power of others have attained such limits as to seem frozen into some supernatural distinction; if, facing nature, or facing death, we can perceive no substantial difference between the SS and ourselves, then we have to say that there is only one human race. And we have to say that everything in the world that masks this unity, everything that places beings in situations of exploitation and subjugation and thereby implies the existence of various species of mankind, is false and mad;

and that we have proof of this here, the most irrefutable proof, since the worst of victims cannot do otherwise than establish that, in its worst exercise, the executioner's power cannot be other than one of the powers that men have, the power of murder. He can kill a man, but he can't change him into something else.

THE FORMER YUGOSLAVIA

Rebecca West (1892–1983)

'Croatia'

They were waiting in the rain on the platform of the real Zagreb, our three friends. There was Constantine, the poet, a Serb, that is to say a Slav member of the Orthodox Church, from Serbia. There was Valetta, a lecturer in mathematics at Zagreb University, a Croat, that is to say a Slav member of the Roman Catholic Church, from Dalmatia. There was Marko Gregorievitch, the critic and journalist, a Croat from Croatia. They were all different sizes and shapes, in body and mind.

Constantine is short and fat, with a head like the best-known satyr in the Louvre, and an air of vine-leaves about the brow, though he drinks little. He is perpetually drunk on what comes out of his mouth, not what goes into it. He talks incessantly. In the morning he comes out of his bedroom in the middle of a sentence; and at night he backs into it, so that he can just finish one more sentence. Automatically he makes silencing gestures while he speaks, just in case somebody should take it into his head to interrupt. Nearly all his talk is good, and sometimes it runs along in a coloured shadow show, like Heine's *Florentine Nights*, and sometimes it crystallizes into a little story the essence of hope or love or regret, like a Heine lyric. Of all human beings I have ever met he is the most like Heine: and since Heine was the most Jewish of writers it follows that Constantine is Jew as well as Serb. His father was a Jewish doctor of revolutionary sympathies, who fled from Russian Poland about fifty years ago and settled in a rich provincial town in Serbia and became one of the leaders of the medical profession, which has always been more advanced there than one might have supposed. His mother was also Polish Jewish, and was a famous musician. He is by adoption only, yet quite completely, a Serb. He fought in the Great War very gallantly, for he is a man of great physical courage, and to him Serbian history is his history, his life is a part of the life of the Serbian people. He is now a Government official; but that is not the reason why he believes in Yugoslavia. To him a state of Serbs, Slovenes, and Croats, controlled by a central government in Belgrade, is a necessity if these peoples are to maintain themselves against Italian and Central European pressure on the west, and Bulgarian pressure, which might become in effect Central European pressure, on the east.

Valetta comes from a Dalmatian town which was settled by the Greeks some hundreds of years before Christ, and he has the strong delicacy and the morning freshness of an archaic stature. They like him everywhere he goes, Paris and London and Berlin and Vienna, but he is hallmarked as a Slav, because his charm is not associated with any of those defects that commonly go with it in other races. He might suddenly stop smiling and clench his long hands, and offer himself up to martyrdom for an idea. He is anti-Yugoslavian; he is a federalist and believes in an autonomous Croatia.

Gregorievitch looks like Pluto in the Mickey Mouse films. His face is grooved with grief at the trouble and lack of gratitude he has encountered while defending certain fixed and noble standards in a chaotic world. His long body is like Pluto's in its extensibility. As he sits in his armchair, resentment at what he conceives to be a remediable injustice will draw him inches nearer to the ceiling, despair at an inevitable wrong will crumple him up like a concertina. Yugoslavia is the Mickey Mouse this Pluto serves. He is ten years older than Constantine, who is forty-six, and thirty years older than Valetta. This means that for sixteen years before the war he was an active revolutionary, fighting against the Hungarians for the right of Croats to govern themselves and to use their own language. In order that the Croats might be united with their free brother Slavs the Serbs, he endured poverty and imprisonment and exile. Therefore Yugoslavia is to him the Kingdom of Heaven on earth. Who speaks more lightly of it spits on those sixteen years of sorrow, who raises his hand against it violates the Slav sacrament. So to him Constantine, who was still a student in Paris when the Great War broke out, and who had been born a free Serb, seems impious in the way he takes Yugoslavia for granted. There is the difference between them that there was between the Christians of the first three centuries, who fought for their faith when it seemed a lost cause, and the Christians of the fourth century, who fought for it when it was victorious.

And to Gregorievitch, Valetta is quite simply a traitor. He is more than an individual who has gone astray, he is the very essence of treachery incarnate. Youth should uphold the banner of the right against unjust authority, and should practise that form of obedience to God which is rebellion against tyranny; and it seems to Gregoriev-itch that Valetta is betraying that ideal, for to him Yugoslavia represents a supreme gesture of defiance against the tyranny of the Austro-Hungarian Empire. Only a sorcerer could make him realize that the Austro-Hungarian Empire ceased to be when Valetta was six years old, and that he has never known any other symbol of unjust authority except Yugoslavia.

They were standing in the rain, and they are all different and they are all the same. They greet us warmly, and in their hearts they cannot greet each other, and they dislike us a little because it is to meet us that they are standing beside their enemies in the rain. We are their friends, but we are made from another substance. The rich passions of Constantine, the intense, graceful, selected joys and sorrow of Valetta, and Gregorievitch's gloomy Great Danish nobility are all cut from the same primary stuff, though in very dissimilar shapes. Sitting in our hotel room, drinking wine, they showed their unity of origin. A door opens, they twitch and swivel their heads and the movement is the same. When these enemies advance on each other, they must move at the same tempo.

My husband has not met any of them before. I see him transfixed by their strangeness. He listens amazed to Constantine's beautiful French, which has preserved in it all the butterfly brilliances of his youth, when he was one of Bergson's favourite students, and was making his musical studies with Wanda Landowska. He falls under the spell of Constantine. He strains forward to hear the perfect phrase that is bound to come when Constantine's eyes catch the light, and each of his tight black curls spins on his head, and his lips shoot out horizontally, and his hands grope in the air before him as if he were unloosing the neckcloth of the strangling truth. Now Constantine was talking of Bergson and saying that it was to miss the very essence in him to regard him only as a philosopher. He was a magician who had taken philosophy as his subject matter. He did not analyse phenomena, he uttered incantations that invoked understanding. 'We students,' said Constantine, 'we were not the pupils of a great professor, we were the sorcerer's apprentices. We did strange things that are not in most academic courses. On Sundays we would talk together in the forest of Fontainebleau, all day long sometimes, reconstituting his lectures by pooling our memories. For, you see, in his classroom it was not possible to take notes. If we bent our heads for one moment to take down a point, we missed an organic phrase, and the rest of the lecture appeared incomprehensible. That shows he was a magician . . . I was able to recognize that at once, for in my town, which is Shabats, there were three houses in a row, and in one house lived my father who was the greatest doctor in our country, and in the next there lived a priest who was the greatest saint in my country, and in the next there lived an old woman who was the greatest witch in my country, and when I was a little boy I lived in the first of these houses and I went as I would into the other two, for the holy man and the witch liked me very much, and I tell you in each of these houses there was magic, so I know all about it as most men do not.'

A line of light ran along the dark map of Europe we all of us hold in our minds; at one end a Serbian town, unknown to me as Ur, peopled with the personnel of fairy-tales, and at the other end the familiar idea of Bergson. My husband, I could see, was enraptured. He loves to learn what he did not know before. But in a minute I could see that he was not so happy. Valetta had said that he was making plans for our pleasure in Yugoslavia, and that he hoped that we would be able to go up into the snow mountains, particularly if we liked winter sports. My husband said he was very fond of Switzerland, and how he enjoyed going over there when he was tired and handing himself over to the care of the guides. 'Yes, the guides are so good for us, who are over-civilized,' said Constantine. 'They refresh us immensely, when we are with them. For they succeed at every point where we fail. We can be responsible for what we love, our families and our countries, and the causes we think just, but where we do not love we cannot muster the necessary attention. That is just what the guides do, with such a wealth of attention that it amounts to nothing comparable to our attention at all, to a mystical apprehension of the whole universe.

'I will give you,' he said, 'an example. I made once a most beautiful journey in Italy with my wife. She is a German, you know, and she worships Goethe, so this was a pilgrimage. We went to see where he had lived in Venice and Rome, and she was so delighted, you cannot believe, delighted deep in herself, so that her intuition told her many things. "That is the house where he lived!" she cried in Venice, jumping up and down in the gondola, and it was so. At length we came to Naples, and we took a guide and went up Vesuvius, because Goethe went up Vesuvius. Do you remember the passage where he said he was on the edge of a little crater, and he slipped? That was much in my wife's mind, and suddenly it was given to her to know by intuition that a certain little crater we saw was that same one where Goethe had slipped, so before we could stop it she ran down to it. I saw, of course, that she might be killed at any moment, so I ran after her. But so did the guide, though she was nothing to him. And then came the evidence of this mystic apprehension which is given by the constant vigilance of a guide's life. Just then this crater began to erupt, and the lava burst out here and there and here. But always the guide knew where it was coming, and took us to the left or the right, wherever it was not. Sometimes there was barely time for us to be there for more than a second; that was proved afterwards because the soles of our shoes were scorched. For three quarters of an hour we ran thus up and down, from right to left and from left to right, before we could get to safety; and I was immensely happy the whole time because the guide was doing something I could not have done, which it is good to do!'

During the telling of this story my husband's eyes rested on me with an expression of alarm. It was apparent from Constantine's tone that nothing in the story had struck him as odd except the devotion of the guide to his charges. 'Are not her friends very dotty?' he was plainly asking himself. 'Is this how she wants to live?' But the conversation took a businesslike turn, and we were called on to consider our plans. We must meet So-and-so and Such-and-such, of course. It became obvious from certain reticences that the strained relations between Croats and Serbs were making themselves felt over our plans. For So-and-so, it appeared, would not meet Such-and-such, and that, it could be deduced, was the reason. Suddenly such reticences were blown away by a very explicit wrangle about Y., the editor of a certain newspaper. 'Oh, you should meet him, he would interest you,' said Valetta. 'Yes, he has a very remarkable mind,' admitted Constantine. 'No,' exploded Gregorievitch. They squabbled for a time in Serbian. Then Gregorievitch shrugged his shoulders and said to us, with heavy lightness, 'Y. is not an honest man, that is all!' 'He is perfectly honest,' said Valetta coldly. 'Gregorievitch, you are an impossibilist,' said Constantine mildly. 'Let our English guests judge,' said Pluto grimly.

It appeared that one day some years before, Pluto had rung up Y. and reminded him that next week was the centenary of a certain Croat poet, and asked him if he would like an article on him. Y. said that he would, and Pluto sent an article four columns long, including two quotations concerning liberty. But the article had to be submitted to the censor, who at that particular time and in that particular place happened to be Pluto. He sent it back to Y., cut by a column and a half, including both quotations. Then, if we would believe it, Y. had rung up Pluto on the telephone and been most abusive, and never since then had he accepted one single article from Pluto. 'Surely,' said Pluto, immensely tall and grey and wrinkled, 'he must have seen that I had to do what I did. To be true to myself as a critic I had to write the article as I did. But to be true to myself as a censor, I had to cut it as I did. In which capacity did he hope that I would betray my ideals?' As he related this anecdote his spectacles shone with the steady glare of a strong man justly enraged.

But that story I could understand. It proceeds not, as might be thought, from incoherence but from a very high and too rigid sense of order. There lingers here a survival of an old attitude towards status that the whole world held, in days which were perhaps happier. Now, we think that if a man takes an office, he will modify it according to what he is as a man, according to his temperament and official standards. But then it was taken for granted that a man would modify his temperament and his ethical standards according to his office, provided it were of any real importance. In the third and fourth centuries Christian congregations were constantly insisting on electing people as bishops who were unwilling to accept the office, perhaps for some such valid reason as that they were not even Christians, but who seemed to have the ability necessary for the semi-magisterial duties of the episcopacy. Sometimes these men were so reluctant that the congregations were obliged to kidnap them and ordain them forcibly. But once they were installed as bishops, they often performed their duties admirably. They had a sense of social structure, they were aware that bishops, who had by then taken over most of the civil administration that the crumbling Roman Empire could no longer handle, must work well if society was not to fall to pieces. Even so Gregorievitch must have been conscious, all his life, of the social value of patriotic poets and, for the last unhappy twenty years, of censors. Therefore it seemed to him that he must do his best in both capacities, not that he should modify his performances to uphold the consistence of his personality. That I could perfectly understand, but it was so late I did not feel able to explain it to my husband, whom I saw, when I forced open my eyelids, undressing slowly, with his eyes set pensively on the window curtains, wondering what strange city they were going to disclose next day.

SLOVAKIA

CLAUDIO MAGRIS (1939–)

'Deambulatory Therapy'

According to tradition it was at Ulm, during the seventeenth century, that they preserved the shoe of Ahasverus, the Wandering Jew. With those soles which had lasted for centuries one could undertake any journey, and doctors at one time considered walking as very good for preserving mental balance. A footnote in the Italian edition of the complete *Tales of Hoffmann*, concerning a real character used by the writer as a model, informs us: 'F. Wilhelm C. L. von Grotthus (1747–1801) attempted to combat the mental disease hereditary to his family by making very long journeys on foot. He died insane at Bayreuth.'

RUSSIA

STENDHAL (1783–1842)

from *The Private Diaries of Stendhal*

[The Author Complains of Toothache While Moscow Burns!]

Smolensk, August 19. The fire appeared such a fine spectacle to us that, although it was seven o'clock, and in spite of the fear of missing dinner (a thing unheard of in such a town), and the fear of the shells which the Russians were firing through the flames at any Frenchmen who might be on the banks of the Borysthenes (Dnepr), we went down to the city gate which is next to a pretty chapel; a shell had just burst there, and everything was still smoking. We advanced a score of paces by running bravely; we crossed the river on a bridge that General Kirgener had ordered to be constructed in great haste. We went right to the edge of the fire, where we found a large number of dogs and a few horses that had been driven out of the city by the general conflagration.

We were about to drink in this rare spectacle when Marignier was approached by an infantry major whom he knew through having taken his place in a lodging at Rostock. This worthy fellow told us at length of his battles that morning and the day before, and then launched out in interminable praise of a dozen Rostock ladies whom he mentioned by name; but he praised one of them more than the others. Reluctance to interrupt a man so full of his subject, and the impulse to laugh, retained us till ten o'clock, when the bullets started raining down again.

We deplored the loss of our dinner, and I was arranging with Marignier that he should return the first to receive our deserved reprimand from M. Daru, when we saw an extraordinary light in the upper town.

We approached, we found all our calashes in the middle of the street, eight large houses near our own were belching flames sixty feet in the air and casting hot embers as big as fists on the house which had been ours for the past few hours; we had the roof pierced in five or six places, half a dozen grenadiers of the Guard were armed with long poles to beat off the sparks and make them fall; they handled their jobs very well. M. Daru took care of everything. Activity, fatigue, tumult till midnight.

Our house caught fire three times and we put it out. Our headquarters were in the courtyard, where, sitting on some straw, we kept watch on the roofs of the house and its dependencies, informing the grenadiers by our shouts where the falling embers were the thickest.

We were there, Messrs Daru, Comte Dumas, Besnard, Jacqueminot, General Kirgener – all of us so exhausted that we dropped off to sleep as we talked; the master of the house (M. Daru) was the only one who resisted sleep.

The dinner we had looked forward to so much appeared at last; but, for all our appetite, since we hadn't eaten anything since ten o'clock in the morning, it was very amusing to see one of us after the other drop off to sleep in his chair, fork in hand.

*

Moscow, Oct 4. I left my general supping at the Apraxin Palace. As we were coming out and were taking leave of M. Z in the courtyard, we noticed that, in addition to the fire in the Chinese village, which had been burning away for several hours, we had one near us; we went to it. The centre of it was very intense. I got a toothache on this expedition. We were foolish enough to stop a soldier who'd just given a couple of whacks with his bayonet to a man who'd drunk too much beer; I went as far as to draw my sword, and I was even on the verge of stabbing the scoundrel. Bourgeois took him to the governor, who set him free.

We retired at one o'clock after spouting numerous commonplaces about fires – all of which didn't produce much effect, at least as far as we could see. Returning to the Casa Apraxin, we tested out a pump. I went to bed, plagued by my toothache. It appears that several of those gents were chickenhearted enough to let themselves be alarmed and to go running out at about two and five o'clock. As for myself, I awoke at seven o'clock, had my carriage loaded and had it driven to the rear of those belonging to M. Daru.

They were strung along the boulevard, opposite the club. There I found Mme B, who was about to throw herself at my feet; that made a very ridiculous recognition. I noticed that there wasn't a shade of naturalness in what Mme B told me, a fact which naturally chilled me. Nevertheless, I did a lot for her by putting her fat sister-in-law in my calash, and inviting her to put her droshkies behind my carriage. She told me that Mme Saint-Albe [Mélanie Guilbert] had often spoken of me.

The fire was rapidly approaching the house we'd left. Our carriages remained on the boulevard five or six hours. Weary of this inaction, I went to see the fire, and stopped an hour or two at Joinville's. I admired the voluptuousness inspired by the furnishings of his house; together with Billet and Busche, we drank three bottles of wine, which revived us.

I read a few lines of an English translation of *Virginie*, which, amid the general coarseness, revived me a bit morally.

I went with Louis [Joinville] to see the fire. We saw a drunken mounted cannoneer named Savoye strike an officer with the flat of his sword, and heap insults on him. He was in the wrong, and was obliged to end up by begging his pardon. One of his pillaging mates went forth through the flaming street, and was probably roasted alive. I saw a further demonstration of the general lack of character in the French. Louis found amusement in calming this man for the benefit of an officer of the Guard who'd have done him a bad turn at the first opportunity; instead of having the scorn for all this disorder that it deserved, he exposed himself to the risk of getting into trouble. For my part, I admired the patience of the officer of the Guard; I'd have given Savoye a sabre blow on the nose – which might have led to trouble with the colonel. The officer acted more prudently.

At three o'clock, I returned to the line of our carriages and dismal colleagues. Stores of flour and oats had just been discovered in the neighbouring frame houses; I told my servants to take some. They made a great show of being busy, put on the appearance of taking great quantities, and in the end their work amounted to very little. That's the way it is with everything everywhere in the Army, and it makes you irritated. It's all well and good to tell yourself it doesn't matter a damn anyway, but, as they're always bellyaching, you finish by getting out of patience, and I pass whole days of unhappiness. I'm far less impatient than another would be in my place, but I lose my temper. I envy certain of my colleagues to whom you could say, I believe, that they're the scum of the earth without their really getting mad; they raise their voices, and that's all. They wiggle their ears, as the Comtesse Palfy used to say. 'A person would be unhappy indeed if he didn't do the same thing,' she would add. She was right: but how are you going to display resignation like that if you have a sensitive soul?

About half past three, Billet and I went to visit the home of Count Petr Soltykov; it appeared to us to be suitable for His Excellency. We went to the Kremlin to notify him; we stopped at General Dumas's quarters, which dominate the square.

General Kirgener said to Louis in front of me, 'If they want to give me four thousand men, I'll guarantee to take care of the fire in six hours, and it will be put out.' These words impressed me. (I doubt if he would succeed. Rostopchin continually had the fire spread to new places; if it were extinguished on the right, it would break out in a score of places on the left.)

We saw M. Daru and the amiable Marignier arrive from the Kremlin; we took them to the Soltykov mansion, which was inspected from cellar to roof; as M. Daru did not find all to his liking in the Soltykov house, he was requested to go to inspect some others in the direction of the club. We saw the club, decorated in the French manner, majestic and blackened by smoke. There is nothing of the kind in Paris that can be compared with it. After the club, we looked over a neighbouring house, vast and superb; finally, a handsome square white house that they decided to occupy.

We were very tired, I more than the others. Ever since Smolensk, I've been completely without strength, and I was childish enough to interest myself and bustle around in this house-hunting. Interest is saying too much, but a great deal of bustle.

We finally moved into this house, which looked as though it had been lived in by a wealthy art lover. It was comfortably arranged, full of statuettes and pictures. There were some good books, notably Buffon, Voltaire – who's to be found everywhere here – and *La Galerie du Palais-Royal.*

A violent epidemic of diarrhoea made everyone fear that the wine would give out. We heard the excellent news that we might help ourselves in the cellar of the fine club I have already mentioned. I persuaded Father Billet to go there. We entered it through a superb stable and a garden that would have been beautiful if the trees of this country did not have such a poverty-stricken aspect for me.

We sent our servants down into the cellar; they brought us up a large quantity of bad white wine, damask tablecloths and badly worn napkins of the same. We pillaged all these things to make sheets out of them.

A little M. J., from the Intendant General's office, who'd come over to do his bit of *pilfering* like us, set about making us presents of all we were taking. He said he was taking over the building for the Intendant General, and started in to moralize; I called him to order a little.

My servant was completely drunk; he heaped tablecloths, wine, a violin he had pillaged for himself and a thousand other things in the carriage. We had a little wine repast with two or three other colleagues.

The servants put the house in order, the fire was far from us and filled the air with copper-coloured smoke; we had set ourselves in order, and were at last about to breathe freely when M. Daru came in and announced that we had to leave. I accepted the thing with courage, but it utterly disheartened me.

My carriage was crammed full, I put the poor pale-faced and boring de B, whom I pitied, in it. He's the most asinine and boring spoiled child I know.

Before leaving the house, I pillaged a volume of Voltaire, the one entitled *Facéties*.

My carriages that François was in charge of kept us waiting. We had barely got under way by seven o'clock. We encountered M. Daru, who was furious. We went directly toward the fire, following a part of the boulevard. Little by little, we advanced through the smoke, breathing became difficult; we finally went between blazing houses. None of our enterprises are ever perilous except through the utter lack of order and caution. Here was a long procession of wagons plunging into the midst of the flames in order to escape them. This manœuvre would have had some sense to it only had the city been surrounded by a circle of fire. This wasn't the case in the least; the fire was limited to one side of the city, it was necessary to get out of it, but it wasn't necessary to go through the fire; what should have been done was to go around it.

The impossibility of the thing stopped us short; we turned back.

As I was thinking of the great spectacle before me, I forgot for a moment that I'd turned my carriage around before the others. I was worn out, I was proceeding on foot because my carriage was full of the servant's plunder, and the paleface was perched on it. I thought my carriage was lost in the fire. François galloped headlong. The carriage wouldn't have been in any danger, but my servants, like those of everyone else, were drunk and quite capable of going to sleep in the middle of a blazing street.

On the boulevard as we returned, we found General Kirgener, with whom I was very satisfied that day. He restored our audacity – in other words, our good sense – and showed us that there were three or four roads by which we could get out of the city.

We followed one of them about eleven o'clock, we broke through the lines, arguing with some of the King of Naples' carters. I later noticed that we were following the Tverskoï, or Tver Street. We left the city, illuminated by the finest fire in the world, which formed an immense pyramid, which, like the prayers of the faithful, had its base on earth and its apex in heaven. The moon appeared above this atmosphere of flame and smoke. It was an imposing sight, but it would have been necessary to be alone, or else surrounded by intelligent people, in order to enjoy it. What has spoiled the Russian campaign for me is to have taken part in it with people who would have belittled the Colosseum or the Bay of Naples.

* * *

FYODOR DOSTOYEVSKY (1820–1881)

from A Writer's Diary Volume 1, 1873–1876

It is a long trip from Petersburg to Berlin – almost two days – and so I took along two pamphlets and a few newspapers just in case. And I truly meant 'just in case', because I have always been afraid of being left in a crowd of strange Russians of our educated class, wherever it may be – in a railway carriage, a steamship, or in any kind of public gathering. I admit this is a weakness and blame it, above all, on my own suspicious nature. When I am abroad among foreigners I always feel more at ease: there, when some foreigner wants to get somewhere he heads straight to his destination, but our Russian goes on looking around the whole time, thinking, 'What will people say about me?' He may look decisive and unshakeable, but in actual fact there is no one more uncertain and lacking in self-confidence. If a Russian stranger begins a conversation with you, it is always in an extremely confidential and friendly manner; but from the first word he utters you can see his deep mistrust and even his underlying suspicious irritation, which will burst out in the form of some biting or even downright rude remark the moment he finds something not to his liking, and this despite all his 'good upbringing'. What's significant is that this can happen for the very slightest of reasons. Every one of these people seems to want to avenge himself on someone else for his own insignificance, yet he may not be an insignificant person at all – sometimes just the reverse. There is no person who will say oftener than a Russian: 'What do I care what people say about me?' or 'I don't worry a bit about public opinion.' And there is no person who is more afraid than a Russian (again, I mean a civilized Russian), who has more fear and trepidation of public opinion and of what people will say or think of him. This comes precisely from his deep-seated lack of self-respect, which, of course, is concealed behind his boundless egotism and vanity. These two opposing factors are always present in *almost* every educated Russian, and he is also the first to find them intolerable, so that each one of them bears his own 'hell' in his soul, as it were. It is especially awkward to meet a Russian stranger abroad somewhere, face to face (shut up with him in a railway car, for instance), so that there is no possibility of running away should something disastrous happen. And yet, it would seem, 'It's so nice to meet a fellow countryman on foreign shores.' And the conversation almost always begins with that very phrase. Once he's found out that you're a Russian, your fellow countryman will be certain to begin: 'So you're a Russian? How nice to meet a fellow countryman on foreign shores. I'm here as well . . .' And then at once come some candid remarks in a most cordial and, so to say, brotherly manner appropriate to two compatriots who have embraced each other on some foreign shore. But don't be misled by the manner: although your compatriot may be smiling, he already has his suspicions of you, and that's obvious from his eyes, from the little lisp he has when he speaks, and from the careful way he stresses his words. He's sizing you up; he's certainly afraid of you already; he already wants to tell you some lies. And, indeed, he can't help but regard you suspiciously and tell lies simply because you are also a Russian and he, willy-nilly, is measuring himself against you; and also, perhaps, because you really deserve such treatment. It's worth noting as well that a Russian stranger abroad (more often when abroad, and indeed almost always when abroad) will always, or at least frequently, hasten to put in after the first three sentences he utters that he has only just met so-and-so or has only just heard something from so-and-so, i.e., from some prominent or famous Russian personage. But he brings up this person in the nicest and most familiar manner, as if he were one of his friends and one of yours as well: 'You know him, of course. The poor fellow has been making pilgrimages from one local medical luminary to another. They send him off to watering places, and the fellow is absolutely worn out. You know him, do you not?' If you reply that you don't know him at all, the stranger will at once find something personally offensive in this circumstance: 'Surely you didn't think that I wanted to boast of my acquaintance with a prominent person?' You can already read that question in his eyes, and yet that may be precisely what he wanted to imply. And if you reply that you do know the person, he will take even more offence; but just why that is I truly don't know. In short, insincerity and animosity grow on both sides; the conversation suddenly breaks off, and you fall silent. Your compatriot suddenly turns away from you. He is prepared to go on chatting the whole while with some German baker sitting opposite, as long as he doesn't speak to you, and he does this specifically so that you will notice it. Having begun in such a friendly fashion, he now will have nothing more to do with you and rudely ignores you altogether. When night comes he stretches out on the cushions if there is room enough, almost putting his feet on you or perhaps even deliberately putting his feet on you; and when the journey is over he leaves the carriage without even nodding good-bye. 'Why did he take such offence?' you think to yourself, saddened and greatly confused. Best of all is an encounter with a Russian general. The Russian general abroad is most concerned with ensuring that none of the Russians he meets ventures to address him in a manner inappropriate to his rank, trying to take advantage by assuming that 'we're abroad, and so we're all equal'. And so, for instance, when he's travelling he sinks into a stern, marmorial silence from the very beginning. So much the better: he doesn't disturb anyone. By the way, a Russian general setting off for foreign parts is sometimes very fond of putting on a civilian suit he's ordered from the best tailor in Petersburg. And when he arrives at the spa, where there are always so many pretty ladies from all over Europe, he is very fond of making a show. When the season is over he takes particular pleasure in being photographed in civilian clothes so that he can give out pictures to his friends in Petersburg or use one to gladden the heart of a devoted subordinate. But in any case, keeping a book or a newspaper on a journey is a great help, particularly to ward off Russians: it tells them, 'I'm reading; leave me alone.'

* * *

NADEZHDA MANDELSTAM (1899–1980)

'Voronezh'

Voronezh

M.'s identity papers were taken from him at the time of his arrest. When we arrived in Voronezh, his only document was the travel warrant issued to him by the Cherdyn GPU Commandant which enabled him to buy tickets in the military booking offices. M. now handed it over at a special window in the shabby premises of the Voronezh GPU and was given a new document which only entitled him to a temporary residence permit. He had to make do with this while it was being established whether he would be kept in Voronezh itself or sent off into the countryside somewhere. Moreover, our new overlords had not decided which category of exile we belonged to. There are several types, of which the two main ones known to me are 'with reporting' and 'without reporting'. In the first case, one had to make regular visits to the GPU offices. In Cherdyn M. had to go and report every three days. If one does not have to report, one may be either permitted or forbidden to travel in the region to which one has been exiled. In the autumn M. was called to the police and given identity papers with a permit to reside in Voronezh. The type of exile was thus the easiest – with identity papers! It was now that we learned what a privilege it is to have identity papers, a privilege not granted to everybody.

The granting of identity papers is an enormous event in the life of an exile, since it gives the illusion of having some rights as a citizen. The first few months of our life in Voronezh were marked by constant visits to the police to get a piece of paper known as a 'temporary permit'. Seven or eight months running we had to renew this permit, which was valid for only one month at a time. A week before it expired, M had to begin collecting the necessary documents needed for its renewal: a note from the local housing department to certify that he had been properly registered to live in such-and-such a house, references from the GPU and his place of work. There was no problem about the note from the GPU, since his standing with them was clear enough, but what was he to do about the second reference? At first he had to ask the local branch of the Union of Soviet Writers. This was never a straightforward procedure. The officials of the Union would gladly have made out any kind of certificate, but they were frightened, and some of them trembled at the thought of exercising their right to put the Union's stamp on a scrap of paper, in case they found themselves issuing a certificate to a bad writer. Every time the heads of the local branch applied to some higher authority for permission to issue a paper stating that M. really was engaged in literary work. At first there was whispering, dark looks and much scurrying about, but once they received clearance from higher up, the Voronezh writers were all smiles: they, too, were glad when all ended well. Those were still comparatively innocent days.

Each piece of paper meant at least two visits to the relevant office: first to apply for it, and then to collect it. Often one had to come again because it wasn't yet ready. When they were ready, all these references had to be handed to the head of the identity-papers section of the local police, where there was always a long line. Two or three days later M. again had to stand in line there to collect his temporary identity paper, which then had to be taken next day and stamped with the residence permit. This meant standing in line once more at the appropriate window in the police station. Fortunately, the girl clerk who entered residence permits was very kind to M. Ignoring the murmurs of concierges fretting in the line with their enormous registers under their arms (all arrivals and departures had to be entered in them), she always called M. to the window straightaway and took his identity paper so that she could return it to him next morning, duly stamped, without his having to wait in line.

In the summer of 1935 M. was granted the favour of receiving an identity paper valid for three months, accompanied by a residence permit for the same period. This made our lives much easier, particularly since the lines for papers had lengthened considerably after the purge in Leningrad: the lucky ones, who had been sent no further than Voronezh, now had to go through the lengthy ordeal of getting permits and papers to live there.

People who live in countries without identity papers will never know what joys can be extracted from these magic little documents. In the days when M.'s were still a precious novelty, the gift of a benevolent fate, Yakhontov came to Voronezh on tour. In Moscow M. and he had amused themselves by reading from the ration books which were used in the excellent store open only to writers. M. refers to this in his poem 'The Apartment': 'I read ration books and listen to hempen speeches.' Now Yakhontov and M. did the same thing with their identity papers, and it must be said that the effect was even more depressing. In the ration book they read off the coupons solo and in chorus: 'Milk, milk, milk . . . cheese, meat . . .' When Yakhontov read from the identity papers, he managed to put ominous and menacing inflections in his voice: 'Basis on which issued . . . issued . . . by whom issued . . . special entries . . . permit to reside, permit to reside, permit to reside . . .' Ration books reminded one of the literary fare that was doled out to us in the magazines and by the State publishing houses, and every time he opened *Novy Mir* or *Krasnaya Nov*, M. would say, 'Today they're dishing out Gladkov' (or Zenkevich or Fadeyev). The line quoted above was intended in this double sense. Allusions to his identity papers are also to be found in M.'s verse: 'Clutching in my fist a worn year of birth, herded with the herd, I whisper with my bloodless lips: I was born on the night between the second and third of January in the unreliable year of eighteen ninety something or other, and the centuries surround me with their fire.'

Another amusement of this type (it was rather like a schoolboy thumbing his nose behind the teacher's back) took the form of a public stage performance by Yakhontov. In a turn entitled 'Travelling Poets' he read passages from Pushkin's 'Journey to Erzrum' and from Mayakovski in such a way as to suggest that poets could travel abroad only under the Soviet regime. The audience reacted with total indifference: nobody then imagined that anybody could travel abroad and as they left at the end of this baffling evening, the only comment they could manage was, 'That's what comes of living too well.' To keep his spirits up in the face of such an impassive audience, Yakhontov had to keep playing little tricks. And one point he would recite from Mayakovski's poem about the 'Soviet Passport' and, taking his own identity papers from his pocket, brandish them in front of the audience, looking all the time straight at M. – M. took his brand-new papers out of his pocket, and they exchanged knowing glances. The authorities would have taken a poor view of such antics, but they are very literal-minded, and there were no instructions to cover cases of this kind.

Another thing about identity papers was that they gave rise to guessing games. Since every general renewal of people's papers was also the occasion for a quiet purge, I decided not to go to Moscow to renew mine, but to do it in Voronezh. The result of this was that I lost my right to live in the capital and did not recover it until twenty-eight years later. But in any case I had no hope of getting my Moscow papers renewed – where would I have got a reference about my employment, how would I have explained the whereabouts of my husband, in whose name the title to our Moscow apartment was made out? When we both got our brand-new Voronezh papers, we noticed that they had the same serial letters before the numbers. It was thought that these letters were a secret-police code indicating the category to which one belonged – i.e. that one was an exile or had been convicted of some offence. 'Now you are really trapped,' M. said, examining the numbers and serial letters. Our more optimistic friends consoled us by saying that it wasn't so, but rather that the police had forgotten that M. was an exile and failed to mark his papers accordingly. We were so convinced that all citizens were numbered and registered according to categories that it never occurred to any of us to doubt the significance of these letters and numbers. Not until a few years after M.'s death did it turn out that these serial numbers had no special significance – apart from showing that my frightened fellow-citizens had imaginations more lively than even the GPU and the police.

We were not too upset by the loss of my Moscow residence permit. 'If I return,' M. said, 'they'll register you as well. But until then they won't let you live there in any case.' Sure enough, I was thrown out of the capital in 1938 and after that was allowed to come back only for brief periods of a month or so on academic business. At last Surkov proposed that I return ('you've been in exile long enough'). Throwing up my work, I returned to Moscow to move into the room offered me by the Union of Writers. I was kept hanging around for six months, and then Surkov informed me that there would be neither a room for me nor a permit to reside in the city. 'They say that you left it of your own free will,' he explained to me, adding that he had no time to 'talk with the comrades about you'. And it is only now at last, in 1964, that I have suddenly been granted the right to live here. No end of people have written letters and pleaded on my behalf, but perhaps it has only happened now because a certain magazine is about to print some of M.'s poems. This means that he has at last returned to Moscow. During thirty-two years not a line of his work has appeared in print. It is twenty-five years since his death, and thirty since his first arrest.

It really was a great relief when M. was given proper papers in Voronezh. The business of renewing the temporary ones not only took up a great deal of time, but was accompanied by constant anxiety and speculation as to whether they would be issued or not. In the GPU office and the police station one heard the same conversations all the time: some complained to the man behind the window that they had been refused a permit to reside, others begged for it to be granted. But the official never argued – he just stretched out his hand for your application and told you when it had been turned down. Those who were refused permits to live in Voronezh had to move into the countryside, where it was impossible to earn one's living and conditions were unbearable. And every time we joined all the other people making the rounds of offices to get our bits of paper, we trembled in case we should be unlucky and be forced to move on in some unknown direction for reasons not revealed to us. 'And clutching in my fist a worn year of birth, herded with the herd . . .' When M. read these lines to Mikhoels, he took out his papers and held them in his clenched hand.

Doctors and Illnesses

When we first got to Voronezh, we stayed in the hotel. Those in charge of us evidently permitted this to exiles arriving at their destination, even when they had no papers. We were not actually given rooms, only beds in rooms (separate for men and women) shared by a number of people. We were put on different floors, and I had to keep running up the stairs because I was worried about M.'s condition. But every day it got harder to climb the stairs. After several days my temperature shot up, and I realized I must be falling ill with spotted typhus, which I had no doubt picked up on the journey. The first symptoms of spotted typhus are unmistakable and cannot be confused with anything else, certainly not with flu. But this meant many weeks in the hospital, in the isolation wing, and I kept picturing the scene of M. throwing himself out of the window. Hiding my temperature from him – it was still going up – I begged him to see a psychiatrist. 'If that's what you want,' he said, and we went together. M. described the whole course of his illness himself, and there was nothing for me to add. He was completely objective and lucid. He told the doctors that at moments of tiredness and distraction he still had hallucinations. Most of all this happened when he was falling asleep. He said he now understood the nature of the voices and had learned to stop them with an effort of the will, but that in the hotel there were many irritants that made it difficult for him to fight his illness – it was very noisy and he couldn't rest during the day. But the most unpleasant thing was the constant closing of doors, even though he knew they closed from the inside, not the outside.

Prison was ever present to our minds. Vasilisa Shklovski cannot stand closed doors – because of all the time she spent in prison as a young woman, when she learned at first hand what it meant to be closed in. And even people who had no experience of prison cells were not always free of this kind of association. When Yakhontov stayed in the same hotel during his visit to Voronezh a year and a half later, he immediately noticed how the keys ground in the locks. 'Oho,' he said, as we closed the door on leaving his room. 'It's a different sound,' said M. reassuringly. They understood each other perfectly. This is why M. is so insistent in his verse on the right to 'breathe and open doors' – it was a right he was terrified of losing.

The psychiatrist was careful about what he said to us. We all suspected each other of being police spies, and there were many among people who had suffered like M. – a man who had undergone a psychological trauma was often incapable of resistance. But without waiting for M. to finish, the psychiatrist said that such 'complexes' were very often observed in 'psychostenic types' who spent any length of time in prison.

I then told the doctor about my own illness (at this moment M.

understood my purpose in bringing him here and became terribly alarmed) and asked whether it wouldn't be best for M. to go into a clinic while I was in the hospital. The doctor replied that it would be perfectly all right to leave M. where he was since there were scarcely any traces left of his traumatic psychosis. He added that he had often observed the same condition among people exiled to Voronezh. It was caused by a few weeks, or even days, of imprisonment, and always cleared up, leaving no trace. M. then asked him why it was that people got into this state after a few days in prison, whereas in the old days prisoners spent years in dungeons without being affected like this. The doctor only shrugged his shoulders.

But is it true that they were unaffected? Perhaps prison always causes mental trouble, if not psychological damage. Is this really a specific feature of our prisons? Or is it perhaps that before we go to prison our mental health is undermined by anxieties and brooding on 'prison themes'? Nobody here is able to go into this question – and abroad the facts are not known, because we are only too good at keeping our secrets from the outside world.

I have heard that somebody abroad recently published his memories about life in a Soviet camp, and that the author was struck by the large number of mentally sick people he encountered among the prisoners. As a foreigner, he had lived in the Soviet Union in somewhat special conditions, and his knowledge of our life was very superficial. The conclusion he reaches is that certain psychotic conditions are just not treated in this country, and that people suffering from them get sent to camps for infringement of discipline and other offences caused by their illness. The percentage of mentally unbalanced people in the country is indeed enormous, and among those sentenced for hooliganism and petty theft there are, I believe, many psychotics, not to mention psychopaths. They are given several years for breaking into a store and stealing a few bottles of vodka, and when they come out they immediately do the same thing again and are sent back to prison and the labour camps for a good ten years. Under Stalin much less attention was paid to them, and far fewer of them went to the camps than nowadays. But the question remains as to why so many intellectuals and nervous or sensitive people in general are so strongly affected by their arrest and often fall prey to this mysterious trauma which quickly passes after their release. The foreign author of the book about the camps does not say *where* the prisoners he saw had become mentally sick, in prison

or 'outside'. Nor does he say who they were – youths who had
stolen to buy drink, or peaceful citizens. And were they psychopaths
or were they suffering from the prison trauma I have described?
All these questions will remain open, both for foreigners and for
ourselves, until we are able to speak up about our past, present
and future.

After I came out of the hospital, M. again went to see a psychiatrist, an eminent specialist who had come from Moscow to
inspect the local lunatic asylum. M. went on his own initiative to tell
him the story of his illness and to ask whether it might not be the
consequence of some organic trouble. He mentioned that he had
earlier noted in himself a tendency towards obsessive ideas – for
instance, at times when he was in conflict with the writers' organization he could think of nothing else. Moreover, he actually was
very sensitive to external shocks. I had noticed the same thing, inci-
dentally, in M.'s two brothers. Though they were both of a very
different make-up, they also tended to become obsessional about
any difficult event in their lives.

The Moscow psychiatrist did an unexpected thing: he asked M.
and me to walk around the wards with him. Afterwards he asked
whether M. thought he had anything in common with the patients
he had seen in the clinic, and if so, how he would describe it: senility?
schizophrenia? hysteria? They parted friends.

Nevertheless, without telling M., I went back to see the doctor
myself next morning. I was worried in case the fearful things he had
shown us the day before might produce a new shock in M. The
doctor reassured me, saying that he had deliberately shown his
patients to M. because better knowledge of these things would help
him to get over the painful memories of his own illness. As for M.'s
nervous sensitivity and inability to withstand traumas, the psychiatrist
saw nothing pathological about this: the traumas had been pretty
severe, and one could only wish that there were fewer of them in
our life.

I was now struck by the light-heartedness with which M. made
fun of his illness and how quickly he managed to forget the days he
had spent in a state of delirium. 'Nadia,' he said a month and a half
after our arrival in Voronezh, complaining about a bad meal I had
made for him, 'I just can't eat stuff like this – I'm not out of my
mind now, you know.'

The only thing that seemed to me an after-effect of his illness was an occasional desire he now had to come to terms with reality and make excuses for it. This happened in sudden fits and was always accompanied by a nervous state, as though he were under hypnosis. At such moments he would say that he wanted to be with everybody else, and that he feared the Revolution might pass him by if, in his short-sightedness, he failed to notice all the great things happening before our eyes. It must be said that the same feeling was experienced by many of our contemporaries, including the most worthy of them, such as Pasternak. My brother Evgeni Yakovlevich used to say that the decisive part in the subjugation of the intelligentsia was played not by terror or bribery (though, God knows, there was enough of both), but by the word 'Revolution' – which none of them could bear to give up. It is a word to which whole nations have succumbed, and its force was such that one wonders why our rulers still needed prisons and capital punishment.

Fortunately, M. was only seldom overcome by these bouts of what is now called 'patriotism', and once he had come to his senses he himself dismissed them as madness. It is interesting to note that in the case of people concerned with art or literature, total rejection of the existing state of affairs led to silence, while complete acceptance had a disastrous effect on their work, reducing it to mediocrity. Unfortunately, only their doubts were productive, but these brought down the wrath of the authorities on their heads.

Another factor which made for reconciliation with reality was simple love of life. M. had no taste for martyrdom, but the price one had to pay to live was much too high. By the time M. had decided to pay a first instalment, it was in any case too late.

To come back to my own illness, I was put in the wing for spotted-typhus cases. I overheard the head doctor saying to some superintendent or other that I was very sick and that I was in the charge of the secret police. At first I thought I must have imagined this in my delirium, but the doctor, who was to prove a good friend, later confirmed to me after my recovery that he really had said these words. Subsequently, during my wanderings around the country, I was often told by people connected (whether openly or secretly) with the secret police – officials of personnel departments and informers – that I was 'in the charge of Moscow'. What this meant I do not know. To understand it, one would have to learn more about the structure of the agency in whose charge I was. Personally, I think it is better not to be in anybody's charge, but I just cannot imagine how to achieve this. It would be interesting to know whether we were all accounted for in the same way, or only a select few of us.

The kindly woman doctor who looked after our ward told me that her husband, an agronomist, was at that time coming to the end of his sentence in a camp, to which he had been sent, together with many others of his profession, for allegedly poisoning the wells in his village. This is not the invention of a lively mind, but a fact. Later on, when I was better, and began to make trips to Moscow, she gave me packages to mail to him in his camp. In those years such food parcels could be mailed only from Moscow, whereas nowadays they can be sent only from small provincial towns. For a number of years Emma Gerstein used to go out to all kinds of outlandish places, lugging heavy parcels which Akhmatova wanted mailed to her son Lev.

When the 'poisoner of the wells' returned at the end of his sentence, we were invited to a party in his honour and toasted him in sweet wine while he sang songs in his soft baritone and rejoiced in his freedom. In 1937 he was arrested once more.

I got a lot of attention in the hospital from a nurse called Niura. Her husband worked at a flour mill. Once he had brought home a handful of grain for his hungry family and had been sentenced to five years. The nurses greedily ate anything the typhus and dysentery patients left on their plates, and they were always talking about their misfortunes and poverty.

I came out of the hospital with a shaved head, and M. said that I looked like a real convict.

* * *

BRUCE CHATWIN (1940–1989)

'Nadezhda Mandelstam: A Visit'

It was snowing hard the afternoon I went to see Nadezhda Mandelstam. The snow melted off my coat and boots and made puddles on her kitchen floor. The kitchen smelled of kerosene and stale bread. On a table there were sticky purple rings, a vase full of begonias, and dried glasses left over from the lightness of a Russian summer.

A fat man in spectacles came out of the bedroom. He glared at me as he wound a grey scarf around his jowls, and then went out.

She called me in. She lay on her left side, on her bed, amid the rumpled sheets, resting her temple on a clenched fist. She greeted me without moving.

'What did you think of my doctor?' she sneered. 'I am sick.'

The doctor, I assume, was her KGB man.

The room was hot and cramped and strewn with clothes and books. Her hair was coarse, like lichen, and the light from the bedside lamp shone through it. White metal fastenings glittered among the brown stumps of her teeth. A cigarette stuck to her lower lip. Her nose was a weapon. You knew for certain she was one of the most powerful women in the world, and knew she knew it.

A friend in England advised me to take her three things: champagne, cheap thrillers and marmalade. She looked at the champagne and said, 'Bollinger!' without enthusiasm. She looked at the thrillers and said, '*Romans policiers!* Next time you come to Moscow you must bring me real TRASH!' But when I pulled out three jars of my mother's Seville orange marmalade, she stubbed out the cigarette and smiled.

'Thank you, my dear. Marmalade, it is my childhood.'

'Tell me, my dear . . .' She waved me to a chair and, as she waved, one of her breasts tumbled out of her nightie. 'Tell me,' she shoved it back, 'are there any grand poets left in your country? I mean grand poets . . . of the stature of Joyce or Eliot?'

Auden was alive, in Oxford. Weakly, I suggested Auden.

'Auden is *not* what I would call a grand poet!'

'Yes,' I said. 'Most of the voices are silent.'

'And in prose?'

'Not much.'

'And in America? Are there poets?'

'Some.'

'Tell me, was Hemingway a grand novelist?'

'Not always,' I said. 'Not towards the end. But he's underrated now. The early short stories are wonderful.'

'But the wonderful American novelist is Faulkner. I am helping a young friend translate Faulkner into Russian. I must tell you, we are having difficulties.

'And in Russia,' she growled, 'we have no grand writers left. Here also the voices are silent. We have Solzhenitsyn and even that is not so good. The trouble with Solzhenitsyn is this. When he thinks he is telling the truth, he tells the most terrible falsehoods. But when he thinks he is making a story from his imagination, then, sometimes, he catches the truth.'

'What about that story . . .?' I faltered. 'I forget its name . . . the one where the old woman gets run over by a train?'

'You mean *Matryona's House*?'

'I do,' I said. 'Does that catch the truth?'

'It could never have happened in Russia!'

On the wall across from the bed there was a white canvas, hung askew. The painting was all white, white on white, a few white bottles on a blank white ground. I knew the work of the artist: a Ukrainian Jew, like herself.

'I see you've got a painting by Weissberg,' I said.

'Yes. And I wonder if you'd mind straightening it for me? I threw a book and hit it by mistake. A disgusting book by an Australian woman!'

I straightened the picture.

'Weissberg,' she said. 'He is our best painter. Perhaps that is all one can do today in Russia? Paint whiteness!'

1978

* * *

JAKOB WALTER (1788–1864)

from *The Diary of a Napoleonic Foot Soldier*

Now, as the march went on, I had to leave my sled behind and to lay my baggage on the horse, upon which I also mounted often during the day. The cold increased again that same day, and the road became as smooth as a mirror from the rain so that the horses fell down in great numbers and could not get up again. Since my horse was a native of the country, it had no horseshoes and could always help itself up again when it had fallen. It had even the good custom, whenever we went downhill, of sitting down on its rump, bracing its front feet forward, and sliding into the valley in this fashion without my dismounting. Other German horses, though, had shoes which were ground entirely smooth and for this reason could not keep themselves from slipping; nor could these irons be torn off, since no one had a tool for that.

Until now I had not seen my major again and believed nothing else than that he must be dead. I always cared for my horse by riding out at night where some village blazed brightly, in order to get some rye sheaves for the horse and rye grains for myself. I often could not get feed for four or five days, but my *goniak* [trotter] was indifferent if only from time to time he could get some old straw from the camp or some thatch straw from a burned house, nor could I notice that he was getting thin. If I found some rest at night, I served as a crib for him. I always hung the halter strap on my arm or foot so that I could notice any attempts to take him away. I laid myself squarely before his feet; and, when he had something to eat, he ground away with his teeth for a short time. When he had nothing, he sniffed and snorted all over me. Not once did his hoof touch me. At the most he pressed my fur coat a little. Unless you tied your horse to yourself, the horse was stolen immediately.

After leaving Smolensk, we arrived on November 16, amid a thousand kinds of danger at Krasnoë, where the Russians received us, having in the meantime circled around to our front. Here the French Guard, with the remaining armed forces that could still be brought together, took its position along the highway and kept up the firing against the enemy as well as possible. Although the enemy had to yield, any movements on our part drew vigorous firing upon us. Unfortunately, all the time the greatest misery fell upon the poor sick, who usually had to be thrown from the wagons just to keep us from losing horses and wagons entirely and who were left to freeze among the enemies, for whoever remained lying behind could not hope to be rescued.

Here I once heard my master speak (rather yell) close in front of me, whereupon I called, 'Major, is it you?' He glanced at me and cried out for joy, 'Oh, God, dear valet, is it you? Oh, now I am glad that I have you again. Oh, I am so happy that you are still alive.' I also showed my joy over this reunion, for my master still had his old German chestnut, his horse from home, and his other attendant was also with him with a second horse. Now he asked me whether I still had part of his sugar loaf and coffee. Sadly I had to say that once when I lay down behind a battlement near a fire-razed village at night a group of Cuirassier Guards pressed upon me and tore away from me the sack with the sugar and coffee; and I almost failed to keep my horse. I gave in, therefore, and chose another place to lie down, and in occupying my second spot I found straw lying about, with which my horse could still his hunger. I myself lay down on a spot that was soft and not frozen. Before departing I thought I would see why it was so soft and warm under me, and I saw a dead man whose unfrozen belly had served as my good bed. 'And I set out upon my journey again, Major, without being able to meet you again.' The major then said, 'That does not matter now. I am glad that you are here again.'

General Ney, about whom no one knew anything anymore, was in charge of the rearguard. He fought his way through to us. However, his forces were half gone. The march had to go on; and the striking, clubbing, and skirmishing commenced so frightfully that the cry of murder echoed all about. The Cossacks advanced upon the army from all sides. We came toward Dubrovna, and the throng was so great that those on foot were usually beaten and cudgelled to the right and the left of the roadway at such narrow passages as marshes, rivers, and bridges. Here my major and I were pushed apart and lost each other again. It was not possible to recognize one another except by voice. Everyone was disguised in furs, rags, and pieces of cloth; they wore round hats and peasant caps on their heads, and many had priest's robes from the churches. It was like a world turned upside down. I had had enough of my helmet at the very beginning of the retreat. I put on a round hat, wrapped my head with silk and muslin cloths and my feet with thick woollen cloth. I had on two vests and over my doublet a thick and large Russian coat which I had taken from a Russian in exchange for my own at Smolensk on the trip into Russia; and over all this I wore my thick fur. I was so enwrapped that only my eyes had an opening out of which I could breathe. From time to time I had to break off from this opening the ice that would immediately form again from my breath.

At night in Dubrovna, when the enemy had given up their manoeuvres, everyone settled down in and around the place. Every night, the fires for warming could be seen over a region four hours' long and wide, reddening the sky like red cloth. The burning villages at the side contributed most to this sight, and the shrieking, beating, and lamenting did not stop for a minute. Again and again people died, and sometimes froze to death; these were people who pressed toward the fire but were seldom permitted to get there; so they died away from the fire, and very often they were even converted into cushions in order that the living would not have to sit in the snow.

In every bivouac soldiers who looked like spectres crept around at night. The colour of their faces, their husky breathing, and their dull muttering were horribly evident; for wherever they went they remained hopeless; and no one allowed these shades of death to drag themselves to the fire. Usually six, eight, or ten of us had to combine to build a fire, since no other wood was to be had except rafter pieces from burned houses, or trees lying around, shattered wagons, etc., and without the cooperation of the men nothing could be accomplished. Neither did we dare to fall asleep at the fire all at the same time, because no one was safe from stealing and robbery.

As we came to Orscha, it was said that we would get shoes and bread from a magazine, also oats for the horses; but this was impossible. In spite of the guards stationed around the storehouses, none of the doors could be opened, since everyone hit and shoved each other in order to get close to a door. I hurried there at first to obtain oats, but that was impossible until the guards could no longer stand their ground and the doors were sprung open. Then I climbed through a window opening, took several sacks of oats with the help of my comrades, and brought them to the camp fire. Immediately thereafter a soldier who also shared in my fire came with two loaves of bread. Now everyone's heart beat with eagerness, and everyone sprang toward the bread store. When we arrived, no one could get inside anymore, and those within could not come out because of the pressure. What was to be done? Many weak soldiers lay on the floor and were trampled down, screaming frightfully. I made for a window opening again; tore out the shutter, the wooden grating, and the window; and got five of the loaves, though they were trampled and broken. This was since Moscow the second bit of bread, for which I thanked God anew with tears.

Now we were all happy by the fire, and with renewed spirits we resumed our journey toward whatever fate had in store for us. Always I set my mind to it and constantly made my way toward the front of the army rather than to the rear. Very often I had to go back because of the Cossacks roaming about; then I joined the front of the column again so as not to be cut off from behind.

Between Orscha and Kochanova I again rode off to the side of the army toward a village which stood in flames, in order to warm myself for a short time in the night and to seek for whatever was available. No sooner had I lain down than the Cossacks came and caught whomever of us they could get. My horse had a peculiar intelligence; for, as soon as shots were fired, it turned and ran of its own accord with all its strength. In the absence of danger, however, striking it often did no good when I wanted to ride fast. Thus it saved me by flight, and we headed toward the army again. Those on foot who had also made the side march were caught and plundered. The Frenchmen were usually struck down by the Russians and not pardoned. Those who were German could reckon on pardon with certainty because, as it was said, the Russian Emperor had commanded that the Germans be spared, since the Empress, as is known, was a descendant of the house of Baden.

While on my side march I saw lying on the ground a beautiful black bearskin with head and claws, which fugitives had had to throw away. With cries of 'hurrah' I took possession of this in the hope of bringing my belongings to Germany, for I had various silver vessels from Moscow which were worth from three to four hundred florins. Besides this, I had silk goods, muslin, etc., such as I was able to take in abundance from the stalled wagons. Nevertheless, all this came to nothing. The retreat led through Kochanova, Toloczin, Krupky, Bobr, and Liecnize to Borissov. In the bustle by day and by night that hardly let me rest or sleep even a few hours in four or five nights, my horse, which was tied to my arm by a strap, was cut off and led away unnoticed. Since I was always accustomed to pulling on the strap on waking up to see whether my horse was still there, I pulled and this time felt no horse. I jumped up – and now what? I thought to myself, even if I had the whole night to spend looking, only a miracle could lead me to my horse, and the likelihood was all the more uncertain if my horse was already on the march. However, I had to do something. I ran left and right, back and forth; and, whenever I tried to run close to a horse, my life was endangered by whipping and beating, for one could not take enough precaution against theft and robbery: usually one of those sitting by the fire had to keep watch. All at once I saw my *goniak* standing before a chapel door with his strap tied to a soldier who was sleeping inside the doorway. Very softly now I in my turn cut the strap and rode toward my fire. I dared not sleep anymore, I thought, so that if my horse lover returned I could speak with him . . .

This night I came by chance upon a comrade from B. by the

name of Sch. This was the third man from my district whom I met on the way from Smolensk to Moscow and back to this place. An officer also had this man with him as a faithful friend, for he no longer could be distinguished as 'Johan' or servant [?]. Indeed, every soldier was like an officer now, since none of the uniforms showed any distinction in rank and no superior could command a private. Officers were beaten away from the fire just as privates were whenever they tried to press forward without merited claim. Only mutual support still procured true friendship. This aforesaid countryman, whom I had once liked so well, still had some rice from Moscow, though only a handful. Along with this, I had a little piece of meat which I cut off next to the ears from a dog's pelt with the whole head on it that lay not far from our fire. Just to give the water flavour and to warm our stomachs, we boiled the two together. Now, when it was only half cooked, we started eating; and, although the meat already stunk a good deal and there was no salt with it, we devoured everything with the best appetite, feeling ourselves lucky to have for once obtained something warm.

Some time before the departure, he said to me, 'I had a loaf of bread for my master. You have taken it from me.' This was a pain to my feelings which I can never in my life forget. It is noteworthy how an opinion which is entirely false can turn a friend into a scoundrel and change him into a shameful caricature of a human being on account of a bit of bread. Here I saw truly how low reason had sunk with us: our brains were frozen, and there was no feeling left. I swore and said, 'Comrade, you are wrong. I have not seen or taken any bread. I would rather give you bread than take it.' It did no good. He remained firm in his opinion, and death soon found him.

Before I came to Borissov, we bivouacked behind a forest around eleven o'clock at night, and it seemed as though the Russians had surrounded us entirely, for the cannonades thundered upon us from all sides, and it was necessary to retreat hurriedly until the enemy gave up from weariness. Everyone among us let loose with slugging, hitting, and chasing, as if we were enemies among ourselves. Every time in bivouac the Germans joined together and made the fires in groups I was also included. They were mostly Württemberg sergeants and soldiers who joined with me at the fire; and here each one fried the horse meat which he had cut off laboriously along the way often with scuffling and slugging; for, as soon as a horse plunged and did not get up immediately, men fell upon it in heaps and often cut at it alive from all sides. The meat, unfortunately, was very lean, and the only skin with a little red meat could be wrested away. Each of us stuck his piece on a stick or sabre, burned off the hair in the fire, and waited until the outside was burned black. Then the piece was bitten off all around and stuck into the fire again. One seldom had time for boiling, and not one among twenty men had a pot.

When the night meal was ended here, we all lay down, and I went to sleep. My horse was tied to my arm as was my custom. In a short time one of my sincere comrades cried, 'You, look after your horse so that it won't be stolen.' I said, 'It's here all right.' I was not awakened again the second time. My countrymen cut the strap and sneaked away. Then I woke up to find myself forsaken. 'God,' I thought, 'who is it that can save me? What is to be done? Mine and my master's possessions I cannot bring any farther. I cannot carry even my fur because of my weakness, and I must freeze to death without it.' These thoughts made me despondent, and increasing pain consumed my body. Now I had to risk something even if my life should be lost; besides, it was already half gone, I thought. Only about a hundred paces away lay the French Cuirassier Guards who earlier had forcibly taken my coffee and sugar loaf while in camp. I will risk taking a horse! I crept near the front, observing which of the men did not move and might be sleeping, cut off a strap, and came away with a very large black horse. I went to a place some distance away where no one was about, then ran hurriedly to get my luggage, laid it on, and rode on without delay. Indeed, I thought, if only the owner will not see me! Because of this fear, I later traded off the horse.

Before daylight, as I rode thoughtfully along, I heard my master again, Major von Schaumberg. I called him by name, whereupon he heartily rejoiced and said, 'Now we are together again.' He told of his preservation until now, and I also told him of mine. He was particularly glad about my care for his luggage and about my reconquest of a horse. After we came to Borissov, we bivouacked again. We came to a lumberyard and built a fire there. When the major had become somewhat warm, his 'subjects' plagued him with unusual wickedness, and for this reason he asked me to kill the tormentors in his shirt collar. I did it; but, when I had his collar open, his raw flesh showed forth where the greedy beasts had gnawed in. I had to turn my eyes away with abhorrence and reassure the master that I saw nothing, telling him that my eyes hurt so much from the smoke that I could not see anything. These pests, however, were no less to be found on me, thousands of them. However, because of my constant restlessness they could not get to the point of forcing me to treat them with flesh. Besides, I remembered the saying, 'Lice stay on healthy people only,' and I did not count this a plague in view of the greater one.

As I walked about within the court, I saw about twenty dead cows which must have died from hunger and cold. When I tried to cut something off from them with my sabre, they were all frozen as hard as a rock, and only with the greatest effort did I finally rip a belly open. Since I could cut or tear nothing loose but the entrails, I took the tallow and supplied myself with a goodly amount of it. Each time I would stick a little of this tallow on my sabre and let it get just hot enough in the fire for the greatest part of it to remain unmelted, and I would eat one piece after another with the greatest eagerness. What I had heard before – namely, that tallow-eating drove sleep away, I now found to be true. For about fourteen days I had tallow, which I always ate only in the greatest emergency and which I thriftily saved; and, truly, sleep did not bother me any more: I could always be active then throughout the night and could forage for myself and my horse in various ways.

It was November 25, 1812, when we reached Borissov. Now the march went toward the Beresina River, where the indescribable horror of all possible plagues awaited us. On the way I met one of my countrymen, by the name of Brenner, who had served with the Light Horse Regiment. He came toward me completely wet and half frozen, and we greeted each other. Brenner said that the night before he and his horse had been caught and plundered but that he had taken to flight again and had come through a river which was not frozen. Now, he said, he was near death from freezing and starvation. This good, noble soldier had run into me not far from Smolensk with a little loaf of bread weighing about two pounds and had asked me whether I wanted a piece of bread, saying that this was his last supply. 'However, because you have nothing at all, I will share it with you.' He had dismounted, laid the bread on the ground, and cut it in two with his sabre. 'Dear, good friend,' I had replied, 'you treat me like a brother. I will not forget as long as I live this good deed of yours but will rather repay you many times if we live!' He had then a Russian horse, a huge dun, mounted it, and each of us had to work his way through, facing his own dangers. This second meeting, with both of us in the most miserable condition because no aid was available, caused a pang in my heart which sank in me unforgettably. Both of us were again separated, and death overtook him.

When we came nearer the Beresina River, there was a place where Napoleon ordered his pack horses to be unharnessed and where he ate. He watched his army pass by in the most wretched condition. What he may have felt in his heart is impossible to surmise. His outward appearance seemed indifferent and unconcerned over the wretchedness of his soldiers; only ambition and lost honour may have made themselves felt in his heart; and, although the French and Allies shouted into his ears many oaths and curses about his own guilty person, he was still able to listen to them unmoved. After his Guard had already disbanded and he was almost abandoned, he collected a voluntary corps at Dubrovna which was enrolled with many promises and received the name of 'Holy Squadron'. After a short time, however, this existed in name only, for the enemy reduced even them to nothing.

In this region we came to a half-burnt village away from the road, in which a cellar was found under a mansion. We sought for potatoes, and I also pressed down the broad stairway, although the cellar was already half filled with people. When I was at the bottom of the steps, the screaming began under my feet. Everyone crowded in, and none could get out. Here people were trampled to death and suffocated; those who wanted to stoop down for something were bowled over by those standing and had to be stepped upon. In spite of the murderous shrieking and frightful groaning, the pressure from outside increased; the poor, deathly weak men who fell had to lie there until dead under the feet of their own comrades. When I reflected on the murderous shrieking, I gave up pushing into the cellar, and I thought in cold fear: how will I get out again? I pressed flat against the wall so that it afforded me shelter and pushed myself vigorously little by little up the steps; this was almost impossible with others treading on my long coat. In the village of Sembin, where Napoleon ate, there was a burned house, under which was a low, timber-covered cellar with a small entrance from the outside. Here again, as potatoes and the like were being hunted for, suddenly the beams fell in and those who were inside and were not entirely burned up or suffocated were jumping about with burned clothes, screaming, whimpering, and freezing to death in terrible pain.

When I had gone somewhat farther from that place, I met a man who had a sack of raw bran in which there was hardly a dust of flour. I begged him ceaselessly to sell me a little of the bran, pressing a silver rouble into his hand; so he put a few handfuls in my little cloth, although very unwillingly, whereupon I happily continued on my journey. When I and my master came closer to the Beresina, we camped on a near-by hill, and by contributing wood I obtained a place at a fire. I immediately mixed some snow with my bran; balled it together into a lump about the size of my fist, which because of its brittleness fell into three or four pieces again in the fire; and allowed it to heat red on the outside in order to obtain something like bread from the inside; and I and my master ate it all with the heartiest appetite.

After a time, from about two till four o'clock in the afternoon, the Russians pressed nearer and nearer from every side, and the murdering and torturing seemed about to annihilate everyone. Although our army used a hill, on which what was left of our artillery was placed, and fired at the enemy as much as possible, the question was: what chance was there of rescue? That day we expected that everyone must be captured, killed, or thrown into the water. Everyone thought that his last hour had come, and everyone was expecting it; but, since the ridge was held by the French artillery, only cannon and howitzer balls could snatch away a part of the men. There was no hospital for the wounded; they died also of hunger, thirst, cold, and despair, uttering complaints and curses with their last breath. Also our sick, who had been conveyed to this point in wagons and consisted almost entirely of officers, were left to themselves; and only deathly white faces and stiffened hands stretched toward us.

When the cannonade had abated somewhat, I and my master set out and rode down the stream for about half an hour to where there was a village with several unburned houses. Here was also the general staff of Württemberg. In the hiding places here, I sought for something to eat at night; with this purpose I lighted candles that I had found; and I did find some cabbage (*kapusk*) which looked green, spotted, and like rubbish. I placed it over a fire and cooked it for about half an hour. All at once cannon balls crashed into the village, and with a wild cheer the enemy sprang upon us. With all the speed we succeeded in escaping, since we mounted and rode away as fast as possible. I couldn't leave my pot of cabbage behind, to be sure, but held it firmly in my arms on the horse, and the fear that I might lose my half-cooked meal made me forget entirely the bullets which were flying by. When we were a little distance from the place, my master and I reached our hands into the pot and ate our cabbage (*kapuska*) in haste with our fingers. Neither could leave his hands bare because of the cold, and because of our hunger and the cold we vied with each other in grabbing swiftly into the warm pot, and the only meal for the entire day was at an end again in short time.

When it became day again, we stood near the stream approximately a thousand paces from the two bridges, which were built of wood near each other. These bridges had the structure of sloping saw-horses suspended like trestles on shallow-sunk piles; on these lay long stringers and across them only bridge ties, which were not fastened down. However, one could not see the bridges because of the crowd of people, horses, and wagons. Everyone crowded together into a solid mass, and nowhere could one see a way out or a means of rescue. From morning till night we stood unprotected from cannonballs and grenades which the Russians hurled at us from two sides. At each blow from three to five men were struck to the ground, and yet no one was able to move a step to get out of the path of the cannonballs. Only by the filling up of the space where a cannonball made room could one make a little progress forward. All the powder wagons also stood in the crowd; many of these were ignited by the grenades, killing hundreds of people and horses standing about them.

I had a horse to ride and one to lead. The horse I led I was soon forced to let go, and I had to kneel on the one which I rode in order not to have my feet crushed off, for everything was so closely packed that in a quarter of an hour one could move only four or five steps forward. To be on foot was to lose all hope of rescue. Indeed, whoever did not have a good horse could not help falling over the horses and people lying about in masses. Everyone was screaming under the feet of the horses, and everywhere was the cry, 'Shoot me or stab me to death!' The fallen horses struck off their feet many of those still standing. It was only by a miracle that anyone was saved.

★　★　★

CLARA SCHUMANN (1819–1896)

from *An Artist's Life*

Dorpat, Feb. 20 1844. I have long been wanting to write to you, dear Father, but I could never manage it, for you must know that I have given five concerts, one after another. That I may forget nothing I will begin at the very beginning, as I think you will be interested in everything.

We spent two days in Berlin, and were most kindly received, especially by the Mendelssohns, who were pleased to have a breath of Leipsic air. Mendelssohn gave me six *Lieder ohne Worte* (among which were two that you know already) which he is dedicating to me, and Madame Mendelssohn gave me a pair of fur muffetees, which I have already found very useful, and which also look very nice (that is for Mother's benefit). We left Berlin on Saturday evening by the flying coach (the most comfortable in which I ever travelled), and reached Königsberg on Monday evening, where we were most kindly received. It is an ugly town, but that makes the people all the nicer; I gave concerts in the theatre on Friday and Saturday, and had full houses, but the cold was dreadful, for the hall is large and is not warmed. On Sunday we left for Tilsit, where we spent the evening with the post-master, Nernst (a most pleasant family); I played a great deal, in spite of the fact that I had spent half the night packing after the concert in Königsberg, had got up at five, and had been travelling all day. On Monday we got up at three, and at four we set out for the frontier. I must add that in Königsberg there was a pianoforte maker on whose instruments I had played (he was called Marty); he lent us his sleigh as far as the frontier (from here on, we went entirely by sleighs – half-way to Königsberg we found tracks made for them), to which we went with an extra post, which was delightful. At Tauroggen, the frontier, Nernst had already bespoken places for us in the flying coach for Riga, which was also very handsome and comfortable, and had only two inside places. In Königsberg the Russian consul had given us a letter to the custom-house inspector (a very nice man), and we were treated very kindly. As at every other frontier, our boxes were just opened, glanced at, and fastened up again. They never so much as looked at the music. In Tauroggen itself we found a fine posting house and a most appetizing breakfast; moreover the consul had recommended us to one of the frontier officials, who looked after everything connected with our passport and luggage etc. Thus we came to Riga very comfortably, but what a hideous city it is! When we reached the posting house we found neither a hackney-coach nor anyone to take charge of our luggage; we had to take possession of a large peasant-sleigh which was standing in the courtyard, put the boxes into it, and sit on them, and so we came to the *City of London*, after threading our way with difficulty through the hundreds of peasants' sleighs in the market, and through tiny little alleys. Here we were told that there was not a single room to be had except on the third floor, which looked dreadful. We once more sat ourselves down on our boxes and drove off to the *City of St Petersburg*, where we got a room, a back room, so dirty that it was quite impossible to sit down in it; Robert at once ran off to Herr von Lutzau, to whom David had given us an introduction. He had ordered the best room in the *City of London* for us, which we had never dreamed of, and now he carried us back to it. You can imagine how unpleasant an impression Riga made on us. We found friendly and obliging people here, but we could not feel quite comfortable. The concert could not be arranged immediately, and in the end this made everything come with a rush. Fancy; on Sunday we had to go to Mitau (the capital of Courland, where in winter all the aristocracy of Courland is gathered together, and where they live for nothing but balls, and concerts, and balls again).

Mitau is three hours' journey from Riga, and is a charming little town in which there is a great deal of artistic culture (all the artists have given concerts here), and far more culture than in Riga. There is no artistic feeling in Riga, so it seemed to me (except in a few people), and no real culture. I gave concerts on Sunday in Mitau, Monday and Tuesday in Riga, Wednesday in Mitau again, and Thursday, the last concert, in Riga. Those were hard days, what with perpetually going backwards and forwards, packing, etc., but I gave all the concerts by myself, without anyone to support me, as I mean always to do in future; it is much the best. I found a wonderfully good pianoforte of Wirth's, in Riga – the Wirth piano in Dresden cannot give you any idea of it; these instruments are the best English make that I have yet seen; from top to bottom they have the most splendid tone, soft and yet so forcible! My husband, whom hardly any piano satisfies, was delighted with the tone of this one as soon as he touched it. I am glad to have such good instruments in St Petersburg. It was difficult to get here from Riga as there are only two coaches a week, and the places are taken weeks in advance, and even if there is room those coming from the frontier have the first claim. We did not want to post, as that is very uncomfortable, so we took an *extra-diligence* as far as St Petersburg, which gives us a guard all the way so that we have no need to trouble ourselves about anything. We can spend five days here, and mean to do so. Dorpat is a very pretty town, of far more importance, from the point of view of culture, than Riga, with great feeling for art, and of a very friendly appearance. In Professor von Brocker we found a very pleasant man, who has made arrangements for our concert, and has placed his carriage at our disposal, as everybody does at once in this country; everybody who can possibly manage it has his sleigh and horses. They are extraordinarily hospitable and friendly especially towards artists. I give my first concert tomorrow, and the second on Friday, and on Saturday we continue our journey towards St Petersburg, where we expect to arrive early Monday morning, or possibly Sunday evening; in any case we shall sleep one night on the road, so as to reach St Petersburg by day; you must know that there is a good inn at every posting-station here, where one can spend the night and have anything one likes to eat and drink, and it will be like this all the way to St Petersburg. The journey is not nearly so difficult and dreadful as we expected. German is spoken everywhere – everything is German here, and Russia does not really begin until ten miles from St Petersburg. Thanks to our furs and fur rugs, we have not suffered from the cold at all so far, though already we have travelled for two days with the thermometer showing 12–15° of frost. All the houses are warm here, there is an even temperature throughout all the rooms, which is very comfortable. Dorpat really does seem northerly, for here, for the first time, we felt real cold – this morning we had 23° of frost.

Now I will leave you alone for a few days – on Saturday I will write again and tell you about the concerts here.

I have just remembered some adventures which Marie will find specially interesting: we have driven, in carriages and sleighs, across the ice of three rivers, all larger than the Elbe; on the Duna, near Riga, the peasants hold their wood-market; hundreds of sleighs, laden with wood, stand in the middle of the river, people walk about as if they were in a street, and as if it were quite natural, and we too, drove about for half an hour. There are many wolves in the forests here, they often appear beside the high way and watch the travellers as they pass, quite quietly; so far we have not seen any, but everybody who goes from here to St Petersburg meets with some, and I am looking forward to seeing some.

The concert takes place today. I have got the university hall, which is very rarely granted as it is by no means intended for concerts. It is not very good for sound, but I like it because of the honour it is to have it. Addio for now.

Tuesday Feb. 27. I have given three brilliant concerts since last I wrote to you, and have aroused wild enthusiasm – I know no more enthusiastic, and at the same time artistic audiences than those here. The third concert took place last night, and after it a fine male chorus serenaded me delightfully, singing among other things a quartet of my husband's. Robert has caught a bad cold, he has been in bed for the last six days, and got up for the first time today. He was not able to be at the two last concerts, and of course we have not been able to leave, though we hope to get off on Thursday. The journey from here to St Petersburg is said to be dreadful! ten miles from St Petersburg the holes in the road begin, and they are enough to make one sea-sick. I wish we had got it over; Dorpat is full of nice people, for the most part the people whom we have got to know have been members of the aristocracy, but they have really been so kind to us that often we have not known what to say. Every day (for the last six days) they have sent us various things for lunch – stewed fruit, good soup, wine, as well as eau de Cologne etc.

Thursday the 3rd, we went to dine at the villa in the *Plauenschen Grunde* and revelled in the exquisite scenery – we little guessed what was happening in the city at that moment. We had hardly been at home for half-an-hour, when the drums sounded a general alarm, bells rang from every tower, and soon we heard firing. The King had refused to recognize the imperial constitution before Prussia had done so, and they had taken out the poles of his carriage – in which he meant to flee – and so compelled him to remain; they had also attempted to gain possession of the arsenal, from which, however, the crowd had been fired upon. It can easily be imagined that this aroused the greatest bitterness. The night passed fairly quietly, but on Friday, the 4th, we found all the streets barricaded when we went into the city, and on the barricades stood men armed with scythes, and republicans who made them keep on building the barricades higher. The utmost lawlessness prevailed everywhere, hatches and paving-stones were torn up as well as the stones from the streets and were turned into barricades. In the town hall the democrats were gathered together, and they chose a provisional government (the King had fled to Königstein during the night) which issued various proclamations concerning the soldiers, who were encamped with cannon in front of the castle and in *Neustadt*.

As we walked through the city we saw the terrible sight of fourteen dead bodies, men who had fallen the day before and now lay in dreadful array in the court of the hospital, a spectacle for the people. I could not forget this sight for a long time, and only the great tumult which was yet to follow obliterated the terrible impression. That day and the following night passed without fighting, the barricades grew into regular fortresses, the tension was dreadful; how would it all end? in what spilling of blood!

Saturday 5th: a terrible morning! A guard of safety formed itself in our street, and they wanted Robert to join. After I had twice denied that he was in, they threatened to search for him; we escaped with Marie, by the garden door, to the Bohemian Station. Here we met Oberländer, amongst other people, who wanted to go to the King at Königstein in order to make one more effort for concession. Here stood men with scythes, who gave warning that no one would be allowed to depart armed. At 1 o'clock we went as far as Mügeln. I was very distressed that we had not at least taken Elise with us, but we went off as best we could, and had no time to take the children with us; besides Robert thought we should be back by the evening, though I did not believe it, especially as shortly before we left they began to storm the city and to fight.

From Mügeln we went on foot to Dohna, there we ate, and waited for news by the next train, which brought nothing comforting, and at 7 o'clock we went to Maxen, where we found a fair number of people.

My anxiety all day was frightful, for continually one could hear the thunder of the cannon, and my children were in the city. In the evening I wanted to go into the city and fetch them, but it was too late, and I found no one who would accompany me so late. Robert could not come with me, for it was reported that the insurgents were searching the neighbourhood for all men capable of bearing arms, and were compelling them to take part in the battle. On Monday, 7th, I went to the city at three in the morning, accompanied by the daughter of the estate agent. Frau von Berg also went with us. It was a terrible drive. I was anxious lest I should never come out of the city again! I did not think that I should return that self-same way, today. We drove to Strehla, and there Frau von Berg went her way, and we went ours across the field to the Reitbahngasse. We entered amidst the continuous thunder of the cannon, and suddenly we saw forty men with scythes coming towards us. At first we did not know what to do, but we plucked up heart and went quietly through (and with us a man whom we had met in the field).

We arrived safely in Reitbahngasse, where the doors of all the houses were shut. It was horrible! Dead silence here; in the city incessant firing. I found the children still asleep, tore them at once from their beds, had them dressed, put together a few necessaries, and in an hour we were once more together in the field outside. Henriette, who was ill when I left, I found still suffering, she lay quietly in one place and took no notice of anything. This made me very anxious, especially just now when I needed her so much. In Strehla we got into the carriage again, and before dinner we were back in Maxen, where at last we were all reunited once more; my poor Robert had been spending anxious hours, and was therefore doubly happy now.

NORTH AMERICA

GONTRAN DE PONCINS (1900–1962)

from *Kabloona: Among the Inuit*

It goes without saying that this tundra is barren of vegetation. No tree flourishes here, no bush is to be seen, the land is without pasture, without oases; neither the camel nor the wild ass could survive here where man is able to live. The Eskimo, preeminently a nomad and a sea-hunter, is driven by the need to feed his family from point to point round an irregular circle, and it is the revolution of the seasons that directs his march. When the run of Arctic salmon in the river is over, he goes down to the lakes to jig through the ice. Meanwhile, he has begun also to trap the white fox. As the winter advances, as the ice thickens too deep for jigging and the big fish lie on the lake bottom refusing to be lured up, the Eskimo is forced to move on, for his family and his dogs consume about fifty pounds of food a day, an average terribly hard to maintain. The next curve on his circle is sealing and polar-bear hunting on the frozen sea. Then with the spring the caribou pass through on their way north; the great season of visiting opens; and in the autumn the river fish return. Thus the Eskimo is constantly on the march, driven by hunger through a cycle of peregrination whose signal characteristic is hardship and whose highest reward is not possession, nor leisure, but a full belly.

This cycle has its grandeur. Nowhere in the world have I known the seasons to speak so commandingly, ordain so precisely and inescapably what man must do to survive. And yet this imperious voice, if I am to judge by the cheerfulness with which the Eskimos listen to it, the serenity with which they set about obeying it, is full of solicitude, too. The Eskimos do not look upon their country as a harsh land, and among the variety of reasons for this I should put first the reason that it is their own, their unchallenged kingdom. Not only are they the undisputed owners of this land, but they are alone in it. All the caribou of the plains are theirs; theirs all the fish in the lakes, all the seal in the sea. No man disputes their prizes with them. No marauders burst in to steal their poor possessions and enslave their children, as among certain peoples of Africa. No armies, as in Europe, invade them to deprive them of their dominion over the snows. Because theft is unknown in this quasi-communist community, because their poverty is unenvied, and they have no neighbours to hate them, they are able to do as they did when we left the lake one morning to go out on the sea – store in their igloos what will not be needed for sealing, plant their fishing tackle upright on the round boss of the snowhouses as landmarks, and start down the trail without so much as turning their heads to see if all is safe – the front door, as it were, locked, the windows all shut, the gate pulled to.

Looking at them as they loaded their sleds, seeing how each was helped by the rest, how all laboured in common with no hint of selfishness as they ran from igloo to igloo, from sled to sled, with what smiles and laughter they chatted and drank their final mugs of tea before the great whips whistled in the air that a moment before had been coiled like lassos on the snow, it came to me that here was indeed the communal life, the Biblical clan which hitherto I had imagined only against a background of sand and date-palm. I watched the procession move out on the lake and into the valley that lay beyond the opposite shore, and though from tip to end the sleds stretched out half a mile, in the perspective lent by distance they formed a common being, a black caterpillar whose rings moved in response to a close and unified life and instinct.

The departure itself was a wonderful sight – sleds piled high, dogs barking and choking as they tugged at the heavy loads and had to be helped by the shoulders of the men at the rear, the excited cries and calls of the wives gesticulating ahead, while the old women, tied high in place on the loads, moaned as their ancient bones were shaken. Once away, there was a ceaseless bustling. Men and women ran alongside, the long whip flashed out at one or another of the dogs: here was a crone who complained and was given a word of comfort, there an old pot swinging loose that had to be retied; and of a sudden a sled would sway, guided so that the runners would not meet the fresh dog-droppings whose momentary warmth would melt the carefully spread coat of ice.

And with all this, we seemed hardly to advance through the wide and monotonous expanse. Our first stop was near a fish camp, where each man had his cache and provisions were to be taken on. The stones were removed, the cache opened, a great chunk of frozen fish hacked off with an axe; and this was to be their food pending the catching of the first seal. Whenever we stopped like this, the driver would stand off to right or left of the dogs, and with a long slow flick of the whip caress each husky that remained standing. At that gentle stroke, the dog would lie down; but indeed most were so trained and habituated to this, that as soon as they stopped they lay down in their tracks. Then there were a hundred things to do: unload the old woman, for her muscles ached; give suck to the baby; disentangle the crossed harness of the dogs; drink tea; after which the men would stand apart with their pipes and talk shop. The Eskimo is never at a loss for reasons to linger by the way. Because his life is hard, his leisure is precious; and except among peasants and common labourers, there is no such pleasure taken from an hour's idleness in our civilized world. I was learning, besides, that the Eskimo always does what he wants to do the moment the notion comes to him of doing it. This day was the first on which I began to see in the Eskimo something attractive, and in his existence something that a civilized man might envy.

* * *

SIMONE DE BEAUVOIR (1908–1986)

'Harlem'

Of course I wanted to know Harlem, but it is not the only coloured district in New York. There is an important coloured community in Brooklyn, another (Jamaica) at Queens, and others too at the city boundaries; even in New York itself you find districts here and there lived in by coloured families. Until 1900, except for Brooklyn, the most important coloured community in New York was near Fifty-seventh Street West. The Harlem tenements were built to house white people; but at the beginning of the century transport was insufficient and property owners had difficulty in letting houses on the East side of the district: adopting the proposal of a coloured man, Philip A. Payton, in the real estate business, it was suggested to the coloured folk that they should install themselves in some apartments on One Hundred and Fortieth Street, and in this way two blocks were filled, and filled to advantage as it soon turned out. At first the white people did not notice the invasion of coloured folk, and when they tried to stop it it was too late. The coloured people rented one by one all the apartments to let and began to buy private houses then being built between Lenox and Seventh Avenues. White people moved out; as soon as a coloured family was detected in a row of houses, all the whites fled as though fleeing from the plague. Soon the whole district was coloured, civic and social centres were formed and a coloured community developed. Above all it was after 1914 that Harlem expanded in such an extraordinary way.

Those who worship American power on their knees are even more servile than Americans themselves in adopting their prejudices. One Frenchman said to me: 'If you like, we will drive through Harlem; you can motor through it, but do not on any account go there on foot.' Another, who was bolder, said: 'If you insist on seeing Harlem, at least do not wander off the avenues: if something happens you can always take refuge in the underground; but avoid the side streets.' And trembling with fear they told me how white people had been found with their throats cut in the gutters at dawn. But I had in the course of my life explored so many places where prudent people said *one couldn't possibly go* that I was not too impressed: I deliberately walked towards Harlem.

I walked towards Harlem, but my steps were not altogether casual; this was not just a walk but something of an adventure. Some force seemed to hold me back, a force emanating from the coloured district which somehow repelled me: fear. But it was not my fear: it was other people's; the fear of all those people who never venture into Harlem, and who sense some vast, mysterious and forbidden zone in the northern part of their city, where they are changed into enemies. I turned a corner and my heart stood still; the scene had changed completely. I had been told: 'There is nothing to see in Harlem: it is an odd corner of New York where people have coloured skins.' And indeed in One Hundred and Twenty-fifth Street I found again the movies, drugstores, shops, bars and restaurants of Forty-second and Fourteenth Streets, but the atmosphere was as changed as though I had crossed a mountain range or an arm of the sea.

There was suddenly a caterwauling of coloured children dressed in bright shirts chequered with red and green squares, school children with woolly hair and deep brown legs, chattering away on the kerb; darkies were slumbering in doorways, while others sauntered about with their hands in their pockets; their relaxed features did not seem concentrated on some invisible point in the future, but reflected the scene as it appeared then under the sky. There was nothing frightening: and I even felt a growing sense of joy and an inner calm that New York had never given me until this moment. If on turning a corner, say in Lille or Lyons, I had suddenly found myself on the Canebière, I would have felt the same pleasure. But the change of scene was not just picturesque: there was nothing frightening about it, yet fear was there and weighed heavily on this great gathering of people.

Crossing the street I advanced through layers of fear; fear inspired by these children with livid eyes, these men in light-coloured suits and these women without haste. One Hundred and Twenty-fifth Street is a frontier: there are still a few white people to be found there. But on Lenox Avenue there is not a face to be seen that is not black or brown. No one paid any attention to me. There was the same *décor* as on the Manhattan avenues and these people, with all their indolence and gaiety, did not seem any more different from the inhabitants of Lexington than are the people of Marseilles from those of Lille. One could *walk* down Lenox Avenue and I asked myself just what I should have done to have had to flee from here, screaming towards the protection of an underground station; it seemed as difficult to provoke rape or murder as it would have been in Columbus Circle at midday. Strange orgies must take place in the minds of serious-thinking people; as for me, this broad, gay, peaceful boulevard acted like a brake on my imagination. I looked into the side streets; there were scarcely more than a few children milling round on roller skates, to disturb the quiet, *petit-bourgeois* atmosphere; they did not look dangerous.

I walked down avenues and in the side streets; when I grew tired I sat down in the squares; nothing could happen to me. And if my feeling of security was not absolutely serene, it was on account of that fear in the hearts of people whose skin was of the same colour as mine. If some rich businessman is frightened when he ventures into districts where people go hungry, that is natural: he walks in a world which does not accept his own, and which may triumph over it some day. But Harlem is a society on its own, with its middle class and proletarians, rich and poor who are not blended together in some revolutionary movement, and who wish to integrate themselves with America, not destroy it. These people will not suddenly roll forward in a flood heading for Wall Street, nor do they constitute any immediate threat. The unreasonable fear they inspire cannot be other than the reverse side of some hatred or some kind of remorse. Clamped to the heart of New York, Harlem weighs on the good conscience of the white people in the same way that original sin does on that of the Christian.

★   ★   ★

MARTIN LUTHER KING, JR. (1929–1968)

from 'A Letter From Birmingham Jail'[1]

Martin Luther King, Jr.
Birmingham City Jail
April 16, 1963

My dear Fellow Clergymen

While confined here in the Birmingham City Jail, I came across your recent statement calling our present activities 'unwise and untimely'. Seldom, if ever, do I pause to answer criticism of my work and ideas. If I sought to answer all of the criticisms that cross my desk, my secretaries would be engaged in little else in the course of the day and I would have no time for constructive work. But since I feel that you are men of genuine good will and your criticisms are sincerely set forth, I would like to answer your statement in what I hope will be patient and reasonable terms.

I think I should give the reason for my being in Birmingham, since you have been influenced by the argument of 'outsiders coming in'. I have the honor of serving as president of the Southern Christian Leadership Conference, an organization operating in every Southern

---

1. Written in the Birmingham, Alabama, jail in 1963, to eight clergymen. King had been jailed, along with his supporters, for demonstrating against the segregation of the city's lunch counters.

state with headquarters in Atlanta, Georgia. We have some eighty-five affiliate organizations all across the South – one being the Alabama Christian Movement for Human Rights. Whenever necessary and possible we share staff, educational, and financial resources with our affiliates. Several months ago our local affiliate here in Birmingham invited us to be on call to engage in a nonviolent direct action program if such were deemed necessary. We readily consented and when the hour came we lived up to our promises. So I am here, along with several members of my staff, because we were invited here. I am here because I have basic organizational ties here. Beyond this, I am in Birmingham because injustice is here. Just as the eighth century prophets left their little villages and carried their 'thus saith the Lord' far beyond the boundaries of their home town, and just as the Apostle Paul left his little village of Tarsus and carried the gospel of Jesus Christ to practically every hamlet and city of the Graeco-Roman world, I too am compelled to carry the gospel of freedom beyond my particular home town. Like Paul, I must constantly respond to the Macedonian call for aid.

* * *

TOBIAS WOLFF (1945–)

from This Boy's Life

Our car boiled over again just after my mother and I crossed the Continental Divide. While we were waiting for it to cool we heard, from somewhere above us, the bawling of an airhorn. The sound got louder and then a big truck came around the corner and shot past us into the next curve, its trailer shimmying wildly. We stared after it. 'Oh, Toby,' my mother said, 'he's lost his brakes.'

The sound of the horn grew distant, then faded in the wind that sighed in the trees all around us.

By the time we got there, quite a few people were standing along the cliff where the truck went over. It had smashed through the guardrails and fallen hundreds of feet through empty space to the river below, where it lay on its back among the boulders. It looked pitifully small. A stream of thick black smoke rose from the cab, feathering out in the wind. My mother asked whether anyone had gone to report the accident. Someone had. We stood with the others at the cliff's edge. Nobody spoke. My mother put her arm around my shoulder.

For the rest of the day she kept looking over at me, touching me, brushing back my hair. I saw that the time was right to make a play for souvenirs. I knew she had no money for them, and I had tried not to ask, but now that her guard was down I couldn't help myself. When we pulled out of Grand Junction I owned a beaded Indian belt, beaded moccasins, and a bronze horse with a removable, tooled-leather saddle.

*

It was 1955 and we were driving from Florida to Utah, to get away from a man my mother was afraid of and to get rich on uranium. We were going to change our luck.

We'd left Sarasota in the dead of summer, right after my tenth birthday, and headed West under low flickering skies that turned black and exploded and cleared just long enough to leave the air gauzy with steam. We drove through Georgia, Alabama, Tennessee, Kentucky, stopping to cool the engine in towns where people moved with arthritic slowness and spoke in thick, strangled tongues. Idlers with rotten teeth surrounded the car to press peanuts on the pretty Yankee lady and her little boy, arguing among themselves about shortcuts. Women looked up from their flower beds as we drove past, or watched us from their porches, sometimes impassively, sometimes giving us a nod and a flutter of their fans.

Every couple of hours the Nash Rambler boiled over. My mother kept digging into her little grubstake but no mechanic could fix it. All we could do was wait for it to cool, then drive on until it boiled over again. (My mother came to hate this machine so much that not long after we got to Utah she gave it away to a woman she met in a cafeteria.) At night we slept in boggy rooms where headlight beams crawled up and down the walls and mosquitoes sang in our ears, incessant as the tires whining on the highway outside. But none of this bothered me. I was caught up in my mother's freedom, her delight in her freedom, her dream of transformation.

Everything was going to change when we got out West. My mother had been a girl in Beverly Hills, and the life we saw ahead of us was conjured from her memories of California in the days before the Crash. Her father, Daddy as she called him, had been a navy officer and a paper millionaire. They'd lived in a big house with a turret. Just before Daddy lost all his money and all his shanty-Irish relatives' money and got himself transferred overseas, my mother was one of four girls chosen to ride on the Beverly Hills float in the Tournament of Roses. The float's theme was 'The End of the Rainbow' and it won that year's prize by acclamation. She met Jackie Coogan. She had her picture taken with Harold Lloyd and Marion Davies, whose movie *The Sailor Man* was filmed on Daddy's ship. When Daddy was at sea she and her mother lived a dream life in which, for days at a time, they played the part of sisters.

And the *cars* my mother told me about as we waited for the Rambler to cool – I should have seen the cars! Daddy drove a Franklin touring car. She'd been courted by a boy who had his own Chrysler convertible with a musical horn. And of course there was the Hernandez family, neighbors who'd moved up from Mexico after finding oil under their cactus ranch. The family was large. When they were expected to appear somewhere together they drove singly in a caravan of identical Pierce-Arrows.

Something like that was supposed to happen to us. People in Utah were getting up poor in the morning and going to bed rich at night. You didn't need to be a mining engineer or a mineralogist. All you needed was a Geiger counter. We were on our way to the uranium fields, where my mother would get a job and keep her eyes open. Once she learned the ropes she'd start prospecting for a claim of her own.

And when she found it she planned to do some serious compensating: for the years of hard work, first as a soda jerk and then as a novice secretary, that had gotten her no farther than flat broke and sometimes not that far. For the breakup of our family five years earlier. For the misery of her long affair with a violent man. She was going to make up for lost time, and I was going to help her.

*

We got to Utah the day after the truck went down. We went too late – months too late. Moab and the other mining towns had been overrun. All the motels were full. The locals had rented out their bedrooms and living rooms and garages and were now offering trailer space in their front yards for a hundred dollars a week, which was what my mother could make in a month if she had a job. But there were no jobs, and people were getting ornery. There'd been murders. Prostitutes walked the streets in broad daylight, drunk and bellicose. Geiger counters cost a fortune. Everyone told us to keep going.

My mother thought things over. Finally she bought a poor man's Geiger counter, a black light that was supposed to make uranium trace glow, and we started for Salt Lake City. She figured there must be ore somewhere around there. The fact that nobody else had found any meant that we would have the place pretty much to ourselves. To tide us over she planned to take a job with the Kennecott Mining Company, whose personnel officer had responded to a letter of inquiry she'd sent from Florida some time back. He had warned her against coming, said there was no work in Salt Lake and that his own company was about to go out on strike. But his letter was so friendly! My mother just knew she'd get a job out of him. It was as good as guaranteed.

So we drove on through the desert. As we drove, we sang – Irish ballads, folk songs, big-band blues. I was hooked on 'Mood Indigo.' Again and again I world-wearily crooned 'You ain't been blue, no, no, no' while my mother eyed the temperature gauge and babied the engine. Then my throat dried up on me and left me croaking. I was too excited anyway. Our trail was ending. Burma Shave ads and bullet-riddled mileage signs ticked past. As the numbers on those signs grew smaller we began calling them out at the top of our lungs.

*   *   *

JOHN CAGE (1912–1992)

from *Silence*

Morris Graves introduced Xenia and me to a miniature island in Puget Sound at Deception Pass. To get there we traveled from Seattle about seventy-five miles north and west to Anacortes Island, then south to the Pass, where we parked. We walked along a rocky beach and then across a sandy stretch that was passable only at low tide to another island, continuing through some luxuriant woods up a hill where now and then we had views of the surrounding waters and distant islands, until finally we came to a small foot-bridge that led to our destination – an island no larger than, say, a modest home. This island was carpeted with flowers and was so situated that all of Deception Pass was visible from it, just as though we were in the best seats of an intimate theatre. While we were lying there on that bed of flowers, some other people came across the footbridge. One of them said to another, 'You come all this way and then when you get here there's nothing to see.'

*   *   *

ISABELLA BIRD (1831–1904)

from A Lady's Life in the Rocky Mountains

Canyon, September

The absence of a date shows my predicament. *They* have no news-paper; *I* have no almanack; the father is away for the day, and none of the others can help me, and they look contemptuously upon my desire for information on the subject. The monotony will come to an end tomorrow, for Chalmers offers to be my guide over the mountains to Estes Park, and has persuaded his wife 'for once to go for a frolic'; and with much reluctance, many growls at the waste of time, and many apprehensions of danger and loss, she has consented to accompany him. My life has grown less dull from theirs having become more interesting to me, and as I have 'made myself agree-able', we are on fairly friendly terms. My first move in the direction of fraternizing was, however, snubbed. A few days ago, having finished my own work, I offered to wash up the plates, but Mrs C., with a look which conveyed more than words, a curl of her nose, and a sneer in her twang, said, 'Guess you'll make more work nor you'll do. Those hands of yours' (very brown and coarse they were) 'ain't no good; never done nothing, I guess.' Then to her awkward daughter: 'This woman says she'll wash up! Ha! ha! look at her arms and hands!' This was the nearest approach to a laugh I have heard, and have never seen even a tendency towards a smile. Since then I have risen in their estimation by improvising a lamp – Hawaiian fashion – by putting a wisp of rag into a tin of fat. They have actually condescended to sit up till the stars come out since. Another advance was made by means of the shell-pattern quilt I am knitting for you. There has been a tendency towards approving of it, and a few days since the girl snatched it out of my hand, saying, 'I want this,' and apparently took it to the camp. This has resulted in my having a knitting class, with the woman, her married daughter, and a woman from the camp, as pupils. Then I have gained ground with the man by being able to catch and saddle a horse. I am often reminded of my favourite couplet,

> Beware of desperate steps; the darkest day,
> Live till to-morrow, will have passed away.

But oh! what a hard, narrow life it is with which I am now in contact! A narrow and unattractive religion, which I believe still to be genuine, and an intense but narrow patriotism, are the only higher influences. Chalmers came from Illinois nine years ago, pronounced by the doctors to be far gone in consumption, and in two years he was strong. They are a queer family; somewhere in the remote Highlands I have seen such another. Its head is tall, gaunt, lean, and ragged, and has lost one eye. On an English road one would think him a starving or a dangerous beggar. He is slightly intelligent, very opinionated, and wishes to be thought well-informed, which he is not. He belongs to the straitest sect of Reformed Presbyterians ('Psalm-singers'), but exaggerates anything of bigotry and intolerance which may characterize them, and rejoices in truly merciless fashion over the excision of the philanthropic Mr Stuart, of Philadelphia, for worshipping with congregations which sing hymns. His great boast is that his ancestors were Scottish Covenanters. He considers himself a profound theologian, and by the pine logs at night discourses to me on the mysteries of the eternal counsels and the divine decrees. Colorado, with its progress and its future, is also a constant theme. He hates England with a bitter, personal hatred, and regards any allusions which I make to the progress of Victoria as a personal insult. He trusts to live to see the downfall of the British monarchy and the disintegration of the empire. He is very fond of talking, and asks me a great deal about my travels, but if I speak favourably of the climate or resources of any other country, he regards it as a slur on Colorado.

They have one hundred and sixty acres of land, a 'squatter's claim', and an invaluable water-power. He is a lumberer, and has a sawmill of a very primitive kind. I notice that every day something goes wrong with it, and this is the case throughout. If he wants to haul timber down, one or other of the oxen cannot be found; or if the timber is actually under way, a wheel or a part of the harness gives way, and the whole affair is at a standstill for days. The cabin is hardly a shelter, but is allowed to remain in ruins because the foundation of a frame-house was once dug. A horse is always sure to be lame for want of a shoe-nail, or a saddle to be useless from a broken buckle, and the wagon and harness are a marvel of temporary shifts, patchings, and insecure linkings with strands of rope. Nothing is ever ready or whole when it is wanted. Yet Chalmers is a frugal, sober, hard-working man, and he, his eldest son, and a 'hired man' 'rise early', 'going forth to their work and labour till the evening', and if they do not 'late take rest', they truly 'eat the bread of carefulness'. It is hardly surprising that nine years of persevering shiftlessness should have resulted in nothing but the ability to procure the bare necessaries of life.

Of Mrs C. I can say less. She looks like one of the English poor women of our childhood – lean, clean, toothless, and speaks, like some of them, in a piping, discontented voice, which seems to convey a personal reproach. All her waking hours are spent in a large sun-bonnet. She is never idle for one minute, is severe and hard, and despises everything but work. I think she suffers from her husband's shiftlessness. She always speaks of me as 'this' or 'that woman'. The family consists of a grown-up son, a shiftless, melancholy-looking youth, who possibly pines for a wider life; a girl of sixteen, a sour, repellent-looking creature, with as much manners as a pig; and three hard, unchildlike younger children. By the whole family all courtesy and gentleness of act or speech seem regarded as 'works of the flesh', if not of 'the devil'. They knock over all one's things without apologizing or picking them up, and when I thank them for anything they look grimly amazed. I feel that they think it sinful that I do not work as hard as they do. I wish I could show them 'a more excellent way'. This hard greed, and the exclusive pursuit of gain, with the indifference to all which does not aid in its acquisition, are eating up family love and life throughout the West. I write this reluctantly, and after a total experience of nearly two years in the United States. They seem to have no 'Sunday clothes', and few of any kind. The

sewing-machine, like most other things, is out of order. One comb
serves the whole family. Mrs C. is cleanly in her person and dress,
and the food, though poor, is clean. Work, work, work, is their
day and their life. They are thoroughly ungenial, and have that air
of suspicion in speaking of every one which is not unusual in the
land of their ancestors. Thomas Chalmers is the man's ecclesiastical
hero, in spite of his own severe Puritanism. Their livestock consists
of two wretched horses, a fairly good *broncho* mare, a mule, four
badly-bred cows, four gaunt and famished-looking oxen, some swine
of singularly active habits, and plenty of poultry. The old saddles are
tied on with twine; one side of the bridle is a worn-out strap and
the other a rope. They wear boots, but never two of one pair,
and never blacked, of course, but no stockings. They think it quite
effeminate to sleep under a roof, except during the severest months
of the year. There is a married daughter across the river, just the
same hard, loveless, moral, hard-working being as her mother. Each
morning, soon after seven, when I have swept the cabin, the family
come in for 'worship'. Chalmers 'wales' a psalm, in every sense of
the word wail, to the most doleful of dismal tunes; they read a
chapter round, and he prays. If his prayer has something of the tone
of the imprecatory psalms, he has high authority in his favour; and
if there be a tinge of the Pharisaic thanksgiving, it is hardly surprising
that he is grateful that he is not as other men are when he contem-
plates the general godlessness of the region.

Sunday was a dreadful day. The family kept the Commandment
literally, and did no work. Worship was conducted twice, and was
rather longer than usual. Chalmers does not allow of any books in
his house but theological works, and two or three volumes of dull
travels, so the mother and children slept nearly all day. The man
attempted to read a well-worn copy of *Boston's Fourfold State*, but
shortly fell asleep, and they only woke up for their meals. Friday and
Saturday had been passably cool, with frosty nights, but on Saturday
night it changed, and I have not felt anything like the heat of Sunday
since I left New Zealand, though the mercury was not higher than
91°. It was sickening, scorching, melting, unbearable, from the mere
power of the sun's rays. It was an awful day, and seemed as if it
would never come to an end. The cabin, with its mud roof under
the shade of the trees, gave a little shelter, but it was occupied by the
family, and I longed for solitude. I took the *Imitation of Christ*, and
strolled up the canyon among the withered, crackling leaves, in much

dread of snakes, and lay down on a rough table which some passing emigrant had left, and soon fell asleep. When I awoke it was only noon. The sun looked wicked as it blazed like a white magnesium light. A large tree-snake (quite harmless) hung from the pine under which I had taken shelter, and looked as if it were going to drop upon me. I was covered with black flies. The air was full of a busy, noisy din of insects, and snakes, locusts, wasps, flies, and grasshoppers were all rioting in the torrid heat. Would the sublime philosophy of Thomas à Kempis, I wondered, have given way under this? All day I seemed to hear in mockery the clear laugh of the Hilo streams, and the drip of Kona showers, and to see as in a mirage the perpetual green of windward Hawaii. I was driven back to the cabin in the late afternoon, and in the evening listened for two hours to abuse of my own country, and to sweeping condemnations of all religionists outside of the brotherhood of 'Psalm-singers'. It is jarring and painful, yet I would say of Chalmers, as Dr Holland says of another:

> If ever I shall reach the home in heaven,
> For whose dear rest I humbly hope and pray,
> In the great company of the forgiven
> I shall be sure to meet old Daniel Gray.

The night came without coolness, but at daylight on Monday morning a fire was pleasant. You will now have some idea of my surroundings. It is a moral, hard, unloving, unlovely, unrelieved, unbeautified, grinding life. These people live in a discomfort and lack of ease and refinement which seems only possible to people of British stock. A 'foreigner' fills his cabin with ingenuities and elegancies, and a Hawaiian or South Sea Islander makes his grass house both pretty and tasteful. Add to my surroundings a mighty canyon, impassable both above and below, and walls of mountains with an opening some miles off to the vast prairie sea.

An English physician is settled about half a mile from here over a hill. He is spoken off as holding 'very extreme opinions'. Chalmers rails at him for being 'a thick-skulled Englishman', for being 'fine, polished', etc. To say a man is 'polished' here is to give him a very bad name. He accuses him also of holding views subversive of all morality. In spite of all this, I thought he might possess a map, and I induced Mrs C. to walk over with me. She intended it as a formal morning call, but she wore the inevitable sun-bonnet, and had her dress tied up as when washing. It was not till I reached the gate that

I remembered that I was in my Hawaiian riding-dress, and that I still wore the spurs with which I had been trying a horse in the morning! The house was in a grass valley which opened from the tremendous canyon through which the river had cut its way. The Foot Hills, with their terraces of flaming red rock, were glowing in the sunset, and a pure green sky arched tenderly over a soft evening scene. Used to the meanness and baldness of settlers' dwellings, I was delighted to see that in this instance the usual log cabin was only the lower floor of a small house, which bore a delightful resemblance to a Swiss chalet. It stood in a vegetable garden fertilized by an irrigating ditch, outside of which were a barn and cowshed. A young Swiss girl was bringing the cows slowly home from the hill, an English-woman in a clean print dress stood by the fence holding a baby, and a fine-looking Englishman in a striped Garibaldi shirt, and trousers of the same tucked into high boots, was shelling corn. As soon as Mrs Hughes spoke I felt she was truly a lady; and oh! how refreshing her refined, courteous, graceful English manner was, as she invited us into the house! The entrance was low, through a log porch festooned and almost concealed by a 'wild cucumber'. Inside, though plain and poor, the room looked a home, not like a squatter's cabin. An old tin was completely covered by a graceful clematis mixed with streamers of Virginia creeper, and white muslin curtains, and above all two shelves of admirably-chosen books, gave the room almost an air of elegance. Why do I write almost? It was an oasis. It was barely three weeks since I had left 'the communion of educated men', and the first tones of the voices of my host and hostess made me feel as if I had been out of it for a year. Mrs C. stayed an hour and a half, and then went home to the cows, when we launched upon a sea of congenial talk. They said they had not seen an educated lady for two years, and pressed me to go and visit them. I rode home on Dr Hughes's horse after dark, to find neither fire nor light in the cabin. Mrs C. had gone back saying, 'Those English talked just like savages, I couldn't understand a word they said.' I made a fire, and extemporized a light with some fat and a wick of rag, and Chalmers came in to discuss my visit and to ask me a question concerning a matter which had roused the latent curiosity of the whole family. I had told him, he said, that I knew no one hereabouts, but 'his woman' told him that Dr H. and I spoke constantly of a Mrs Grundy, whom we both knew and disliked, and who was settled, as we said, not far off! He had never heard of her, he said, and he was the pioneer settler of the canyon, and there was a man up here from Longmount who said he was sure there was not a Mrs Grundy in the district, unless it was a woman who went by two names! The wife and family had then come in, and I felt completely nonplussed, I longed to tell Chalmers that it was he and such as he, there or anywhere, with narrow hearts, bitter tongues, and harsh judgments, who were the true 'Mrs Grundys', dwarfing individuality, checking lawful freedom of speech, and making men 'offenders for a word', but I forebore. How I extricated myself from the difficulty, deponent sayeth not. The rest of the evening has been spent in preparing to cross the mountains. Chalmers says he knows the way well, and that we shall sleep tomorrow at the foot of Long's Peak. Mrs Chalmers repents of having consented, and conjures up doleful visions of what the family will come to when left headless, and of disasters among the cows and hens. I could tell her that the eldest son and the 'hired man' have plotted to close the saw-mill and go on a hunting and fishing expedition, that the cows will stray, and that the individual spoken respectfully of as 'Mr Skunk' will make havoc in the hen-house.

Nameless Region, Rocky Mountains, September

This is indeed far removed. It seems farther away from you than any place I have been to yet, except the frozen top of the volcano of Mauna Loa. It is so little profaned by man that if one were compelled to live here in solitude one might truly say of the bears, deer, and elk which abound, 'Their tameness is shocking to me.' It is the world of 'big game'. Just now a heavy-headed elk, with much-branched horns fully three feet long, stood and looked at me, and then quietly trotted away. He was so near that I heard the grass, crisp with hoar frost, crackle under his feet. Bears stripped the cherry-bushes within a few yards of us last night. Now two lovely blue birds, with crests on their heads, are picking about within a stone's-throw. This is 'The Great Lone Land', until lately the hunting-ground of the Indians, and not yet settled or traversed, or likely to be so, owing to the want of water. A solitary hunter has built a log cabin up here, which he occupies for a few weeks for the purpose of elk-hunting, but all the region is unsurveyed, and mostly unexplored. It is 7 a.m. The sun has not yet risen high enough to melt the hoar-frost, and the air is clear, bright, and cold. The stillness is profound. I hear nothing but the far-off mysterious roaring of a river in a deep canyon, which we spent two hours last night in trying to find. The horses are lost, and if I were disposed to retort upon my companions the term they invariably apply to me, I should now write, with bitter emphasis, '*that* man' and '*that* woman' have gone in search of them.

The scenery up here is glorious, combining sublimity with beauty, and in the elastic air fatigue has dropped off from me. This is no region for tourists and women, only for a few elk and bear hunters at times, and its unprofaned freshness gives me new life. I cannot by any words give you an idea of scenery so different from any that you or I have ever seen. This is an upland valley of grass and flowers, of glades and sloping lawns, and cherry-fringed beds of dry streams, and clumps of pines artistically placed, and mountain sides densely pine-clad, the pines breaking into fringes as they come down upon the 'park', and the mountains breaking into pinnacles of bold grey rock as they pierce the blue of the sky. A single dell of bright green grass, on which dwarf clumps of the scarlet poison-oak look like beds of geraniums, slopes towards the west, as if it must lead to the river which we seek. Deep, vast canyons, all trending westwards, lie in purple gloom. Pine-clad ranges rising into the blasted top of Storm Peak, all run westwards too, and all the beauty and glory are but the frame out of which rises – heaven-piercing, pure in its pearly lustre, as glorious a mountain as the sun tinges red in either hemisphere – the splintered, pinnacled, lonely, ghastly, imposing, double-peaked summit of Long's Peak, the Mont Blanc of Northern Colorado.[1]

This is a view to which nothing needs to be added. This is truly the 'lodge in some vast wilderness' for which one often sighs when in the midst of 'a bustle at once sordid and trivial'. In spite of Dr Johnson, these 'monstrous protuberances' do 'inflame the imagination and elevate the understanding'. This scenery satisfies my soul. Now, the Rocky Mountains realize – nay, exceed – the dream of my childhood. It is magnificent, and the air is life-giving. I should like to spend some time in these higher regions, but I know that this will turn out an abortive expedition, owing to the stupidity and pigheadedness of Chalmers.

1. Gray's Peak and Pike's Peak have their partisans, but after seeing them all under favourable aspects, Long's Peak stands in my memory as it does in that vast congeries of mountains, alone in imperial grandeur.

There is a most romantic place called Estes Park, at a height of 7500 feet, which can be reached by going down to the plains and then striking up the St Vrain Canyon, but this is a distance of fifty-five miles, and as Chalmers was confident that he could take me over the mountains, a distance, as he supposed, of about twenty miles, we left at midday yesterday, with the fervent hope, on my part, that I might not return. Mrs C. was busy the whole of Tuesday in preparing what she called 'grub', which, together with 'plenty of bedding', was to be carried on a pack mule; but when we started I was disgusted to find that Chalmers was on what should have been the pack animal, and that two thickly-quilted cotton 'spreads' had been disposed of under my saddle, making it broad, high, and uncomfortable. Any human being must have laughed to see an expedition start so grotesquely 'ill found'. I had a very old iron-grey horse, whose lower lip hung down feebly, showing his few teeth, while his fore-legs stuck out forwards, and matter ran from both his nearly-blind eyes. It is a kindness to bring him up to abundant pasture. My saddle is an old McLellan cavalry saddle, with a battered brass peak, and the bridle is a rotten leather strap on one side and a strand of rope on the other. The cotton quilts covered the Rosinante from mane to tail. Mrs C. wore an old print skirt, an old short-gown, a print apron, and a sun-bonnet, with the flap coming down to her waist, and looked as careworn and clean as she always does. The inside horn of her saddle was broken; to the outside one hung a saucepan and a bundle of clothes. The one girth was nearly at the breaking-point when we started.

My pack, with my well-worn umbrella upon it, was behind my saddle. I wore my Hawaiian riding-dress, with a handkerchief tied over my face and the sun-cover of my umbrella folded and tied over my hat for the sun was very fierce. The queerest figure of all was the would-be guide. With his one eye, his gaunt, lean form, and his torn clothes, he looked more like a strolling tinker than the honest worthy settler that he is. He bestrode rather than rode a gaunt mule, whose tail hair had all been shaven off, except a tuft for a tassel at the end. Two flour bags which leaked were tied on behind the saddle, two quilts were under it, and my canvas bag, a battered canteen, a frying-pan, and two lariats hung from the horn. On one foot C. wore an old high boot, into which his trouser was tucked, and on the other an old brogue, through which his toes protruded.

We had an ascent of four hours through a ravine which gradually opened out upon this beautiful 'park', but we rode through it for some miles before the view burst upon us. The vastness of this range, like astronomical distances, can hardly be conceived of. At this place, I suppose, it is not less than 250 miles wide, and with hardly a break in its continuity, it stretches almost from the Arctic circle to the Straits of Magellan. From the top of Long's Peak, within a short distance, twenty-two summits, each above 12,000 feet in height, are visible, and the Snowy Range, the backbone or 'divide' of the continent, is seen snaking distinctly through the wilderness of ranges, with its waters starting for either ocean. From the first ridge we crossed after leaving Canyon we had a singular view of range beyond range cleft by deep canyons, and abounding in elliptical valleys, richly grassed. The slopes of all the hills, as far as one could see, were waving with fine grass ready for the scythe, but the food of wild animals only. All these ridges are heavily timbered with pitch pines, and where they come down on the grassy slopes they look as if the trees had been arranged by a landscape gardener. Far off, through an opening in a canyon, we saw the prairie simulating the ocean. Far off, through an opening in another direction, was the glistening outline of the Snowy Range. But still, till we reached this place, it was monotonous, though grand as a whole: a grey-green or buff-grey, with outbreaks of brilliantly-coloured rock, only varied by the black green of pines, which are not the stately pyramidal pines of the Sierra Nevada, but much resemble the natural Scotch fir. Not many miles from us is North Park, a great tract of land said to be rich in gold, but those who have gone to 'prospect' have seldom returned, the region being the home of tribes of Indians who live in perpetual hostility to the whites and to each other.

At this great height, and most artistically situated, we came upon a rude log camp tenanted in winter by an elk hunter, but now deserted. Chalmers without any scruple picked the padlock; we lighted a fire, made some tea, and fried some bacon, and after a good meal mounted again and started for Estes Park. For four weary hours we searched hither and thither along every indentation of the ground which might be supposed to slope towards the Big Thompson River, which we knew had to be forded. Still, as the quest grew more tedious, Long's Peak stood before us as a landmark in purple glory; and still at his feet lay a hollow filled with deep blue atmosphere, where I knew that Estes Park must lie, and still between us and it lay never-lessening miles of inaccessibility, and the sun was ever westering, and the shadows ever lengthening, and Chalmers, who had started confident, bumptious, blatant, was ever becoming more bewildered, and his wife's thin voice more piping and discontented, and my stumbling horse more insecure, and I more determined (as I am at this moment) that somehow or other I would reach that blue hollow, and even stand on Long's Peak where the snow was glittering. Affairs were becoming serious, and Chalmers's incompetence a source of real peril, when, after an exploring expedition, he returned more bumptious than ever, saying he knew it would be all right, he had found a trail, and we could get across the river by dark, and camp out for the night. So he led us into a steep, deep, rough ravine, where we had to dismount, for trees were lying across it everywhere, and there was almost no footing on the great slabs of shelving rock. Yet there was a trail, tolerably well worn, and the branches and twigs near the ground were well broken back. Ah! it was a wild place. My horse fell first, rolling over twice, and breaking off a part of the saddle, in his second roll knocking me over a shelf of three feet of descent. Then Mrs C.'s horse and the mule fell on the top of each other, and on recovering themselves bit each other savagely. The ravine became a wild gulch, the dry bed of some awful torrent; there were huge shelves of rock, great overhanging walls of rock, great prostrate trees, cedar spikes and cacti to wound the feet, and then a precipice fully 500 feet deep! The trail was a trail made by bears in search of bear cherries, which abounded!

It was getting dusk as we had to struggle up the rough gulch we had so fatuously descended. The horses fell several times; I could hardly get mine up at all, though I helped him as much as I could; I was cut and bruised, scratched and torn. A spine of a cactus penetrated my foot, and some vicious thing cut the back of my neck. Poor Mrs C. was much bruised, and I pitied her, for she got no fun out of it as I did. It was an awful climb. When we got out of the gulch, C. was so confused that he took the wrong direction, and after an hour of vague wandering was only recalled to the right one by my pertinacious assertions acting on his weak brain. I was inclined to be angry with the incompetent braggart, who had boasted that he could take us to Estes Park 'blindfold'; but I was sorry for him too, so said nothing, even though I had to walk during these meanderings to save my tired horse. When at last, at dark, we reached the open, there was a snow-flurry, with violent gusts of wind, and the shelter of the camp, dark and cold as it was, was desirable. We had no food, but made a fire. I lay down on some dry grass, with my inverted saddle for a pillow, and slept soundly, till I was awoke by the cold of an intense frost, and the pain of my many cuts and bruises. Chalmers promised that we should make a fresh start at six, so I woke him at five, and here I am alone at half past eight! I said to him many times that unless he hobbled or picketed the horses, we should lose them. 'Oh,' he said, 'they'll be all right.' In truth he had no picketing-pins. Now, the animals are merrily trotting homewards. I saw them two miles off an hour ago with him after them. His wife, who is also after them, goaded to desperation, said, 'He's the most ignorant, careless, good-for-nothing man I ever saw,' upon which I dwelt upon his being well-meaning. There is a sort of well here, but our 'afternoon tea' and watering the horses drained it, so we have had nothing to drink since yesterday, for the canteen, which started without a cork, lost all its contents when the mule fell. I have made a monstrous fire, but thirst and impatience are hard to bear, and preventible misfortunes are always irksome. I have found the stomach of a bear with fully a pint of cherrystones in it, and have spent an hour in getting the kernels; and lo! now, at half past nine, I see the culprit and his wife coming back with the animals!

*   *   *

HUNTER S. THOMPSON (1939-)

from *Fear and Loathing in Las Vegas*

We were somewhere around Barstow on the edge of the desert when the drugs began to take hold. I remember saying something like 'I feel a bit lightheaded; maybe you should drive . . .' And suddenly there was a terrible roar all around us and the sky was full of what looked like huge bats, all swooping and screeching and diving around the car, which was going about a hundred miles an hour with the top down to Las Vegas. And a voice was screaming: 'Holy Jesus! What are these goddamn animals?'

Then it was quiet again. My attorney had taken his shirt off and was pouring beer on his chest, to facilitate the tanning process. 'What the hell are you yelling about?' he muttered, staring up at the sun with his eyes closed and covered with wraparound Spanish sunglasses. 'Never mind,' I said. 'It's your turn to drive.' I hit the brakes and aimed the Great Red Shark toward the shoulder of the highway. No point mentioning those bats, I thought. The poor bastard will see them soon enough.

It was almost noon, and we still had more than a hundred miles to go. They would be tough miles. Very soon, I knew, we would both be completely twisted. But there was no going back, and no time to rest. We would have to ride it out. Press registration for the fabulous Mint 400 was already underway, and we had to get there by four to claim our sound-proof suite. A fashionable sporting magazine in New York had taken care of the reservations, along with this huge red Chevy convertible we'd just rented off a lot on the Sunset Strip . . . and I was, after all, a professional journalist; so I had an obligation to *cover the story*, for good or ill.

The sporting editors had also given me $300 in cash, most of which was already spent on extremely dangerous drugs. The trunk of the car looked like a mobile police narcotics lab. We had two bags of grass, seventy-five pellets of mescaline, five sheets of high-powered blotter acid, a salt shaker half full of cocaine, and a whole galaxy of multi-colored uppers, downers, screamers, laughers . . . and also a quart of tequila, a quart of rum, a case of Budweiser, a pint of raw ether and two dozen amyls.

All this had been rounded up the night before, in a frenzy of high-speed driving all over Los Angeles County – from Topanga to Watts, we picked up everything we could get our hands on. Not that we *needed* all that for the trip, but once you get locked into a serious drug collection, the tendency is to push it as far as you can.

The only thing that really worried me was the ether. There is nothing in the world more helpless and irresponsible and depraved than a man in the depths of an ether binge. And I knew we'd get into that rotten stuff pretty soon. Probably at the next gas station. We had sampled almost everything else, and now – yes, it was time for a long snort of ether. And then do the next hundred miles in a horrible, slobbering sort of spastic stupor. The only way to keep alert on ether is to do up a lot of amyls – not all at once, but steadily, just enough to maintain the focus at ninety miles an hour through Barstow.

'Man, this is the way to travel,' said my attorney. He leaned over to turn the volume up on the radio, humming along with the rhythm section and kind of moaning the words: 'One toke over the line, Sweet Jesus . . . One toke over the line . . .'

One toke? You poor fool! Wait till you see those goddamn bats. I could barely hear the radio . . . slumped over on the far side of the seat, grappling with a tape recorder turned all the way up on 'Sympathy for the Devil.' That was the only tape we had, so we played it constantly, over and over, as a kind of demented counterpoint to the radio. And also to maintain our rhythm on the road. A constant speed is good for gas mileage – and for some reason that seemed important at the time. Indeed. On a trip like this one *must* be careful about gas consumption. Avoid those quick bursts of acceleration that drag blood to the back of the brain.

My attorney saw the hitchhiker long before I did. 'Let's give this boy a lift,' he said, and before I could mount any argument he was stopped and this poor Okie kid was running up to the car with a big grin on his face, saying, 'Hot damn! I never rode in a convertible before!'

'Is that right?' I said. 'Well, I guess you're about ready, eh?'

The kid nodded eagerly as we roared off.

'We're your friends,' said my attorney. 'We're not like the others.'

O Christ, I thought, he's gone around the bend. 'No more of that talk,' I said sharply. 'Or I'll put the leeches on you.' He grinned, seeming to understand. Luckily, the noise in the car was so awful – between the wind and the radio and the tape machine – that the kid in the back seat couldn't hear a word we were saying. Or could he?

How long can we *maintain*? I wondered. How long before one of us starts raving and jabbering at this boy? What will he think then? This same lonely desert was the last known home of the Manson family. Will he make that grim connection when my attorney starts screaming about bats and huge manta rays coming down on the car? If so – well, we'll just have to cut his head off and bury him somewhere. Because it goes without saying that we can't turn him loose. He'll report us at once to some kind of outback nazi law enforcement agency, and they'll run us down like dogs.

Jesus! Did I *say* that? Or just think it? Was I talking? Did they hear me? I glanced over at my attorney, but he seemed oblivious – watching the road, driving our Great Red Shark along at a hundred and ten or so. There was no sound from the back seat.

Maybe I'd better have a chat with this boy, I thought. Perhaps if I *explain* things, he'll rest easy.

Of course. I leaned around in the seat and gave him a fine big smile . . . admiring the shape of his skull.

'By the way,' I said. 'There's one thing you should probably understand.'

He stared at me, not blinking. Was he gritting his teeth?

'Can you *hear* me?' I yelled.

He nodded.

'That's good,' I said. 'Because I want you to know that we're on our way to Las Vegas to find the American Dream.' I smiled. 'That's why we rented this car. It was the only way to do it. Can you grasp that?'

He nodded again, but his eyes were nervous.

'I want you to have all the background,' I said. 'Because this is a very ominous assignment – with overtones of extreme personal danger . . . Hell, I forgot all about this beer; you want one?'

He shook his head.

'How about some ether?' I said.

'What?'

'Never mind. Let's get right to the heart of this thing. You see, about twenty-four hours ago we were sitting in the Polo Lounge of the Beverly Hills Hotel – in the patio section, of course – and we were just sitting there under a palm tree when this uniformed dwarf came up to me with a pink telephone and said, "This must be the call you've been waiting for all this time, sir."'

I laughed and ripped open a beer can that foamed all over the back seat while I kept talking. 'And you know? He was right! I'd been *expecting* that call, but I didn't know who it would come from. Do you follow me?'

The boy's face was a mask of pure fear and bewilderment.

I blundered on: 'I want you to understand that this man at the wheel is my *attorney*! He's not just some dingbat I found on the Strip. Shit, *look* at him! He doesn't look like you or me, right? That's because he's a foreigner. I think he's probably Samoan. But it doesn't matter, does it? Are you prejudiced?'

'Oh, hell *no*!' he blurted.

'I didn't think so,' I said. 'Because in spite of his race, this man is extremely valuable to me.' I glanced over at my attorney, but his mind was somewhere else.

I whacked the back of the driver's seat with my fist. 'This is *important*, goddamnit! This is a *true story!*' The car swerved sickeningly, then straightened out. 'Keep your hands off my fucking neck!' my attorney screamed. The kid in the back looked like he was ready to jump right out of the car and take his chances.

Our vibrations were getting nasty – but why? I was puzzled, frustrated. Was there no communication in this car? Had we deteriorated to the level of *dumb beasts*?

Because my story *was* true. I was certain of that. And it was extremely important, I felt, for the *meaning* of our journey to be made absolutely clear. We had actually been sitting there in the Polo Lounge – for many hours – drinking Singapore Slings with mescal on the side and beer chasers. And when the call came, I was ready.

The Dwark approached our table cautiously, as I recall, and when he handed me the pink telephone I said nothing, merely listened. And then I hung, up, turning to face my attorney. 'That was headquarters,' I said. 'They want me to go to Las Vegas at once, and make contact with a Portuguese photographer named Lacerda. He'll have the details. All I have to do is check into my suite and he'll seek me out.'

My attorney said nothing for a moment, then he suddenly came alive in his chair. 'God *hell!*' he exclaimed. 'I think I see the *pattern*. This one sounds like real trouble!' He tucked his khaki undershirt into his white rayon bellbottoms and called for more drink. 'You're going to need plenty of legal advice before this thing is over,' he said. 'And my first advice is that you should rent a very fast car with no top and get the hell out of LA for at least forty-eight hours.' He shook his head sadly. 'This blows my weekend, because naturally I'll have to go with you – and we'll have to arm ourselves.'

'Why not?' I said. 'If a thing like this is worth doing at all, it's worth doing right. We'll need some decent equipment and plenty of cash on the line – if only for drugs and a super-sensitive tape recorder, for the sake of a permanent record.'

'What kind of a story is this?' he asked.

'The Mint 400,' I said. 'It's the richest off-the-road race for motorcycles and dune-buggies in the history of organized sport – a fantastic spectacle in honor of some fatback *grossero* named Del Webb, who owns the luxurious Mint Hotel in the heart of downtown Las Vegas . . . at least that's what the press release says; my man in New York just read it to me.'

'Well,' he said, 'as your attorney I advise you to buy a motorcycle. How else can you cover a thing like this righteously?'

'No way,' I said. 'Where can we get hold of a Vincent Black Shadow?'

'What's that?'

'A fantastic bike,' I said. 'The new model is something like two thousand cubic inches, developing two hundred brake-horsepower at four thousand revolutions per minute on a magnesium frame with two styrofoam seats and a total curb weight of exactly two hundred pounds.'

'That sounds about right for this gig,' he said.

'It is,' I assured him. 'The fucker's not much for turning, but it's pure hell on the straightaway. It'll outrun the F-111 until takeoff.'

'Takeoff?' he said. 'Can we handle that much torque?'

'Absolutely,' I said. 'I'll call New York for some cash.'

* * *

MARGARET FOUNTAINE (1862–1940)

from *Butterflies and Late Loves*

Mid-winter in Hollywood, where I had taken up my abode, is like a prolonged and lovely spring. The gardens are one blaze of flowers, and though the continuous drought made the hills bare, the irrigation system is so perfect, like most things in this highly favoured land, that the lack of rain is scarcely felt. Through a somewhat back-stair acquaintance I had managed to obtain with Dr John Adams Comstock (Curator of the South West Museum) I was brought into contact with several local entomologists, some of whom, such as Mr Piazza and Mr H. M. Simms, I got to know quite well. Mr Simms was a young Englishman twice invalided home from the trenches, and here to regain his health. Mr Piazza was half Italian, and though quite English in his manners was not the least like an Englishman in his appearance; in fact typical of a certain type of man who would be described by a certain type of woman as 'very foreign-looking'; a middle-aged man with pleasing manners and any amount of keenness for entomology. I found, almost without thinking of it, that I was getting on very friendly terms with this man, and it began to strike me that Charles might object to my being so constantly seen with him poking around the Hollywood gardens after larvae (they only occurred on a cultivated Cassia which always grew in private grounds, but the people were just as genial as their climate, so we never failed to obtain permission to search their trees). I also began to suspect that Mr Piazza, a man of anything but ample means, was contemplating that the addition of a few extra hundreds per annum to his rather slender income might not be an altogether undesirable arrangement.

So I decided I would go to Arizona, having been told that Yuma was the best locality for *Euchloë Pima* and several other good species of butterflies. Mr Piazza at once discovered that Yuma would be a good place for moths (which was his speciality) and announced that he might follow me there, asking me to write and let him know how I got on, so I promised a card, inwardly resolving that I would *not* find Yuma a good place for moths. There was no need for any duplicity, for I found practically nothing at Yuma, and in the Arizona Hotel, of a strictly commercial character, I passed many a lonely hour.

However, I found a good horse in a corral in Thirs Street; black, with white fetlocks, slender and well made, and with quite a good canter. How different everything is from the standpoint of a middle-aged woman. In the old days, when I might be starting on horseback from some hotel, half the establishment would turn out to see me mount, while waiters would be running about with chairs; now I simply went to the corral, fetched the horse myself and hitched him up outside the Arizona Hotel, while I brought down my saddle and saddled him up myself, not a man standing by offering to lend me the slightest assistance or apparently taking the slightest notice of my proceedings; and when he was saddled I would promptly mount and ride away, nobody troubling themselves about me. I must own I found this way much more to my liking, for if there is a thing I hate, it is being fussed over. I enjoyed long rides into the desert, though the desert was parched up by the drought and I got no butterflies.

★ ★ ★

EL SALVADOR

JOAN DIDION (1934–)

'In El Salvador'

The three-year-old El Salvador International Airport is glassy and white and splendidly isolated, conceived during the waning of the Molina 'National Transformation' as convenient less to the capital (San Salvador is forty miles away, until recently a drive of several hours) than to a central hallucination of the Molina and Romero regimes, the projected beach resorts, the Hyatt, the Pacific Paradise, tennis, golf, waterskiing, condos, Costa del Sol; the visionary invention of a tourist industry in yet another republic where the leading natural cause of death is gastrointestinal infection. In the general absence of tourists these hotels have since been abandoned, ghost resorts on the empty Pacific beaches, and to land at this airport built to service them is to plunge directly into a state in which no ground is solid, no depth of field reliable, no perception so definite that it might not dissolve into its reverse.

The only logic is that of acquiescence. Immigration is negotiated in a thicket of automatic weapons, but by whose authority the weapons are brandished (army or national guard or national police or customs police or treasury police or one of a continuing proliferation of other shadowy and overlapping forces) is a blurred point. Eye contact is avoided. Documents are scrutinized upside-down. Once clear of the airport, on the new highway that slices through green hills rendered phosphorescent by the cloud cover of the tropical rainy season, one sees mainly underfed cattle and mongrel dogs and armored vehicles, vans, and trucks and Cherokee Chiefs fitted with reinforced steel and bulletproof Plexiglas an inch thick.

Such vehicles are a fixed feature of local life, and are popularly associated with disappearance and death. There was the Cherokee

Chief seen following the Dutch television crew killed in Chalatenango province in March. There was the red Toyota three-quarter-ton pickup sighted near the van driven by the four American Maryknoll workers on the night they were killed in December 1980. There are the three Toyota panel trucks, one yellow, one blue, and one green, none bearing plates, reported present at each of the summer mass detentions (a 'detention' is another fixed feature of local life, and often precedes a 'disappearance') in the Amatepec district of San Salvador. These are the details – the models and colors of armored vehicles, the makes and calibers of weapons, the particular methods of dismemberment and decapitation used in particular instances – on which the visitor to Salvador learns immediately to concentrate, to the exclusion of past or future concerns, as in a prolonged amnesiac fugue.

*

Terror is the given of the place. Black-and-white police cars cruise in pairs, each with the barrel of a rifle extruding from an open window. Roadblocks materialize at random, soldiers fanning out from trucks and taking positions, fingers always on triggers, safetys clicking on and off. Aim is taken as if to pass the time. Every morning *El Diario de Hoy* and *La Prensa Gráfica* carry cautionary stories. *'Una madre y sus dos hijos fueron asesinados con arma cortante (corvo) por ocho sujetos desconocidos el lunes en la noche'*: a mother and her two sons hacked to death in their beds by eight *desconocidos*, unknown men. The same morning's paper: the unidentified body of a young man, strangled, found on the shoulder of a road. Same morning, different story: the unidentified bodies of three young men, found on another road, their faces partially destroyed by bayonets, one face carved to represent a cross.

It is largely from these reports in the newspapers that the United States embassy compiles its body counts, which are transmitted to Washington in a weekly dispatch referred to by embassy people as 'the grim-gram'. These counts are presented in a kind of tortured code that fails to obscure what is taken for granted in El Salvador, that government forces do most of the killing. In a January 15 memo to Washington, for example, the embassy issued a 'guarded' breakdown on its count of 6,909 'reported' political murders between September 16, 1980, and September 15, 1981. Of these 6,909, 922 were 'believed committed by security forces,' 952 'believed committed by leftist terrorists,' 136 'believed committed by rightist terrorists,' and 4,889 'committed by unknown assailants,' the famous *desconocidos* favored by those San Salvador newspapers still publishing. (By whom the remaining ten were committed is unclear.) The memo continued:

> The uncertainty involved here can be seen in the fact that responsibility cannot be fixed in the majority of cases. We note, however, that it is generally believed in El Salvador that a large number of the unexplained killings are carried out by the security forces, officially or unofficially. The Embassy is aware of dramatic claims that have been made by one interest group or another in which the security forces figure as the primary agents of murder here. El Salvador's tangled web of attack and vengeance, traditional criminal violence and political mayhem make this an impossible charge to sustain. In saying this, however, we make no attempt to lighten the responsibility for the deaths of many hundreds, and perhaps thousands, which can be attributed to the security forces . . .

*

The body count kept by what is generally referred to in San Salvador as 'the Human Rights Commission' is higher than the embassy's, and documented periodically by a photographer who goes out looking for bodies. The bodies he photographs are often broken into unnatural positions, and the faces to which the bodies are attached (when they are attached) are equally unnatural, sometimes unrecognizable as human faces, obliterated by acid or beaten to a mash of misplaced ears and teeth or slashed ear to ear and invaded by insects. '*Encontrado en Antiguo Cuscatlán el día 25 de marzo 1982: camison de dormir celeste,*' the typed caption reads on one photograph: found in Antiguo Cuscatlán March 25, 1982, wearing a sky-blue night shirt. The captions are laconic. Found in Soyapango May 21, 1982. Found in Mejicanos June 11, 1982. Found at El Playón May 30, 1982, white shirt, purple pants, black shoes.

The photograph accompanying that last caption shows a body with no eyes, because the vultures got to it before the photographer did. There is a special kind of practical information that the visitor to El Salvador acquires immediately, the way visitors to other places acquire information about the currency rates, the hours for the museums. In El Salvador one learns that vultures go first for the soft tissue, for the eyes, the exposed genitalia, the open mouth. One learns that an open mouth can be used to make a specific point, can be stuffed with something emblematic; stuffed, say, with a penis, or, if the point has to do with land title, stuffed with some of the dirt in question. One learns that hair deteriorates less rapidly than flesh, and that a skull surrounded by a perfect corona of hair is not an uncommon sight in the body dumps.

All forensic photographs induce in the viewer a certain protective numbness, but dissociation is more difficult here. The disfigurement is too routine. The locations are too near, the dates too recent. There is the presence of the relatives of the disappeared: the women who sit every day in this cramped office on the grounds of the archdiocese, waiting to look at the spiral-bound photo albums in which the photographs are kept. These albums have plastic covers bearing soft-focus color photographs of young Americans in dating situations (strolling through autumn foliage on one album, recumbent in a field of daisies on another), and the women, looking for the bodies of their husbands and brothers and sisters and children, pass them from hand to hand without comment or expression.

> One of the more shadowy elements of the violent scene here [is] the death squad. Existence of these groups has long been disputed, but not by many Salvadorans . . . Who constitutes the death squads is yet another difficult question. We do not believe that these squads exist as permanent formations but rather as *ad hoc* vigilante groups that coalesce according to perceived need. Membership is also uncertain, but in addition to civilians we believe that both on- and off-duty members of the security forces are participants. This was unofficially confirmed by right-wing spokesman Maj. Roberto D'Aubuisson who stated in an interview in early 1981 that security force members utilize the guise of the death squad when a potentially embarrassing or odious task needs to be performed.
>
> —*from the confidential but later declassified January 15, 1982, memo previously cited, drafted for the State Department by the political section at the embassy in San Salvador*

The dead and pieces of the dead turn up in El Salvador everywhere, every day, as taken for granted as in a nightmare, or a horror movie. Vultures of course suggest the presence of a body. A knot of children on the street suggests the presence of a body. Bodies turn up in the brush of vacant lots, in the garbage thrown down ravines in the richest districts, in public rest rooms, in bus stations. Some are dropped in Lake Ilopango, a few miles east of the city, and wash up near the lakeside cottages and clubs frequented by what remains in San Salvador of the sporting bourgeoisie. Some still turn up at El Playón, the lunar lava field of rotting human flesh visible at one time or another on every television screen in America but characterized as recently as June in the *El Salvador News Gazette*, an English-language weekly edited by an American named Mario Rosenthal, as an 'uncorroborated story ... dredged up from the files of leftist propaganda'. Others turn up at Puerta del Diablo, above Parque Balboa, a national *Turicentro* still described, in the April-July 1982 issue of *Aboard TACA*, the magazine provided passengers on the national airline of El Salvador, as 'offering excellent subjects for color photography'.

*

I drove up to Puerta del Diablo one morning last summer, past the Casa Presidencial and the camouflaged watchtowers and heavy concentrations of troops and arms south of town, on up a narrow road narrowed further by landslides and deep crevices in the roadbed, a drive so insistently premonitory that after a while I began to hope that I would pass Puerta del Diablo without knowing it, just miss it, write it off, turn around and go back. There was however no way of missing it. Puerta del Diablo is a 'view site' in an older and distinctly literary tradition, nature as lesson, an immense cleft rock through which half of El Salvador seems framed, a site so romantic and 'mystical', so theatrically sacrificial in aspect, that it might be a cosmic parody of nineteenth-century landscape painting. The place presents itself as pathetic fallacy: the sky 'broods', the stones 'weep', a constant seepage of water weighting the ferns and moss. The foliage is thick and slick with moisture. The only sound is a steady buzz, I believe of cicadas.

Body dumps are seen in El Salvador, as a kind of visitors' must-do, difficult but worth the detour. 'Of course you have seen El Playón,' an aide to President Alvaro Magaña said to me one day, and proceeded to discuss the site geologically, as evidence of the country's geothermal resources. He made no mention of the bodies. I was unsure if he was sounding me out or simply found the geothermal aspect of overriding interest. One difference between El Playón and Puerta del Diablo is that most bodies at El Playón appear to have been killed somewhere else, and then dumped; at Puerta del Diablo the executions are believed to occur in place, at the top, and the bodies thrown over. Sometimes reporters will speak of wanting to spend the night at Puerta del Diablo, in order to document an actual execution, but at the time I was in Salvador no one had.

The aftermath, the daylight aspect, is well documented. 'Nothing fresh today, I hear,' an embassy officer said when I mentioned that I had visited Puerta del Diablo. 'Were there any on top?' someone else asked. 'There were supposed to have been three on top yesterday.' The point about whether or not there had been any on top was that usually it was necessary to go down to see bodies. The way down is hard. Slabs of stone, slippery with moss, are set into the vertiginous cliff, and it is down this cliff that one begins the descent to the bodies, or what is left of the bodies, pecked and maggoty masses of flesh, bone, hair. On some days there have been helicopters circling, tracking those making the descent. Other days there have been militia at the top, in the clearing where the road seems to run out, but on the morning I was there the only people on top were a man and a woman and three small children, who played in the wet grass while the woman started and stopped a Toyota pickup. She appeared to be learning how to drive. She drove forward and then back toward the edge, apparently following the man's signals over and over again.

We did not speak, and it was only later, down the mountain and back in the land of the provisionally living, that it occurred to me that there was a definite question about why a man and a woman might choose a well-known body dump for a driving lesson. This was one of a number of occasions, during the two weeks my husband and I spent in El Salvador, on which I came to understand, in a way I had not understood before, the exact mechanism of terror.

*

Whenever I had nothing better to do in San Salvador I would walk up in the leafy stillness of the San Benito and Escalón districts, where the hush at midday is broken only by the occasional crackle of a walkie-talkie, the click of metal moving on a weapon. I recall a day in San Benito when I opened my bag to check an address, and heard the clicking of metal on metal all up and down the street. On the whole no one walks up here, and pools of blossoms lie undisturbed on the sidewalks. Most of the houses in San Benito are more recent than those in Escalón, less idiosyncratic and probably smarter, but the most striking architectural features in both districts are not the houses but their walls, walls built upon walls, walls stripped of the usual *copa de oro* and bougainvillea, walls that reflect successive generations of violence: the original stone, the additional five or six or ten feet of brick, and finally the barbed wire, sometimes concertina, sometimes electrified; walls with watch-towers, gun ports, closed-circuit television cameras, walls now reaching twenty and thirty feet.

San Benito and Escalón appear on the embassy security maps as districts of relatively few 'incidents', but they remain districts in which a certain oppressive uneasiness prevails. In the first place there are always 'incidents' – detentions and deaths and disappearances – in the barrancas, the ravines lined with shanties that fall down behind the houses with the walls and the guards and the walkie-talkies; one day in Escalón I was introduced to a woman who kept the lean-to that served as a grocery store in a barranca just above the Hotel Sheraton. She was sticking prices on bars of Camay and Johnson's baby soap, stopping occasionally to sell a plastic bag or two filled with crushed ice and Coca-Cola, and all the while she talked in a low voice about her fear, about her eighteen-year-old son, about the boys who had been taken out and shot on successive nights recently in a neighboring barranca.

*

In the second place there is, in Escalón, the presence of the Sheraton itself, a hotel that has figured rather too prominently in certain local stories involving the disappearance and death of Americans. The Sheraton always seems brighter and more mildly festive than either the Camino Real or the Presidente, with children in the pool and flowers and pretty women in pastel dresses, but there are usually several bulletproofed Cherokee Chiefs in the parking area, and the men drinking in the lobby often carry the little zippered purses that in San Salvador suggest not passports or credit cards but Browning 9-mm pistols.

It was at the Sheraton that one of the few American *desaparacidos*, a young freelance writer named John Sullivan, was last seen, in December of 1980. It was also at the Sheraton, after eleven on the evening of January 3, 1981, that the two American advisers on agrarian reform, Michael Hammer and Mark Pearlman, were killed, along with the Salvadoran director of the Institute for Agrarian Transformation, José Rodolfo Viera. The three were drinking coffee in a dining room off the lobby, and whoever killed them used an Ingram MAC-10 without sound suppressor, and then walked out through the lobby, unapprehended. The Sheraton has even turned up in the investigation into the December 1980 deaths of the four American Maryknoll workers. In *Justice in El Salvador: A Case Study*, prepared and released this summer in New York by the Lawyers Committee for International Human Rights, there appears this note:

> On December 19, 1980, the [Duarte government's] Special Investigative Commission reported that 'a red Toyota ¾-ton pick-up was seen leaving (the crime scene) at about 11:00 PM on December 2' and that 'a red splotch on the burned van' of the churchwomen was being checked to determined whether the paint splotch 'could be the result of a collision between that van and the red Toyota pick-up.' By February 1981, the Maryknoll Sisters' Office of Social Concerns, which has been actively monitoring the investigation, received word from a source which it considered reliable that the FBI had matched the red splotch on the burned van with a red Toyota pick-up belonging to the Sheraton hotel in San Salvador . . .
>
> Subsequent to the FBI's alleged matching of the paint splotch and a Sheraton truck, the State Department has claimed, in a communication with the families of the churchwomen, that 'the FBI could not determine the source of the paint scraping.'

There is also mention in this study of a young Salvadoran businessman named Hans Christ (his father was a German who arrived in El Salvador at the end of World War II), a part-owner of the Sheraton. Hans Christ lives now in Miami, and that his name should have even come up in the Maryknoll investigation made many people uneasy, because it was Hans Christ, along with his brother-in-law, Ricardo Sol Meza, who, in April of 1981, were first charged with the murders of Michael Hammer and Mark Pearlman and José Rodolfo Viera at the Sheraton. These charges were later dropped, and were followed by a series of other charges, arrests, releases, expressions of 'dismay' and 'incredulity' from the US Embassy, and even, recently, confessions to the killings from two former National Guard corporals, who testified that Hans Christ had led them through the lobby and pointed out the victims. Christ and Ricardo Sol Meza have said that the dropped case against them was a government frame-up, and that they were only having drinks at the Sheraton the night of the killings, with a National Guard intelligence officer. It was logical for Hans Christ and Ricardo Sol Meza to have drinks at the Sheraton because they both had interests in the hotel, and Ricardo Sol Meza had just opened a roller disco, since closed, off the lobby into which the killers walked that night. The killers were described by witnesses as well dressed, their faces covered. The room from which they walked is no longer a restaurant, but the marks left by the bullets are still visible, on the wall facing the door.

Whenever I had occasion to visit the Sheraton I was apprehensive, and this apprehension came to color the entire Escalon district for me, even its lower reaches, where there were people and movies and restaurants. I recall being struck by it on the canopied porch of a restaurant near the Mexican embassy, on an evening when rain or sabotage or habit had blacked out the city and I became abruptly aware, in the light cast by a passing car, of two human shadows, silhouettes illuminated by the headlights and then invisible again. One shadow sat behind the smoked-glass windows of a Cherokee Chief parked at the curb in front of the restaurant; the other crouched between the pumps at the Esso station next door, carrying a rifle. It seemed to me unencouraging that my husband and I were the only people seated on the porch. In the absence of the headlights the candle on our table provided the only light, and I fought the impulse to blow it out. We continued talking, carefully. Nothing came of this, but I did not forget the sensation of having been in a single instant demoralized, undone, humiliated by fear, which is what I meant when I said that I came to understand in El Salvador the mechanism of terror . . .

*

The place brings everything into question. One afternoon when I had run out of the Halazone tablets I dropped every night in a pitcher of tap water (a demented *gringa* gesture, I knew even then, in a country where anyone who had not been born there was at least mildly ill, including the nurse at the American embassy), I walked across the street from the Camino Real to the Metrocenter, which is referred to locally as 'Central America's Largest Shopping Mall'. I found no Halazone at the Metrocenter but became absorbed in making notes about the mall itself, about the Muzak playing 'I Left My Heart in San Francisco' and 'American Pie' (. . . *singing, This will be the day that I die* . . .) although the record store featured a cassette called *Classics of Paraguay*, about the pâté de foie gras for sale in the supermarket, about the guard who did the weapons-check on everyone who entered the supermarket, about the young matrons in tight Sergio Valente jeans, trailing maids and babies behind them and buying towels, big beach towels printed with maps of Manhattan that featured Bloomingdale's; about the number of things for sale that seemed to suggest a fashion for 'smart drinking', to evoke modish cocktail hours. There were bottles of Stolichnaya vodka packaged with glasses and mixer, there were ice buckets, there were bar carts of every conceivable design, displayed with sample bottles.

This was a shopping center that embodied the future for which El Salvador was presumably being saved, and I wrote it down dutifully, this being the kind of 'color' I knew how to interpret, the kind of inductive irony, the detail that was supposed to illuminate the story. As I wrote it down I realized that I was no longer much interested in this kind of irony, that this was a story that would not be illuminated by such details, that this was a story that would perhaps not be illuminated at all, that this was perhaps even less a 'story' than a true *noche obscura*. As I waited to cross back over the Boulevard de los Heroes to the Camino Real I noticed soldiers herding a young civilian into a van, their guns at the boy's back, and I walked straight ahead, not wanting to see anything at all.

CUBA

Esteban Montejo (1860–1973)

'Life in the Forest'

I have never forgotten the first time I tried to escape. That time I failed, and I stayed a slave for several years longer from fear of having the shackles put on me again. But I had the spirit of a runaway watching over me, which never left me. And I kept my plans to myself so that no one could give me away. I thought of nothing else; the idea went round and round my head and would not leave me in peace; nothing could get rid of it, at times it almost tormented me. The old Negroes did not care for escaping, the women still less. There were few runaways. People were afraid of the forest. They said anyone who ran away was bound to be recaptured. But I gave more thought to this idea than the others did. I always had the feeling that I would like the forest and I knew that it was hell working in the fields, for you couldn't do anything for yourself. Everything went by what the master said.

One day I began to keep my eye on the overseer. I had already been sizing him up for some time. That son-of-a-bitch obsessed me, and nothing could make me forget him. I think he was Spanish. I remember that he was tall and never took his hat off. All the blacks respected him because he would take the skin off your back with a single stroke of his whip. The fact is I was hot-headed that day. I don't know what came over me, but I was filled with a rage which burned me up just to look at the man.

I whistled at him from a distance, and he looked round and then turned his back; that was when I picked up a stone and threw it at his head. I know it must have hit him because he shouted to the others to seize me. But that was the last he saw of me, because I took to the forest there and then.

I spent several days walking about in no particular direction. I had never left the plantation before. I walked uphill, downhill, in every direction. I know I got to a farm near the Siguanea, where I was forced to rest. My feet were blistered and my hands were swollen and festering. I camped under a tree. I made myself a shelter of banana-leaves in a few hours and I stayed there four or five days. I only had to hear the sound of a human voice to be off like a bullet. It was a terrible thing to be captured again after you had run away.

Then I had the idea of hiding in a cave. I lived there for something like a year and a half. The reason I chose it was that I thought it might save me wandering about so much and also that all the pigs in the district, from the farms and smallholdings and allotments, used to come to a sort of marsh near the mouth of the cave to bathe and wallow in the water. I caught them very easily because they came up one behind the other. I used to cook myself up a pig every week. This cave of mine was very big and as black as a wolf's mouth. Its name was Guajabán, near the village of Remedios. It was very dangerous because there was no other way out; you had to enter and leave by the mouth. I was very curious to find another exit, but I preferred to stay in the mouth of the cave with the *majases* which are very dangerous snakes.[1] They knock a person down with their breath, a snake breath you cannot feel, and then they put you to sleep to suck your blood. That was why I was always on guard and lit a fire to frighten them off. Anyone who dozes off in a cave is in a bad way. I did not want to see a snake even from a distance. The Congolese, and this is a fact, told me that the *majases* lived for over a thousand years, and when they got to a thousand they turned into marine creatures and went off to live in the sea like any other fish.

The cave was like a house inside, only a little darker, as you would expect. Ah, and the stink! Yes, it stank of bat droppings! I used to walk about on them because they were as soft as a feather bed. The bats lead a free life in caves. They were and are the masters of caves. It is the same everywhere in the world. As no one kills them they live for scores of years, though not as long as the *majases*. Their droppings turn to dust and are thrown on the ground to make pasture for animals and to fertilize crops.

Once I almost set fire to the place. I struck a spark and flames leapt through the cave. It was because of the bat droppings. After

1. In fact they are harmless.

Abolition I told a Congolese the story of how I lived with the bats, and the liar – the Congolese were even worse than you could imagine – said, 'A Creole like you doesn't know a thing. In my country what you call a bat is as big as a pigeon.' I knew this was untrue. They fooled half the world with their tales. But I just listened and was inwardly amused.

The cave was silent. The only sound was the bats going 'Chui, chui, chui'. They didn't know how to sing, but they spoke to each other, they understood each other. I noticed that one of them would go 'Chui, chui, chui' and the whole band would follow him wherever he went. They were very united in everything. Bats don't have wings. They are nothing but a scrap of black rag with a little black head, very dark and ugly, and if you look closely at them they are like mice. In that cave I was, as it were, just summering. What I really liked was the forest, and after a year and a half I left that dark place and took to the forest tracks. I went into the Siguanea forests again and spent a long time there. I cared for myself as if I were a pampered child. I didn't want to be taken into slavery again. It was repugnant to me, it was shameful. I have always felt like that about slavery. It was like a plague – it still seems like that today.

I was careful about making sounds or showing lights. If I left a trail they would follow me and catch me. I walked up and down so many hills that my arms and legs became as hard as wood. I came to know the forest gradually, and I began to like it. Sometimes I forgot I was a runaway and started whistling. I used to whistle to dispel the fear of the first days. They say whistling drives away evil spirits. But in the forest a runaway had to be on his guard, and I stopped in case the *ranchadores* came after me. To track down runaway slaves, the masters used to send for a posse of *ranchadores*, brutal white countrymen with hunting dogs which would drag you out of the forest with their teeth. I never ran into any of them or even saw one close up. They were trained to catch Negroes; if one of them saw a Negro he would give chase. If I happened to hear barking near by I would take off my clothes immediately, because once you are naked the dogs can't smell anything. Now I see a dog and it doesn't mean a thing, but if I had seen one then you wouldn't have seen my heels for miles around. I have never felt drawn to dogs. To my mind they have wicked instincts.

When a *ranchador* caught a slave, the master would give him money, a gold onza or more. In those days an onza was worth seventeen pesos. There's no knowing how many white countrymen were involved in that business!

To tell the truth, I lived very well as a runaway, hidden but comfortable. I did not let the other runaways catch sight of me: 'Runaway meets runaway, sells runaway.' There were many things I didn't do. For a long time I didn't speak to a soul. I liked this solitude. The other runaways always stayed in groups of twos and threes, but this was dangerous because when it rained their footprints showed up in the mud, and lots of idiots were caught that way.

*

There were some freed slaves around. I saw them going into the forest to look for herbs and *jutías*, edible rats. I never spoke to them or went near them, in fact I took good care to hide from them. Some of them worked on the land, and as soon as they left the coast clear, I took advantage of their absence to steal their vegetables and pigs. Most of them raised pigs on their plots of land. But I preferred to steal from the smallholdings because there was more of everything and it was easier. The smallholdings were bigger than the plots, far bigger, almost like big farms. The Negroes didn't have such luxuries. Those *guajíros* really lived very well in their palm-bark houses. I used to watch them at their music-making from a safe distance. Sometimes I could even hear them. They played small accordions, kettledrums, gourds, maraccas and calabashes. Those were their favourite instruments. I didn't learn their names till after I left the forest because, as a runaway, I was ignorant of everything.

They enjoyed dancing. But they didn't dance to the black man's music. They liked the *zapateo* and the *caringa*.[2] They all used to get together to dance the *zapateo* in the evenings, around five o'clock. The men wore coloured scarves around their necks and the women wore them around their heads. If one man excelled in the dance, his woman would come up and put a hat on top of the one he was wearing. This was the prize. I watched it all from a safe distance, taking it all in. I even saw them playing their pianolas. They played every sort of instrument there. They made a lot of noise, but it was as pretty as could be. From time to time one of the men would grab

2. Folk dances popular in the nineteenth century, especially among white country people. The *caringa* was of African origin and usually took the form of a scurrilous song accompanied by a dance.

a gourd to accompany the pianola. The pianolas played the music that was popular at the time, the *danzón*.

On Sundays the *guajiros* wore white and their women put flowers on their heads and wore their hair loose, then they joined the rest of the festive company and got together in the taverns to celebrate. The men liked linen and drill. They made themselves long shirts like jackets, with big pockets. The *guajiros* in those days lived better than people realize. They got tips from the masters almost every day. Naturally the two got along very well and did their dirty work together. But in my view the runaway lived better than the *guajiro;* he had greater freedom.

I had to forage for food for a long time, but there was always enough. 'The careful tortoise carries his house on his back.' I liked vegetables and beans and pork best. I think it is because of the pork that I have lived so long. I used to eat it every day, and it never disagreed with me. I would creep up to the smallholdings at night to catch piglets, taking care that no one heard me. I grabbed the first one I saw by the neck, clapped a halter round it, slung it over my shoulder and started to run, keeping my hand over its snout to stop it squealing. When I reached my camp I set it down and looked it over. If it was well fed and weighed twenty pounds or so, I had meals for a fortnight.

I led a half-wild existence as a runaway. I hunted animals like *jutías*. The *jutía* runs like the devil, and you need wings on your feet to catch it. I was very fond of smoked *jutía*. I don't know what people think of it today, but they never eat it. I used to catch one and smoke it without salt, and it lasted me months. The *jutía* is the healthiest food there is, though vegetables are better for the bones. The man who eats vegetables daily, particularly malanga roots, has no trouble from his bones. There are plenty of these wild vegetables in the forest. The malanga has a big leaf which shines at night. You can recognize it at once.

All the forest leaves have their uses. The leaves of tobacco plants and mulberry-trees cure stings. If I saw some insect bite was festering, I picked a tobacco leaf and chewed it thoroughly, then I laid it on the sting and the swelling went. Often, when it was cold, my bones would ache, a dry pain which would not go away. Then I made myself an infusion of rosemary leaves to soothe it, and it was cured at once. The cold also gave me bad coughs. When I got catarrh and a cough, I would pick this big leaf and lay it on my chest. I never knew its name, but it gave out a whitish liquid which was very warming; that soothed my cough. When I caught a cold, my eyes used to itch maddeningly, and the same used to happen as a result of the sun; in that case I laid a few leaves of the *ítamo* plant out to catch the dew overnight, and the next day I washed my eyes carefully with them. *Ítamo* is the best thing for this. The stuff they sell in pharmacies today is *ítamo*, but what happens is that they put it into little bottles and it looks like something else. As one grows older this eye trouble disappears. I have not had any itching bouts for years now.

The macaw-tree leaf provided me with smokes. I made tight-rolled neat little cigarettes with it. Tobacco was one of my relaxations. After I left the forest I stopped smoking tobacco, but while I was a runaway I smoked all the time.

And I drank coffee which I made with roast *guanina* leaves. I had to grind the leaves with the bottom of a bottle. When the mixture was ground right down, I filtered it and there was my coffee. I could always add a little wild honey to give it flavour. Coffee with honey strengthens the organism. You were always fit and strong in the forest.

Townsfolk are feeble because they are mad about lard. I have never liked lard because it weakens the body. The person who eats a lot of it grows fat and sluggish. Lard is bad for the circulation and it strangles people. Bees' honey is one of the best things there is for health. It was easy to get in the forest. I used to find it in the hollows of hardwood trees. I used it to make *chanchanchara*, a delicious drink made of stream-water and honey, and best drunk cold. It was better for you than any modern medicine; it was natural. When there was no stream near by I hunted around till I found a spring. In the forest there are springs of sweet water – the coldest and clearest I have seen in my life – which run downhill.

The truth is I lacked for nothing in the forest. The only thing I could not manage was sex. Since there were no women around I had to keep the appetite in check. It wasn't even possible to fuck a mare because they whinnied like demons, and if the white countrymen had heard the din they would have come rushing out immediately. I was not going to have anyone clap me in irons for a mare.

I was never short of fire. During my first few days in the forest I had matches. Then they ran out, and I had to use my *yesca*, a black ash that I kept in one of the tinderboxes the Spaniards sold in taverns.

It was easy to get a fire going. All you had to do was rub a stone on the tinderbox till it sparked. I learned this from the Canary Islanders while I was a slave. I never liked them as they were domineering and petty. The Galicians were nicer and got on better with the Negroes.

As I have always liked being my own man, I kept well away from everyone. I even kept away from the insects. To frighten off snakes I fired a big log and left it burning all night. They did not come near because they thought the log was a devil or an enemy of theirs. That's why I say I enjoyed my life as a runaway. I looked after myself, and I protected myself too. I used knives and half-sized machetes made by the firm of Collins, which were the ones used by the rural police, to clear the undergrowth and hunt animals, and I kept them ready in case a *ranchador* tried to take me by surprise – though that would have been difficult, as I kept on the move. I walked so much in the sun that at times my head began to burn and become, I imagined, quite red. Then I would be seized with a strong fever which I got rid of by wrapping myself up a bit or putting fresh leaves on my forehead, plantain as a rule. The problem was that I had no hat. I used to imagine the heat must be getting into my head and softening my brain.

When the fever passed, and it sometimes lasted several days, I dipped myself in the first river I came across and came out like new. The river water did me no harm. I think river water is the best thing for health, because it's so cold. This is good, because it hardens you. The bones feel firm. The rain used to give me a touch of catarrh which I cured with a brew of *cuajani* berries and bees' honey. So as not to get wet I sheltered myself with palm-leaves, piling them on top of a frame made of four forked sticks to make a hut. These huts were often seen after slavery and during the war. They looked like Indian shacks.

I spent most of the time walking or sleeping. At midday and at five in the afternoon I could hear the *fotuto*,[3] which the women blew to call their husbands home. It sounded like this: 'Fuuuu, fu, fu, fu, fu.' At night I slept at my ease. That was why I got so fat. I never thought about anything. My life was all eating, sleeping and keeping watch. I liked going to the hills at night, they were quieter and safer. *Ranchadores* and wild animals found difficulty in getting there. I went

3. A large conch used as a trumpet in the country districts.

as far as Trinidad. From the top of those hills you could see the town and the sea.

The nearer I got to the coast the bigger the sea got. I always imagined the sea like an immense river. Sometimes I stared hard at it and it went the strangest white colour and was swallowed up in my eyes. The sea is another great mystery of Nature, and it is very important, because it can take men and close over them and never give them up. Those are what they call shipwrecked men.

One thing I remember really clearly is the forest birds. They are something I cannot forget. I remember them all. Some were pretty and some were hellishly ugly. They frightened me a lot at first, but then I got used to hearing them. I even got so I felt they were taking care of me. The *contunto* was a real bastard. It was a black, *black* bird, which said, 'You, you, you, you, you, you, you ate the cheese up.' And it kept on saying this till I answered, 'Get away!' and it went. I heard it crystal clear. There was another bird which used to answer it as well; it went, 'Cu, cu, cu, cu, cu, cu,' and sounded like a ghost.

The *sijú* was one of the birds which tormented me most. It always came at night. That creature was the ugliest thing in the forest! It had white feet and yellow eyes. It shrieked out something like this: 'Cus, cus, cuuuus.'

The barn-owl had a sad song, but then it was a witch. It looked for dead mice. It cried, 'Chua, chua, chua, kui, kui,' and flew off like a ray of light. When I saw a barn-owl in my path, especially when it was flying to and fro, I used to take a different way because I knew it was warning me of an enemy near by, or death itself. The barn-owl is wise and strange. I recollect that the witches had a great respect for her and worked magic with her, the *sunsundamba*, as she is called in Africa. The barn-owl may well have left Cuba. I have never seen one again. Those birds go from country to country.

The sparrow came here from Spain and has founded an immense tribe here. Also the *tocororo*, which is half a greenish colour. It wears a scarlet sash across its breast, just like one the King of Spain has. The overseers used to say that it was a messenger from the King. I know it was forbidden even to look at a *tocororo*. The Negro who killed one was killing the King. I saw lots of men get the lash for killing sparrows and *tocororo*. I liked the *tocororo* because it sang as if it was hopping about, like this: 'Có, co, có, co, có, co.'

A bird which was a real son-of-a-bitch was the *ciguapa*. It whistled just like a man and it froze the soul to hear it. I don't like to think how often those creatures upset me.

★

I got used to living with trees in the forest. They have their noises too, because the leaves hiss in the air. There is one tree with a big white leaf which looks like a bird at night. I could swear that tree spoke. It went, 'Uch, uch, uch, ui, ui, ui, uch, uch.' Trees also cast shadows which do no harm, although one should not walk on them at night. I think trees' shadows must be like men's spirits. The spirit is the reflection of the soul, this is clear.

One thing it is not given to us men to see is the soul. We cannot say whether it is of such or such a colour. The soul is one of the greatest things in the world. Dreams are there to put us in touch with it. The Congolese elders used to say that the soul was like a witchcraft inside you and that there were good spirits and bad spirits, or rather, good souls and bad souls, and that everybody had them. As far as I can see, some people only have the magic sort of souls, while others have ordinary ones. But the ordinary ones are better, I think, because the others are in league with the Devil. It can happen that the soul leaves the body – when a person dies or sleeps – and joins the other souls wandering in space. It does this to rest itself, because so much strife at all times would be unbearable. There are people who don't like being called while they are asleep, because they are easily frightened and could die suddenly. This is because the soul travels far away during sleep and leaves the body empty. I sometimes get the shivers at night, and the same used to happen in the forest. Then I cover myself well because this is God's warning to one to take care of oneself. People who get the shivers need to pray a lot.

The heart is very different. It never leaves its post. If you put your hand on your left side you can make sure that it is beating. But the day it stops no one can help but go stiff. That is why you should not trust it.

Now the most important thing of all is the guardian angel. It is he who makes you go forwards or back. To my mind, the angel ranks higher than the soul or heart. He is always at your feet, watching over you and seeing everything. Nothing will ever make him go. I have thought a lot about these things, and I still find them a bit obscure. These are the thoughts which come when one is alone.

Man is thinking at all times. Even when he dreams, it is as though he were thinking. It is not good to speak of these thoughts. There is danger of decadence setting in. You cannot put much trust in people. How many people ask you questions so as to be able to use the information against you afterwards! Besides, this business of the spirits is infinite, like debts which keep piling up. No one knows the end. The truth is I don't even trust the Holy Ghost. That was why I stayed on my own as a runaway. I did nothing except listen to the birds and trees, and eat, but I never spoke to a soul. I remember I was so hairy my whiskers hung in ringlets. It was a sight to inspire fear. When I came out of the forest and went into the villages an old man called Ta Migue cropped me with a big pair of scissors. He gave me such a close crop I looked like a thoroughbred. I felt strange with all that wool gone, tremendously cold. The hair started growing again in a few days. Negroes have this tendency – I have never seen a bald Negro, not one. It was the Galicians who brought baldness to Cuba.

All my life I have liked the forest, but when slavery ended I stopped being a runaway. I realized from the way the people were cheering and shouting that slavery had ended, and so I came out of the forest. They were shouting, 'We're free now.' But I didn't join in, I thought it might be a lie. I don't know . . . anyway, I went up to a plantation and let my head appear little by little till I was out in the open. That was while Martinez Campos was Governor, the slaves said it was he who had freed them. All the same, years passed and there were still slaves in Cuba. It lasted longer than people think.

When I left the forest and began walking, I met an old woman carrying two children in her arms. I called to her, and when she came up I asked her, 'Tell me, is it true we are no longer slaves?' She replied, 'No, son, we are free now.' I went on walking the way I was going and began to look for work. Lots of Negroes wanted to be friends with me, and they used to ask me what I had done as a runaway. I told them, 'Nothing.' I have always been one for my independence. Idle gossip never helped anyone. I went for years and years without talking to anyone at all.

ANTILLES

DEREK WALCOTT (1930–)

'The Antilles: Fragments of Epic Memory'

[Acceptance Speech for the Nobel Prize for Literature]

Felicity is a village in Trinidad on the edge of the Caroni plain, the wide central plain that still grows sugar and to which indentured cane cutters were brought after emancipation, so the small population of Felicity is East Indian, and on the afternoon that I visited it with friends from America, all the faces along its road were Indian, which, as I hope to show, was a moving, beautiful thing, because this Saturday afternoon *Ramleela*, the epic dramatization of the Hindu epic the *Ramayana*, was going to be performed, and the costumed actors from the village were assembling on a field strung with different-coloured flags, like a new gas station, and beautiful Indian boys in red and black were aiming arrows haphazardly into the afternoon light. Low blue mountains on the horizon, bright grass, clouds that would gather colour before the light went. Felicity! What a gentle Anglo-Saxon name for an epical memory.

Under an open shed on the edge of the field, there were two huge armatures of bamboo that looked like immense cages. They were parts of the body of a god, his calves or thighs, which, fitted and reared, would make a gigantic effigy. This effigy would be burnt as a conclusion to the epic. The cane structures flashed a predictable parallel: Shelley's sonnet on the fallen statue of Ozymandias and his empire, that 'colossal wreck' in its empty desert.

Drummers had lit a fire in the shed and they eased the skins of their tablas nearer the flames to tighten them. The saffron flames, the bright grass, and the hand-woven armatures of the fragmented god who would be burnt were not in any desert where imperial power had finally toppled but were part of a ritual, evergreen season that, like the cane-burning harvest, is annually repeated, the point of such sacrifice being its repetition, the point of the destruction being renewal through fire.

Deities were entering the field. What we generally call 'Indian music' was blaring from the open platformed shed from which the epic would be narrated. Costumed actors were arriving. Princes and gods, I supposed. What an unfortunate confession! 'Gods, I suppose' is the shrug that embodies our African and Asian diasporas. I had often thought of but never seen *Ramleela*, and had never seen this theatre, an open field, with village children as warriors, princes, and gods. I had no idea what the epic story was, who its hero was, what enemies he fought, yet I had recently adapted the *Odyssey* for a theatre in England, presuming that the audience knew the trials of Odysseus, hero of another Asia Minor epic, while nobody in Trinidad knew any more than I did about Rama, Kali, Shiva, Vishnu, apart from the Indians, a phrase I use pervertedly because that is the kind of remark you can still hear in Trinidad: 'apart from the Indians'.

It was as if, on the edge of the Central Plain, there was another plateau, a raft on which the *Ramayana* would be poorly performed in this ocean of cane, but that was my writer's view of things, and it is wrong. I was seeing the *Ramleela* at Felicity as theatre when it was faith.

Multiply that moment of self-conviction when an actor, made-up and costumed, nods to his mirror before stepping on stage in the belief that he is a reality entering an illusion and you would have what I presumed was happening to the actors of this epic. But they were not actors. They had been chosen; or they themselves had chosen their roles in this sacred story that would go on for nine afternoons over a two-hour period till the sun set. They were not amateurs but believers. There was no theatrical term to define them. They did not have to psych themselves up to play their roles. Their acting would probably be as buoyant and as natural as those bamboo arrows crisscrossing the afternoon pasture. They believed in what they were playing, in the sacredness of the text, the validity of India, while I, out of the writer's habit, searched for some sense of elegy, of loss, even of degenerative mimicry in the happy faces of the boy-warriors or the heraldic profiles of the village princes. I was polluting the afternoon with doubt and with the patronage of admiration. I misread the event through a visual echo of History – the cane fields, indenture, the evocation of vanished armies, temples, and trumpeting elephants – when all around me there was quite the opposite: elation, delight in the boys' screams, in the sweets-stalls, in more and more costumed characters appearing; a delight of conviction, not loss. The name Felicity made sense.

Consider the scale of Asia reduced to these fragments: the small white exclamations of minarets or the stone balls of temples in the cane fields, and one can understand the self-mockery and embarrassment of those who see these rites as parodic, even degenerate. These purists look on such ceremonies as grammarians look at a dialect, as cities look on provinces and empires on their colonies. Memory that yearns to join the centre, a limb remembering the body from which it has been severed, like those bamboo thighs of the god. In other words, the way that the Caribbean is still looked at, illegitimate, rootless, mongrelized. 'No people there', to quote Froude, 'in the true sense of the word.' No people. Fragments and echoes of real people, unoriginal and broken.

The performance was like a dialect, a branch of its original language, an abridgement of it, but not a distortion or even a reduction of its epic scale. Here in Trinidad I had discovered that one of the greatest epics of the world was seasonally performed, not with that desperate resignation of preserving a culture, but with an openness of belief that was as steady as the wind bending the cane lances of the Caroni plain. We had to leave before the play began to go through the creeks of the Caroni Swamp, to catch the scarlet ibises coming home at dusk. In a performance as natural as those of the actors of the *Ramleela*, we watched the flocks come in as bright as the scarlet of the boy archers, as the red flags, and cover an islet until it turned into a flowering tree, an anchored immortelle. The sigh of History meant nothing here. These two visions, the *Ramleela* and the arrowing flocks of scarlet ibises, blent into a single gasp of gratitude. Visual surprise is natural in the Caribbean; it comes with the landscape, and faced with its beauty, the sigh of History dissolves.

We make too much of that long groan which underlines the past. I felt privileged to discover the ibises as well as the scarlet archers of Felicity.

The sigh of History rises over ruins, not over landscapes, and in the Antilles there are few ruins to sigh over, apart from the ruins of sugar estates and abandoned forts. Looking around slowly, as a camera would, taking in the low blue hills over Port of Spain, the village road and houses, the warrior-archers, the god-actors and their handlers, and music already on the sound track, I wanted to make a film that would be a long-drawn sigh over Felicity. I was filtering the afternoon with evocations of a lost India, but why 'evocations'? Why not 'celebrations of a real presence'? Why should India be 'lost' when none of these villagers ever really knew it, and why not 'continuing', why not the perpetuation of joy in Felicity and in all the other nouns of the Central Plain: Couva, Chaguanas, Charley Village? Why was I not letting my pleasure open its windows wide? I was enticed like any Trinidadian to the ecstasies of their claim, because ecstasy was the pitch of the sinuous drumming in the loudspeakers. I was entitled to the feast of Husein, to the mirrors and crepe-paper temples of the Muslim epic, to the Chinese Dragon Dance, to the rites of that Sephardic Jewish synagogue that was once on Something Street. I am only one-eighth the writer I might have been had I contained all the fragmented languages of Trinidad.

Break a vase, and the love that reassembles the fragments is stronger than that love which took its symmetry for granted when it was whole. The glue that fits the pieces is the sealing of its original shape. It is such a love that reassembles our African and Asiatic fragments, the cracked heirlooms whose restoration shows its white scars. This gathering of broken pieces is the care and pain of the Antilles, and if the pieces are disparate, ill-fitting, they contain more pain than their original sculpture, those icons and sacred vessels taken for granted in their ancestral places. Antillean art is this restoration of our shattered histories, our shards of vocabulary, our archipelago becoming a synonym for pieces broken off from the original continent.

And this is the exact process of the making of poetry, or what should be called not its 'making' but its remaking, the fragmented memory, the armature that frames the god, even the rite that surrenders it to a final pyre; the god assembled cane by cane, reed by weaving reed, line by plaited line, as the artisans of Felicity would erect his holy echo.

Poetry, which is perfection's sweat but which must seem as fresh as the raindrops on a statue's brow, combines the natural and the marmoreal; it conjugates both tenses simultaneously: the past and the present, if the past is the sculpture and the present the beads of dew or rain on the forehead of the past. There is the buried language and there is the individual vocabulary, and the process of poetry is one of excavation and of self-discovery. Tonally the individual voice is a dialect; it shapes its own accent, its own vocabulary and melody in defiance of an imperial concept of language, the language of Ozymandias, libraries and dictionaries, law courts and critics, and churches, universities, political dogma, the diction of institutions. Poetry is an island that breaks away from the main. The dialects of my archipelago seem as fresh to me as those raindrops on the statue's forehead, not the sweat made from the classic exertion of frowning marble, but the condensations of a refreshing element, rain and salt.

Deprived of their original language, the captured and indentured tribes create their own, accreting and secreting fragments of an old, an epic vocabulary, from Asia and from Africa, but to an ancestral, an ecstatic rhythm in the blood that cannot be subdued by slavery or indenture, while nouns are renamed and the given names of places accepted like Felicity village or Choiseul. The original language dissolves from the exhaustion of distance like fog trying to cross an ocean, but this process of renaming, of finding new metaphors, is the same process that the poet faces every morning of his working day, making his own tools like Crusoe, assembling nouns from necessity, from Felicity, even renaming himself. The stripped man is driven back to that self-astonishing, elemental force, his mind. That is the basis of the Antillean experience, this shipwreck of fragments, these echoes, these shards of a huge tribal vocabulary, these partially remembered customs, and they are not decayed but strong. They survived the Middle Passage and the *Fatel Rozack*, the ship that carried the first indentured Indians from the port of Madras to the cane fields of Felicity, that carried the chained Cromwellian convict and the Sephardic Jew, the Chinese grocer and the Lebanese merchant selling cloth samples on his bicycle.

And here they are, all in a single Caribbean city, Port of Spain, the sum of history, Trollope's 'non-people'. A downtown babel of shop signs and streets, mongrelized, polyglot, a ferment without a history, like heaven. Because that is what such a city is, in the New World, a writer's heaven.

A culture, we all know, is made by its cities.

Another first morning home, impatient for the sunrise – a broken sleep. Darkness at five, and the drapes not worth opening; then, in the sudden light, a cream-walled, brown-roofed police station bordered with short royal palms, in the colonial style, back of it frothing trees and taller palms, a pigeon fluttering into the cover of an cave, a rain-stained block of once-modern apartments, the morning side road into the station without traffic. All part of a surprising peace. This quiet happens with every visit to a city that has deepened itself in me. The flowers and the hills are easy, affection for them predictable; it is the architecture that, for the first morning, disorients. A return from American seductions used to make the traveller feel that something was missing, something was trying to complete itself, like the stained concrete apartments. Pan left along the window and the excrescences rear – a city trying to soar, trying to be brutal, like an American city in silhouette, stamped from the same mould as Columbus or Des Moines. An assertion of power, its decor bland, its air conditioning pitched to the point where its secretarial and executive staff sport competing cardigans; the colder the offices the more important, an imitation of another climate. A longing, even an envy of feeling cold.

In serious cities, in grey, militant winter with its short afternoons, the days seem to pass by in buttoned overcoats, every building appears as a barracks with lights on in its windows, and when snow comes, one has the illusion of living in a Russian novel, in the nineteenth century, because of the literature of winter. So visitors to the Caribbean must feel that they are inhabiting a succession of postcards. Both climates are shaped by what we have read of them. For tourists, the sunshine cannot be serious. Winter adds depth and darkness to life as well as to literature, and in the unending summer of the tropics not even poverty or poetry (in the Antilles poverty is poetry with a V, *une vie*, a condition of life as well as of imagination) seems capable of being profound because the nature around it is so exultant, so resolutely ecstatic, like its music. A culture based on joy is bound to be shallow. Sadly, to sell itself, the Caribbean encourages the delights of mindlessness, of brilliant vacuity, as a place to flee not only winter but that seriousness that comes only out of culture with four seasons. So how can there be a people there, in the true sense of the word?

They know nothing about seasons in which leaves let go of the year, in which spires fade in blizzards and streets whiten, of the erasures of whole cities by fog, of reflection in fireplaces; instead, they inhabit a geography whose rhythm, like their music, is limited to two stresses: hot and wet, sun and rain, light and shadow, day and night, the limitations of an incomplete metre, and are therefore a people incapable of the subtleties of contradiction, of imaginative complexity. So be it. We cannot change contempt.

Ours are not cities in the accepted sense, but no one wants them to be. They dictate their own proportions, their own definitions in particular places and in a prose equal to that of their detractors, so that now it is not just St James but the streets and yards that Naipaul commemorates, its lanes as short and brilliant as his sentences; not just the noise and jostle of Tunapuna but the origins of C. L. R. James's *Beyond the Boundary*, not just Felicity village on the Caroni plain, but Selvon Country, and that is the way it goes up the islands now: the old Dominica of Jean Rhys still very much the way she wrote of it; and the Martinique of the early Cesaire; Perse's Guadeloupe, even without the pith helmets and the mules; and what delight and privilege there was in watching a literature – one literature in several imperial languages, French, English, Spanish – bud and open island after island in the early morning of a culture, not timid, not derivative, any more than the hard white petals of the frangipani are derivative and timid. This is not a belligerent boast but a simple celebration of inevitability: that this flowering had to come.

On a heat-stoned afternoon in Port of Spain, some alley white with glare, with love vine spilling over a fence, palms and a hazed mountain appear around a corner to the evocation of Vaughan or Herbert's 'that shady city of palm-trees', or to the memory of a Hammond organ from a wooden chapel in Castries, where the congregation sang 'Jerusalem, the Golden'. It is hard for me to see such emptiness as desolation. It is that patience that is the width of Antillean life, and the secret is not to ask the wrong thing of it, not to demand of it an ambition it has no interest in. The traveller reads this as lethargy, as torpor.

Here there are not enough books, one says, no theatres, no museums, simply not enough to do. Yet, deprived of books, a man must fall back on thought, and out of thought, if he can learn to order it, will come the urge to record, and in extremity, if he has no means of recording, recitation, the ordering of memory which leads to metre, to commemoration. There can be virtues in deprivation, and certainly one virtue is salvation from a cascade of high mediocrity, since books are now not so much created as remade. Cities create a culture, and all we have are these magnified market towns, so what are the proportions of the ideal Caribbean city? A surrounding, accessible countryside with leafy suburbs, and if the city is lucky, behind it, spacious plains. Behind it, fine mountains; before it, an indigo sea. Spires would pin its centre and around them would be leafy, shadowy parks. Pigeons would cross its sky in alphabetic patterns, carrying with them memories of a belief in augury, and at the heart of the city there would be horses, yes, horses, those animals last seen at the end of the nineteenth century drawing broughams and carriages with top-hatted citizens, horses that live in the present tense without elegiac echoes from their hooves, emerging from paddocks at the Queen's Park Savannah at sunrise, when mist is unthreading from the cool mountains above the roofs, and at the centre of the city seasonally there would be races, so that citizens could roar at the speed and grace of these nineteenth-century animals. Its docks, not obscured by smoke or deafened by too much machinery, and above all, it would be so racially various that the cultures of the world – the Asiatic, the Mediterranean, the European, the African – would be represented in it, its humane variety more exciting than Joyce's Dublin. Its citizens would intermarry as they chose, from instinct, not tradition, until their children find it increasingly futile to trace their genealogy. It would not have too many avenues difficult or dangerous for pedestrians, its mercantile area would be a cacophony of accents, fragments of the old language that would be silenced immediately at five o'clock, its docks resolutely vacant on Sundays.

This is Port of Spain to me, a city ideal in its commercial and human proportions, where a citizen is a walker and not a pedestrian, and this is how Athens may have been before it became a cultural echo.

The finest silhouettes of Port of Spain are idealizations of the craftsman's handiwork, not of concrete and glass, but of baroque woodwork, each fantasy looking more like an involved drawing of itself than the actual building. Behind the city is the Caroni plain, with its villages, Indian prayer flags, and fruit vendors' stalls along the highway over which ibises come like floating flags. Photogenic poverty! Postcard sadnesses! I am not re-creating Eden; I mean, by 'the Antilles', the reality of light, of work, of survival. I mean a house on the side of a country road, I mean the Caribbean Sea, whose smell is the smell of refreshing possibility as well as survival. Survival is the triumph of stubbornness, and spiritual stubbornness, a sublime stupidity, is what makes the occupation of poetry endure, when there are so many things that should make it futile. Those things added together can go under one collective noun: 'the world'.

This is the visible poetry of the Antilles, then. Survival.

If you wish to understand that consoling pity with which the islands were regarded, look at the tinted engravings of Antillean forests, with their proper palm trees, ferns, and waterfalls. They have a civilizing decency, like Botanical Gardens, as if the sky were a glass ceiling under which a colonized vegetation is arranged for quiet walks and carriage rides. Those views are incised with a pathos that guides the engraver's tool and the topographer's pencil, and it is this pathos which, tenderly ironic, gave villages names like Felicity. A century looked at a landscape furious with vegetation in the wrong light and with the wrong eye. It is such pictures that are saddening rather than the tropics itself. These delicate engravings of sugar mills and harbours, of native women in costume, are seen as a part of History, that History which looked over the shoulder of the engraver and, later, the photographer. History can alter the eye and the moving hand to conform a view of itself; it can rename places for the nostalgia in an echo; it can temper the glare of tropical light to elegiac monotony in prose, the tone of judgement in Conrad, in the travel journals of Trollope.

These travellers carried with them the infection of their own malaise, and their prose reduced even the landscape to melancholia and self-contempt. Every endeavour is belittled as imitation, from architecture to music. There was this conviction in Froude that since History is based on achievement, and since the history of the Antilles was so genetically corrupt, so depressing in its cycles of massacres, slavery, and indenture, a culture was inconceivable and nothing could ever be created in those ramshackle ports, those monotonously feudal sugar estates. Not only the light and salt of Antillean mountains defied this, but the demotic vigour and variety of their inhabitants. Stand close to a waterfall and you will stop hearing its roar. To be still in the nineteenth century, like horses, as Brodsky has written, may not be such a bad deal, and much of our life in the Antilles still seems to be in the rhythm of the last century, like the West Indian novel.

By writers even as refreshing as Graham Greene, the Caribbean is looked at with elegiac pathos, a prolonged sadness to which Levi-Strauss has supplied an epigraph: *Tristes Tropiques*. Their *tristesse* derives from an attitude to the Caribbean dusk, to rain, to uncontrollable vegetation, to the provincial ambition of Caribbean cities where brutal replicas of modern architecture dwarf the small houses and streets. The mood is understandable, the melancholy as contagious as the fever of a sunset, like the gold fronds of diseased coconut palms, but there is something alien and ultimately wrong in the way such a sadness, even a morbidity, is described by English, French, or some of our exiled writers. It relates to a misunderstanding of the light and the people on whom the light falls.

These writers describe the ambitions of our unfinished cities, their unrealized, homiletic conclusion, but the Caribbean city may conclude just at that point where it is satisfied with its own scale, just as Caribbean culture is not evolving but already shaped. Its proportions are not to be measured by the traveller or the exile, but by its own citizenry and architecture. To be told you are not yet a city or a culture requires this response. I am not your city or your culture. There might be less of *Tristes Tropiques* after that.

Here, on the raft of this dais, there is the sound of the applauding surf: our landscape, our history recognized, 'at last'. *At Last* is one of the first Caribbean books. It was written by the Victorian traveller Charles Kingsley. It is one of the early books to admit the Antillean landscape and its figures into English literature. I have never read it but gather that its tone is benign. The Antillean archipelago was there to be written about, not to write itself, by Trollope, by Patrick Leigh-Fermor, in the very tone in which I almost wrote about the village spectacle at Felicity, as a compassionate and beguiled outsider, distancing myself from Felicity village even while I was enjoying it. What is hidden cannot be loved. The traveller cannot love, since love is stasis and travel is motion. If he returns to what he loved in a landscape and stays there, he is no longer a traveller but in stasis and concentration, the lover of that particular part of earth, a native. So many people say they 'love the Caribbean', meaning that someday they plan to return for a visit but could never live there, the usual benign insult of the traveller, the tourist. These travellers, at their kindest, were devoted to the same patronage, the islands passing in profile, their vegetal luxury, their backwardness and poverty. Victorian prose dignified them. They passed by in beautiful profiles and were forgotten, like a vacation.

Alexis Saint-Leger Leger, whose writer's name is Saint-John Perse, was the first Antillean to win this prize for poetry. He was born in

Guadeloupe and wrote in French, but before him, there was nothing as fresh and clear in feeling as those poems of his childhood, that of a privileged white child on an Antillean plantation, *Pour Fêter une Enfance*, *Éloges*, and later *Images a Crusoe*. At last, the first breeze on the page, salt-edged and self-renewing as the trade winds, the sound of pages and palm trees turning as 'the odour of coffee ascends the stairs'.

Caribbean genius is condemned to contradict itself. To celebrate Perse, we might be told, is to celebrate the old plantation system, to celebrate the beque or plantation rider, verandahs and mulatto servants, a white French language in a white pith helmet, to celebrate a rhetoric of patronage and hauteur; and even if Perse denied his origins, great writers often have this folly of trying to smother their source, we cannot deny him any more than we can the African Aime Cesaire. This is not accommodation, this is the ironic republic that is poetry, since, when I see cabbage palms moving their fronds at sunrise, I think they are reciting Perse.

The fragrant and privileged poetry that Perse composed to celebrate his white childhood and the recorded Indian music behind the brown young archers of Felicity, with the same cabbage palms against the same Antillean sky, pierce me equally. I feel the same poignancy of pride in the poems as in the faces. Why, given the history of the Antilles, should this be remarkable? The history of the world, by which of course we mean Europe, is a record of intertribal lacerations, of ethnic cleansings. At last, islands not written about but writing themselves! The palms and the Muslim minarets are Antillean exclamations. At last! the royal palms of Guadeloupe recite *Éloges* by heart.

Later, in *Anabase*, Perse assembled fragments of an imaginary epic, with the clicking teeth of frontier gates, barren wadis with the froth of poisonous lakes, horsemen burnoosed in sandstorms, the opposite of cool Caribbean mornings, yet not necessarily a contrast any more than some young brown archer at Felicity, hearing the sacred text blared across the flagged field, with its battles and elephants and monkey-gods, in a contrast to the white child in Guadeloupe assembling fragments of his own epic from the lances of the cane fields, the estate carts and oxens, and the calligraphy of bamboo leaves from the ancient languages, Hindi, Chinese, and Arabic, on the Antillean sky. From the *Ramayana* to Anabasis, from Guadeloupe to Trinidad, all that archaeology of fragments lying around, from the broken African kingdoms, from the crevasses of Canton, from Syria and Lebanon, vibrating not under the earth but in our raucous, demotic streets.

A boy with weak eyes skims a flat stone across the flat water of an Aegean inlet, and that ordinary action with the scything elbow contains the skipping lines of the *Iliad* and the *Odyssey*, and another child aims a bamboo arrow at a village festival, another hears the rustling march of cabbage palms in a Caribbean sunrise, and from that sound, with its fragments of tribal myth, the compact expedition of Perse's epic is launched, centuries and archipelagoes apart. For every poet it is always morning in the world. History a forgotten, insomniac night; History and elemental awe are always our early beginning, because the fate of poetry is to fall in love with the world, in spite of History.

There is a force of exultation, a celebration of luck, when a writer finds himself a witness to the early morning of a culture that is defining itself, branch by branch, leaf by leaf, in that self-defining dawn, which is why, especially at the edge of the sea, it is good to make a ritual of the sunrise. Then the noun, the 'Antilles' ripples like brightening water, and the sounds of leaves, palm fronds, and birds are the sounds of a fresh dialect, the native tongue. The personal vocabulary, the individual melody whose metre is one's biography, joins in that sound, with any luck, and the body moves like a walking, a waking island.

This is the benediction that is celebrated, a fresh language and a fresh people, and this is the frightening duty owed.

I stand here in their name, if not their image – but also in the name of the dialect they exchange like the leaves of the trees whose names are suppler, greener, more morning-stirred than English – *laurier canelles*, *bois-flot*, *bois-canot* – or the valleys the trees mention – Fond St Jacques, Matoonya, Forestier, Roseau, Mahaut – or the empty beaches – L'Anse Ivrogne, Case en Bas, Paradis – all songs and histories in themselves, pronounced not in French – but in patois.

One rose hearing two languages, one of the trees, one of school children reciting in English:

> I am monarch of all I survey,
> My right there is none to dispute;
> From the centre all round to the sea
> I am lord of the fowl and the brute.

ANTILLES 221

Oh, solitude! where are the charms
That sages have seen in thy face?
Better dwell in the midst of alarms,
Than reign in this horrible place . . .

While in the country to the same metre, but to organic instruments,
handmade violin, *chac-chac*, and goatskin drum, a girl named Sen-
senne singing:

> Si mwen di 'ous ca fait mwen la peine
> 'Ous kai dire ca vrai.
> (If I told you that caused me pain
> You'll say, 'It's true.')
> Si mwen di 'ous ca penetrait mwen
> 'Ous peut dire ca vrai
> (If I told you you pierced my heart
> You'd say, 'It's true.')
> Ces mamailles actuellement
> Pas ka faire l'amour z'autres pour un rien.
> (Children nowadays
> Don't make love for nothing.)

It is not that History is obliterated by this sunrise. It is there in
Antillean geography, in the vegetation itself. The sea sighs with the
drowned from the Middle Passage, the butchery of its aborigines,
Carib and Aruac and Taino, bleeds in the scarlet of the *immortelle*,
and even the actions of surf on sand cannot erase the African memory,
or the lances of cane as a green prison where indentured Asians, the
ancestors of Felicity, are still serving time.

That is what I have read around me from boyhood, from the
beginnings of poetry, the grace of effort. In the hard mahogany of
woodcutters: faces, resinous men, charcoal burners; in a man with a
cutlass cradled across his forearm, who stands on the verge with the
usual anonymous khaki dog; in the extra clothes he put on this
morning, when it was cold when he rose in the thinning dark to go
and make his garden in the heights – the heights, the garden, being
miles away from his house, but that is where he has his land – not
to mention the fishermen, the footmen on trucks, groaning up
mornes, all fragments of Africa originally but shaped and hardened
and rooted now in the island's life, illiterate in the way leaves are

illiterate; they do not read, they are there to be read, and if they are properly read, they create their own literature.

But in our tourist brochures the Caribbean is a blue pool into which the republic dangles the extended foot of Florida as inflated rubber islands bob and drinks with umbrellas float towards her on a raft. This is how the islands from the shame of necessity sell themselves; this is the seasonal erosion of their identity, that high-pitched repetition of the same images of service that cannot distinguish one island from the other, with a future of polluted marinas, land deals negotiated by ministers, and all of this conducted to the music of Happy Hour and the rictus of a smile. What is the earthly paradise for our visitors? Two weeks without rain and a mahogany tan, and, at sunset, local troubadours in straw hats and floral shirts beating 'Yellow Bird' and 'Banana Boat Song' to death. There is a territory wider than this – wider than the limits made by the map of an island – which is the illimitable sea and what it remembers.

All of the Antilles, every island, is an effort of memory; every mind, every racial biography culminating in amnesia and fog. Pieces of sunlight through the fog and sudden rainbows, *arcs-en-ciel*. That is the effort, the labour of the Antillean imagination, rebuilding its gods from bamboo frames, phrase by phrase.

Decimation from the Aruac downwards is the blasted root of Antillean history, and the benign blight that is tourism can infect all of those island nations, not gradually, but with imperceptible speed, until each rock is whitened by the guano of white-winged hotels, the arc and descent of progress.

Before it is all gone, before only a few valleys are left, pockets of an older life, before development turns every artist into an anthropologist or folklorist, there are still cherishable places, little valleys that do not echo with ideas, a simplicity of rebeginnings, not yet corrupted by the dangers of change. Not nostalgic sites but occluded sanctities as common and simple as their sunlight. Places as threatened by this prose as a headland is by the bulldozer or a sea almond grove by the surveyor's string, or from blight, the mountain laurel.

One last epiphany: A basic stone church in a thick valley outside Soufrière, the hills almost shoving the houses around into a brown river, a sunlight that looks oily on the leaves, a backward place, unimportant, and one now being corrupted into significance by this prose. The idea is not to hallow or invest the place with anything, not even memory. African children in Sunday frocks come down the ordinary concrete steps into the church, banana leaves hang and glisten, a truck is parked in a yard, and old women totter towards the entrance. Here is where a real fresco should be painted, one without importance, but one with real faith, mapless, Historyless.

How quickly it could all disappear! And how it is beginning to drive us further into where we hope are impenetrable places, green secrets at the end of bad roads, headlands where the next view is not of a hotel but of some long beach without a figure and the hanging question of some fisherman's smoke at its far end. The Caribbean is not an idyll, not to its natives. They draw their working strength from it organically, like trees, like the sea almond or the spice laurel of the heights. Its peasantry and its fishermen are not there to be loved or even photographed; they are trees who sweat, and whose bark is filmed with salt, but every day on some island, rootless trees in suits are signing favourable tax breaks with entrepreneurs, poisoning the sea almond and the spice laurel of the mountains to their roots. A morning could come in which governments might ask what happened not merely to the forests and the bays but to a whole people.

They are here again, they recur, the faces, corruptible angels, smooth black skins and white eyes huge with an alarming joy, like those of the Asian children of Felicity at *Ramleela*; two different religions, two different continents, both filling the heart with the pain that is joy.

But what is joy without fear? The fear of selfishness that, here on this podium with the world paying attention not to them but to me, I should like to keep these simple joys inviolate, not because they are innocent, but because they are true. They are as true as when, in the grace of this gift, Perse heard the fragments of his own epic of Asia Minor in the rustling of cabbage palms, that inner Asia of the soul through which imagination wanders, if there is such a thing as imagination as opposed to the collective memory of our entire race, as true as the delight of that warrior-child who flew a bamboo arrow over the flags in the field at Felicity; and now as grateful a joy and a blessed fear as when a boy opened an exercise book and, within the discipline of its margins, framed stanzas that might contain the light of the hills on an island blest by obscurity, cherishing our insignificance.

BRAZIL

EUCLIDES DA CUNHA (1866–1909)

'The Moreira Cesar Expedition'

A View of Canudos

Here at last was that enormous weed patch which previous
expeditions had not succeeded in reaching. It came into view all at
once, lying there in a broadened depression of the rolling plain. At
first glimpse, before his eye had become accustomed to this pile of
huts and labyrinth of narrow alleys, some of which came out on the
wide square where the churches stood, the observer had the precise
impression of having unexpectedly stumbled upon a large city.
Forming a huge, deepened moat to the left, at the foot of the highest
hills, the Vasa-Barris half-circled the village and then took a sharp
turn directly to the east, as the first waters of the flood season rolled
slowly along. The compact cluster of huts about the square gradually
spread out, sprawling over the hills to the east and north, with the
last of the outlying houses taking on the appearance of scattered
sentry boxes; and, meanwhile, there was not a single white wall or
rubble-strewn roof to break the monotony of this monstrous collection of five thousand shacks dropped down in a furrow of the earth.
The two churches stood out sharply. The new one, on the observer's
left, was still unfinished, and its main walls, high and thick, could
be seen covered with scaffoldings, with wooden joists, beams, and
planks, while from this maze there emerged the rigid outlines of the
cranes with their swaying pulleys. This structure towered above
the others in the village and overlooked the broad expanse of plains;
it was large, rectangular, solidly built, its walls consisting of great
stone blocks laid one upon another with perfect skill, which gave it
the exact appearance of a formidable bastion. More humble in aspect,

built like the common run of back-country chapels, the old church stood facing it. Still farther to the right, roughly circular in shape, dotted with little rudely fashioned crosses, but without a single flower bed, a single bloom, a single shrub, was the cemetery of levelled graves, a mournful *tybicuera*. Directly opposite the cemetery, on the other side of the river, was a small plot whose level surface was in contrast to the barren rolling hills around it; a few scattered trees stood here, a few rows of bright-hued palmatorias, and half a dozen quixabeira stalks with their verdant branches, all of which gave the place the aspect of a rustic garden. A spur of Mount Favella comes down here, jutting out into the river, where it ends abruptly in a cliff. These last foothills bear the appropriate name of 'Bald Pates', owing to the denudation of their slopes. Halfway down the rounded hillsides one could see the ruins of a dwelling, the 'Old Ranch House', and overhanging it a steep terrace, 'Mount Mario'. And there on the top of the mountain were the troops.

Arrival of the Troops

The vanguard of the Seventh was the first detachment to arrive, along with the artillery; they were engaged in repulsing a violent attack on the right while the rest of the infantry climbed the last slopes. They paid little attention to the settlement itself, meanwhile. The cannon were aligned in battle formation, as the first platoons came up, their ranks in confusion, the men panting; and a cannonading then began, with all the guns firing at once, without co-ordination. There was no missing a mark as big as this one. The effects of the initial rounds were visible at various points: huts were shattered, ripped apart and buried in debris by cannon balls exploding in their midst; the splintered roofs of clay and wood were sent hurtling through their air; the adobe walls were pulverized; the first fires were started.

The bombarded village was now enveloped in a dense cloud of dust and smoke which hid it completely from view. The rest of the troops could not be seen. The solemn thunder of the artillery rent the air, awakening a far, deep resonance throughout the breadth of the desert lands, as the deafening echoes came back from the mountainsides.

Disconcerting Incident

But, as the minutes passed, there were to be heard, sounding clear above the roar of the cannons, the sudden silvery notes of a bell. It was the bell of the old church down below, summoning the faithful to battle.

The battle had not yet started. Aside from a light flank attack made by a few guerrillas upon the artillery, the *sertanejos* so far had put up no resistance. The troops spread out over the sloping summit without their manoeuvres being disturbed by a single shot; and when the shooting did begin, it was a sustained but aimless running fire. Eight hundred rifles blazing, eight hundred rifles aimed in a line down the drop of the hill.

As the smoke cleared away now and again, the settlement could be glimpsed. It was a beehive in commotion: innumerable groups here and there, weaving in and out of the square, scattering down the paths along the riverbank, making for the church, dashing down the alleyways with weapons in their hands, climbing up onto the roofs.

A few, at the far end of the village, appeared to be in flight; they could be seen wandering along the edge of the caatingas and disappearing behind the hills. Others displayed an incredible non-chalance by crossing the square at a leisurely pace, oblivious to the tumult and the stubborn spatter of bullets from the mountain.

One whole company of the Seventh at this moment trained its fire for several minutes upon a *jagunço* who was coming along the Uauá Road, but the *sertanejo* did not so much as quicken his step; indeed, he even came to a dead stop at times. His impassive face could be seen in the distance as he raised his head to gaze at the troops for a few seconds and then went tranquilly on his way. This was an irritating challenge. In surprise, the soldiers nervously concentrated their fire upon this exceptional being, who had now become the bull's-eye for an army. At one moment he seated himself beside the road and appeared to be striking a light for his pipe. The soldiers laughed. Then he got to his feet and, still at the same leisurely pace, was gradually lost from sight among the outlying houses.

From the village not a shot was fired. The commotion in the square had died down. The last of the stragglers were now coming in, among them a number of women with children in their arms or dragging them by the hand, as they went on in the direction of the arbour, seeking the barrier afforded by the big walls of the new church.

The Order of the Battle

The bell had finally stopped ringing. The troops now began the descent along the gentler slopes, hundreds of bayonets gleaming in the sun. As he surveyed them, the commander-in-chief of the expedition remarked to the commanding officer of one of the companies in his own regiment, beside whom he happened to be standing: 'We're going to take the town without firing another shot – at the point of the bayonet!'

It was one o'clock in the afternoon. When the descent had been made, a part of the infantry took up its position in the vale where the quixabeiras stood; on its right was the Seventh, lined up along the course of the Vasa-Barris; and, on its left, the Ninth and Sixteenth, badly placed on unsuitable ground. The artillery was in the centre, upon the last spur of the hills, in an advanced position directly above the river, facing the new church and on a level with its cornices; it thus became the axis of a pincers designed to close in and grip the flanks of the settlement. This was the most rudimentary of battle lines, a simple parallel formation, adapted to those rare cases of battle in the open country where a superiority in the matter of numbers and of bravery renders more complex manoeuvres unnecessary and permits of a simultaneous and equal action on the part of all the fighting units upon a uniform terrain.

Character of the Terrain; Critical Observations

Such a line of assault was inconceivable here. Centring at the eminence where the cannons were, the various parts of the line were confronted with absolutely different topographical conditions. On the right was a small level area that rendered an attack easy, for the reason that the river at this point had an even bed and its banks were low. On the left the land was more rugged, falling away in rolling hillocks and, moreover, was separated from the village by a deep trench. The most hasty observation would accordingly indicate

that, while conditions on the extreme left were wholly unfavourable
for combatants running forward to an assault, they were, on the
other hand, a tactical asset of the first order if a reserve force
were to be promptly stationed there, either as a slight diversionary
movement, or in order that it might opportunely intervene,
depending upon how the engagement developed. Thus it may be
seen that the general configuration of the terrain in itself dictated an
oblique line, either a simple one, or reinforced on one of its wings,
and, in place of a simultaneous attack, a partial attack on the right,
firmly supported by the artillery, the effect of whose fire, at a range
of a little more than a hundred yards from the enemy, would be
terrific.

Furthermore, such an arrangement would not permit of any
surprises, and in case the enemy should display unexpected powers
of resistance, the reserve troops, being outside the mêlée, would be
able to move about more freely in accordance with the contingencies
that might arise and would be able to engage in decisive manoeuvres,
with definite objectives. Colonel Moreira Cesar, however, disdained
to take these imperative considerations into account and insisted
upon lining up all his forces at once. He appeared to be relying not
so much upon the bravery of his men and the loyalty and competence
of their officers as upon a doubtful supposition: the fright and
terror of the fleeing *sertanejos* as they found themselves suddenly
hemmed in by hundreds of bayonets. This supposition was clearly
an unjustifiable one, revealing an ignorance of the rudimentary prin-
ciples of his profession and a forgetfulness of what had happened to
previous expeditions; and he now topped it off by planning an assault
under the most disastrous of circumstances.

The fact of the matter is that, with the battalions attacking at
once from two sides and bearing down upon a single objective,
within a short space of time they would be facing each other and
exchanging bullets intended for the *jagunço*. While the artillery at
the beginning might bombard the churches and the centre of the
town, the scope of its action would gradually be limited as the troops
advanced, until finally it would be obliged to fall silent just as the
battle reached its decisive phase, from fear of firing upon the troops
themselves as they mingled in hand-to-hand combat with the enemy
in that labyrinth of huts.

It did not require the eagle eye of any master-strategist to foresee
all this; it was revealed plainly enough in the first minutes of action.

'Weed-trap Citadel'

The battle began heroically, with all the troops moving into action at once and with all the bugles blowing. The church bell was once more ringing, and an intense rifle fire had broken out from the walls and roofs of the dwellings nearest to the river, while the blunderbusses of the guerrillas massed within the new church produced the effect of a single explosion. With the advantage of a favourable terrain, the Seventh Battalion marched forward on the double-quick, amid a hail of lead and pebbles, down to the river; and it was not long before, having climbed the opposite bank, the first of the soldiers were to be seen at the entrance to the *praça*; they were in small groups, without anything whatsoever to suggest a battle formation. Some of them fell at the river crossing, or tumbled into the stream to be swept away by the current, which was streaked with blood; but the majority continued to advance under heavy fire from the front and sides. On the extreme left, one wing of the Ninth, having overcome the obstacles in its path, had taken up a position at the rear of the new church, while the Sixteenth and the right wing of the Seventh attacked in the centre. A pitched battle was now raging around the column which was advancing in so rash a manner; and from then on, there was not the simplest military movement or joint manoeuvre such as might have revealed the presence of a commander.

The battle was now breaking up into smaller skirmishes which were at once futile and dangerous, with much fine bravery ingloriously thrown away. This was inevitable. Canudos, less than a couple of yards from the square, became a hopeless maze of alleys, winding and crossing in all directions. With its mud-built huts, the town may have given the impression of fragility, but this was an illusion; it was in reality more formidable than a polygonal citadel or one protected by strong armoured walls. Lying wide open to attackers, who might destroy it with their rifle butts, who might with a blow knock down the clay walls and roofs or send them flying in all directions, it yet possessed the lack of consistency and the treacherous flexibility of a huge net. It was easy to attack it, overcome it, conquer it, knock it down, sending it hurtling – the difficult thing was to leave it. A complement to the dangerous tactics of the *sertanejo*, it was formidable for the very reason that it offered no resistance. There was not so much as a hard-surface tile to break the percussion of the grenades, which fell without exploding, piercing dozens of roofs at once. There was nothing to cause the smallest band of attackers to waver, from whatever side they might come, once they had crossed the river. Canudos invited attacks; it exerted an irresistible attraction for the enemy who would bombard it; but when the invaders, drunken with a feeling of victory, began separating and scattering out down the winding lanes, it then had a means of defence that was at once amazing and tremendously effective.

In the sombre story of cities taken by storm, this humble village must stand out as an extraordinary and a tragic instance. Intact, it was very weak indeed; reduced to a rubbish heap, it was redoubtable. Yielding in order to conquer, it suddenly appeared before the victor's astonished gaze as an inexpugnable pile of ruins. For while an army with its iron grip might shake it, crush it, rend it asunder, leaving it a shapeless mass of mud walls and wooden stakes, that same army would of a sudden find itself with its hands tied, trapped between the tottering partitions of timber and liana stalks, like a clumsy puma powerfully but vainly struggling to free itself from the meshes of a well-made snare. The *jagunços* were experienced hunters, and this it was, perhaps, which led them to create this 'weed-trap citadel'.

Colonel Moreira Cesar's troops were now engaged in springing that trap upon themselves.

Skirmishes

At first, after they had crossed the river in spite of a few losses, the attack appeared easy enough. One detachment, led by valorous subalterns, boldly assaulted the new church, but without any compensating effect, and with the further loss of two officers and several men. Others, making a detour about this nucleus of resistance, fell upon the outlying houses along the river. They took them and set fire to them, as the inhabitants fled for shelter elsewhere. The latter were pursued as they fled by the soldiers; and it was in the course of this tumultuous pursuit that the one very grave peril of this monstrous undertaking became apparent: the platoons began to break up. The men now dashed down the narrow lanes, two abreast, in great confusion. There were hundreds of corners to be turned, one after another, from house to house, and the soldiers rounded them in disorderly fashion, some of them without making use of their weapons, while others fired at random, straight ahead. In this manner the entire outfit gradually became split up into small wandering detachments, and these in their turn broke up into bewildered groups with numbers diminishing all the while as the forces became more and more scattered, until finally they were reduced to isolated combatants here and there.

From a distance the spectacle was a weird one, with whole battalions being suddenly swallowed up among the huts, as in some dark cave, while over the clay roofs there hovered a dense cloud of smoke from the first of the conflagrations. All in all, the attack was anything but military in character. It was no longer a battle but a series of skirmishes at the corners of the lanes and in the doorways of the houses.

Here, however, the attack was a fierce one, for there were no obstacles in the way. A blow from a rifle butt would effect an entrance through doors or walls, shattering them to bits and opening a free passage from any side. Many of the houses were empty. In others, the intruders would unexpectedly find a musket barrel against their chests, or else they would drop, riddled with bullets at close range fired from chinks in the wall. Their nearest comrades would then run to their assistance, and there would be a brutal hand-to-hand struggle, until the soldiers who outnumbered the inmates had forced their way through the narrow doorway of the hut. On the inside, crouching in a dark corner, a lone remaining inmate would fire his last shot at them and flee. Or it might be that he would stand his ground and stubbornly defend his humble dwelling, fighting terribly – and alone – to avenge himself on the victorious ruffians, boldly having recourse to any weapons at hand, repelling them with knife and bullet, slashing at them with scythe or cattle prong, hurling the wretched household furniture at their heads, or, weak and gasping for breath, rushing upon them in an effort to strangle the first on whom he could lay his brawny arms. The womenfolk, meanwhile, would burst into sobs and cower in the corner, until at last the bold warrior lay on the ground, pierced with a bayonet, clubbed by gunstocks, trampled under the soldiers' bootheels. Scenes such as these were many.

Plunder Before Victory

Almost always, after capturing a house, the famished soldier was unable to resist the longing he felt to have some breakfast – at last – in Canudos. Suspended from the ceiling were the food containers, and these he would search. In them he would find sun-dried meats, clay cups filled with passoca (the *sertanejo*'s wartime flour), and bags brimming with the savoury fruit of the urucuri. In a corner would be pouches with the moisture standing on them, swollen with water crystalline and fresh. The temptation was too much for him. Rashly, he would fall to for a minute's repast, topping it off with a large drink of water. Sometimes, however, he had a dessert of a cruel and bitter-sort – a volley of lead.

The *jagunços*, coming in the door, would fall upon him, and the struggle would be repeated with the roles reversed this time, until the imprudent warrior lay on the ground, slashed with a knife, clubbed, trampled by the *sertanejo*'s coarse sandals.

Disquieting Situation

Stationed in front of his headquarters on the right bank of the river, the commander-in-chief of the expedition was observing the attack, without quite being able to come to a decision regarding it. All he could make out was his men disappearing from sight among the thousand and one holes and hiding-places of Canudos, followed by a great uproar in which curses and shrill cries mingled with the sound of rifle fire. All that he could see was small groups, detachments of soldiers without any formation and small bands of *jagunços* suddenly coming into view now and then in the open space of the square, only to disappear once more amid the smoke, in a confused hand-to-hand struggle.

That was all, but it was enough to alarm him; the situation was now a disquieting one. There was nothing to indicate that the *sertanejos* were giving up the struggle. The sharpshooters at the new church were standing their ground, and were able with practical impunity to fire in all directions; for the artillery had finally ceased, from fear of striking some of the soldiers with a stray ball. And now, above all the din of battle, the bell of the old church was steadily ringing out once more. Only about half the village was involved in the fray; the other half, on the right, where the Geremoabo Highway came in, was unaffected by it. Less compactly built, it was at the same time less open to assault. Spread out over a large elevated plain, it could be defended on a line of fire level with the enemy, obliging the latter to the dangerous expedient of trying to take it by storm. Consequently, after the other part of the village had been stormed and taken, it still remained intact, and this, perhaps, meant that an even greater amount of effort must be expended here.

The truth is, while there were not the winding lanes to contend with, as down below, these scattered houses nonetheless, by the nature of their distribution which was vaguely reminiscent of a chessboard, afforded an extraordinarily good opportunity for cross-fire, so that a single marksman might command all four points of the compass without leaving his own small square. When one took this portion of the town into consideration, the full gravity of the situation became apparent. Even assuming that they had met with success in the centre of the village, the victorious but exhausted troops would have to engage in a futile attack on that slope, which was separated from the *praça* by a deep gully. Colonel Moreira Cesar's eye took this in at a glance. Accordingly, when the rear guard consisting of the police detachment and the squadron of cavalry came up, he ordered the police to proceed to the extreme right and attack this unscathed portion of the settlement as a complement to the action which was taking place on the left. The cavalry, meanwhile, was to attack in the centre, in the vicinity of the churches.

A cavalry charge in Canudos! This, surely, was an eccentric procedure. The cavalry is the classic arm of the service for use on open plains; its strength lies in the shock of a charge, when the mounted force comes in suddenly after a spirited attack by the infantry. Here, however, its movements were restricted by the walls of the huts and it had to charge, one man at a time, down those narrow corridors.

The cavalry – their winded mounts swaying on their unsteady legs – set off at a half-gallop down to the river's edge, where bullets were spattering in the water. That was as far as they could go, for their frightened steeds balked there. By digging in their spurs and lashing the animals with the flat of their swords, the cavalryman barely succeeded in making it to the middle of the stream, where, rearing and bounding, taking the bit in their teeth and sprawling their riders from the saddle, the horses made a wild rush for the bank from which they had started. The police for their part, after crossing the river in a downstream direction, in water up to their knees, came to a halt when they beheld the deep and slippery bed of the gully which at this point runs from north to south, separating from the rest of the town the 'suburb' which they were supposed to attack. The complementary movement was thus frustrated at the very start; and it was then that the commander-in-chief of the expedition left the place where he had been stationed, halfway up the 'Bald Pates' slope, between the artillery and the plain where the quixabeiras stood.

'I'm going to put a little mettle into those fellows,' he said.

Moreira Cesar hors de combat

He started off but was no more than halfway there when, letting go the reins, he lurched forward over the saddlebow. A bullet had struck him in the abdomen. His staff now gathered about him.

'It is nothing,' he said, 'a slight wound,' endeavouring to allay the fears of his devoted comrades. He was, as a matter of fact, mortally wounded.

He did not descend from his horse but, supported by Lieutenant Avila, returned to the place where he had been stationed, when another bullet struck him. He was *hors de combat* now, and Colonel Tamarindo, who was at once notified of the disastrous event, was the one who should have replaced him. The latter, however, was so preoccupied with saving his own battalion, on the other bank of the river, that he could not think of taking over the command. A simple, good-natured, jovial fellow, going on sixty and looking forward to retirement and a peaceful old age, he was by nature averse to showy exploits. What was more, he had been assigned to the expedition against his will; and, even had he possessed the ability to deal with the present crisis, there was no way of remedying matters.

The Troops Fall Back

Already, however, before night came, the troops had begun falling back. On the left bank of the river scattered groups, the first of the fleeing detachments, could now be seen running about in confusion, and they were soon joined by others; breaking ranks entirely, dashing out from the corners of the churches and from behind the huts along the riverbank, officers and men together, filthy-looking, singed, their uniforms ripped to pieces, took to their heels in whatever direction seemed most favourable depending upon the rifle fire of the enemy, a crazed, shouting, terror-stricken, staggering, fleeing mob.

Beginning on the left wing, this impulse spread to the far right. Compelled to retreat to its original positions, the entire battle line, raked by enemy fire, fell back in a writhing mass to the river's edge down below. Without anyone to give the word of command, it was every man for himself. As they came to the river, a few small groups would split off, still, to set fire to the nearest houses or to engage in brief skirmishes, while the others, wounded or with no weapons left, were only interested in crossing the stream. It was a veritable rout.

And then, of a sudden, having fallen back to their last positions, under the hypnotic spell of panic and amid an indescribable tumult, the men, deserting their platoons, leaped headlong into the level-flowing current of the river! Struggling with one another, trampling the wounded, brutally beating off the maimed and exhausted, pushing them under and stifling them, the first of the fugitives made their way to the right bank and started to scramble up it. Getting such a hold as they could on the scant grass, propping themselves on their weapons, grasping the legs of their fortunate comrades ahead of them who were already clambering over the top, they became once more on the other side of the river a clamouring, fleeing mass. All that could be seen was a swarm of human bodies up and down the river, accompanied by loud, discordant cries. It was as if, as the result of some downpour, the Vasa-Barris had suddenly risen and leaped from its bed, bubbling, foaming, raging.

On Mount Mario

Having crossed the river, the soldiers gathered about the artillery. They were now a panic-stricken mob, without any resemblance whatever to a military force; they were an army in an advanced state of decomposition, all that was left being a number of terrified and useless individuals whose one thought now was to avoid the enemy with whom they had previously been so anxious to come to grips.

The hill where they were at present was much too close to that enemy, who might, possibly, attack them there under cover of darkness, and it was accordingly necessary to abandon it. Still without any kind of order, dragging the cannons after them, they accordingly made their way to Mount Mario, four hundred yards father on. There they improvised an incorrect square formation, with their broken ranks, their officers, the ambulances with the wounded, and the artillery and supply trains. In the centre of their 'camp' were the ruins of the 'Old Ranch House', and here their commander-in-chief lay dying. All that was left of the expedition now was this hodgepodge of men, animals, uniforms, and rifles, dumped in a fold of the mountains.

Night had come, one of those intensely bright nights which are common in the backlands, when every star – fixed, not twinkling – seems to radiate heat, as the cloudless horizons light up from moment to moment with the reflected lightning gleams of distant tempests.

The settlement was invisible now; or, rather, all that was visible was a few smouldering fires where the wood beneath the mud walls and roofs was still being consumed, or the pale glow of a lantern shimmering in the darkness here and there and moving slowly about, as if the bearer were engaged in a mournful search of some sort. These lights showed that the enemy was keeping watch, but the firing had ceased and there was not a sound to be heard. The brilliant starlight made it barely possible to discern the faint outlines of the church buildings, standing out from the rest; but the compact mass of huts, the hills round about, the distant mountains – all were lost in the night.

The disorder of the camp afforded a contrast to the peaceful surrounding. Huddled in between their comrades more than a hundred maimed and wounded men, tortured with pain and thirst, writhed in agony or crept about on their hands and knees, in grave peril of being trampled by the frightened, neighing horses of the supply train. It was out of the question to undertake to treat them here in the darkness, where the careless lighting of a match would have been an incredibly foolhardy act. In addition to this, there were not enough surgeons to go round, one of them – either dead, strayed, or captured – having disappeared that afternoon, never to return.

Colonel Tamarindo

What was lacking, above all, was a commander possessed of the requisite firmness. The burdens laid upon him were too heavy for Colonel Tamarindo, who inwardly cursed the turn of fate which had forced him into this catastrophic position. He made no plans, and to an officer who anxiously enquired as to what he meant to do he replied with a wry humour by quoting a popular north-country refrain: *E'temp de muricy cada umcuide de si* . . . 'The time has come to die; every man for himself . . .' That was his only order of the day. Seated on a drum case, sucking on his pipe in pained but stoic discouragement, he gave a similar reply or muttered a few monosyllables to all who sought his counsel; he had entirely abdicated his function of bringing order out of this disheartened mob by performing the miracle of dividing them into fresh combat units.

There were, assuredly, men of valour among them, and their officers were ready to sacrifice themselves; but the old commander's intuition told him that, under such conditions, the numerical aggregate was not equal to the sum of individual energies, and he could not but take into account those circumstances which, in the case of crowds that are a prey to violent emotions, always tend to offset the most brilliant of personal qualities. He therefore remained impassive, aloof from the general anxiety, thus tacitly yielding his command to the men at large. On their own account the indefatigable officers took those precautions which were most urgent, by rectifying as best they could the alleged square formation in which men of all companies were mixed together at random, by organizing the ambulance train and arranging for litters, and by attempting to raise the spirits of the soldiers. Many of them were inspired by the thought that the next morning at daybreak they would renew the assault by descending full force and launching a violent attack on the fanatics, after the latter had been given a taste of a stronger bombardment than the one they had had the day before. With such an idea in mind, they put their heads together in laying plans that would retrieve, through daring acts of valour, the defeat they had suffered; for victory must be obtained, no matter what the cost. Within the four sides of this ill-formed square, so their thoughts ran, the destinies of the Republic were at stake. They simply must win; they were revolted and painfully humiliated by this grave yet ridiculous situation in which they found themselves, surrounded by modern cannon, with the best weapons made, seated on packing cases filled to the brim with cartridges – and penned in a corner by a horde of riotous backwoodsmen.

The majority, however, took a dispassionate view of the matter. They were under no illusions. They had but to picture to themselves the troops as they had arrived a few hours before, enthusiastic and confident of victory, and contrast that picture with the one before them; when they did this, it was clear to them that there was but one solution possible – a retreat.

Proposed Retreat

There was no other recourse to be thought of; they must retreat and retreat at once.

It was eleven o'clock at night when the officers unanimously adopted this plan, and a captain of infantry was appointed to make known their resolution to Colonel Moreira Cesar. The latter was surprised and dismayed when he learned of it. He remained calm at first, as he spoke of military obligations that must be fulfilled, pointing out that they still possessed sufficient resources to make another attempt of some sort, more than two-thirds of the troops being fit for combat duty and the supply of ammunition being adequate. Then, as his anguish and indignation grew, he began casting aspersions on the riffraff who would soil his name forever; and, finally, he could restrain himself no longer but burst out: No! he would not give in to such unbelievable cowardice.

In spite of this, however, the officers adhered to the resolution which they had adopted.

Moreira Cesar's Protest

This was all that was needed to complete the agony of the unfortunate hero. In deep disgust he gave his last word of command: let them put all this in writing, leaving space in the margin for him to enter his protest, along with his resignation. Even this grievous reprimand on the part of their twice-wounded superior failed to sway his able-bodied staff from their decision. It was true enough that they still had hundreds of soldiers, eight hundred, it might be; they likewise had two-thirds of their ammunition intact and were in a position overlooking the enemy.

But this very night the backlands conflict had begun to take on that mysterious aspect which it was to preserve until the end. The majority of the soldiers were *mestizos*, of the same racial stock as the backwoodsmen; and in their discouragement over the inexplicable defeat which they had suffered and the loss of their commander who had been reputed to be invincible, they readily fell victim to the power of suggestion and, seeing in it all an element of the marvellous and the supernatural, were filled with an unreasoning terror – a terror that was further increased by the extravagant stories that were going round.

The burly and brutal *jagunço* was now transformed into an intangible hobgoblin. Most of the combatants, even those who had been wounded in the recent engagement, had not so much as laid eyes on a single one of the enemy. Others, who had been members of the previous expedition, were dumbfounded to behold, resurrected in the flesh as they believed, two or three of the rebel leaders who, they asserted with conviction, had died at Cambaio. And to all of them, even the most incredulous, there did begin to appear to be something abnormal about these ghostlike, all but invisible fighters with whom they had struggled so impotently, having had no more than a glimpse of a few of them here and there, dodging boldly in and out among the ruins and dashing unscathed through what was left of the blazing huts. Many of the soldiers were from the North, and they, upon hearing Antonio Conselheiro's name, were inclined to associate him with the heroes of childhood tales. The extravagant legend which had grown up about him, his miracles, his unrivalled exploits as a sorcerer, now appeared to them to have been overwhelmingly verified by this tremendous catastrophe.

Along toward midnight their apprehensions were greatly increased, when the drowsing sentinels who had been posted to guard the laxly organized camp suddenly awoke in terror, uttering cries of alarm. The silence of the night was broken by a strange sound coming up the mountainside. It was not, however, the dull tramp of an attacking party. It was something worse than that. The enemy down below, in that invisible town – was praying. This extraordinary occurrence, at this time of night – mournful litanies, with feminine in place of masculine voices predominating, welling up from the ruins of a battlefield – all this was formidable indeed. The effect was heightened by contrast. As the astounded soldiers whispered in fear, those sorrowful-sounding tag ends of 'Kyrie's' seemed worse to them than forthright threats would have been. In this eloquent manner they were being told that there was no contending with an enemy who was thus transfigured by religious faith.

Retreat was now more of a necessity than ever; and at dawn the next day a disturbing piece of news rendered it most urgent. Colonel Moreira Cesar had died.

The Retreat

This was all that was needed to complete the feeling of general discouragement. The preparations for departure were made in great haste and amid an indescribable tumult. At the first break of day a contingent made up of men from all the corps set out as a vanguard, closely followed by the supply trains and the ambulances and litters bearing the wounded, on one of which lay the body of the ill-fated commander of the expedition. There was nothing in all this to indicate that a serious military operation was under way.

The retreat was in reality a flight. Advancing over the summit, in the direction of Mount Favella, and then descending the steep slopes on the other side by the road which runs there, the expeditionaries spread out over the hills in a long and scattering line, without any semblance of military formation. In thus turning their back on the enemy down below, who, though alert, was not troubling them as yet, they appeared to be trusting solely to the swiftness of their movements to get them out of their plight. There was no defensive-offensive alignment by successive stages such as is the characteristic procedure in military crises of this sort. All that they did was to rush down the roads at top speed, with no thought of order or direction. They were not falling back; they were taking to their heels. One division alone, with two Krupp guns, under the command of a valorous subaltern, and strengthened by an infantry detachment, stood its ground for some time on Mount Mario by way of holding off the inevitable pursuit.

The Drama Ends in Hisses

When it did finally get under way, this self-sacrificing detachment was fiercely assaulted. The enemy now had the impetus that comes from taking the offensive and was further aware of the dread he inspired in the fleeing troops. To the accompaniment of loud and enthusiastic *vivas*, he attacked violently from all sides, in a circling movement. Down below, the bell was ringing wildly, and there was a burst of rifle fire from the new church, as the entire population of Canudos thronged into the square or dashed over the hilltops to view the scene, conferring upon the tragic episode an irritatingly mocking note, as thousands and thousands of throats gave vent to a prolonged, shrill, deadly intentioned whistling.

Once again, the fearful drama of backlands warfare was ending in lugubrious hoots and hisses.

The evacuation of the camp was accomplished within a short space of time. The final division of artillery returned the enemy's fire for a few moments and then in turn slowly lumbered off down the slope, in full retreat.

It was afternoon; and, as far as the eye could reach, the expedition, sprawled along the roadways, was from place to place flanked by *jagunços*.

Broken Ranks; Flight

The ranks were now completely broken. Eight hundred men were engaged in flight, throwing their rifles away, dropping the litters on which the wounded were writhing, abandoning their equipment, undoing their belts that they might be able to run the faster – running, running, in any direction, without weapons, in small groups and wandering bands, running down the road and along the intersecting paths, making for the depths of the caatingas, terrified, out of their senses, leaderless.

Among the burdens deposited along the side of the road when the panic broke out was – mournful detail! – the body of the commander. There was no effort to protect his remains, not the slightest effort to repel the enemy whom they had not glimpsed, but who made his presence known by noisy shouts of defiance and by scattering shots at irregular intervals, like those of a hunter in the brush. At the first sound of those shots, the battalions melted away.

Salomão da Rocha

Vainly, a few indignant officers thrust revolvers against the fugitives' chests; there was no restraining them. On, on, they ran, ran madly, running from their officers, running from the *jagunços*; and, when those who brought up the rear were shot down, they did not so much as turn their heads. Captain Villarim fought valiantly and almost alone, and, as he lay dying, there was not a one of his men to place an arm beneath him. The maimed and wounded were left to stagger along, dragging themselves over the ground and cursing out their more active comrades.

Over all this tumult the notes of the bugler went unheard, unheeded. At last the bugles ceased. There were no longer any troops to summon. The infantry had disappeared.

Along the side of the road were to be seen scattered pieces of equipment, knapsacks and rifles, belts and sabres, thrown away at random as useless objects. Entirely alone, without a single orderly, Colonel Tamarindo dashed down the road – deserted now – at a desperate gallop, as if he were bent on personally heading off the vanguard. As for the artillery, it was wholly abandoned, finally, before reaching 'Angico', and the *jagunços* at once fell upon it. This was the end. Captain Salomão now had about him barely half a dozen loyal men; the enemy closed in upon him and he fell, cut to pieces with the blows of a scythe, beside the cannon which he had never abandoned. The catastrophe was complete.

Not long after this, as he was galloping along the ravine to 'Angico', Colonel Tamarindo was knocked from his horse by a bullet. He was still alive when the army engineer, Alfredo do Nascimento, reached his side. Lying beside the road, the old commander whispered his last order in his comrade's ear: 'Get Cunha Mattos.'

That order was a difficult one to carry out.

An Open-air Arsenal

The third expedition was now done for, dispersed; it had vanished utterly. Most of the fugitives, avoiding the highroad, lost their way and wandered aimlessly, with no sense of direction, over the desert wastes; and many of them here – many of the wounded, especially – were left to breathe their last in absolute abandonment. Some, striking off from the main route, made for Cumbe or points more remote. The rest of them, one day or another, showed up at Monte Santo. Colonel Souza Menezes, commander of the garrison, was not expecting them and, upon learning of the disaster, galloped away at top speed to Queimadas, which had become a terminus of this human stampede.

In the meanwhile, the *sertanejos* were gathering up the spoils. Along the road and in near-by spots weapons and munitions lay strewn, together with pieces of the soldiers' uniforms, military capes and crimson-striped trousers, which, standing out against the grey of the caatingas, would have made their wearers too conspicuous as they fled. From which it may be seen that the major portion of the troops not only had thrown away their weapons but had stripped themselves of their clothing as well.

Thus it was that, midway between 'Rosario' and Canudos, the *jagunços* came to assemble a helter-skelter open-air arsenal; they now had enough and more than enough in the way of arms to satisfy their needs. The Moreira Cesar expedition appeared to have achieved this one objective: that of supplying the enemy with all this equipment, making him a present of all those modern weapons and munitions.

A Cruel Diversion

The *jagunços* took the four Krupps back to the settlement, their front-line fighters now equipped with formidable Mannlichers and Comblains in place of the ancient, slow-loading muskets. As for the uniforms, belts, military bonnets, anything that had touched the bodies of the cursed soldiery, they would have defiled the epidermis of these consecrated warriors, and so the latter disposed of them in a manner that was both cruel and gruesome.

The successes they had thus far achieved had exacerbated, at one and the same time, their sense of mysticism and their inclinations to brutality. The prestige of the soldier was gone, and the *sertanejos'* rude and swaggering leaders proceeded to make the most of every incident and detail. The government's strength was now, in truth, the government's *weakness*; and this term ('government weakling') was one that was destined to be employed by them throughout the balance of the campaign. They had seen this force arrive, impressive and terrifying, equipped with weapons compared to which their own crude firearms were mere children's toys; they had seen the troops fall upon the settlement, attack it, invade it, set fire to it, overrun it; and then they had beheld them falling back, had seen them in flight, a flight that became a wild stampede, as they tossed their arms and equipment along the roadside. It was, without doubt, a miracle. The aspect of events troubled their minds, and they could see but one possible interpretation of it all: they were obviously under the protection of Divinity itself and its superior powers. This conviction, strengthened by the brutal nature of the conflict, continued to grow, and resulted in a revival of all their barbarous instincts, to the deterioration of their character.

There was a strange occurrence which bore witness to this, a kind of sinister diversion reminiscent of the tragically perverted religious sense of the Ashantis, which came as a sequel to the events narrated. Having concluded their search of the roads and trails, and having gathered up and brought in all the weapons and munitions of war that they found, the *jagunços* then collected all the corpses that were lying here and there, decapitated them, and burned the bodies; after which they lined the heads up along both sides of the highway, at regular intervals, with the faces turned toward the road. Above these, from the tallest shrubbery, they suspended the remains of the uniforms and equipment, the trousers and multi-coloured dolmans, the saddles, belts, red-striped kepis, the capes, blankets, canteens and knapsacks.

The barren, withered caatinga now blossomed forth with an extravagant-coloured flora: the bright red of officers' stripes, the pale blue of dolmans, set off by the brilliant gleam of shoulder straps and swaying stirrups.

There is one painful detail which must be added to complete this cruel picture: at one side of the road, impaled on a dried angico bough, loomed the body of Colonel Tamarindo.

It was a horrifying sight. Like a terribly macabre manikin, the drooping corpse, arms and legs swaying in the wind as it hung from the flexible, bending branch, in these desert regions took on the appearance of some demoniac vision. It remained there for a long time.

And when, three months later, a fresh expeditionary force set out for Canudos, this was the scene that greeted their eyes: rows of skulls bleaching along the roadside, with the shreds of one-time uniforms stuck up on the tree branches round about, while over at one side – mute protagonist of a formidable drama – was the dangling spectre of the old colonel.

* * *

ELIZABETH BISHOP (1911–1979)

'A Trip to Vigia'

The shy poet, so soiled, so poor, so polite, insisted on taking us in his own car. A friend would go along as *mechanista*. The car was on its last legs; it had broken down twice just getting us around Belem the day before. But what could we do? I couldn't very well flaunt my dollars in his face and hire a better one.

He arrived at our hotel at nine (he had said eight) with José Augusto, one of his little boys, aged eleven, fair, and also very shy. Ruy, the poet, was dark, quiet, and softly heavy, his waxy face spattered with fine black moles like shot. His other children, four or five of them, were at home with 'fever'. They were sick all the time we were in Belem. This José Augusto scarcely spoke, but in the course of the long day his expression became by degrees more animated, more childlike. By mid-afternoon he grew restless, even active; he slept all the way back from the expedition in his father's arms.

Ruy was nervous. He kept telling us we probably wouldn't like the famous church at Vigia; it would be too 'baroque' for us. Each time he said this, our imaginations added more belfries and a slightly wilder wave of carved stone. M. and I got into the back seat that slanted downwards so that our bottoms felt as if they were gently grazing the road. The *mechanista*, José Augusto, and Ruy were in front. Most of the time they kept their heads bent as if in prayer. Perhaps they were praying to the tired heart of the car to keep on beating just a little longer, until the expedition was safely over.

We had met Ruy just two days before. That morning I asked M. to let me know when the mystic moment arrived and she'd shift gears from addressing him as 'Dr Ruy' to 'you.' This use of the *você* or second person is always a delicate problem and I wanted to see how M., who has the nicest Brazilian manners, would solve it. Since Ruy was a poet and therefore could be considered sensitive, and since we found him very sympathetic, I felt it would be happening very soon.

Outside Belem we crossed a dead-looking railroad yard with old red freight cars scattered about in it, the end of the line. We passed under a fretwork arch, decorated with a long and faded banner and with cut bamboos turned sere brown. It had been set up to celebrate the opening of the new highway to Brasilia. Just beyond it, the paved road stopped for good. However, the very thought of this new road to the capital had cheered up all of Belem considerably. Even the resigned Ruy spoke about the future optimistically.

Vigia was about a hundred kilometers away. We went off toward it on another narrower road to the left that went up and down, up and down, in low wavy hills, mostly through bushes. Because of the two daily rains (it was the rainy season), there was little dust. Slowly, slowly we rose and fell over the gravel. The silent *mechanista* was like a mother teaching the car to walk. But after a while it stopped.

He got out and lifted the hood. M. talked gaily of this and that. After fifteen minutes or so, the car started again: up a slight grade; down faster; up. The day was getting hot. The car was getting hot. But still it seemed as if we had just left Belem. We passed fields of pepper, big leafy pillars. It is grown on poles, like string beans, and is called Pimenta da Rainha, Queen's Pepper, because it originally belonged to the crown. They say that the whole history of Portugal since the fourteenth century is the history of pepper. It had recently become a big crop in the north. Ruy complained about it, saying it was already overplanted, the way any successful crop always is in Brazil, and the price was dropping. On the left, where an unseen stream ran, were occasional plantations of jute, a bright and tender green.

More pepper. A mud-and-wattle house or two. An oxcart: mild, lovely zebus with high humps and long hanging ears, blue-gray, a well-matched team. Skinny horses scrambled off into the bushes, or stood pat while we edged around them. A dismal mud-and-wattle church, half-painted bright blue: IGREJA BATISTA. Then a little bridge with half the planks missing. The *mechanista* got out and squatted to study it from the far side, before taking us over.

Fine and blue, the morning rain arrived. The gravel darkened and spurted away slowly on either side. We plowed dreamily along. Ruy was talking about T. S. Eliot. He read English, some, but spoke not a word. I tried a story about Ezra Pound. It was very well received but, I felt, not understood. I undertook some more literary anecdotes. Smiling politely, Ruy waited for every joke until the faithful M. had helped me put them into Portuguese. Often they proved to be untranslatable. The car stopped.

This time the *mechanista* took much longer. M. talked ever more gaily. Suddenly the rain came down hard, great white lashings. The bushes crouched and the gravel danced. M. nudged me, whispered 'Now,' and in her next sentence to Ruy used a noticeable *você*; the mystic moment was past. The *mechanista* got back in, his clothes several shades darker with wet, and said we would stop at the next village for repairs.

*

The rains stopped and the sun came out. Certain varieties of glazed tropical leaves reflected the light like nickel or white enamel, but as the car passed they returned to their actual grey-green. It was confusing, and trying to the eyes. Palm trees, more pepper and jute, more bushes. Here and there a great jungle tree had been left standing, and black specks were busy high around the tops; each tree held a whole community of birds. At least two hundred feet high, a Brazil nut tree blossomed; one could tell only by a smell like that of a thousand lilacs.

Three teams of zebus, loaded with jute. A small shower, like an afterthought right through the sunshine. We were driving north-northeast, skirting the great bay of Marajó, but we might as well have been in the middle of Africa or the Yucatan. (It *looked* a bit like the Yucatan.) More wretched little houses, with pigs, and naked children shining from the rain. The 'village' was a crossroads, with a combined drink-shop and grocery store, a *botequim*, beside a spreading flamboyant tree. It took a moment to realize the car had really stopped; we stopped talking, and got out.

The store had been raided, sacked. Oh, that was its normal state. It was quite large, no color inside or cloud-color perhaps, with holes in the floor, holes in the walls, holes in the roof. A barrel of kerosene stood in a dark stain. There were a coil of blue cotton rope, a few mattock heads, and a bundle of yellow-white handles, fresh cut from hard *ipé* wood. Lined up on the shelves were many, many bottles of *cachaça*, all alike: Esperança, Hope, Hope, Hope. There was a counter where you could drink, if you wanted. A bunch of red-striped lamp wicks hung beside a bunch of rusty frying pans. A glass case offered brown toffees leaking through their papers, and old, old, old sweet buns. Some very large ants were making hay there while the sun shone. Our eyes negotiated the advertisements for Orange Crush and Guaraná on the cloud-colored walls, and we had seen everything. That was all.

The shopkeeper had gone off with our *mechanista*, so Ruy helped us to warm Orange Crush and over our protests put the money for it on the counter. 'No cheese?' he inquired, poking about in back, as if he were in the habit of eating quantities of cheese with an Orange Crush every morning. He asked if we'd like a toffee, and urged us to take another *crooshy.* Then he said, 'Let's go see the manioc factory.'

This was right behind the *botequim*. It was an open-air affair of three thatched roofs on posts, one a round toadstool. A dozen women and girls sat on the ground, ripping the black skins off the long roots with knives. We were the funniest things they had seen in years. They tried not to laugh in our faces, but we 'slayed' them. M. talked to them, but this did not increase their self-control. Zebus stood looking on, chewing their cuds. A motor, with belts slanting up under the thatch, chugged away, grinding up the raw manioc. The place smelled of zebu, gasoline, and people. Everyone talked, but it was murky and peaceful.

The greatest attraction was the revolving metal floor, a big disk, for drying out the flour. It was heated underneath by a charcoal fire and the area was partly railed off, like a small rink, so one could lean over and watch. The coarse white flour went slowly round and round, pushed back and forth in drifts by two men with long wooden hoes. The flour got whiter and whiter, but they were careful not to let it brown. In the north, people usually eat it white; in the south, they prefer it roasted to a pale tan.

We almost forgot we were on our way to Vigia. Then the *mechanista* collected us; in we got, out again, in again, and finally off. The motor now sounded languid and half sick but uncomplaining, like the poet himself.

★

Another ten kilometers and we came to a small house on the left, set among fruit and banana trees growing directly from the bare, swept earth. A wash was strung on the barbed-wire fence. Several skinny dogs appeared and a very fat young woman came out, carrying a baby, with two little boys tagging along behind. We all shook hands, even the baby boys. Her husband, a friend of Ruy's, was away but she invited us in – 'for lunch', said the poor woman. We quickly explained we had brought our lunch with us. Ruy did the honors. 'Ah! the water here is a *delicia*, isn't it, Dona Sebastiana? It's the best water, the only water, from here to Vigia. People come for miles to get water here. Wait till you try it.'

Pegged to the side of the house was a fresh snake skin, a monster over ten feet long the husband had shot two days before. Dona Sebastiana brought out three glass jars, and a large tin can full of fat she'd rendered from the snake. She said it was the best remedy in the world for a great variety of ailments, including tuberculosis and 'sore legs'. Then she hurried in to make the coffee.

There were several small rooms in her house, and they were almost bare. There was no glass in the windows, and only the front room had a floor. It also had the *oratorio*, a yellowed print of Our Lady of Nazareth, with red paper roses in front of it, and that other light of the world, the sewing machine, a hand-run *Sin-ger*.

In the kitchen Dona Sebastiana was fanning hard, with a plaited palm leaf held in both hands, a charcoal fire in a clay trough. We admired a hanging lamp of tin, homemade, cleverly constructed to stay upright. It was the only thing to admire. 'Oh,' she said, 'my girl friend left that to me when she died. We went to school together.' There was almost nothing in her kitchen except a black pot or two. The only signs of food were some overripe cucumbers on the windowsill. How had she managed to be so fat? The upside-down *cafezinho* cups were modestly hidden under a fringed napkin, with a little boy pushing a wheelbarrow embroidered in red outline. Dona

Sebastiana had no white sugar, and she apologized for the cake of brown she scraped for us herself. We drank it down, the hot, bad, sad coffee, and went out back to see her river.

It really was a beautiful river. It was four yards across, dark, clear, running rapidly, with white cascades and deep pools edged with backed-up foam, and its banks were a dream of the tropics. It splashed, it sang, it glittered over white pebbles. Little did it reck that it had almost reached the vast muddy bay, the mouth of the Amazon. It made up for a lot, and Dona Sebastiana was proud of it. José Augusto and the little boys went wading. The thin dogs stood in the water, and gulped at it, then looked back at us over their shoulders from *their* river.

It was one o'clock by now and we were starving. The hotel had given us a lunch, a good-sized roast hen, fresh rolls, butter, oranges, a hunk of desirable white cheese. But no one would eat a bite. They *never* ate lunch – what an idea! I made a chicken sandwich and offered it to José Augusto. He looked shocked and frightened, and moved closer to his father's knee. Finally M. and I miserably gobbled up some lunch by ourselves. The *mechanista* soaked his feet, and rolled and smoked corn-husk cigarettes. Ruy let José Augusto accept one orange; Dona Sebastiana let her little boys accept two oranges. Then we shook hands all around, and back in our car we crawled away.

*

After a while, we got there. But first, from far off, we could see the pinnacled tops of two square towers, dazzling white against the dark rainclouds. The church looked like a sacred bull, a great white zebu. The road was level now, the landscape low and flat; we were near the coast. The church towers could be seen a long way off, rising very high above the tops of the tall green-black mango trees around them.

The plaza was dark red, laid out with cement benches and lamp-posts stuck with round globes, like artificial pearls. Smack in the middle was a blue-and-white bandstand. It was hideous, but because it was so small it didn't spoil the effect at all – rather as if these absurd offerings had been laid out on the ground in front of the great, indifferent, sacred white zebu. The dark green mango trees were dwarfed by the church. On either side the little old houses were tile-covered, with Gothic blue-and-white, or yellow-and-white, tile-covered *azulejos*.

Ruy watched us. But we liked the church very much and said so. He looked greatly relieved. The church danced in the light. I climbed on a stone wall, the remains of another abandoned house, to get a photograph of the whole thing, if possible, but there was nothing high enough to take it all in. It started to rain. I got a picture, jumped down – a dozen people had gathered to watch me, all looking scandalized – tripped, and tore my petticoat, which fell down below my skirt. The rain poured.

The others were all inside the church. It was mostly blue and white – bare, cold, huge, echoing. Little children followed us and ran shouting up and down; Ruy's little boy joined in. We went out on the second-story galleries, beneath the row of huge whitewashed pillars. You could see a pattern of tile roofs and mango trees through the rain tapestry, red-brown, down to the river, where the masts of ships and boats showed. A battered blue truck ground along below, and the driver came in, too – another friend of Ruy's.

The sacristan, an old fisherman, appeared. There was little enough to be seen in the sacristy. He went to a cupboard, with the little children pressing close around him and me, crying, 'Show her Father! Show her Father!' and he handed me – a bone. A skull. The children reached up for it. He patted the skull and said yes, that was Father So-and-So, a saint if ever there was one, a really holy man. Never went anywhere, thought of nothing but prayer, meditated and prayed seven hours a day. I thought he was speaking of some forgotten saint of the seventeenth century who had never been properly recognized. No, Father had died two years before. I kept trying to hand the skull back. He was too busy telling me about the final illness, his *agonia*, his death. It was the most wonderful thing in Vigia. The sacristan put the skull back in the corner of the bare cupboard. It was so dark in the sacristy we could scarcely see.

We went out. Huge thunderclouds rolled back and forth, the river was higher, the tide had turned. All the lights went on in the forsaken plaza, although it was not dark. The pearly, silent, huge church of Vigia had made us all feel somehow guilty at abandoning it once again. The town's little white houses were turning mauve. In the high, high skies, shafts of long golden beams fell through the thunderclouds. Nature was providing all the baroque grandeur the place lacked. We started back to Belem, and it soon began to get really dark.

*

The car didn't stop all the way home, except once on purpose for gasoline. The trip seemed to take forever and we all fell silent. The little boy fell sound asleep. There wasn't even a light for miles, and never a car; we met two trucks and overtook two. Our eyes fastened on the slightest light or movement – an oil lamp, like an ancient Greek lamp, on a bicycle; a few people on foot carrying umbrellas.

Then lights. We were coming to Belem. Lights on the mud walls and their political posters and endless slogans, with all the ns and ss written backwards. Tall narrow doorways, the murky light of an oil lamp, warm, yellow and black. A man carrying a lantern – oh, he's leading a cow and a calf. Goats. Look out, a zebu! We almost hit him, a high bony gray wall across the road. He lowered his horns sharply and snorted softly.

Suddenly we are in Belem. Huge black mango trees. Cars bumping over the cobblestones, bumpety-bump. How very, very bright this dim city can look! We ache in the dark. The church at Vigia, huge, white, alone on our consciences, has become a ghost story.

The hotel at last. It is almost nine o'clock. We invite Ruy in for a drink, at least. He comes, but will take only another *cafezinho*. The dingy café looks brilliant. The young literary men are there, with their rolled umbrellas, moving hands and black neckties, their hair slicked back. They all greet Ruy. Half asleep, we swallow the coffee and, behind our backs, Ruy pays for it.

1967

SOUTHERN OCEAN

Joseph Conrad (1857–1924)

from *The Mirror of the Sea*

The unholy fascination of dread dwells in the thought of the last moments of a ship reported as 'missing' in the columns of the *Shipping Gazette*. Nothing of her ever comes to light – no grating, no lifebuoy, no piece of boat or branded oar – to give a hint of the place and date of her sudden end. The *Shipping Gazette* does not even call her 'lost with all hands'. She remains simply 'missing'; she has disappeared enigmatically into a mystery of fate as big as the world, where your imagination of a brother-sailor, of a fellow-servant and lover of ships, may range unchecked.

And yet sometimes one gets a hint of what the last scene may be like in the life of a ship and her crew, which resembles a drama in its struggle against a great force bearing it up, formless, ungraspable, chaotic, and mysterious as fate.

It was on a grey afternoon in the lull of a three days' gale that had left the Southern Ocean tumbling heavily upon our ship, under a sky hung with rags of clouds that seemed to have been cut and hacked by the keen edge of a sou'-west gale.

Our craft, a Clyde-built barque of 1000 tons, rolled so heavily that something aloft had carried away. No matter what the damage was, but it was serious enough to induce me to go aloft myself with a couple of hands and the carpenter to see the temporary repairs properly done.

Sometimes we had to drop everything and cling with both hands to the swaying spars, holding our breath in fear of a terribly heavy roll. And, wallowing as if she meant to turn over with us, the barque, her decks full of water, her gear flying in bights, ran at some ten knots an hour. We had been driven far south – much farther that way than we had meant to go; and suddenly, up there in the slings of the foreyard, in the midst of our work, I felt my shoulder gripped with such force in the carpenter's powerful paw that I positively yelled with unexpected pain. The man's eyes stared close in my face, and he shouted, 'Look, sir! Look! What's this?' pointing ahead with his other hand.

At first I saw nothing. The sea was one empty wilderness of black and white hills. Suddenly, half-concealed in the tumult of the foaming rollers I made out awash, something enormous, rising and falling – something spread out like a burst of foam, but with a more bluish, more solid look.

It was a piece of an ice-floe melted down to a fragment, but still big enough to sink a ship, and floating lower than any raft, right in our way, as if ambushed among the waves with murderous intent. There was no time to get down on deck. I shouted from aloft till my head was ready to split. I was heard aft, and we managed to clear the sunken floe which had come all the way from the Southern ice-cap to have a try at our unsuspecting lives. Had it been an hour later, nothing could have saved the ship, for no eye could have made out in the dusk that pale piece of ice swept over by the white-crested waves.

And as we stood near the taffrail side by side, my captain and I, looking at it, hardly discernible already, but still quite close-to on our quarter, he remarked in a meditative tone:

'But for the turn of that wheel just in time, there would have been another case of a "missing" ship.'

Nobody ever comes back from a 'missing' ship to tell how hard was the death of the craft, and how sudden and overwhelming the last anguish of her men. Nobody can say with what thoughts, with what regrets, with what words on their lips they died. But there is something fine in the sudden passing away of these hearts from the extremity of struggle and stress and tremendous uproar – from the vast, unrestful rage of the surface to the profound peace of the depths, sleeping untroubled since the beginning of ages.

ANTARCTICA

APSLEY CHERRY-GARRARD (1886–1959)

from *The Worst Journey in the World*

The horror of the nineteen days it took us to travel from Cape Evans to Cape Crozier would have to be re-experienced to be appreciated; and any one would be a fool who went again: it is not possible to describe it. The weeks which followed them were comparative bliss, not because later our conditions were better – they were far worse – but because we were callous. I for one had come to that point of suffering at which I did not really care if only I could die without much pain. They talk of the heroism of the dying – they little know – it would be so easy to die, a dose of morphia, a friendly crevasse, and blissful sleep. The trouble is to go on . . .

It was the darkness that did it. I don't believe minus seventy temperatures would be bad in daylight, not comparatively bad, when you could see where you were going, where you were stepping, where the sledge straps were, the cooker, the primus, the food; could see your footsteps lately trodden deep into the soft snow that you might find your way back to the rest of your load; could see the lashings of the food bags; could read a compass without striking three or four different boxes to find one dry match; could read your watch to see if the blissful moment of getting out of your bag was come without groping in the snow all about; when it would not take you five minutes to lash up the door of the tent, and five hours to get started in the morning . . .

But in these days we were never less than four hours from the moment when Bill cried 'Time to get up' to the time when we got into our harness. It took two men to get one man into his harness, and was all they could do, for the canvas was frozen and our clothes were frozen until sometimes not even two men could bend them into the required shape.

The trouble is sweat and breath. I never knew before how much of the body's waste comes out through the pores of the skin. On the most bitter days, when we had to camp before we had done a four-hour march in order to nurse back our frozen feet, it seemed that we must be sweating. And all this sweat, instead of passing away through the porous wool of our clothing and gradually drying off us, froze and accumulated. It passed just away from our flesh and then became ice: we shook plenty of snow and ice down from inside our trousers every time we changed our foot-gear, and we could have shaken it from our vests and from between our vests and shirts, but of course we could not strip to this extent. But when we got into our sleeping-bags, if we were fortunate, we became warm enough during the night to thaw this ice: part remained in our clothes, part passed into the skins of our sleeping-bags, and soon both were sheets of armour-plate.

As for our breath – in the daytime it did nothing worse than cover the lower parts of our faces with ice and solder our balaclavas tightly to our heads. It was no good trying to get your balaclava off until you had had the primus going quite a long time, and then you could throw your breath about if you wished. The trouble really began in your sleeping-bag, for it was far too cold to keep a hole open through which to breathe. So all night long our breath froze into the skins, and our respiration became quicker and quicker as the air in our bags got fouler and fouler: it was never possible to make a match strike or burn inside our bags!

Of course we were not iced up all at once: it took several days of this kind of thing before we really got into big difficulties on this score. It was not until I got out of the tent one morning fully ready to pack the sledge that I realized the possibilities ahead. We had had our breakfast, struggled into our foot-gear, and squared up inside the tent, which was comparatively warm. Once outside, I raised my head to look round and found I could not move it back. My clothing had frozen hard as I stood – perhaps fifteen seconds. For four hours I had to pull with my head stuck up, and from that time we all took care to bend down into a pulling position before being frozen in.

By now we had realized that we must reverse the usual sledging routine and do everything slowly, wearing when possible the fur mitts which fitted over our woollen mitts, and always stopping whatever we were doing, directly we felt that any part of us was getting frozen, until the circulation was restored. Henceforward it was common for one or other of us to leave the other two to continue the camp work while he stamped about in the snow, beat his arms, or nursed some exposed part. But we could not restore the circulation of our feet like this – the only way then was to camp and get some hot water into ourselves before we took our foot-gear off. The difficulty was to know whether our feet were frozen or not, for the only thing we knew for certain was that we had lost all feeling in them. Wilson's knowledge as a doctor came in here: many a time he had to decide from our descriptions of our feet whether to camp or to go on for another hour. A wrong decision meant disaster, for if one of us had been crippled the whole party would have been placed in great difficulties. Probably we should all have died.

On 29 June the temperature was −50° all day and there was sometimes a light breeze which was inclined to frost-bite our faces and hands. Owing to the weight of our two sledges and the bad surface our pace was not more than a slow and very heavy plod: at our lunch camp Wilson had the heel and sole of one foot frost-bitten, and I had two big toes. Bowers was never worried by frost-bitten feet.

That night was very cold, the temperature falling to −66°, and it was −55° at breakfast on 30 June. We had not shipped the eider-down linings to our sleeping-bags, in order to keep them dry as long as possible. My own fur bag was too big for me, and throughout this journey was more difficult to thaw out than the other two: on the other hand, it never split, as did Bill's.

We were now getting into that cold bay which lies between the Hut Point Peninsula and Terror Point. It was known from old *Discovery* days that the Barrier winds are deflected from this area, pouring out into McMurdo Sound behind us, and into the Ross Sea at Cape Crozier in front. In consequence of the lack of high winds the surface of the snow is never swept and hardened and polished as elsewhere: it was now a mass of the hardest and smallest snow crystals, to pull through which in cold temperatures was just like pulling through sand. I have spoken elsewhere of Barrier surfaces, and how, when the cold is very great, sledge runners cannot melt the crystal points but only advance by rolling them over and over upon one another. That was the surface we met on this journey, and in soft snow the effect is accentuated. Our feet were sinking deep at every step.

And so when we tried to start on 30 June we found we could not move both sledges together. There was nothing for it but to take one on at a time and come back for the other. This has often been done in daylight when the only risks run are those of blizzards which may spring up suddenly and obliterate tracks. Now in darkness it was more complicated. From 11 a.m. to 3 p.m. there was enough light to see the big holes made by our feet, and we took on one sledge, trudged back in our tracks, and brought on the second. Bowers used to toggle and untoggle our harnesses when we changed sledges. Of course in this relay work we covered three miles in distance for every one mile forward, and even the single sledges were very hard pulling. When we lunched the temperature was −61°. After lunch the little light had gone, and we carried a naked lighted candle back with us when we went to find our second sledge. It was the weirdest kind of procession, three frozen men and a little pool of light. Generally we steered by Jupiter, and I never see him now without recalling his friendship in those days.

We were very silent, it was not very easy to talk: but sledging is always a silent business. I remember a long discussion which began just now about cold snaps – was this the normal condition of the Barrier, or was it a cold snap? – what constituted a cold snap? The discussion lasted about a week. Do things slowly, always slowly, that was the burden of Wilson's leadership: and every now and then the question, Shall we go on? and the answer Yes. 'I think we are all right as long as our appetites are good,' said Bill. Always patient, self-possessed, unruffled, he was the only man on earth, as I believe, who could have led this journey.

That day we made 3¼ miles, and travelled 10 miles to do it. The temperature was −66° when we camped, and we were already pretty badly iced up. That was the last night I lay (I had written slept) in my big reindeer bag without the lining of eider-down which we each carried. For me it was a very bad night: a succession of shivering fits which I was quite unable to stop, and which took possession of my body for many minutes at a time until I thought my back would break, such was the strain placed upon it. They talk of chattering teeth: but when your body chatters you may call yourself cold. I can only compare the strain to that which I have been unfortunate enough to see in a case of lock-jaw. One of my big toes was frost-bitten, but I do not know for how long. Wilson was fairly comfortable in his smaller bag, and Bowers was snoring loudly. The minimum temperature that night as taken under the sledge was −69° and as taken on the sledge was −75°. That is a hundred and seven degrees of frost.

We did the same relay work on 1 July, but found the pulling harder still; and it was all that we could do to move the one sledge forward. From now onwards Wilson and I, but not to the same extent as Bowers, experienced a curious optical delusion when returning in our tracks for the second sledge. I have said that we found our way back by the light of a candle, and we found it necessary to go back in our same footprints. These holes became to our tired brains not depressions but elevations: hummocks over which we stepped, raising our feet painfully and draggingly. And then we remembered, and said what fools we were, and for a while we compelled ourselves to walk through these phantom hills. But it was no lasting good, and as the days passed we realized that we must suffer this absurdity, for we could not do anything else. But of course it took it out of us.

During these days the blisters on my fingers were very painful. Long before my hands were frost-bitten, or indeed anything but cold, which was of course a normal thing, the matter inside these big blisters, which rose all down my fingers with only a skin between them, was frozen into ice. To handle the cooking gear or the food bags was agony; to start the primus was worse; and when, one day, I was able to prick six or seven of the blisters after supper and let the liquid matter out, the relief was very great. Every night after that I treated such others as were ready in the same way until they gradually disappeared. Sometimes it was difficult not to howl.

I *did* want to howl many times every hour of these days and nights, but I invented a formula instead, which I repeated to myself continually. Especially, I remember, it came in useful when at the end of the march with my feet frost-bitten, my heart beating slowly, my vitality at its lowest ebb, my body solid with cold, I used to seize the shovel and go on digging snow on to the tent skirting while the cook inside was trying to light the primus. 'You've got it in the neck – stick it – stick it – you've got it in the neck,' was the refrain, and I wanted every little bit of encouragement it would give me: then I would find myself repeating 'Stick it – stick it – stick it – stick it,' and then 'You've got it in the neck.' One of the joys of summer sledging is that you can let your mind wander thousands of miles away for weeks and weeks. Oates used to provision his little yacht (there was a pickled herring he was going to have); I invented the compactest little revolving bookcase which was going to hold not books, but pemmican and chocolate and biscuit and cocoa and sugar, and have a cooker on the top, and was going to stand always ready to quench my hunger when I got home; and we visited restaurants and theatres and grouse moors, and we thought of a pretty girl, or girls, and . . . But now that was all impossible. Our conditions forced themselves upon us without pause: it was not possible to think of anything else. We got no respite. I found it best to refuse to let myself think of the past or the future – to live only for the job of the moment, and to compel myself to think only how to do it most efficiently. Once you let yourself imagine . . .

*

That evening, for the first time, we discarded our naked candle in favour of the rising moon. We had started before the moon on purpose, but as we shall see she gave us little light. However, we owed our escape from a very sticky death to her on one occasion.

It was a little later on when we were among crevasses, with Terror above us, but invisible, somewhere on our left, and the Barrier pressure on our right. We were quite lost in the darkness, and only knew that we were running downhill, the sledge almost catching our heels. There had been no light all day, clouds obscured the moon, we had not seen her since yesterday. And quite suddenly a little patch of clear sky drifted, as it were, over her face, and she showed us three paces ahead a great crevasse with just a shining icy lid not much thicker than glass. We should all have walked into it, and the sledge would certainly have followed us down. After that I felt we had a chance of pulling through: God could not be so cruel as to have saved us just to prolong our agony.

But at present we need not worry about crevasses; for we had not reached the long stretch where the moving Barrier, with the weight of many hundred miles of ice behind it, comes butting up against the slopes of Mount Terror, itself some eleven thousand feet high. Now we were still plunging ankle-deep in the mass of soft sandy snow which lies in the windless area. It seemed to have no bottom at all, and since the snow was much the same temperature as the air, our feet, as well as our bodies, got colder and colder the longer we marched: in ordinary sledging you begin to warm up after a quarter of an hour's pulling, here it was just the reverse. Even now I find myself unconsciously kicking the toes of my right foot against the heels of my left: a habit I picked up on this journey by doing it every time we halted. Well no. Not always. For there was one halt when we just lay on our backs and gazed up into the sky, where, so the others said, there was blazing the most wonderful aurora they had ever seen. I did not see it, being so near-sighted and unable to wear spectacles owing to the cold. The aurora was always before us as we travelled east, more beautiful than any seen by previous expeditions wintering in McMurdo Sound, where Erebus must have hidden the most brilliant displays. Now most of the sky was covered with swinging, swaying curtains which met in a great whirl overhead: lemon yellow, green and orange.

The minimum this night was −65°, and during 3 July it ranged between −52° and −58°. We got forward only 2½ miles, and by this time I had silently made up my mind that we had not the ghost of a chance of reaching the penguins. I am sure that Bill was having a very bad time these nights, though it was an impression rather than anything else, for he never said so. We knew we did sleep, for we heard one another snore, and also we used to have dreams and nightmares; but we had little consciousness of it, and we were now beginning to drop off when we halted on the march.

Our sleeping-bags were getting really bad by now, and already it took a long time to thaw a way down into them at night. Bill spread his in the middle, Bowers was on his right, and I was on his left. Always he insisted that I should start getting my legs into mine before *he* started: we were rapidly cooling down after our hot supper, and this was very unselfish of him. Then came seven shivering hours and first thing on getting out of sleeping-bags in the morning we stuffed our personal gear into the mouth of the bag before it could freeze: this made a plug which when removed formed a frozen hole for us to push into as a start in the evening.

We got into some strange knots when trying to persuade our limbs into our bags, and suffered terribly from cramp in consequence. We would wait and rub, but directly we tried to move again down it would come and grip our legs in a vice. We also, especially Bowers, suffered agony from cramp in the stomach. We let the primus burn on after supper now for a time – it was the only thing which kept us going – and when one who was holding the primus was seized with cramp we hastily took the lamp from him until the spasm was

over. It was horrible to see Birdie's stomach cramp sometimes: he
certainly got it much worse than Bill or I. I suffered a lot from
heartburn, especially in my bag at nights: we were eating a great
proportion of fat and this was probably the cause. Stupidly I said
nothing about it for a long time. Later when Bill found out, he soon
made it better with the medical case.

Birdie always lit the candle in the morning – so called, and this
was an heroic business. Moisture collected on our matches if you
looked at them. Partly I suppose it was bringing them from outside
into a comparatively warm tent; partly from putting boxes into
pockets in our clothing. Sometimes it was necessary to try four or
five boxes before a match struck. The temperature of the boxes and
matches was about a hundred degrees of frost, and the smallest
touch of the metal on naked flesh caused a frost-bite. If you wore
mitts you could scarcely feel anything – especially since the tips of
our fingers were already very callous. To get the first light going in
the morning was a beastly cold business, made worse by having to
make sure that it was at last time to get up. Bill insisted that we
must lie in our bags seven hours every night.

In civilization men are taken at their own valuation because there
are so many ways of concealment, and there is so little time, perhaps
even so little understanding. Not so down South. These two men
went through the Winter Journey and lived: later they went through
the Polar Journey and died. They were gold, pure, shining, unalloyed.
Words cannot express how good their companionship was.

Through all these days, and those which were to follow, the worst
I suppose in their dark severity that men have ever come through
alive, no single hasty or angry word passed their lips. When, later,
we were sure, so far as we can be sure of anything, that we must
die, they were cheerful, and so far as I can judge their songs and
cheery words were quite unforced. Nor were they ever flurried,
though always as quick as the conditions would allow in moments
of emergency. It is hard that often such men must go first when
others far less worthy remain.

There are those who write of Polar Expeditions as though the
whole thing was as easy as possible. They are trusting, I suspect, in
a public who will say, 'What a fine fellow this is! We know what
horrors he has endured, yet see, how little he makes of all his
difficulties and hardships.' Others have gone to the opposite extreme.
I do not know that there is any use in trying to make a −18°

temperature appear formidable to an uninitiated reader by calling it fifty degrees of frost. I want to do neither of these things. I am not going to pretend that this was anything but a ghastly journey, made bearable and even pleasant to look back upon by the qualities of my two companions who have gone. At the same time I have no wish to make it appear more horrible than it actually was: the reader need not fear that I am trying to exaggerate . . .

*

The temperature that night was −75.8°, and I will not pretend that it did not convince me that Dante was right when he placed the circles of ice below the circles of fire. Still we slept sometimes, and always we lay for seven hours. Again and again Bill asked us how about going back, and always we said no. Yet there was nothing I should have liked better: I was quite sure that to dream of Cape Crozier was the wildest lunacy. That day we had advanced 1½ miles by the utmost labour, and the usual relay work. This was quite a good march – and Cape Crozier is 67 miles from Cape Evans!

More than once in my short life I have been struck by the value of the man who is blind to what appears to be a common-sense certainty: he achieves the impossible. We never spoke our thoughts: we discussed the Age of Stone which was to come, when we built our cosy warm rock hut on the slopes of Mount Terror, and ran our stove with penguin blubber, and pickled little Emperors in warmth and dryness. We were quite intelligent people, and we must all have known that we were not going to see the penguins and that it was folly to go forward. And yet with quiet perseverance, in perfect friendship, almost with gentleness those two men led on. I just did what I was told.

It is desirable that the body should work, feed and sleep at regular hours, and this is too often forgotten when sledging. But just now we found we were unable to fit eight hours marching and seven hours in our sleeping-bags into a 24-hour day: the routine camp work took more than nine hours, such were the conditions. We therefore ceased to observe the quite imaginary difference between night and day, and it was noon on Friday (7 July) before we got away. The temperature was −68° and there was a thick white fog: generally we had but the vaguest idea where we were, and we camped at 10 p.m. after managing 1¾ miles for the day. But what a relief. Instead of labouring away, our hearts were beating more naturally: it was easier to camp, we had some feeling in our hands, and our feet had not gone to sleep. Birdie swung the thermometer and found it only −55°. 'Now if we tell people that to get only 87 degrees of frost can be an enormous relief they simply won't believe us,' I remember saying. Perhaps you won't, but it was, all the same: and I wrote that night: 'There is something after all rather good in doing something never done before.' Things were looking up, you see.

Our hearts were doing very gallant work. Towards the end of the march they were getting beaten and were finding it difficult to pump the blood out to our extremities. There were few days that Wilson and I did not get some part of our feet frost-bitten. As we camped, I suspect our hearts were beating comparatively slowly and weakly. Nothing could be done until a hot drink was ready – tea for lunch, hot water for supper. Directly we started to drink then the effect was wonderful: it was, said Wilson, like putting a hot-water bottle against your heart. The beats became very rapid and strong and you felt the warmth travelling outwards and downwards. Then you got your foot-gear off – puttees (cut in half and wound round the bottom of the trousers), finnesko, saennegrass, hair socks, and two pairs of woollen socks. Then you nursed back your feet and tried to believe you were glad – a frost-bite does not hurt until it begins to thaw. Later came the blisters, and then the chunks of dead skin. . . .

*

On 8 July we found the first sign that we might be coming to an end of this soft, powdered, arrowrooty snow. It was frightfully hard pulling; but every now and then our finnesko pierced a thin crust before they sank right in. This meant a little wind, and every now and then our feet came down on a hard slippery patch under the soft snow. We were surrounded by fog which walked along with us, and far above us the moon was shining on its roof. Steering was as difficult as the pulling, and four hours of the hardest work only produced 1¼ miles in the morning, and three more hours one mile in the afternoon – and the temperature was −57° with a breeze – horrible!

In the early morning of the next day snow began to fall and the fog was dense: when we got up we could see nothing at all anywhere. After the usual four hours to get going in the morning we settled that it was impossible to relay, for we should never be able to track ourselves back to the second sledge. It was with very great relief that we found we could move both sledges together, and I think this was mainly due to the temperature which had risen to −36°.

This was our fourth day of fog in addition to the normal darkness, and we knew we must be approaching the land. It would be Terror Point, and the fog is probably caused by the moist warm air coming up from the sea through the pressure cracks and crevasses; for it is supposed that the Barrier here is afloat.

I wish I could take you on to the great Ice Barrier some calm evening when the sun is just dipping in the middle of the night and show you the autumn tints on Ross Island. A last look round before turning in, a good day's march behind, enough fine fat pemmican inside you to make you happy, the homely smell of tobacco from the tent, a pleasant sense of soft fur and the deep sleep to come. And all the softest colours God has made are in the snow; on Erebus to the west, where the wind can scarcely move his cloud of smoke; and on Terror to the east, not so high, and more regular in form. How peaceful and dignified it all is.

That was what you might have seen four months ago had you been out on the Barrier plain. Low down on the extreme right or east of the land there was a black smudge of rock peeping out from great snow-drifts: that was the Knoll, and close under it were the cliffs of Cape Crozier, the Knoll looking quite low and the cliffs invisible, although they are eight hundred feet high, a sheer precipice falling to the sea.

It is at Cape Crozier that the Barrier edge, which runs for four hundred miles as an ice-cliff up to 200 feet high, meets the land. The Barrier is moving against this land at a rate which is sometimes not much less than a mile in a year. Perhaps you can imagine the chaos which it piles up: there are pressure ridges compared to which the waves of the sea are like a ploughed field. These are worst at Cape Crozier itself, but they extend all along the southern slopes of Mount Terror, running parallel with the land, and the disturbance which Cape Crozier makes is apparent at Corner Camp some forty miles back on the Barrier in the crevasses we used to find and the occasional ridges we had to cross.

In the *Discovery* days the pressure just where it hit Cape Crozier formed a small bay, and on the sea-ice frozen in this bay the men of the *Discovery* found the only Emperor penguin rookery which had ever been seen. The ice here was not blown out by the blizzards which cleared the Ross Sea, and open water or open leads were never far away. This gave the Emperors a place to lay their eggs and an opportunity to find their food. We had therefore to find our way along the pressure to the Knoll, and thence penetrate *through* the pressure to the Emperors' Bay. And we had to do it in the dark.

Terror Point, which we were approaching in the fog, is a short twenty miles from the Knoll, and ends in a long snow-tongue running out into the Barrier. The way bad been travelled a good many times in *Discovery* days and in daylight, and Wilson knew there was a narrow path, free from crevasses, which skirted along between the mountain and the pressure ridges running parallel to it. But it is one thing to walk along a corridor by day, and quite another to try to do so at night, especially when there are no walls by which you can correct your course – only crevasses. Anyway, Terror Point must be somewhere close to us now, and vaguely in front of us was that strip of snow, neither Barrier nor mountain, which was our only way forward.

We began to realize, now that our eyes were more or less out of action, how much we could do with our feet and ears. The effect of walking in finnesko is much the same as walking in gloves, and you get a sense of touch which nothing else except bare feet could give you. Thus we could feel every small variation in surface, every crust through which our feet broke, every hardened patch below the soft snow. And soon we began to rely more and more upon the sound of our footsteps to tell us whether we were on crevasses or solid ground. From now onwards we were working among crevasses fairly constantly. I loathe them in full daylight when much can be done to avoid them, and when if you fall into them you can at any rate see where the sides are, which way they run and how best to scramble out; when your companions can see how to stop the sledge to which you are all attached by your harness; how most safely to hold the sledge when stopped; how, if you are dangling fifteen feet down in a chasm, to work above you to get you up to the surface again. And then our clothes were generally something like clothes. Even under the ideal conditions of good light, warmth and no wind, crevasses are beastly, whether you are pulling over a level and uniform snow surface, never knowing what moment will find you dropping into some bottomless pit, or whether you are rushing for the Alpine rope and the sledge, to help some companion who has disappeared. I dream sometimes now of bad days we had on the Beardmore and elsewhere, when men were dropping through to be caught up and hang at the full length of the harnesses and toggles many times in an hour. On the same sledge as myself on the Beardmore one man went down once head first, and another eight times to the length of his harness in 25 minutes. And always you wondered whether your harness was going to hold when the jerk came. But those days were a Sunday School treat compared to our days of blind-man's-bluff with the Emperor penguins among the crevasses of Cape Crozier.

Our troubles were greatly increased by the state of our clothes. If we had been dressed in lead we should have been able to move our arms and necks and heads more easily than we could now. If the same amount of icing had extended to our legs I believe we should still be there, standing unable to move: but happily the forks of our trousers still remained movable. To get into our canvas harness was the most absurd business. Quite in the early days of our journey we met with this difficulty, and somewhat foolishly decided not to take off our harness for lunch. The harnesses thawed in the tent, and froze back as hard as boards. Likewise our clothing was hard as boards and stuck out from our bodies in every imaginable fold and angle. To fit one board over the other required the efforts of the would-be wearer and his two companions, and the process had to be repeated for each one of us twice a day. Goodness knows how long it took; but it cannot have been less than five minutes' thumping at each man.

As we approached Terror Point in the fog we sensed that we had risen and fallen over several rises. Every now and then we felt hard slippery snow under our feet. Every now and then our feet went through crusts in the surface. And then quite suddenly, vague, indefinable, monstrous, there loomed a something ahead. I remember having a feeling as of ghosts about as we untoggled our harnesses from the sledge, tied them together, and thus roped walked upwards on that ice. The moon was showing a ghastly ragged mountainous edge above us in the fog, and as we rose we found that we were on a pressure ridge. We stopped, looked at one another, and then *bang* – right under our feet. More bangs, and creaks and groans; for that ice was moving and splitting like glass. The cracks went off all round us, and some of them ran along for hundreds of yards. Afterwards we got used to it, but at first the effect was very jumpy. From first

to last during this journey we had plenty of variety and none of that
monotony which is inevitable in sledging over long distances of
Barrier in summer. Only the long shivering fits following close one
after the other all the time we lay in our dreadful sleeping-bags,
hour after hour and night after night in those temperatures – they
were as monotonous as could be. Later we got frost-bitten even as
we lay in our sleeping-bags. Things are getting pretty bad when you
get frost-bitten in your bag.

There was only a glow where the moon was; we stood in a
moonlit fog, and this was sufficient to show the edge of another
ridge ahead, and yet another on our left. We were utterly bewildered.
The deep booming of the ice continued, and it may be that the tide
has something to do with this, though we were many miles from
the ordinary coastal ice. We went back, toggled up to our sledges
again and pulled in what we thought was the right direction, always
with that feeling that the earth may open underneath your feet
which you have in crevassed areas. But all we found were more
mounds and banks of snow and ice, into which we almost ran before
we saw them. We were clearly lost. It was near midnight, and I
wrote, 'it may be the pressure ridges or it may be Terror, it is
impossible to say, – and I should think it is impossible to move till it
clears. We were steering N.E. when we got here and returned S.W.
till we seemed to be in a hollow and camped.'

The temperature had been rising from −36° at 11 a.m. and it was
now −27°; snow was falling and nothing whatever could be seen.
From under the tent came noises as though some giant was banging
a big empty tank. All the signs were for a blizzard, and indeed we
had not long finished our supper and were thawing our way little
by little into our bags when the wind came away from the south.
Before it started we got a glimpse of black rock, and knew we must
be in the pressure ridges where they nearly join Mount Terror.

It is with great surprise that in looking up the records I find that
blizzard lasted three days, the temperature and wind both rising till
it was +9° and blowing force 9 on the morning of the second day
(11 July). On the morning of the third day (12 July) it was blowing
storm force (10). The temperature had thus risen over eighty degrees.

It was not an uncomfortable time. Wet and warm, the risen
temperature allowed all our ice to turn to water, and we lay steaming
and beautifully liquid, and wondered sometimes what we should be

like when our gear froze up once more. But we did not do much wondering, I suspect: we slept. From that point of view these blizzards were a perfect Godsend . . .

*

When we started next morning (15 July) we could see on our left front and more or less on top of us the Knoll, which is a big hill whose precipitous cliffs to seaward form Cape Crozier. The sides of it sloped down towards us, and pressing against its ice-cliffs on ahead were miles and miles of great pressure ridges, along which we had travelled, and which hemmed us in. Mount Terror rose ten thousand feet high on our left, and was connected with the Knoll by a great cup-like drift of wind-polished snow. The slope of this in one place runs gently out on to the corridor along which we had sledged, and here we turned and started to pull our sledges up. There were no crevasses, only the great drift of snow, so hard that we used our crampons just as though we had been on ice, and as polished as the china sides of a giant cup which it resembled. For three miles we slogged up, until we were only 150 yards from the moraine shelf where we were going to build our hut of rocks and snow. This moraine was above us on our left, the twin peaks of the Knoll were across the cup on our right; and here, 800 feet up the mountain side, we pitched our last camp . . .

We had arrived.

*

Birdie was very disappointed that we could not finish the whole thing that day: he was nearly angry about it, but there was a lot to do yet and we were tired out. We turned out early the next morning (Tuesday 18th) to try and finish the igloo, but it was blowing too hard. When we got to the top we did some digging but it was quite impossible to get the roof on, and we had to leave it. We realized that day that it blew much harder at the top of the slope than where our tent was. It was bitterly cold up there that morning with a wind force 4–5 and a minus thirty temperature.

The oil question was worrying us quite a lot. We were now well in to the fifth of our six tins, and economizing as much as possible, often having only two hot meals a day. We had to get down to the Emperor penguins somehow and get some blubber to run the stove which had been made for us in the hut. The 19th being a calm fine day we started at 9.30, with an empty sledge, two ice-axes, Alpine rope, harnesses and skinning tools.

Wilson had made this journey through the Cape Crozier pressure ridges several times in the *Discovery* days. But then they had daylight, and they had found a practicable way close under the cliffs which at the present moment were between us and the ridges.

As we neared the bottom of the mountain slope, farther to the north than we had previously gone, we had to be careful about crevasses, but we soon hit off the edge of the cliff and skirted along it until it petered out on the same level as the Barrier. Turning left handed we headed towards the sea-ice, knowing that there were some two miles of pressure between us and Cape Crozier itself. For about half a mile it was fair going, rounding big knobs of pressure but always managing to keep more or less on the flat and near the ice-cliff which soon rose to a very great height on our left. Bill's idea was to try and keep close under this cliff, along that same *Discovery* way which I have mentioned above. They never arrived there early enough for the eggs in those days: the chicks were hatched. Whether we should now find any Emperors, and if so whether they would have any eggs, was by no means certain.

However, we soon began to get into trouble, meeting several crevasses every few yards, and I have no doubt crossing scores of others of which we had no knowledge. Though we hugged the cliffs as close as possible we found ourselves on the top of the first pressure ridge, separated by a deep gulf from the ice-slope which we wished to reach. Then we were in a great valley between the first and second ridges: we got into huge heaps of ice pressed up in every shape on every side, crevassed in every direction: we slithered over snow-slopes and crawled along drift ridges, trying to get in towards the cliffs. And always we came up against impossible places and had to crawl back. Bill led on a length of Alpine rope fastened to the toggle of the sledge; Birdie was in his harness also fastened to the toggle, and I was in my harness fastened to the rear of the sledge, which was of great use to us both as a bridge and a ladder.

Two or three times we tried to get down the ice-slopes to the comparatively level road under the cliffs, but it was always too great a drop. In that dim light every proportion was distorted; some of the places we actually did manage to negotiate with ice-axes and Alpine rope looked absolute precipices, and there were always crevasses at the bottom if you slipped. On the way back I did slip into one of these and was hauled out by the other two standing on the wall above me.

We then worked our way down into the hollow between the first and second large pressure ridges, and I believe on to the top of the second. The crests here rose fifty or sixty feet. After this I don't know where we went. Our best landmarks were patches of crevasses, sometimes three or four in a few footsteps. The temperatures were lowish (−37°), it was impossible for me to wear spectacles, and this was a tremendous difficulty to me and handicap to the party: Bill would find a crevasse and point it out; Birdie would cross; and then time after time, in trying to step over or climb over on the sledge, I put my feet right into the middle of the cracks. This day I went well in at least six times; once, when we were close to the sea, rolling into and out of one and then down a steep slope until brought up by Birdie and Bill on the rope.

We blundered along until we got into a great cul-de-sac which probably formed the end of the two ridges, where they butted on to the sea-ice. On all sides rose great walls of battered ice with steep snow-slopes in the middle, where we slithered about and blundered into crevasses. To the left rose the huge cliff of Cape Crozier, but we could not tell whether there were not two or three pressure ridges between us and it, and though we tried at least four ways, there was no possibility of getting forward.

And then we heard the Emperors calling.

Their cries came to us from the sea-ice we could not see, but which must have been a chaotic quarter of a mile away. They came echoing back from the cliffs, as we stood helpless and tantalized. We listened and realized that there was nothing for it but to return, for the little light which now came in the middle of the day was going fast, and to be caught in absolute darkness there was a horrible idea. We started back on our tracks and almost immediately I lost my footing and rolled down a slope into a crevasse. Birdie and Bill kept their balance and I clambered back to them. The tracks were very faint and we soon began to lose them. Birdie was the best man at following tracks that I have ever known, and he found them time after time. But at last even he lost them altogether and we settled we must just go ahead. As a matter of fact, we picked them up again, and by then were out of the worst: but we were glad to see the tent.

The next morning (Thursday, 20 June) we started work on the igloo at 3 a.m. and managed to get the canvas roof on in spite of a wind which harried us all that day. Little did we think what that roof had in store for us as we packed it in with snow blocks, stretching it over our second sledge, which we put athwartships across the middle of the longer walls. The windward (south) end came right down to the ground and we tied it securely to rocks before packing it in. On the other three sides we had a good two feet or more of slack all round, and in every case we tied it to rocks by lanyards at intervals of two feet. The door was the difficulty, and for the present we left the cloth arching over the stones, forming a kind of portico. The whole was well packed in and over with slabs of hard snow, but there was no soft snow with which to fill up the gaps between the blocks. However, we felt already that nothing could drag that roof out of its packing, and subsequent events proved that we were right.

It was a bleak job for three o'clock in the morning before breakfast, and we were glad to get back to the tent and a meal, for we meant to have another go at the Emperors that day. With the first glimpse of light we were off for the rookery again.

But we now knew one or two things about that pressure which we had not known twenty-four hours ago; for instance, that there was a lot of alteration since the *Discovery* days and that probably the pressure was bigger. As a matter of fact it has been since proved by photographs that the ridges now ran out three-quarters of a mile farther into the sea than they did ten years before. We knew also that if we entered the pressure at the only place where the ice-cliffs came down to the level of the Barrier, as we did yesterday, we could neither penetrate to the rookery nor get in under the cliffs where formerly a possible way had been found. There was only one other thing to do – to go over the cliffs. And this was what we proposed to try and do.

Now these ice-cliffs are some two hundred feet high, and I felt uncomfortable, especially in the dark. But as we came back the day before we had noticed at one place a break in the cliffs from which there hung a snow-drift. It *might* be possible to get down that drift.

And so, all harnessed to the sledge, with Bill on a long lead out in front and Birdie and myself checking the sledge behind, we started down the slope which ended in the cliff, which of course we could not see. We crossed a number of small crevasses, and soon we knew we must be nearly there. Twice we crept up to the edge of the cliff with no success, and then we found the slope: more, we got down it without great difficulty and it brought us out just where we wanted to be, between the land cliffs and the pressure.

Then began the most exciting climb among the pressure that you can imagine. At first very much as it was the day before – pulling ourselves and one another up ridges, slithering down slopes, tumbling into and out of crevasses and holes of all sorts, we made our way along under the cliffs which rose higher and higher above us as we neared the black lava precipices which form Cape Crozier itself. We straddled along the top of a snow ridge with a razor-backed edge, balancing the sledge between us as we wriggled: on our right was a drop of great depth with crevasses at the bottom, on our left was a smaller drop also crevassed. We crawled along, and I can tell you it was exciting work in the more than half darkness. At the end was a series of slopes full of crevasses, and finally we got right in under the rock on to moraine, and here we had to leave the sledge.

We roped up, and started to worry along under the cliffs, which had now changed from ice to rock, and rose 800 feet above us. The tumult of pressure which climbed against them showed no order here. Four hundred miles of moving ice behind it had just tossed and twisted those giant ridges until Job himself would have lacked words to reproach their Maker. We scrambled over and under, hanging on with our axes and cutting steps where we could not find a foothold with our crampons. And always we got towards the Emperor penguins, and it really began to look as if we were going to do it this time, when we came up against a wall of ice which a single glance told us we could never cross. One of the largest pressure ridges had been thrown, end on, against the cliff. We seemed to be stopped, when Bill found a black hole, something like a fox's earth, disappearing into the bowels of the ice. We looked at it: 'Well, here goes!' he said, and put his head in, and disappeared. Bowers likewise. It was a longish way, but quite possible to wriggle along, and presently I found myself looking out of the other side with a deep gully below me, the rock face on one hand and the ice on the other. 'Put your back against the ice and your feet against the rock and lever yourself along,' said Bill, who was already standing on firm ice at the far end in a snow pit. We cut some fifteen steps to get out of that hole. Excited by now, and thoroughly enjoying ourselves, we found the way ahead easier, until the penguins' call reached us again and we stood, three crystallized ragamuffins, above the Emperors' home. They were there all right, and we were going to reach them, but where were all the thousands of which we had heard?

We stood on an ice-foot which was really a dwarf cliff some twelve feet high, and the sea-ice, with a good many ice-blocks strewn upon it, lay below. The cliff dropped straight, with a bit of an overhang and no snow-drift. This may have been because the sea had only frozen recently; whatever the reason may have been it meant that we should have a lot of difficulty in getting up again without help. It was decided that someone must stop on the top with the Alpine rope, and clearly that one should be I, for with short sight and fogged spectacles which I could not wear I was much the least useful of the party for the job immediately ahead. Had we had the sledge we could have used it as a ladder, but of course we had left this at the beginning of the moraine miles back.

We saw the Emperors standing all together huddled under the Barrier cliff some hundreds of yards away. The little light was going fast: we were much more excited about the approach of complete darkness and the look of wind in the south than we were about our triumph. After indescribable effort and hardship we were witnessing a marvel of the natural world, and we were the first and only men who had ever done so; we had within our grasp material which might prove of the utmost importance to science; we were turning theories into facts with every observation we made, – and we had but a moment to give.

The disturbed Emperors made a tremendous row, trumpeting with their curious metallic voices. There was no doubt they had eggs, for they tried to shuffle along the ground without losing them off their feet. But when they were hustled a good many eggs were dropped and left lying on the ice, and some of these were quickly picked up by eggless Emperors who had probably been waiting a long time for the opportunity. In these poor birds the maternal side seems to have necessarily swamped the other functions of life. Such is the struggle for existence that they can only live by a glut of maternity, and it would be interesting to know whether such a life leads to happiness or satisfaction.

The men of the *Discovery* found this rookery where we now stood. They made journeys in the early spring but never arrived early enough to get eggs and only found parents and chicks. They concluded that the Emperor was an impossible kind of bird who, for some reason or other, nests in the middle of the Antarctic winter with the temperature anywhere below seventy degrees of frost, and the blizzards blowing, always blowing, against his devoted back. And they found him holding his precious chick balanced upon his big feet, and pressing it maternally, or paternally (for both sexes squabble for the privilege) against a bald patch in his breast. And when at last he simply must go and eat something in the open leads near by, he just puts the child down on the ice, and twenty chickless Emperors rush to pick it up. And they fight over it, and so tear it that sometimes it will die. And, if it can, it will crawl into any ice-crack to escape from so much kindness, and there it will freeze. Likewise many broken and addled eggs were found, and it is clear that the mortality is very great. But some survive, and summer comes; and when a big blizzard is going to blow (they know all about the weather), the parents take the children out for miles across the sea-ice, until they reach the threshold of the open sea. And there they sit until the wind comes, and the swell rises, and breaks that ice-floe off; and away they go in the blinding drift to join the main pack-ice, with a private yacht all to themselves.

You must agree that a bird like this is an interesting beast, and when, seven months ago, we rowed a boat under those great black cliffs, and found a disconsolate Emperor chick still in the down, we knew definitely why the Emperor has to nest in mid-winter. For if a June egg was still without feathers in the beginning of January, the same egg laid in the summer would leave its produce without practical covering for the following winter. Thus the Emperor penguin is compelled to undertake all kinds of hardships because his children insist on developing so slowly, very much as we are tied in our human relationships for the same reason. It is of interest that such a primitive bird should have so long a childhood.

But interesting as the life history of these birds must be, we had not travelled for three weeks to see them sitting on their eggs. We wanted the embryos, and we wanted them as young as possible, and fresh and unfrozen, that specialists at home might cut them into microscopic sections and learn from the previous history of birds throughout the evolutionary ages. And so Bill and Birdie rapidly collected five eggs, which we hoped to carry safely in our fur mitts to our igloo upon Mount Terror, where we could pickle them in the alcohol we had brought for the purpose. We also wanted oil for our

blubber stove, and they killed and skinned three birds – an Emperor
weighs up to 6½ stones . . .

*

Meanwhile a whole procession of Emperors came round under the
cliff on which I stood. The light was already very bad and it was
well that my companions were quick in returning: we had to do
everything in a great hurry. I hauled up the eggs in their mitts (which
we fastened together round our necks with lampwick lanyards) and
then the skins, but failed to help Bill at all. 'Pull,' he cried, from the
bottom: 'I am pulling,' I said. 'But the line's quite slack down here,'
he shouted. And when he had reached the top by climbing up on
Bowers's shoulders, and we were both pulling all we knew, Birdie's
end of the rope was still slack in his hands. Directly we put on a
strain the rope cut into the ice edge and jammed – a very common
difficulty when working among crevasses. We tried to run the rope
over an ice-axe without success, and things began to look serious
when Birdie, who had been running about prospecting and had
meanwhile put one leg through a crack into the sea, found a place
where the cliff did not overhang. He cut steps for himself, we hauled,
and at last we were all together on the top – his foot being by now
surrounded by a solid mass of ice.

We legged it back as hard as we could go: five eggs in our fur
mitts, Birdie with two skins tied to him and trailing behind, and
myself with one. We were roped up, and climbing the ridges and
getting through the holes was very difficult. In one place where
there was a steep rubble and snow slope down I left the ice-axe halfway up; in another it was too dark to see our former ice-axe footsteps,
and I could see nothing, and so just let myself go and trusted to
luck. With infinite patience Bill said: 'Cherry, you *must* learn how
to use an ice-axe.' For the rest of the trip my wind-clothes were in
rags.

We found the sledge, and none too soon, and now had three
eggs left, more or less whole. Both mine had burst in my mitts: the
first I emptied out, the second I left in my mitt to put into the cooker;
it never got there, but on the return journey I had my mitts far
more easily thawed out than Birdie's (Bill had none) and I believe
the grease in the egg did them good. When we got into the hollows
under the ridge where we had to cross, it was too dark to do anything
but feel our way. We did so over many crevasses, found the ridge

and crept over it. Higher up we could see more, but to follow our tracks soon became impossible, and we plugged straight ahead and luckily found the slope down which we had come. All day it had been blowing a nasty cold wind with a temperature between −20° and 30°, which we felt a good deal. Now it began to get worse. The weather was getting thick and things did not look very nice when we started up to find our tent. Soon it was blowing force 4, and soon we missed our way entirely. We got right up above the patch of rocks which marked our igloo and only found it after a good deal of search.

I have heard tell of an English officer at the Dardanelles who was left, blinded, in no-man's-land between the English and Turkish trenches. Moving only at night, and having no sense to tell him which were his own trenches, he was fired at by Turk and English alike as he groped his ghastly way to and from them. Thus he spent days and nights until, one night, he crawled towards the English trenches, to be fired at as usual. 'Oh God! what can I do!' someone heard him say, and he was brought in.

Such extremity of suffering cannot be measured: madness or death may give relief. But this I know: we on this journey were already beginning to think of death as a friend. As we groped our way back that night, sleepless, icy, and dog-tired in the dark and the wind and the drift, a crevasse seemed almost a friendly gift.

'Things must improve,' said Bill next day, 'I think we reached bed-rock last night.' We hadn't, by a long way.

It was like this.

We moved into the igloo for the first time, for we had to save oil by using our blubber stove if we were to have any left to travel home with, and we did not wish to cover our tent with the oily black filth which the use of blubber necessitates. The blizzard blew all night, and we were covered with drift which came in through hundreds of leaks: in this wind-swept place we had found no soft snow with which we could pack our hard snow blocks. As we flensed some blubber from one of our penguin skins the powdery drift covered everything we had.

Though uncomfortable this was nothing to worry about over-much. Some of the drift which the blizzard was bringing would collect to leeward of our hut and the rocks below which it was built, and they could be used to make our hut more weather-proof. Then with great difficulty we got the blubber stove to start, and it spouted a blob of boiling oil into Bill's eye. For the rest of the night he lay, quite unable to stifle his groans, obviously in very great pain: be told us afterwards that he thought his eye was gone. We managed to cook a meal somehow, and Birdie got the stove going afterwards, but it was quite useless to try and warm the place. I got out and cut the green canvas outside the door, so as to get the roof cloth in under the stones, and then packed it down as well as I could with snow, and so blocked most of the drift coming in.

It is extraordinary how often angels and fools do the same thing in this life, and I have never been able to settle which we were on this journey. I never heard an angry word: once only (when this same day I could not pull Bill up the cliff out of the penguin rookery) I heard an impatient one: and these groans were the nearest approach to complaint. Most men would have howled. 'I think we reached bed-rock last night,' was strong language for Bill. 'I was incapacitated for a short time,' he says in his report to Scott.[1] Endurance was tested on this journey under unique circumstances, and always these two men with all the burden of responsibility which did not fall upon myself, displayed that quality which is perhaps the only one which may be said with certainty to make for success, self-control.

We spent the next day – it was 21 July – in collecting every scrap of soft snow we could find and packing it into the crevasses between our hard snow blocks. It was a pitifully small amount but we could see no cracks when we had finished. To counteract the lifting tendency the wind had on our roof we cut some great flat hard snow blocks and laid them on the canvas top to steady it against the sledge which formed the ridge support. We also pitched our tent outside the igloo door. Both tent and igloo were therefore eight or nine hundred feet up Terror: both were below an outcrop of rocks from which the mountain fell steeply to the Barrier behind us, and from this direction came the blizzards. In front of us the slope fell for a mile or more down to the ice-cliffs, so wind-swept that we had to wear crampons to walk upon it. Most of the tent was in the lee of the igloo, but the cap of it came over the igloo roof, while a segment of the tent itself jutted out beyond the igloo wall.

That night we took much of our gear into the tent and lighted the blubber stove. I always mistrusted that stove, and every moment I expected it to flare up and burn the tent. But the heat it gave, as

---

1. *Scott's Last Expedition*, vol. ii, p. 42.

it burned furiously, with the double lining of the tent to contain it, was considerable.

It did not matter, except for a routine which we never managed to keep, whether we started to thaw our way into our frozen sleeping-bags at 4 in the morning or 4 in the afternoon. I think we must have turned in during the afternoon of that Friday, leaving the cooker, our finnesko, a deal of our foot-gear, Bowers's bag of personal gear, and many other things in the tent. I expect we left the blubber stove there too, for it was quite useless at present to try and warm the igloo. The tent floor-cloth was under our sleeping-bags in the igloo . . .

*

And so we spent half an hour or more getting into our bags. Cirrus cloud was moving across the face of the stars from the north, it looked rather hazy and thick to the south, but it is always difficult to judge weather in the dark. There was little wind and the tempera-ture was in the minus twenties. We felt no particular uneasiness. Our tent was well dug in, and was also held down by rocks and the heavy tank off the sledge which were placed on the skirting as additional security. We felt that no power on earth could move the thick walls of our igloo, nor drag the canvas roof from the middle of the embankment into which it was packed and lashed.

'Things must improve,' said Bill.

I do not know what time it was when I woke up. It was calm, with that absolute silence which can be so soothing or so terrible as circumstances dictate. Then there came a sob of wind, and all was still again. Ten minutes and it was blowing as though the world was having a fit of hysterics. The earth was torn in pieces: the indescribable fury and roar of it all cannot be imagined.

'Bill, Bill, the tent has gone,' was the next I remember – from Bowers shouting at us again and again through the door. It is always these early morning shocks which hit one hardest: our slow minds suggested that this might mean a peculiarly lingering form of death. Journey after journey Birdie and I fought our way across the few yards which had separated the tent from the igloo door. I have never understood why so much of our gear which was in the tent remained, even in the lee of the igloo. The place where the tent had been was littered with gear, and when we came to reckon up afterwards we had everything except the bottom piece of the cooker, and the top of the outer cooker. We never saw these again. The most wonderful thing of all was that our finnesko were lying where they were left, which happened to be on the ground in the part of the tent which was under the lee of the igloo. Also Birdie's bag of personal gear was there, and a tin of sweets.

Birdie brought two tins of sweets away with him. One we had to celebrate our arrival at the Knoll: this was the second, of which we knew nothing, and which was for Bill's birthday, the next day. We started eating them on Saturday, however, and the tin came in useful to Bill afterwards.

To get that gear in we fought against solid walls of black snow which flowed past us and tried to hurl us down the slope. Once started nothing could have stopped us. I saw Birdie knocked over once, but he clawed his way back just in time. Having passed everything we could find in to Bill, we got back into the igloo, and started to collect things together, including our very dishevelled minds.

There was no doubt that we were in the devil of a mess, and it was not altogether our fault. We had had to put our igloo more or less where we could get rocks with which to build it. Very naturally we had given both our tent and igloo all the shelter we could from the full force of the wind, and now it seemed we were in danger not because they were in the wind, but because they were not sufficiently in it. The main force of the hurricane, deflected by the ridge behind, fled over our heads and appeared to form by suction a vacuum below. Our tent had either been sucked upwards into this, or had been blown away, because some of it was in the wind while some of it was not. The roof of our igloo was being wrenched upwards and then dropped back with great crashes: the drift was spouting in, not it seemed because it was blown in from outside, but because it was sucked in from within: the lee, not the weather, wall was the worst. Already everything was six or eight inches under snow.

Very soon we began to be alarmed about the igloo. For some time the heavy snow blocks we had heaved up on to the canvas roof kept it weighted down. But it seemed that they were being gradually moved off by the hurricane. The tension became well-nigh unendurable: the waiting in all that welter of noise was maddening. Minute after minute, hour after hour – those snow blocks were off now anyway, and the roof was smashed up and down – no canvas ever made could stand it indefinitely.

We got a meal that Saturday morning, our last for a very long time as it happened. Oil being of such importance to us we tried to use the blubber stove, but after several preliminary spasms it came to pieces in our hands, some solder having melted; and a very good thing too, I thought, for it was more dangerous than useful. We finished cooking our meal on the primus. Two bits of the cooker having been blown away we had to balance it on the primus as best we could. We then settled that in view of the shortage of oil we would not have another meal for as long as possible. As a matter of fact God settled that for us.

We did all we could to stop up the places where the drift was coming in, plugging the holes with our socks, mitts and other clothing. But it was no real good. Our igloo was a vacuum which was filling itself up as soon as possible: and when snow was not coming in a fine black moraine dust took its place, covering us and everything. For twenty-four hours we waited for the roof to go: things were so bad now that we dare not unlash the door.

Many hours ago Bill had told us that if the roof went he considered that our best chance would be to roll over in our sleeping-bags until we were lying on the openings, and get frozen and drifted in.

Gradually the situation got more desperate. The distance between the taut-sucked canvas and the sledge on which it should have been resting became greater, and this must have been due to the stretching of the canvas itself and the loss of the snow blocks on the top: it was not drawing out of the walls. The crashes as it dropped and banged out again were louder. There was more snow coming through the walls, though all our loose mitts, socks and smaller clothing were stuffed into the worst places: our pyjama jackets were stuffed between the roof and the rocks over the door. The rocks were lifting and shaking here till we thought they would fall.

We talked by shouting, and long before this one of us proposed to try and get the Alpine rope lashed down over the roof from outside. But Bowers said it was an absolute impossibility in that wind. 'You could never ask men at sea to try such a thing,' he said. He was up and out of his bag continually, stopping up holes, pressing against bits of roof to try and prevent the flapping and so forth. He was magnificent.

And then it went.

Birdie was over by the door, where the canvas which was bent over the lintel board was working worse than anywhere else. Bill was practically out of his bag pressing against some part with a long stick of some kind. I don't know what I was doing but I was half out of and half in my bag.

The top of the door opened in little slits and that green Willesden canvas flapped into hundreds of little fragments in fewer seconds than it takes to read this. The uproar of it all was indescribable. Even above the savage thunder of that great wind on the mountain came the lash of the canvas as it was whipped to little tiny strips. The highest rocks which we had built into our walls fell upon us, and a sheet of drift came in.

Birdie dived for his sleeping-bag and eventually got in, together with a terrible lot of drift. Bill also – but he was better off: I was already half into mine and all right, so I turned to help Bill. 'Get into your own,' he shouted, and when I continued to try and help him, he leaned over until his mouth was against my ear. 'Please, Cherry,' he said, and his voice was terribly anxious. I know he felt responsible: feared it was he who had brought us to this ghastly end.

The next I knew was Bowers's head across Bill's body. 'We're all right,' he yelled, and we answered in the affirmative. Despite the fact that we knew we only said so because we knew we were all wrong, this statement was helpful. Then we turned our bags over as far as possible, so that the bottom of the bag was uppermost and the flaps were more or less beneath us. And we lay and thought, and sometimes we sang.

I suppose, wrote Wilson, we were all revolving plans to get back without a tent: and the one thing we had left was the floor-cloth upon which we were actually lying. Of course we could not speak at present, but later after the blizzard had stopped we discussed the possibility of digging a hole in the snow each night and covering it over with the floor-cloth. I do not think we had any idea that we could really get back in those temperatures in our present state of ice by such means, but no one ever hinted at such a thing. Birdie and Bill sang quite a lot of songs and hymns, snatches of which reached me every now and then, and I chimed in, somewhat feebly I suspect. Of course we were getting pretty badly drifted up. 'I was resolved to keep warm,' wrote Bowers, 'and beneath my debris covering I paddled my feet and sang all the songs and hymns I knew to pass the time. I could occasionally thump Bill, and as he still moved I knew he was alive all right – what a birthday for him!' Birdie was more drifted up than we, but at times we all had to hummock ourselves up to heave the snow off our bags. By opening the flaps of our bags we could get small pinches of soft drift which we pressed together and put into our mouths to melt. When our hands warmed up again we got some more; so we did not get very thirsty. A few ribbons of canvas still remained in the wall over our heads, and these produced volleys of cracks like pistol shots hour after hour. The canvas never drew out from the walls, not an inch. The wind made just the same noise as an express train running fast through a tunnel if you have both the windows down.

I can well believe that neither of my companions gave up hope for an instant. They must have been frightened, but they were never disturbed. As for me I never had any hope at all; and when the roof went I felt that this was the end. What else could I think? We had spent days in reaching this place through the darkness in cold such as had never been experienced by human beings. We had been out for four weeks under conditions in which no man had existed previously for more than a few days, if that. During this time we had seldom slept except from sheer physical exhaustion, as men sleep on the rack; and every minute of it we had been fighting for the bed-rock necessaries of bare existence, and always in the dark. We had kept ourselves going by enormous care of our feet and hands and bodies, by burning oil, and by having plenty of hot fatty food. Now we had no tent, one tin of oil left out of six, and only part of our cooker. When we were lucky and not too cold we could almost wring water from our clothes, and directly we got out of our sleeping-bags we were frozen into solid sheets of armoured ice. In cold temperatures with all the advantages of a tent over our heads we were already taking more than an hour of fierce struggling and cramp to get into our sleeping-bags – so frozen were they and so long did it take us to thaw our way in. No! Without the tent we were dead men . . .

*

Face to face with real death one does not think of the things that torment the bad people in the tracts, and fill the good people with bliss. I might have speculated on my chances of going to Heaven; but candidly I did not care. I could not have wept if I had tried. I had no wish to review the evils of my past. But the past did seem to have been a bit wasted. The road to Hell may be paved with good intentions: the road to Heaven is paved with lost opportunities.

I wanted those years over again. What fun I would have with

them: what glorious fun! It was a pity. Well has the Persian said that when we come to die we, remembering that God is merciful, will gnaw our elbows with remorse for thinking of the things we have not done for fear of the Day of Judgement.

And I wanted peaches and syrup – badly. We had them at the hut, sweeter and more luscious than you can imagine. And we have been without sugar for a month. Yes – especially the syrup.

Thus impiously I set out to die, making up my mind that I was not going to try and keep warm, that it might not take too long, and thinking I would try and get some morphia from the medical case if it got very bad. Not a bit heroic, and entirely true! Yes! comfortable, warm reader. Men do not fear death, they fear the pain of dying.

And then quite naturally and no doubt disappointingly to those who would like to read of my last agonies (for who would not give pleasure by his death?) I fell asleep. I expect the temperature was pretty high during this great blizzard, and anything near zero was very high to us. That and the snow which drifted over us made a pleasant wet kind of snipe marsh inside our sleeping-bags, and I am sure we all dozed a good bit. There was so much to worry about that there was not the least use in worrying: and we were so *very* tired. We were hungry, for the last meal we had had was in the morning of the day before, but hunger was not very pressing . . .

*

It was in the early morning of Saturday (22 July) that we discovered the loss of the tent. Some time during that morning we had had our last meal. The roof went about noon on Sunday and we had had no meal in the interval because our supply of oil was so low; nor could we move out of our bags except as a last necessity. By Sunday night we had been without a meal for some thirty-six hours . . .

*

In the early hours of Monday there was an occasional hint of a lull. Ordinarily in a big winter blizzard, when you have lived for several days and nights with that turmoil in your ears, the lulls are more trying than the noise: 'the feel of not to feel it'.[2] I do not remember noticing that now. Seven or eight more hours passed, and though it

2. Keats.

was still blowing we could make ourselves heard to one another without great difficulty. It was two days and two nights since we had had a meal.

We decided to get out of our bags and make a search for the tent. We did so, bitterly cold and utterly miserable, though I do not think any of us showed it. In the darkness we could see very little, and no trace whatever of the tent. We returned against the wind, nursing our faces and hands, and settled that we must try and cook a meal somehow. We managed about the weirdest meal eaten north or south. We got the floor-cloth wedged under our bags, then got into our bags and drew the floor-cloth over our heads. Between us we got the primus alight somehow, and by hand we balanced the cooker on top of it, minus the two members which had been blown away. The flame flickered in the draughts. Very slowly the snow in the cooker melted, we threw in a plentiful supply of pemmican, and the smell of it was better than anything on earth. In time we got both tea and pemmican, which was full of hairs from our bags, penguin feathers, dirt and debris, but delicious. The blubber left in the cooker got burnt and gave the tea a burnt taste. None of us ever forgot that meal: I enjoyed it as much as such a meal could be enjoyed, and that burnt taste will always bring back the memory.

It was still dark and we lay down in our bags again, but soon a little glow of light began to come up, and we turned out to have a further search for the tent. Birdie went off before Bill and me. Clumsily I dragged my eider-down out of my bag on my feet, all sopping wet: it was impossible to get it back and I let it freeze: it was soon just like a rock. The sky to the south was as black and sinister as it could possibly be. It looked as though the blizzard would be on us again in a moment.

I followed Bill down the slope. We could find nothing. But, as we searched, we heard a shout somewhere below and to the right. We got on a slope, slipped, and went sliding down quite unable to stop ourselves, and came upon Birdie with the tent, the outer lining still on the bamboos. Our lives had been taken away and given back to us.

We were so thankful we said nothing.

The tent must have been gripped up into the air, shutting as it rose. The bamboos, with the inner lining lashed to them, had entangled the outer cover, and the whole went up together like a shut umbrella. This was our salvation. If it had opened in the air nothing could have prevented its destruction. As it was, with all the accumulated ice upon it, it must have weighed the best part of 100 lbs. It had been dropped about half a mile away, at the bottom of a steep slope: and it fell in a hollow, still shut up. The main force of the wind had passed over it, and there it was, with the bamboos and fastenings wrenched and strained, and the ends of two of the poles broken, but the silk untorn.

If that tent went again we were going with it. We made our way back up the slope with it, carrying it solemnly and reverently, precious as though it were something not quite of the earth. And we dug it in as tent was never dug in before; not by the igloo, but in the old place farther down where we had first arrived. And while Bill was doing this Birdie and I went back to the igloo and dug and scratched and shook away the drift inside until we had found nearly all our gear. It is wonderful how little we lost when the roof went. Most of our gear was hung on the sledge, which was part of the roof, or was packed into the holes of the hut to try and make it drift-proof, and the things must have been blown inwards into the bottom of the hut by the wind from the south and the back draught from the north. Then they were all drifted up. Of course a certain number of mitts and socks were blown away and lost, but the only important things were Bill's fur mitts, which were stuffed into a hole in the rocks of the hut. We loaded up the sledge and pushed it down the slope. I don't know how Birdie was feeling, but I felt so weak that it was the greatest labour. The blizzard looked right on top of us.

We had another meal, and we wanted it: and as the good hoosh ran down into our feet and hands, and up into our cheeks and ears and brains, we discussed what we would do next. Birdie was all for another go at the Emperor penguins. Dear Birdie, he never would admit that he was beaten – I don't know that he ever really was! 'I think he (Wilson) thought he had landed us in a bad corner and was determined to go straight home, though I was for one other tap at the Rookery. However, I had placed myself under his orders for this trip voluntarily, and so we started the next day for home.'[3] There could really be no common-sense doubt: we had to go back, and we were already very doubtful whether we should ever manage to get into our sleeping-bags in very low temperature, so ghastly had they become.

3. Bowers.

I don't know when it was, but I remember walking down that slope – I don't know why, perhaps to try and find the bottom of the cooker – and thinking that there was nothing on earth that a man under such circumstances would not give for a good warm sleep. He would give everything he possessed: he would give – how many – years of his life. One or two at any rate – perhaps five? Yes – I would give five. I remember the sastrugi, the view of the Knoll, the dim hazy black smudge of the sea far away below: the tiny bits of green canvas that twittered in the wind on the surface of the snow: the cold misery of it all, and the weakness which was biting into my heart.

For days Birdie had been urging me to use his eider-down lining – his beautiful dry bag of the finest down – which he had never slipped into his own fur bag. I had refused: I felt that I should be a beast to take it.

We packed the tank ready for a start back in the morning and turned in, utterly worn out. It was only −12° that night, but my left big-toe was frost-bitten in my bag which I was trying to use without an eider-down lining, and my bag was always too big for me. It must have taken several hours to get it back, by beating one foot against the other. When we got up, as soon as we could, as we did every night, for our bags were nearly impossible, it was blowing fairly hard and looked like blizzing. We had a lot to do, two or three hours' work, packing sledges and making a depot of what we did not want, in a corner of the igloo. We left the second sledge, and a note tied to the handle of the pickaxe.

We started down the slope in a wind which was rising all the time and −15°. My job was to balance the sledge behind: I was so utterly done I don't believe I could have pulled effectively. Birdie was much the strongest of us. The strain and want of sleep was getting me in the neck, and Bill looked very bad. At the bottom we turned our faces to the Barrier, our backs to the penguins, but after doing about a mile it looked so threatening in the south that we camped in a big wind, our hands going one after the other. We had nothing but the hardest wind-swept sastrugi, and it was a long business: there was only the smallest amount of drift, and we were afraid the icy snow blocks would chafe the tent. Birdie lashed the full biscuit tin to the door to prevent its flapping, and also got what he called the tent downhaul round the cap and then tied it about himself outside his bag: if the tent went he was going too.

I was feeling as if I should crack, and accepted Birdie's eider-down. It was wonderfully self-sacrificing of him: more than I can write. I felt a brute to take it, but I was getting useless unless I got some sleep which my big bag would not allow. Bill and Birdie kept on telling me to do less: that I was doing more than my share of the work: but I think that I was getting more and more weak. Birdie kept wonderfully strong: he slept most of the night: the difficulty for him was to get into his bag without going to sleep. He kept the meteorological log untiringly, but some of these nights he had to give it up for the time because he could not keep awake. He used to fall asleep with his pannikin in his hand and let it fall: and sometimes he had the primus.

Bill's bag was getting hopeless: it was really too small for an eider-down and was splitting all over the place: great long holes. He never consciously slept for nights: he did sleep a bit, for we heard him. Except for this night, and the next when Birdie's eider-down was still fairly dry, I never consciously slept; except that I used to wake for five or six nights running with the same nightmare – that we were drifted up, and that Bill and Birdie were passing the gear into my bag, cutting it open to do so, or some other variation, – I did not know that I had been asleep at all . . .

*

It was −49° in the night and we were away early in −47°. By midday we were rising Terror Point, opening Erebus rapidly, and got the first really light day, though the sun would not appear over the horizon for another month. I cannot describe what a relief the light was to us. We crossed the point outside our former track, and saw inside us the ridges where we had been blizzed for three days on our outward journey.

The minimum was −66° the next night and we were now back in the windless bight of Barrier with its soft snow, low temperatures, fogs and mists, and lingering settlements of the inside crusts. Saturday and Sunday, the 29th and 30th, we plugged on across this waste, iced up as usual but always with Castle Rock getting bigger. Sometimes it looked like fog or wind, but it always cleared away. We were getting weak, how weak we can only realize now, but we got in good marches, though slow – days when we did 4½, 7¼, 6¾, 6½, 7½ miles. On our outward journey we had been relaying and getting forward about 1½ miles a day at this point. The surface which we had dreaded so much was not so sandy or soft as when we had come out, and the settlements were more marked. These are caused by a crust falling under your feet. Generally the area involved is some twenty yards or so round you, and the surface falls through an air space for two or three inches with a soft 'crush' which may at first make you think there are crevasses about. In the region where we now travelled they were much more pronounced than elsewhere, and one day, when Bill was inside the tent lighting the primus, I put my foot into a hole that I had dug. This started a big settlement: sledge, tent and all of us dropped about a foot, and the noise of it ran away for miles and miles: we listened to it until we began to get too cold. It must have lasted a full three minutes.

In the pauses of our marching we halted in our harness, the ropes of which lay slack in the powdery snow. We stood panting with our backs against the mountainous mass of frozen gear which was our load. There was no wind, at any rate no more than light airs: our breath crackled as it froze. There was no unnecessary conversation: I don't know why our tongues never got frozen, but all my teeth, the nerves of which had been killed, split to pieces. We had been going perhaps three hours since lunch.

'How are your feet, Cherry?' from Bill.

'Very cold.'

'That's all right; so are mine.' We didn't worry to ask Birdie: he never had a frost-bitten foot from start to finish.

Half an hour later, as we marched, Bill would ask the same question. I tell him that all feeling has gone: Bill still has some feeling in one of his but the other is lost. He settled we had better camp: another ghastly night ahead . . .

*

The horrors of that return journey are blurred to my memory and I know they were blurred to my body at the time. I think this applies to all of us, for we were much weakened and callous. The day we got down to the penguins I had not cared whether I fell into a crevasse or not. We had been through a great deal since then. I know that we slept on the march; for I woke up when I bumped against Birdie, and Birdie woke when he bumped against me. I think Bill steering out in front managed to keep awake. I know we fell asleep if we waited in the comparatively warm tent when the primus was alight – with our pannikins or the primus in our hands. I know

that our sleeping-bags were so full of ice that we did not worry if
we spilt water or hoosh over them as they lay on the floor-cloth,
when we cooked on them with our maimed cooker. They were so
bad that we never rolled them up in the usual way when we got out
of them in the morning: we opened their mouths as much as possible
before they froze, and hoisted them more or less flat on to the
sledge. All three of us helped to raise each bag, which looked rather
like a squashed coffin and was probably a good deal harder. I know
that if it was only −40° when we camped for the night we considered
quite seriously that we were going to have a warm one, and that
when we got up in the morning if the temperature was in the minus
sixties we did not inquire what it was. The day's march was bliss
compared to the night's rest, and both were awful. We were about
as bad as men can be and do good travelling: but I never heard a
word of complaint, nor, I believe, an oath, and I saw self-sacrifice
standing every test.

Always we were getting nearer home: and we were doing good
marches. We were going to pull through; it was only a matter of
sticking this for a few more days; six, five, four . . . three perhaps
now, if we were not blizzed. Our main hut was behind that ridge
where the mist was always forming and blowing away, and there was
Castle Rock: we might even see Observation Hill tomorrow, and the
Discovery Hut furnished and trim was behind it, and they would have
sent some dry sleeping-bags from Cape Evans to greet us there. We
reckoned our troubles over at the Barrier edge, and assuredly it was
not far away. 'You've got it in the neck, stick it, you've got it in the
neck' – it was always running in my head.

And we did stick it. How good the memories of those days are.
With jokes about Birdie's picture hat: with songs we remembered
off the gramophone: with ready words of sympathy for frost-bitten
feet: with generous smiles for poor jests: with suggestions of happy
beds to come. We did not forget the Please and Thank You, which
means much in such circumstances, and all the little links with decent
civilization which we could still keep going. I'll swear there was still
a grace about us when we staggered in. And we kept our tempers –
even with God.

We might reach Hut Point tonight: we were burning more oil
now, that one-gallon tin had lasted us well: and burning more candle
too; at one time we feared they would give out. A hell of a morning
we had: − 57° in our present state. But it was calm, and the Barrier

edge could not be much farther now. The surface was getting harder: there were a few windblown furrows, the crust was coming up to us. The sledge was dragging easier: we always suspected the Barrier sloped downwards hereabouts. Now the hard snow was on the surface, peeping out like great inverted basins on which we slipped, and our feet became warmer for not sinking into soft snow. Suddenly we saw a gleam of light in the line of darkness running across our course. It was the Barrier edge: we were all right now.

We ran the sledge off a snow-drift on to the sea-ice, with the same cold stream of air flowing down it which wrecked my hands five weeks ago: pushed out of this, camped and had a meal: the temperature had already risen to −43°. We could almost feel it getting warmer as we went round Cape Armitage on the last three miles. We managed to haul our sledge up the ice foot, and dug the drift away from the door. The old hut struck us as fairly warm.

Bill was convinced that we ought not to go into the warm hut at Cape Evans when we arrived there – tomorrow night! We ought to get back to warmth gradually, live in a tent outside, or in the annexe for a day or two. But I'm sure we never meant to do it. Just now Hut Point did not prejudice us in favour of such abstinence. It was just as we had left it: there was nothing sent down for us there – no sleeping-bags, nor sugar: but there was plenty of oil. Inside the hut we pitched a dry tent left there since Depot Journey days, set two primuses going in it; sat dozing on our bags; and drank cocoa without sugar so thick that next morning we were gorged with it. We were very happy, falling asleep between each mouthful, and after several hours discussed schemes of not getting into our bags at all. But someone would have to keep the primus going to prevent frost-bite, and we could not trust ourselves to keep awake. Bill and I tried to sing a part-song. Finally we sopped our way into our bags. We only stuck *them* three hours, and thankfully turned out at 3 a.m., and were ready to pack up when we heard the wind come away. It was no good, so we sat in our tent and dozed again. The wind dropped at 9.30: we were off at 11. We walked out into what seemed to us a blaze of light. It was not until the following year that I understood that a great part of such twilight as there is in the latter part of the winter was cut off from us by the mountains under which we travelled. Now, with nothing between us and the northern horizon below which lay the sun, we saw as we had not seen for months, and the iridescent clouds that day were beautiful.

We just pulled for all we were worth and did nearly two miles an hour: for two miles a baddish salt surface, then big undulating hard sastrugi and good going. We slept as we walked. We had done eight miles by 4 p.m. and were past Glacier Tongue. We lunched there.

As we began to gather our gear together to pack up for the last time, Bill said quietly, 'I want to thank you two for what you have done. I couldn't have found two better companions – and what is more I never shall.'

I am proud of that.

Antarctic exploration is seldom as bad as you imagine, seldom as bad as it sounds. But this journey had beggared our language: no words could express its horror.

We trudged on for several more hours and it grew very dark. There was a discussion as to where Cape Evans lay. We rounded it at last: it must have been ten or eleven o'clock, and it was possible that someone might see us as we pulled towards the hut. 'Spread out well,' said Bill, 'and they will be able to see that there are three men.' But we pulled along the cape, over the tide-crack, up the bank to the very door of the hut without a sound. No noise from the stable, nor the bark of a dog from the snow drifts above us. We halted and stood there trying to get ourselves and one another out of our frozen harnesses – the usual long job. The door opened – 'Good God! here is the Crozier Party,' said a voice, and disappeared.

Thus ended the worst journey in the world.

And now the reader will ask what became of the three penguins' eggs for which three human lives had been risked three hundred times a day, and three human frames strained to the utmost extremity of human endurance.

Let us leave the Antarctic for a moment and conceive ourselves in the year 1913 in the Natural History Museum in South Kensington. I had written to say that I would bring the eggs at this time. Present, myself, C.-G., the sole survivor of the three, with First or Doorstep Custodian of the Sacred Eggs. I did not take a verbatim report of his welcome; but the spirit of it may be dramatized as follows:

FIRST CUSTODIAN. Who are you? What do you want? This ain't an egg-shop. What call have you to come meddling with our eggs? Do you want me to put the police on to you? Is it the crocodile's egg you're after? I don't know nothing about no eggs. You'd best speak to Mr Brown: it's him that varnishes the eggs.

I resort to Mr Brown, who ushers me into the presence of the Chief Custodian, a man of scientific aspect, with two manners: one, affably courteous, for a Person of Importance (I guess a Naturalist Rothschild at least) with whom he is conversing, and the other, extraordinarily offensive even for an official man of science, for myself.

I announce myself with becoming modesty as the bearer of the penguins' eggs, and proffer them. The Chief Custodian takes them into custody without a word of thanks, and turns to the Person of Importance to discuss them. I wait. The temperature of my blood rises. The conversation proceeds for what seems to me a considerable period. Suddenly the Chief Custodian notices my presence and seems to resent it.

CHIEF CUSTODIAN. You needn't wait.

HEROIC EXPLORER. I should like to have a receipt for the eggs, if you please.

CHIEF CUSTODIAN. It is not necessary: it is all right. You needn't wait.

HEROIC EXPLORER. I should like to have a receipt.

But by this time the Chief Custodian's attention is again devoted wholly to the Person of Importance. Feeling that to persist in over-hearing their conversation would be an indelicacy, the Heroic Explorer politely leaves the room, and establishes himself on a chair in a gloomy passage outside, where he wiles away the time by rehearsing in his imagination how he will tell off the Chief Custodian when the Person of Importance retires. But this the Person of Importance shows no sign of doing, and the Explorer's thoughts and intentions become darker and darker. As the day wears on, minor officials, passing to and from the Presence, look at him doubtfully and ask his business. The reply is always the same, 'I am waiting for a receipt for some penguins' eggs.' At last it becomes clear from the Explorer's expression that what he is really waiting for is not to take a receipt but to commit murder. Presumably this is reported to the destined victim: at all events the receipt finally comes; and the Explorer goes his way with it, feeling that he has behaved like a perfect gentleman, but so very dissatisfied with that vapid consolation that for hours he continues his imaginary rehearsals of what he would have liked to have done to that Custodian (mostly with his boots) by way of teaching him manners.

NEW ZEALAND

CAPTAIN JAMES COOK (1728–1779)

'The Maoris demonstrate their cannibalism on board the Resolution, Queen Charlotte Sound, South Island, November 1773'

Tuesday 23rd November. Calm or light airs from the Northward so that we could not get to Sea as I intended, some of the officers went on shore to amuse themselves among the Natives where they saw the head and bowels of a youth who had lately been killed, the heart was stuck upon a forked stick and fixed to the head of their largest Canoe, the gentlemen brought the head on board with them, I was on shore at this time but soon after returned on board when I was informed of the above circumstances, and found the quarter deck crowded with the Natives. I now saw the mangled head or rather the remains of it for the under jaw, lips &c were wanting, the scul was broke on the left side just above the temple, the face had all the appearance of a youth about fourteen or fifteen, a peice of the flesh had been broiled and eat by one of the Natives in the presince of most of the officers. The sight of the head and the relation of the circumstances just mentioned struck me with horror and filled my mind with indignation against these Canibals, but when I considered that any resentment I could shew would avail but little and being desireous of being an eye wittness to a fact which many people had their doubts about I concealed my indignation and ordered apiece of the flesh to be broiled and brought on the quarter deck were one of these Canibals eat it with a seeming good relish before the whole ships Company had such effect on some of them as to cause them to vomit . . . That the New Zealanders are Canibals can now no longer be doubted . . .

AUSTRALIA

ERNEST GILES (1835–1897)

from *Australia Twice Traversed*

The ants were so troublesome last night, I had to shift my bed several times. Gibson was not at all affected by them, and slept well. We were in our saddles immediately after daylight. I was in hopes that a few miles might bring about a change of country, and so it did, but not an advantageous one to us. At ten miles from camp the horizon became flatter, the sandhills fell off, and the undulations became covered with brown gravel, at first very fine. At fifty-five miles it became coarser, and at sixty miles it was evident the country was becoming firmer, if not actually stony. Here we turned the horses out, having come twenty miles. I found one of our large water-bags leaked more than I expected, and our supply of water was diminishing with distance. Here Gibson preferred to keep the big cob to ride, against my advice, instead of Badger, so, after giving Badger and Darkie a few pints of water each, Gibson drove them back on the tracks about a mile and let them go, to take their own time and find their own way back to the Circus. They both looked terribly hollow and fatigued, and went away very slowly. Sixty miles through such a country as this tells fearfully upon a horse. The poor brutes were very unwilling to leave us, as they knew we had some water, and they also knew what a fearful region they had before them to reach the Circus again.

We gave the two remaining horses all the water contained in the two large water-bags, except a quart or two for ourselves. This allowed them a pretty fair drink, though not a circumstance to what they would have swallowed. They fed a little, while we remained here. The day was warm enough. The two five-gallon kegs with water we hung in the branches of a tree, with the pack-saddles,

empty water-bags, etc. of the other two horses. Leaving the Kegs –
I always called this place by that name – we travelled another twenty
miles by night, the country being still covered with small stones and
thickly clothed with the tall triodia. There were thin patches of
mulga and mallee scrub occasionally. No view could be obtained to
the west; all round us, north, south, east, and west, were alike, the
undulations forming the horizons were not generally more than
seven or eight miles distant from one another, and when we reached
the rim or top of one, we obtained exactly the same view for the
next seven or eight miles. The country still retained all the appearance
of fine, open, dry, grassy downs, and the triodia tops waving in the
heated breeze had all the semblance of good grass. The afternoon
had been very oppressive, and the horses were greatly disinclined to
exert themselves, though my mare went very well. It was late by
the time we encamped, and the horses were much in want of water,
especially the big cob, who kept coming up to the camp all night,
and tried to get at our water-bags, pannikins, etc. The instinct of a
horse when in the first stage of thirst in getting hold of any utensil
that ever had water in it, is surprising and most annoying, but
teaching us by most persuasive reasons how akin they are to human
things. We had one small water-bag hung in a tree. I did not think
of this just at the moment, when my mare came straight up to it
and took it in her teeth, forcing out the cork and sending the water
up, which we were both dying to drink, in a beautiful jet, which,
descending to earth, was irrevocably lost. We now had only a pint
or two left. Gibson was now very sorry he had exchanged Badger
for the cob, as he found the cob very dull and heavy to get on; this
was not usual, for he was generally a most willing animal, but he
would only go at a jog while my mare was a fine walker. There had
been a hot wind from the north all day. The following morning
(23rd) there was a most strange dampness in the air, and I had a
vague feeling, such as must have been felt by augurs, and seers of
old, who trembled as they told, events to come; for this was the last
day on which I ever saw Gibson. It was a lamentable day in the
history of this expedition. The horizon to the west was hid in clouds.
We left the camp even before daylight, and as we had camped on
the top of a rim, we knew we had seven or eight miles to go before
another view could be obtained. The next rim was at least ten miles
from the camp, and there was some slight indications of a change.

We were now ninety miles from the Circus water, and 110 from

Fort McKellar. The horizon to the west was still obstructed by another rise three or four miles away; but to the west-north-west I could see a line of low stony ridges, ten miles off. To the south was an isolated little hill, six or seven miles away. I determined to go to the ridges, when Gibson complained that his horse could never reach them, and suggested that the next rise to the west might reveal something better in front. The ridges were five miles away, and there were others still farther preventing a view. When we reached them we had come ninety-eight miles from the Circus. Here Gibson, who was always behind, called out and said his horse was going to die, or knock up, which are synonymous terms in this region. Now we had reached a point where at last a different view was presented to us, and I believed a change of country was at hand, for the whole western, down to the south-western, horizon was broken by lines of ranges, being most elevated at the south-western end. They were all notched and irregular, and I believed formed the eastern extreme of a more elevated and probably mountainous region to the west ... The hills to the west were twenty-five to thirty miles away, and it was with extreme regret I was compelled to relinquish a farther attempt to reach them. Oh, how ardently I longed for a camel! How ardently I gazed upon this scene! At this moment I would even my jewel eternal, have sold for power to span the gulf that lay between! But it could not be, situated as I was; compelled to retreat – of course with the intention of coming again with a larger supply of water – now the sooner I retreated the better ... Gibson's horse having got so bad had placed us both in a great dilemma; indeed, ours was a most critical position. We turned back upon our tracks, when the cob refused to carry his rider any farther, and tried to lie down. We drove him another mile on foot, and down he fell to die. My mare, the Fair Maid of Perth, was only too willing to return; she had now to carry Gibson's saddle and things, and we went away walking and riding by turns of half an hour. The cob, no doubt, died where he fell; not a second thought could be bestowed on him.

When we got back to about thirty miles from the Kegs I was walking, and having concluded in my mind what course to pursue, I called to Gibson to halt till I walked up to him. We were both excessively thirsty, for walking had made us so, and we had scarcely a pint of water left between us. However, of what we had we each took a mouthful, which finished the supply, and I then said – for I couldn't speak before – 'Look here, Gibson, you see we are in a most terrible fix with only one horse, therefore only one can ride, and one must remain behind. I shall remain: and now listen to me. If the mare does not get water soon she will die; therefore ride right on; get to the Kegs, if possible, tonight, and give her water. Now the cob is dead there'll be all the more for her; let her rest for an hour or two, and then get over a few more miles by morning, so that early tomorrow you will sight the Rawlinson, at twenty-five miles from the Kegs. Stick to the tracks, and never leave them. Leave as much water in one keg for me as you can afford after watering the mare and filling up your own bags, and, remember, I depend upon you to bring me relief. Rouse Mr Tietkens, get fresh horses and more water-bags, and return as soon as you possibly can. I shall of course endeavour to get down the tracks also.'

He then said if he had a compass he thought he could go better at night. I knew he didn't understand anything about compasses, as I had often tried to explain them to him. The one I had was a Gregory's Patent, of a totally different construction from ordinary instruments of the kind, and I was very loth to part with it, as it was the only one I had. However, he was so anxious for it that I gave it him, and he departed. I sent one final shout after him to stick to the tracks, to which he replied, 'All right,' and the mare carried him out of sight almost immediately. That was the last ever seen of Gibson.

I walked slowly on, and the further I walked the more thirsty I became. I had thirty miles to go to reach the Kegs, which I could not reach until late tomorrow at the rate I was travelling, and I did not feel sure that I could keep on at that. The afternoon was very hot. I continued following the tracks until the moon went down, and then had to stop. The night was reasonably cool, but I was parched and choking for water. How I longed again for morning! I hoped Gibson had reached the Kegs, and that he and the mare were all right. I could not sleep for thirst, although towards morning it became almost cold. How I wished this planet would for once accelerate its movements and turn upon its axis in twelve instead of twenty-four hours, or rather that it would complete its revolution in six hours.

April 24th to 1st May. So soon as it was light I was again upon the horse tracks, and reached the Kegs about the middle of the day. Gibson had been here, and watered the mare, and gone on. He had left me a little over two gallons of water in one keg, and it may be imagined how glad I was to get a drink. I could have drunk my whole supply in half an hour, but was compelled to economy, for I could not tell how many days would elapse before assistance could come: it could not be less than five, it might be many more. After quenching my thirst a little I felt ravenously hungry, and on searching among the bags, all the food I could find was eleven sticks of dirty, sandy, smoked horse, averaging about an ounce and a half each, at the bottom of a pack-bag. I was rather staggered to find that I had little more than a pound weight of meat to last me until assistance came. However, I was compelled to eat some at once, and devoured two sticks raw, as I had no water to spare to boil them in.

After this I sat in what shade the trees afforded, and reflected on the precariousness of my position. I was sixty miles from water, and eighty from food, my messenger could hardly return before six days, and I began to think it highly probable that I should be dead of hunger and thirst long before anybody could possibly arrive. I looked at the keg; it was an awkward thing to carry empty. There was nothing else to carry water in, as Gibson had taken all the smaller water-bags, and the large ones would require several gallons of water to soak the canvas before they began to tighten enough to hold water. The keg when empty, with its rings and straps, weighed fifteen pounds, and now it had twenty pounds of water in it. I could not carry it without a blanket for a pad for my shoulder, so that with my revolver and cartridge-pouch, knife, and one or two other small things on my belt, I staggered under a weight of about fifty pounds when I put the keg on my back. I only had fourteen matches.

After I had thoroughly digested all points of my situation, I concluded that if I did not help myself Providence wouldn't help me. I started, bent double by the keg, and could only travel so slowly that I thought it scarcely worthwhile to travel at all. I became so thirsty at each step I took, that I longed to drink up every drop of water I had in the keg, but it was the elixir of death I was burdened with, and to drink it was to die, so I restrained myself. By next morning I had only got about three miles away from the Kegs, and to do that I travelled mostly in the moonlight. The next few days I can only pass over as they seemed to pass with me, for I was quite unconscious half the time, and I only got over about five miles a day.

To people who cannot comprehend such a region it may seem absurd that a man could not travel faster than that. All I can say is, there may be men who could do so, but most men in the position

I was in would simply have died of hunger and thirst, for by the third or fourth day – I couldn't tell which – my horse meat was all gone. I had to remain in what scanty shade I could find during the day, and I could only travel by night.

When I lay down in the shade in the morning I lost all consciousness, and when I recovered my senses I could not tell whether one day or two or three had passed. At one place I am sure I must have remained over forty-eight hours. At a certain place on the road – that is to say, on the horse tracks – at about fifteen miles from the Kegs – at twenty-five miles the Rawlinson could again be sighted – I saw that the tracks of the two loose horses we had turned back from there had left the main line of tracks, which ran east and west, and had turned about east-south-east, and the tracks of the Fair Maid of Perth, I was grieved to see, had gone on them also. I felt sure Gibson would soon find his error, and return to the main line. I was unable to investigate this any farther in my present position. I followed them about a mile, and then returned to the proper line, anxiously looking at every step to see if Gibson's horse tracks returned into them.

They never did, nor did the loose horse tracks either. Generally speaking, whenever I saw a shady desert oak tree there was an enormous bulldog ants' nest under it, and I was prevented from sitting in its shade. On what I thought was the 27th I almost gave up the thought of walking any farther, for the exertion in this dreadful region, where the triodia was almost as high as myself, and as thick as it could grow, was quite overpowering, and being starved, I felt quite light-headed. After sitting down, on every occasion when I tried to get up again, my head would swim round, and I would fall down oblivious for some time. Being in a chronic state of burning thirst, my general plight was dreadful in the extreme. A bare and level sandy waste would have been paradise to walk over compared to this. My arms, legs, thighs, both before and behind, were so punctured with spines, it was agony only to exist; the slightest movement and in went more spines, where they broke off in the clothes and flesh, causing the whole of the body that was punctured to gather into minute pustules, which were continually growing and bursting. My clothes, especially inside my trousers, were a perfect mass of prickly points.

My great hope and consolation now was that I might soon meet the relief party. But where was the relief party? Echo could only answer – where? About the 29th I had emptied the keg, and was still over twenty miles from the Circus. Ah! who can imagine what twenty miles means in such a case? But in this April's ivory moonlight I plodded on, desolate indeed, but all undaunted, on this lone, unhallowed shore. At last I reached the Circus, just at the dawn of day. Oh, how I drank! How I reeled! How hungry I was! How thankful I was that I had so far at least escaped from the jaws of that howling wilderness, for I was once more upon the range, though still twenty miles from home.

There was no sign of the tracks, of any one having been here since I left it. The water was all but gone. The solitary eagle still was there. I wondered what could have become of Gibson; he certainly had never come here, and how could he reach the fort without doing so?

I was in such a miserable state of mind and body, that I refrained from more vexatious speculations as to what had delayed him: I stayed here, drinking and drinking, until about ten a.m., when I crawled away over the stones down from the water. I was very footsore, and could only go at a snail's pace. Just as I got clear of the bank of the creek, I heard a faint squeak, and looking about I saw, and immediately caught, a small dying wallaby, whose marsupial mother had evidently thrown it from her pouch. It only weighed about two ounces, and was scarcely furnished yet with fur. The instant I saw it, like an eagle I pounced upon it and ate it, living, raw, dying – fur, skin, bones, skull, and all. The delicious taste of that creature I shall never forget. I only wished I had its mother and father to serve in the same way. I had become so weak that by late at night, I had only accomplished eleven miles, and I lay down about five miles from the Gorge of Tarns, again choking for water. While lying down here, I thought I heard the sound of the footfalls of a galloping horse going campwards, and vague ideas of Gibson on the Fair Maid – or she without him – entered my head. I stood up, and listened, but the sound had died away upon the midnight air. On the 1st of May, as I afterwards found, at one o'clock in the morning, I was walking again, and reached the Gorge of Tarns long before daylight, and could again indulge in as much water as I desired; but it was exhaustion I suffered from, and I could hardly move.

My reader may imagine with what intense feelings of relief I stepped over the little bridge across the water, staggered into the camp at daylight, and woke Mr Tietkens, who stared at me as though

I had been one, new risen from the dead. I asked him had he seen Gibson, and to give me some food. I was of course prepared to hear that Gibson had never reached the camp; indeed I could see but two people in their blankets the moment I entered the fort, and by that I knew he could not be there. None of the horses had come back, and it appeared that I was the only one of six living creatures – two men and four horses – that had returned, or were now ever likely to return, from that desert, for it was now, as I found, nine days since I last saw Gibson.

★ ★ ★

MOLLY NUNGARRAYI

'How We Fled When I Was a Girl'

When the whitefellas first came to our country a long time ago, they started shooting our people. They shot some dead, and chased others away from their land so that they never returned. The whitefellas chased people from places like Yinapaka, Yilyampuru, Jarralyku and Kunajarrayi. My poor people were chased off their country for ever. They went to places like Tennant Creek and Phillip Creek.

When I was a little girl I saw my people shot at – all because they lived off this country and because they were Aborigines. Some of our parents and grandparents hid us in caves. During the day we'd go without water and hide from the whitefellas. At night our parents would sneak out to the soakages to get water for us to drink. They would leave us little ones in the caves for an hour or two and we'd cry, wondering when they'd return. We were frightened. We knew the whitefellas were after us and could shoot us. But they didn't. Our parents came back carrying water in a large wooden container that they'd put grass around the edges of, to stop the water spilling out. They'd come back to us and say, 'You little ones are still here?', and we'd answer back, 'Yes, we're still here, alive.' Sometimes they'd pour water on our heads to keep us cool. After drinking the water we'd sleep.

We stayed there for a week or two, then we left the cave for another place. We went further and further away from the whitefellas. As we travelled our parents and grandparents hunted meat. They gathered berries and roots, and ground seeds for us to eat. We used to look around to see if there were any whites coming before we went out. During the hot weather we'd tie our feet with vines and grass to protect them from the hot sand. We'd put leafy-branches on top of our heads to shade us from the burning sun. Nowadays we buy things from the shop, but that time we were bone naked, poor things. No boots. We didn't have any clothes at that time. No pubic tassels. We were just naked little girls.

Later the whitefellas went back to where they'd come from and we started going back to the country where we were born. All the way back to our country we found people who had been shot and we mourned them. That is how most of us lived. We left our country because of the cruel whitefellas and their guns. Most of us were lucky, for the whitefellas never saw us.

SOUTH EAST ASIA

MARY MCCARTHY (1912–1989)

from *Vietnam*

A short trip by helicopter from Saigon in almost any direction permits a ringside view of American bombing. Just beyond the truck gardens of the suburbs, you see what at first glance appears to be a series of bonfires evocative of Indian summers; thick plumes of smoke are rising from wooded clumps and fields. Toward the west, great blackish-brown tracts testify to the most recent results of the defoliation program; purplish-brown tracts are last year's work. As the helicopter skims the treetops, and its machine guns lower into position, you can study the fires more closely, and it is possible to distinguish a rice field burned over by peasants from neat bombing targets emitting spirals of smoke. But a new visitor cannot be sure and may tend to discredit his horrified impression, not wishing to jump to conclusions. Flying over the delta one morning, I saw the accustomed lazy smoke puffs mounting from the landscape and was urging myself to be cautious ('How do you *know*?') when I noticed a small plane circling; then it plunged, dropped its bombs, and was away in a graceful movement, having hit the target again; there was a flash of flame, and fresh, blacker smoke poured out. In the distance, a pair of small planes was hovering in the sky, like mosquitoes buzzing near the ceiling, waiting to strike. We flew on.

Coming back to Saigon in the afternoon, I expected to hear about 'my' double air strike in the daily five o'clock press briefing, but no air activity in the sector was mentioned – too trivial to record, said a newsman. On a day taken at random (Washington's Birthday), the Air Force and the Marine Corps reported 460 sorties flown over *South* Vietnam 'in support of ground forces'; whenever a unit is in trouble, they send for the airmen. Quite apart from the main battle areas, where fires and secondary explosions are announced as so many 'scores', the countryside is routinely dotted with fires in various stages, so that they come to seem a natural part of it, like the grave mounds in the rice fields and pastures. The charred patches you see when returning in the afternoon from a morning's field trip are this morning's smoking embers; meanwhile, new curls of smoke, looking almost peaceful, are the afternoon's tally. And the cruel couples of hovering aircraft (they seem to travel in pairs, like FBI agents) appear to be daytime fixtures, almost stationary in the sky.

The Saigonese themselves are unaware of the magnitude of what is happening to their country, since they are unable to use military transport to get an aerial view of it; they only note the refugees sleeping in the streets and hear the B-52s pounding a few miles away. Seeing the war from the air, amid the crisscrossing Skyraiders, Supersabres, Phantoms, observation planes, Psywar planes (dropping leaflets), you ask yourself how much longer the Viet Cong can hold out; the country is so small that at the present rate of destruction there will be no place left for them to hide, not even under water, breathing through a straw. The plane and helicopter crews are alert for the slightest sign of movement in the fields and woods and estuaries below; they lean forward intently, scanning the ground. At night, the Dragon-ships come out, dropping flares and firing mini-guns.

The Air Force seems inescapable, like the Eye of God, and soon, you imagine (let us hope with hyperbole), all will be razed, charred, defoliated by that terrible searching gaze. Punishment can be magistrial. A correspondent, who was tickled by the incident, described flying with the pilot of the little FAC plane that directs a big bombing mission; below, a lone Vietnamese on a bicycle stopped, looked up, dismounted, took up a rifle and fired; the pilot let him have it with the whole bombload of napalm – enough for a platoon. In such circumstances, anyone with a normal sense of fair play cannot help pulling for the bicyclist, but the sense of fair play, supposed to be Anglo-Saxon, has atrophied in the Americans here from lack of exercise. We draw a long face over Viet Cong 'terror', but no one stops to remember that the Viet Cong does not possess that superior instrument of terror, an air force, which in our case, over South Vietnam at least, is acting almost with impunity. The worst thing that could happen to our country would be to win this war.

* * *

ALFRED RUSSEL WALLACE (1823–1913)

'On First Seeing a King Bird of Paradise'

The emotions excited in the mind of a naturalist, who has long desired to see the actual thing which he has hitherto known only by description, drawing, or badly-preserved external covering – especially when that thing is of surpassing rarity and beauty, require the poetic faculty fully to express them. The remote island in which I found myself situated, in an almost unvisited sea, far from the tracks of merchant fleets and navies; the wild luxuriant tropical forest, which stretched far away on every side; the rude uncultured savages who gathered round me – all had their influence in determining the emotions with which I gazed upon this 'thing of beauty'. I thought of the long ages of the past, during which the successive generations of this little creature had run their course – year by year being born, and living and dying amid these dark and gloomy woods, with no intelligent eye to gaze upon their loveliness; to all appearance such a wanton waste of beauty. Such ideas excite a feeling of melancholy. It seems sad, that on the one hand such exquisite creatures should live out their lives and exhibit their charms only in these wild inhospitable regions, doomed for ages yet to come to hopeless barbarism; while on the other hand, should civilized man ever reach these distant lands, and bring moral, intellectual, and physical light into the recesses of these virgin forests, we may be sure that he will so disturb the nicely-balanced relations of organic and inorganic nature as to cause the disappearance, and finally the extinction, of these very beings whose wonderful structure and beauty he alone is fitted to appreciate and enjoy. This consideration must surely tell us that all living things were *not* made for man. Many of them have no relation to him. The cycle of their existence has gone on independently of his, and is disturbed or broken by every advance in man's intellectual development; and their happiness and enjoyments, their loves and hates, their struggles for existence, their vigorous life and early death, would seem to be immediately related to their own well-being and perpetuation alone, limited only by the equal well-being and perpetuation of the numberless other organisms with which each is more or less intimately connected.

*   *   *

RICHARD HAKLUYT (1552/3–1616)

from *The Principall Navigations, Voiages, Traffiques and Discoveries of the English Nation*

As I said before, I was so stunned and shocked by what I had just seen that I wasn't able to weep, let alone speak, for upwards of three hours; the other sailor and myself turned back from the river and waited in the sea until the following morning when we saw a fishing-boat approaching the mouth of the river.

As soon as the boat was close enough we pulled ourselves up onto some rocks and on our knees, naked, with our hands raised in the air, we pleaded with the men on the boat to take us on board. When the men saw us they stopped rowing and rested for a little while; and then, when they saw our wretched condition and realized that we were victims of shipwreck, they pulled in close to the rocks and asked us what we wanted.

We told them that we were Christians from Malacca who had been wrecked nine days earlier on our way back from Aru and we begged them, for the love of God, to take us with them wherever they were going.

The man who seemed to be in charge of the boat answered us:

'From what I can see of you both from here you'll not be worth the food that you'll eat, so for your own good you'd better hand over any money you've got hidden away – and then we'll treat you just as brotherly-like as you're begging us to! Otherwise just forget it!'

Then they made as if to sail off, but we started weeping and pleading with them again just to take us as prisoners and sell us as slaves wherever they wanted. As for myself, I added that I was a Portuguese and a close relative of the commander in Malacca, so wherever they sold me they would certainly receive whatever price they asked for me.

Their leader answered:

'Fair enough. We'll take you, but if you're not who you say you are we'll whip you to shreds and throw you bound hand-and-foot into the sea!'

We said yes, that was all right by us, and four of them jumped ashore and carried us aboard. By this time we were both so weak that we could scarcely lift our hands.

As soon as they had us on board they tied both of us to the foot of the mast. They had planned all along to take any money that we might have and thought that if they whipped and beat us we would break down and tell them where any valuables were hidden. They beat us mercilessly until the blood was pouring out of us. I was as good as dead already, in a worse condition than my companion, so I was spared drinking the potion that they gave to him, poor wretch. It was a mixture of quicklime and piss that made him bring his guts up and he died inside the hour.

They didn't find any trace of gold in what my companion had vomited up (as they had been convinced they would) so by the grace of Our Lord they didn't bother to give me the same treatment; instead they used the same mixture to rub my body all over so that I wouldn't die of my wounds – though the pain was so great that I was as good as dead to the world.

We finally left this river, the Arissumhee, and at evening on the following day we came into sight of a large town of thatched houses called Siaca, in the kingdom of Jambi.

The seven fishermen who had rescued me and who now all had a share in me kept me in their house for twenty-seven days and, praised be Our Lord, I recovered from my wounds; but when they realized that I wouldn't be of any use to them in their fishing they put me up for auction.

On three separate occasions they brought me to the market but didn't so much as get a bid for me. They decided they wouldn't be able to sell me at all: I was of absolutely no use to them, and they threw me out of the house to save the expense of having to feed me.

I spent the next thirty-six days living out in the open like an old donkey without a master, begging from door to door for crumbs and morsels that I was rarely given because the people of Siaca were very poor themselves.

Then one day when I was down on the sea-shore bewailing my

misfortune Our Lord saw fit that a Moor should pass by, a merchant from the island of Palembang who had been to Malacca several times and traded there with the Portuguese. When the Moor saw me lying there, naked on the shore, he asked me if I was Portuguese – and said not to be afraid to tell the truth if I was.

I told him that I was, indeed, Portuguese – and one with very rich relations in Malacca who would pay as much ransom as he asked for me if he brought me there. I said I was a nephew of the commander there, the son of one of his sisters.

The Moor replied:

'If you are who you say you are, what wrong have you done that you have come to the miserable state I see you in here?'

I gave him a detailed account of my shipwreck and how the fishermen had brought me to Siaca and then turned me out of their house because they couldn't find anyone to buy me.

He was amazed by my story and after thinking things over for a while he said:

'As you might have guessed, I am a poor trader, so poor that, with my income not being more than a hundred pardaus I went into the shad's egg business, thinking that it could be the path to an easier life – although with my bad luck it didn't work out that way. Now I know that I could make a good profit at the present time trading in Malacca and I would be glad to go there – if the commander and customs men don't treat me as badly as I've heard they treat some of the traders who go there. So if you think that on your account I could do business in Malacca, secure against any obstacles and abuse, then I will go and see about buying you from these fishermen.'

I answered him through flooding tears:

'You know very well yourself that there's no good reason why you should believe what I have told you. Indeed, you might well think that in order to escape from this poverty and miserable captivity I would make myself out to be more important in Malacca than I actually am. But if you will trust my word – and I have no other bond to give you – I will swear a written oath that if you take me to Malacca the commander there will reward you and will not confiscate the least part of your merchandise and, furthermore, will pay you twenty times over whatever sum you pay to the fishermen for me.'

The Moor replied:

'All right. I'll be glad to buy you out and take you to Malacca but don't say anything to the fishermen about what we have just arranged. We don't want them to raise your price so high that I won't be able to do you the favour I want to do!'

I swore to him that I would do just as he said and added a lot more besides that I thought would help to win him over, and he accepted all my promises readily enough.

*

Four days after I made these arrangements with the Moor he began to bargain for me with the seven fishermen through a third party, a native of Siaca.

The fishermen were already fed up with the sight of me because I was very sick and of absolutely no use to them. It was more than a month since they put me out of the house and by this time the seven who had a share in me were no longer all working together nor even as friendly with each other as they had been. Through these and other means God brought it about that they were not bothered to keep me at all. They asked the Moor's man for seven mazes of gold (that's three and a half cruzados). It was paid straight away and the Moor brought me to his house.

Five days after I was freed from the clutches of the fishermen, and when I was somewhat recovered due to the good treatment I received from my new master, this Moor went to a place called Surabaya, five leagues away, to finish loading up a boat with a cargo of shads' eggs – which is what he traded in, as I mentioned earlier. Shad are so abundant in the local rivers that the people don't make use of anything but the females' eggs, of which they export more than two thousand boat-loads every year, each boat carrying a hundred and fifty or two hundred jars, and each jar holding a thousand eggs, which is as much as the traders are able to handle.

When the merchant had finished loading the *lanchara* (the type of Malayan boat he used for carrying his merchandise) we set sail for Malacca and arrived there three days later. He straight away brought me to the fort to see Pêro de Faria and told him everything that had happened to me.

Pêro de Faria was astonished when he saw the condition I was in, and with tears in his eyes he told me to speak up and let him know that it was really me – because I was so emaciated and changed in face and body that he couldn't believe his eyes. It was more than three months since they had heard from me and they had given me up for dead, but now so many people wanted to see me that there wasn't room in the fort for them, all of them weeping and asking me what on earth had brought me into the sorry state in which they now saw me. When I gave them the full story of my voyage and the ill-fortune that had befallen me they were so amazed that they were left speechless and went on their way again, blessing themselves.

As was the custom at that time there was a collection taken up for me afterwards, so that I ended up a lot better off than I had been.

Pêro de Faria ordered sixty cruzados and two rolls of damask be given to the Moor who had rescued me and he decreed, in the king's name, that the Moor's merchandise be exempted from whatever custom duties might be due on it (which was worth another sixty cruzados to him). The Moor wasn't impeded or harassed at all while he was in Malacca, so he was content and more than satisfied, considering himself very well paid for the bargain he had struck with me.

Pêro de Faria sent me to stay in the house of a married man, a clerk in the trading-post. He thought I would be better looked after there than anywhere else in Malacca – indeed I was: I spent upwards of a month in bed, and I was fully restored to health, thanks be to God.

* * *

ANNA LEONOWENS (1831–1915)

'The English Governess at the Siamese Court'

In 1825 a royal prince of Siam (his birthright wrested from him by an elder half-brother and his life imperilled) took refuge in a Buddhist monastery and assumed the yellow garb of a priest.

Finally in 1851, at the age of forty-five, he emerged from his cloister, and was crowned, with the title of Somedtch-Phra Paramendr Maha Mongkut (duke, and royal bearer of the great crown).

For twenty-five years had the true heir to the throne of the Phrabatts (the Golden-footed), patiently biding his time, lain perdu in his monastery, diligently devoting himself to the study of Sanskrit, Bali, theology, history, geology, chemistry, and especially astronomy.

In the Oriental tongues this progressive king was eminently proficient; and toward priests, preachers, and teachers, of all creeds, sects, and sciences, an enlightened exemplar of tolerance. It was likewise his peculiar vanity to pass for an accomplished English scholar, and to this end he maintained in his palace at Bangkok a private printing establishment, with fonts of English type, which he was at no loss to keep in 'copy'. Perhaps it was the printing-office which suggested, quite naturally, an English governess for the *élite* of his wives and concubines, and their offspring – in number amply adequate to the constitution of a royal school, and in material most attractively fresh and romantic. Happy thought! Wherefore, behold me, just after sunset on a pleasant day in April, 1862, on the threshhold of the outer court of the Grand Palace, accompanied by my own brave little boy, and escorted by a compatriot.

A flood of light sweeping through the spacious Hall of Audience displayed a throng of noblemen in waiting. None turned a glance, or seemingly a thought, on us, and, my child being tired and hungry, I urged Captain B— to present us without delay. At once we mounted the marble steps, and entered the brilliant hall unannounced. Ranged on the carpet were many prostrate, mute, and motionless forms, over whose heads to step was a temptation as drolly natural as it was dangerous. His Majesty spied us quickly, and advanced abruptly, petulantly screaming, 'Who? who? who?'

Captain B— (who, by the by, is a titled nobleman of Siam) introduced me as the English governess, engaged for the royal family. The king shook hands with us, and immediately proceeded to march up and down in quick step, putting one foot before the other with mathematical precision, as if under drill. 'Forewarned, forearmed,' my friend whispered that I should prepare myself for a sharp cross-questioning as to my age, my husband, children, and other strictly personal concerns. Suddenly his Majesty, having cogitated sufficiently in his peculiar manner, with one long final stride halted in front of us, and pointing straight at me with his forefinger, asked, 'How old shall you be?'

Scarcely able to repress a smile at a proceeding so absurd, and with my sex's distaste for so serious a question, I demurely replied, 'One hundred and fifty years old.'

Had I made myself much younger, he might have ridiculed or assailed me; but now he stood surprised and embarrassed for a few moments, then resumed his quick march, and at last, beginning to perceive the jest, coughed, laughed, coughed again, and then in a high, sharp key asked, 'In what year were you borned?'

Instantly I 'struck' a mental balance, and answered, as gravely as I could, 'In 1788.'

At this point the expression of his Majesty's face was indescribably comical. Captain B— slipped behind a pillar to laugh; but the king only coughed, with a significant emphasis that startled me, and addressed a few words to his prostrate courtiers, who smiled at the carpet – all except the prime minister, who turned to look at me. But his Majesty was not to be baffled so: again he marched with vigour, and then returned to the attack with *élan*.

'How many years shall you be married?'

'For several years, your Majesty.'

He fell into a brown study; then suddenly rushed at me, and demanded triumphantly:

'Ha! How many grandchildren shall you now have? Ha! ha! How many? How many? Ha! ha! ha!'

Of course we all laughed with him; but the general hilarity admitted of a variety of constructions.

Then suddenly he seized my hand, and dragged me, *nolens volens*, my little Louis holding fast by my skirt, through several sombre passages along which crouched duennas, shrivelled and grotesque, and many youthful women, covering their faces, as if blinded by the splendour of the passing Majesty. At length he stopped before one of the many-curtained recesses, and, drawing aside the hangings, disclosed a lovely, childlike form. He stooped and took her hand (she naïvely hiding her face), and placing it in mine, said: 'This is my wife, the Lady T. She desires to be educated in English. She is as renowned for her talents as for her beauty, and it is our pleasure to make her a good English scholar. You shall educate her for me.'

I replied that the office would give me much pleasure; for nothing could be more eloquently winning than the modest, timid bearing of that tender young creature in the presence of her lord. She laughed low and pleasantly as he translated my sympathetic words to her, and seemed so enraptured with the graciousness of his act that I took my leave of her with a sentiment of profound pity.

He led me back by the way we had come; and now we met

many children, who put my patient boy to much childish torture for the gratification of their startled curiosity.

'I have sixty-seven children,' said his Majesty, when we had returned to the Audience Hall. 'You shall educate them; and as many of my wives, likewise, as may wish to learn English. And I have much correspondence in which you must assist me. And, moreover, I have much difficulty for reading and translating French letters; for French are fond of using gloomily deceiving terms. You must undertake; and you shall make all their murky sentences and gloomily deceiving propositions clear to me. And, furthermore, I have by every mail many foreign letters whose writing is not easily read by me. You shall copy on round hand, for my readily perusal thereof.'

Nil desperandum; but I began by despairing of my ability to accomplish tasks so multifarious. I simply bowed, however, and so dismissed myself for that evening.

When next I 'interviewed' the king, I was accompanied by the premier's sister, a fair and pleasant woman, whose whole stock of English was, 'Good morning, sir'; and with this somewhat irrelevant greeting, a dozen times in an hour, though the hour were night, she relieved her pent-up feelings and gave expression to her sympathy and regard for me. We found his Majesty in a less genial mood than at my first reception. He approached us coughing loudly and repeatedly, a sufficiently ominous fashion of announcing himself. He then approached me, and said, in a loud and domineering tone, 'It is our pleasure that you shall reside within this palace with our family.'

I replied that it would be quite impossible for me to do so; that, being as yet unable to speak the language, and the gates being shut every evening, I should feel like an unhappy prisoner in the palace.

'Where do you go every evening?' he demanded.

'Not anywhere, your Majesty. I am a stranger here.'

'Then why you shall object to the gates being shut?'

'I do not clearly know,' I replied, with a secret shudder at the idea of sleeping within those walls; 'but I am afraid I could not do it. I beg your Majesty will remember that in your gracious letter you promised me "a residence adjoining the royal palace", not within it.'

He turned and looked at me, his face growing almost purple

with rage. 'I do not know I have promised. I do not know former condition. I do not know anything but you are our servant; and it is our pleasure that you must live in this palace, and *you shall obey*.' Those last three words he fairly screamed.

I trembled in every limb, and for some time I knew not how to reply. At length I ventured to say: 'I am prepared to obey all your Majesty's commands, within the obligation of my duty to your family; but beyond that I can promise no obedience.'

'You *shall* live in palace,' he roared, 'you shall live in palace. I will give woman slaves to wait on you. You shall commence royal school in this pavilion on Thursday next. That is the best day for such undertaking, in the estimation of our astrologers.'

With that, he addressed, in a frantic manner, commands, unintelligible to me, to some of the old women about the pavilion. I turned and saw the king beckoning and calling to me. I bowed to him profoundly, but passed on through the brass door.

But kings who are not mad have their sober second thoughts like other rational people. His Golden-footed Majesty presently repented him of his arbitrary 'cantankerousness', and in due time, my ultimatum was accepted . . .

*

His Majesty was the most capricious of kings as to his working moods – busy when the average man should be sleeping, sleeping while letters, papers, despatches, messengers, mailboats waited. More than once had we been aroused at dead of night by noisy female slaves, and dragged in hot haste and consternation to the Hall of Audience, only to find that his Majesty was, not at his last gasp, as we had feared, but simply bothered to find in Webster's Dictionary some word that was to be found nowhere but in his own fertile brain.

Before my arrival in Bangkok it had been his not uncommon practice to send for a missionary at midnight, have him beguiled or abducted from his bed, and conveyed by boat to the palace, some miles up the river, to inquire if it would not be more elegant to write *murky* instead of *obscure*, or *gloomily dark* rather than *not clearly apparent*. And if the wretched man should venture to declare his honest preference for the ordinary over the extraordinary form of expression, he was forthwith dismissed with irony, arrogance, or even insult, and without a word of apology for the rude invasion of his rest.

His Majesty usually passed his mornings in study or dictating or writing English letters and despatches. His breakfast, though a repast sufficiently frugal for Oriental royalty, was served with awesome forms. In an antechamber adjoining a noble hall, rich in grotesque carvings and gildings, a throng of females waited, while his Majesty sat at a long table, near which knelt twelve women before great silver trays laden with twelve varieties of viands – soups, meats, game, poultry, fish, vegetables, cakes, jellies, preserves, sauces, fruits, and teas. Each tray, in its order, was passed by three ladies to the head wife or concubine, who removed the silver covers, and at least seemed to taste the contents of each dish; and then, advancing on her knees, she set them on the long table before the king.

But his Majesty was notably temperate in his diet, and by no means a gastronome. In his long seclusion in a Buddhist cloister he had acquired habits of severe simplicity and frugality, as a preparation for the exercise of those powers of mental concentration for which he was remarkable. At these morning repasts it was his custom to detain me in conversation, relating to some topic of interest derived from his studies, or in reading or translating. He was more systematically educated, and a more capacious devourer of books and news, than perhaps any man of equal rank in our day. But much learning had made him morally mad; his extensive reading had engendered in his mind an extreme scepticism concerning all existing religious systems. In inborn integrity and steadfast principle he had no faith whatever, and he honestly pitied the delusion that pinned its faith on human truth and virtue.

Ah! if this man could but have cast off the cramping yoke of his intellectual egotism, and been loyal to the free government of his own true heart, what a demigod might he not have been, among the lower animals of Asiatic royalty!

When the sweet, bright little princess, Somdetch Chowfa Chandrmondol (who was so dear to me by her pet name of Fâ-ying), was seized with cholera on the night of the 13th of May, 1863, his Majesty wrote to me:

My Dear Mam:
    Our well-beloved daughter, your favourite pupil, is attacked with cholera, and has earnest desire to see you, and is heard

much to make frequent repetition of your name. I beg that you will favour her wish. I fear her illness is mortal, as there has been three deaths since morning. She is best beloved of my children.

    I am your afflicted friend,
        S. P. P. Maha Mongkut

In a moment I was in my boat. I entreated, I flattered, I scolded, the rowers. How slow they were! how strong the opposing current! And when at last I stood panting at the door of my Fâ-ying's chamber – too late! even Dr Campbell (the surgeon of the British consulate) had come too late.

An attendant hurried me to the king, who, reading the heavy tidings in my silence, covered his face with his hands and wept passionately. Strange and terrible were the tears of such a man. What could I say? What could I do but weep with him; and then steal quietly away, and leave the king to the father?

JAPAN

Matsuo Basho (1644–1694)

'The Narrow Road to the Deep North'

Days and months are travellers of eternity. So are the years that pass by. Those who steer a boat across the sea, or drive a horse over the earth till they succumb to the weight of years, spend every minute of their lives travelling. There are a great number of ancients, too, who died on the road. I myself have been tempted for a long time by the cloud-moving wind – filled with a strong desire to wander.

It was only towards the end of last autumn that I returned from rambling along the coast. I barely had time to sweep the cobwebs from my broken house on the River Sumida before the New Year, but no sooner had the spring mist begun to rise over the field than I wanted to be on the road again to cross the barrier-gate of Shirakawa in due time. The gods seemed to have possessed my soul and turned it inside out, and roadside images seemed to invite me from every corner, so that it was impossible for me to stay idle at home. Even while I was getting ready, mending my torn trousers, tying a new strap to my hat, and applying *moxa* to my legs to strengthen them, I was already dreaming of the full moon rising over the islands of Matsushima.

AFRICA

DORIS LESSING (1919–)

'The Bush'

The family went often to Marandellas, whose name is now again
Marondera, just as the real right name for Umtali would have been
Mutare, if the whites had not overrun these parts. We did not go to
Umtali, for it was then a distant place. I did not get to it until I was
fifteen or so, and then Marandellas had become only one of the way-
stations along a road where I visited farms, sometimes for weeks at
a time. But as a child, Marandellas was the other pole to our farm,
which was in the District of Banket, Lomagundi (or Lo Magondi)
seventy miles to the north-east of Salisbury, and on the road north
to the Zambesi valley. Nothing ever happened on our road but the
routine excitements of flooded rivers, where we might have to sit
waiting for the waters to subside for four or five hours before daring
the drift that could have potholes in it from the flood; or getting
stuck in thick red mud and having to be pushed out over freshly cut
branches laid across the mud; or glimpses of wild animals . . . 'Look,
there's a duiker!' Or a koodoo, or a little herd of eland. These being
the stuff of ordinary life, and what we took for granted, it was only
on the other side of Salisbury that the shock and tug of new
impressions began, a shimmer in the air, like mental heat waves,
which I knew were proper to the road to Umtali. Marandellas was
about fifty miles south-east of Salisbury, but if you ask, What is a
hundred and twenty miles? – then that is from the practical,
unpoetical perspective. Our car was an Overland, contemporary with
the first Fords, now taken out of car museums to star in films of the
Great Depression. It was second-hand when we bought it, and thirty
miles an hour was a great speed. Add this to the characters of my
parents, and the journey became an epic endeavour, to be planned

and prepared for weeks in advance. The most often spoken words
in our house were, 'But we can't afford it!' – usually, triumphantly,
from my father to my mother, to prove something was impossible,
in this case to spend a week near Ruzawi at the Marandellas Hotel.
My brother was at Ruzawi School, a prep-school conducted on
English lines, and the trip would be so we could take part in a Sports
Day, an Open Day, a cricket match, judged as successful according
to how they mirrored similar events at prep-schools at Home. Impossible! – thank the Lord! – and he would not have to leave the farm
and put on respectable clothes instead of his farm khaki and make
small talk with other parents. For his 'We can't afford it,' was not a
symptom of meanness, but rather of his need, by now the strongest
thing in him, to be left in peace to dream.

But my mother triumphed. Rolls of bedding, boxes of food,
suitcases, filled the back of the car where the 'boy' and I fitted
ourselves, and we set off. At the speed my father insisted on travelling,
the seventy miles to Salisbury took three or four hours. ('A man who
has to use a brake doesn't know how to drive a car.') The Packards
and the Studebakers shot past us in tumults of dust (these were the
old strip roads and you overtook on dirt) for the Fords and
the Overlands were already an anachronism. ('Why give up your car
when it is still working perfectly well just because *they* want to sell
you a new one?') To go from Banket to Marandellas in one day, or
an afternoon, even on those roads, was easily done – by everyone
else. We stayed at the old Meikles Hotel, but in the annex at the
back, because it was cheaper. We ate a picnic supper in our room,
because we could not afford the hotel dining-room. Afterwards we
drank coffee in Meikles lounge, where a band played among palm
trees and gilded columns.

Next morning, the car forced to accommodate even more food,
we left early on the road to Marandellas, so there would be plenty
of time to set up camp. The drive went on for ever, the miles made
longer by the need to concentrate on everything. This is sandveld
country, not the heavy red, brown and bright pink soils of Banket,
and the landscape has a light dry airiness. Mountains and more
mountains accompany the road, but at distances that paint them
blue, mauve, purple, while close to the road are clusters of granite
boulders unique in the world; at least, I have not seen anything like
them elsewhere, or in photographs. The boulders erupt from pale
soil to balance on each other so lightly it seems impossible a strong

wind will not topple them. The great stones, a light bright grey, with a sparkle to them if you look close, but patched and patterned with lichens, radiate heat waves against the intense blue of the sky. Everyone who passes speculates about how long they have impossibly balanced there and enjoy notions of giants who have played with pebbles. 'That one, there,' I would think, fixing its exact shape and position in my mind, 'it might have fallen off by the time we come back next week.' But that boulder, the size of a hut or a baobab tree, contacting the one beneath it only for a square inch or two, had won the battle against gravity, and was still there in 1982 on that day I sped past on the road, not to Marandellas and Umtali, but to Marondera and Mutare, after so many rain storms, powerful winds, bolts of lightning; after half a century of history and the years of the civil war: the War of Liberation, the Bush War.

The road went up. The road went down. Roads do this every-where, but never as emphatically as on those journeys at thirty miles an hour, the car labouring to the top of a crest and reaching it in a climax of achievement, then the reward of a descent freewheeling into the valley, then the grind up the next rise, in second gear, because second gear is a solid, responsible state to be in, top gear has something about it of frivolity, even recklessness. Each crest brought another magnificent view, and my mother exclaimed and directed our attention in her way that mingled admiration and regret, as if such beauty must have a penalty to pay in sorrow. Meanwhile I was cramming into my mind, like photographs in an album, these views and vistas that would never stay put, but were changed by memory, as I would find out on the next trip. A 'view' I had believed was fixed for ever, had disappeared. A coil of mountains was lower than I remembered. A peak had come forward and attracted to itself a lesser hill. A river had changed course and acquired a tributary I had simply not noticed. Perhaps there had been a different 'view', and I had been mistaken? No, because *that* hill, there, near the road, had not changed, and I had used it as a marker. Yet how I had laboured over that view, my eyes stretched wide in case a blink shifted a perspective or spoiled my attention, my mind set to receive and record. I was in a contest with Time, and I knew it. I was obsessed with Time, always had been, and my very earliest memories are of how I insisted to myself, Hold this . . . don't forget it – as if I had been born with a knowledge of its sleights and deceptions. When I was very young, perhaps not more than two or three years old,

someone must have said to me, 'I'm telling you, it's like this.' But I
knew that 'it', was like that. They said: '*This* happened, *this* is the
truth' – but I knew *that* had happened, *that* was the truth. Someone
trying to talk me out of what I knew was true, must have been the
important thing that happened to me in my childhood, for I was
continually holding fast to moments, when I said to myself,
'Remember this. Remember what really happened. Don't let yourself
be talked out of what really happened.' Even now I hold a series of
sharp little scenes, like photographs, or eidetic memory, which I refer
to. So when I fought to retain a 'view', a perspective on a road, the
little effort was only one on a long list. Time, like grown-ups,
possessed all these slippery qualities, but if you labour enough over
an event, a moment, you make a solid thing of it, may revisit it . . .
Is it still there? Is it still the same? Meanwhile Time erodes, Time
chips and blurs, Time emits blue and mauve and purple and white
hazes like dry ice in a theatre: 'Here, wait a minute, I can't see.'

Time passed slowly, so very s-l-o-w-l-y, it crept and crawled, and
I knew I was in child-time, because my parents told me I was. 'When
you are our age, the years simply gallop!' But at my age, every day
went on for ever and I was determined to grow up as quickly as I
could and leave behind the condition of being a child, being helpless.
Now I wonder if those who dislike being children, who urge time
to go quickly, experience time differently when they get older: does
it go faster for us than for other people who have not spent years
teaching it to hurry by? The journeys to Marandellas, occurring two
or three times a year, were a way of marking accomplished stages:
another four months gone, another rainy season over, and that's a
whole year done with – and the same point last year seems so far
away. The journeys themselves, slow, painstaking, needing so much
effort by my mother to get everything ready, so much effort by my
father to rouse himself to face life and remain this damned car's
master ('We would have done much better to keep horses and the
use of our feet!') were each one like a small life, distant, different from
the ones before, marked by its own flavour, incidents, adventures.

'That was the trip Mrs C. visited us in our camp. I thought she
was a bit sniffy about it. Well, I think we have the best of it – you
don't lie out all night under the stars if you're in the Marandellas
Hotel!' Or, 'That was the time when our boy – what was his name?
Reuben?' – (These damned missionaries!) – 'went off for two days
on a beer drink because he met a brother in the next village, and he

turned up as calm as you please and said he hadn't seen his brother for five years. Brother my foot! Every second person they meet is a brother, as far as I can see.' 'Now, come on, old thing, be fair! Every second person they meet is a brother – do you remember that letter in the *Rhodesia Herald*? They have a different system of relationships. And anyway, we did quite all right without a servant, didn't we? I don't see what we need a boy for on the trips anyway.' 'It's the principle of the thing,' said my mother, fierce. But what she did not say, could not say, and only her face ever said it for her, like that of an unjustly punished little girl: 'It's all very well for you! Who gets the food ready and packs the car and unpacks everything, and finds the camp site and spreads the bedding and looks after the children? Not you, not you, ever! Surely I am not expected to do everything, always, myself?' And yes, she was; and yes, she did, always.

When we reached Marandellas, we turned off the main road that led to Umtali, drove through the neat little township with its gardens and its jacarandas and its flame trees, and went for a few miles along the road to Ruzawi. Here the bush was full of rocky kopjes and small streams. The sandy earth sparkled. Well before reaching the school, off the road but within sight of it, a space was found among the musasa trees. The 'boy' cut branches to make an enclosure about twenty feet by twenty, but round, in the spirit of the country. This leafy barrier was to keep out leopards, who were still holding on, though threatened, in their caves in the hills. We could have lain out under the trees without the barricade for any leopard worth its salt could have jumped over it in a moment and carried one of us off. No, the walls were an expression of something else, not a keeping out, but a keeping together, strangers in a strange land. My parents needed those encircling branchy arms. But my brother, when he was only a little older, went for days through the bush by himself, or with the son of the black man who worked in our kitchen, and he slept, as they did, as some still do, rolled in a blanket near the fire.

Inside this *boma* were made five low platforms of fresh grass, long and green and sappy, or long and yellow and dry, according to the season, and on these was spread the bedding. My brother was given permission to leave school and join us at these times for at least a night or two. And my parents always insisted that the black man must sleep inside the lager, safe, with us.

This involved all kinds of illogicalities and inconsistencies, but I was used to them, and took them for granted until I was much older. Reuben (or Isaiah, or Jacob, or Simon, or Abraham, or Sixpence, or Tickie – for they never stayed long) made up his own smaller fire outside the *boma*, and cooked his maize porridge on it, eating, too, the foods we were eating, bacon, eggs, steak, cake, bread, jam. While we sat at night around the big fire, gazing at it, watching the sparks whirl up into the trees and the stars, he sat with his back to a tree, turned away from us, looking at his own smaller fire. Later, when we were in our pyjamas inside the blankets, he was called in, and he wrapped himself in his blankets, and lay down, his face turned away from us to the leafy wall. In the early morning when we woke he was already gone, and his fire was lit, he was sitting by it, a blanket around his shoulders, and he was wearing everything he owned – tattered shirt, shorts, a cast-off jersey of my father's. These mornings could be cold, and sometimes frost crusted the edges of leaves in cold hollows. In our part of the country, so much hotter, there was seldom frost.

Later I had to wonder what that man was thinking, taken on this amazing trip in a car (and few of his fellows then had been in a car) to a part of the country too far away for him normally to think of visiting, days and days of walking, with the white family who were choosing – briefly – to live just as his people did, exclaiming all the time how wonderful it was, but preserving their customs as if they were still inside their house. They put on special clothes to sleep in. They washed continually in a white enamel basin set on a soap box under a tree. And they never stopped eating, just like all the white people. 'They eat all the time,' he certainly reported, returning to his own. 'As soon as one meal is finished, they start cooking the next.'

Now I wonder most of all, with the helpless grieving so many of us feel these days, when we remember the destruction of animals and plants, about the reckless cutting down of those boughs, and of young trees. When we left a site the rubbish was well buried, but the wreckage of the encircling boughs remained, and we would see it all there a few months later, on our way to making a new enclosure with fresh boughs. Above where our fires had roared, the scorched leaves hung grey and brittle. In those days the bush, the game, the birds, seemed limitless. Not long before I left Southern Rhodesia to come to London I was a typist for a Parliamentary Committee on sleeping sickness, reporting on the eradication of tsetse fly, recording how, over large areas, the hunters moved, killing out hundreds of thousands of head of game, kudu, sable, bush buck, duiker, particularly duiker, those light-stepping, graceful, dark-liquid-eyed creatures which once filled the bush, so that you could not walk more than a few yards without seeing one.

When I returned to Zimbabwe after that long absence, I expected all kinds of changes, but there was one change I had not thought to expect. The game had mostly gone. The bush was nearly silent. Once, the dawn chorus hurt the ears. Lying in our blankets under the trees on the sandveld of Marandellas, or in the house on the farm in Banket, the shrilling, clamouring, exulting of the birds as the sun appeared was so loud the ears seemed to curl up and complain before – there was nothing else for it – we leaped up into the early morning, to become part of all that tumult and activity. But by the 1980s the dawn chorus had become a feeble thing. Once, everywhere, moving through the bush, you saw duiker, bush buck, wild pig, wild cats, porcupines, anteaters; koodoo stood on the antheaps turning their proud horns to examine you before bounding off; eland went about in groups, like cattle. Being in the bush was to be with animals, one of them.

Lying inside our leafy circle at night, we listened to owls, nightjars, the mysterious cries of monkeys. Sometimes a pair of small eyes gleamed from the trees over our heads, as a monkey or wild cat watched, as we did, how the roaring fire of early evening sent the red sparks rushing up from the flames that reached to the boughs, but then, later, when it died down, the sparks fled up, but fewer, and snapped out one by one, like the meteors that you could watch too, when the fire had died. Or we might wake to hear how some large animal, startled to find this obstruction in its usual path, bounded away into silence. The moon, which had been pushed away by the roar of the fire, had come close, and was standing over the trees in one of its many shapes and sizes, looking straight down at us.

★ ★ ★

DAVID LIVINGSTONE (1813–1873)

'Discovery of the Victoria Falls'

As this was the point from which we intended to strike off to the
north-east, I resolved on the following day to visit the falls of Victoria,
called by the natives Mosioatunya, or more anciently Shongwe. Of
these we had often heard since we came into the country: indeed
one of the questions asked by Sebituane [Sekeletu's father] was, 'Have
you smoke that sounds in your country?' They did not go near
enough to examine them, but, viewing them with awe at a distance,
said, in reference to the vapour and noise, 'Mosi oa tunya' (smoke
does sound there). It was previously called Shongwe, the meaning
of which I could not ascertain. The word for a 'pot' resembles this,
and it may mean a seething cauldron; but I am not certain of it.
Being persuaded that Mr Oswell and myself were the very first
Europeans who ever visited the Zambesi in the centre of the country,
and that this is the connecting link between the known and unknown
portions of that river, I decided to use the same liberty as the
Makololo did, and gave the only English name I have affixed to any
part of the country. No better proof of previous ignorance of this
river could be desired, than that an untravelled gentleman, who had
spent a great part of his life in the study of the geography of Africa,
and knew everything written on the subject from the time of Ptolemy
downwards, actually asserted in the 'Athenaeum,' while I was coming
up the Red Sea, that this magnificent river, the Leeambye, had 'no
connection with the Zambesi, but flowed under the Kalahari Desert,
and became lost', and 'that, as all the old maps asserted, the Zambesi
took its rise in the very hills to which we have now come'. This
modest assertion smacks exactly as if a native of Timbuctu should
declare, that the Thames and the Pool were different rivers, he having
seen neither the one nor the other. Leeambye and Zambesi mean
the very same thing, viz. the RIVER.

Sekeletu intended to accompany me, but, one canoe only having
come instead of the two he had ordered, he resigned it to me. After
twenty minutes' sail from Kalai, we came in sight, for the first time,
of the columns of vapour, appropriately called 'smoke', rising at a

distance of five or six miles, exactly as when large tracts of grass are burned in Africa. Five columns now arose, and bending in the direction of the wind, they seemed placed against a low ridge covered with trees; the tops of the columns at this distance appeared to mingle with the clouds. They were white below, and higher up became dark, so as to simulate smoke very closely. The whole scene was extremely beautiful; the banks and islands dotted over the river are adorned with sylvan vegetation of great variety of colour and form. At the period of our visit several trees were spangled over with blossoms. Trees have each their own physiognomy. There, towering above all, stands the great burly baobab, each of whose enormous arms would form the trunk of a large tree, beside groups of graceful palms, which, with their feathery-shaped leaves depicted on the sky, lend their beauty to the scene. As a heiroglyphic they always mean 'far from home', for one can never get over their foreign air in a picture or landscape. The silvery mohonono, which in the tropics is in form like the cedar of Lebanon, stands in pleasing contrast with the dark colour of the motsouri, whose cypress-form is dotted over at present with its pleasant scarlet fruit. Some trees resemble the great spreading oak, others assume the character of our own elms and chestnuts; but no one can imagine the beauty of the view from anything witnessed in England. It had never been seen before by European eyes; but scenes so lovely must have been gazed upon by angels in their flight. The only want felt, is that of mountains in the background. The falls are bounded on three sides by ridges 300 or 400 feet in height, which are covered with forest, with the red soil appearing among the trees. When about half a mile from the falls, I left the canoe by which we had come down thus far, and embarked in a lighter one, with men well acquainted with the rapids, who, by passing down the centre of the stream in the eddies and still places caused by many jutting rocks, brought me to an island situated in the middle of the river, and on the edge of the lip over which the water rolls. In coming hither, there was danger of being swept down by the streams which rushed along on each side of the island; but the river was now low, and we sailed where it is totally impossible to go when the water is high. But though we had reached the island, and were within a few yards of the spot, a view from which would solve the whole problem, I believe that no one could perceive where the vast body of water went; it seemed to lose itself in the earth, the opposite lip of the fissure into which it disappeared being only 80 feet distant. At least I did not comprehend it until, creeping with awe to the verge, I peered down into a large rent which had been made from bank to bank of the broad Zambesi, and saw that a stream of a thousand yards broad leaped down a hundred feet, and then became suddenly compressed into a space of fifteen or twenty yards. The entire falls are simply a crack made in a hard basaltic rock from the right to the left bank of the Zambesi, and then prolonged from the left bank away through thirty or forty miles of hills . . . In looking down into the fissure on the right of the island, one sees nothing but a dense white cloud, which, at the time we visited the spot, had two bright rainbows on it. (The sun was on the meridian, and the declination about equal to the latitude of the place.) From this cloud rushed up a great jet of vapour exactly like steam, and it mounted 200 or 300 feet high; there condensing, it changed its hue to that of dark smoke, and came back in a constant shower, which soon wetted us to the skin. This shower falls chiefly on the opposite side of the fissure, and a few yards back from the lip there stands a straight hedge of evergreen trees, whose leaves are always wet. From their roots a number of little rills run back into the gulf; but as they flow down the steep wall there, the column of vapour, in its ascent, licks them up clean off the rock, and away they mount again. They are constantly running down, but never reach the bottom.

On the left of the island we see the water at the bottom, a white rolling mass moving away to the prolongation of the fissure, which branches off near the left bank of the river. A piece of the rock has fallen off a spot on the left of the island, and juts out from the water below, and from it, I judged the distance which the water falls to be about 100 feet. The walls of this gigantic crack are perpendicular, and composed of one homogeneous mass of rock. The edge of that side over which the water falls, is worn off two or three feet, and pieces have fallen away, so as to give it somewhat of a serrated appearance. That over which the water does not fall is quite straight, except at the left corner, where a rent appears, and a piece seems inclined to fall off. Upon the whole, it is nearly in the state in which it was left at the period of its formation. The rock is dark brown in colour, except about ten feet from the bottom, which is discoloured by the annual rise of the water to that or a greater height. On the left side of the island we have a good view of the mass of water which causes one of the columns of vapour to ascend, as it leaps quite clear of the rock, and forms a thick unbroken fleece all the way to the bottom. Its whiteness gave the idea of snow, a sight I had not seen for many a day. As it broke into (if I may use the term) pieces of water, all rushing on in the same direction, each gave off several rays of foam, exactly as bits of steel, when burnt in oxygen gas, give off rays of sparks. The snow-white sheet seemed like myriads of small comets rushing on in one direction, each of which left behind its nucleus rays of foam. I never saw the appearance referred to noticed elsewhere. It seemed to be the effect of the mass of water leaping at once clear of the rock, and but slowly breaking up into spray.

I have mentioned that we saw five columns of vapour ascending from this strange abyss. They are evidently formed by the compression suffered by the force of the water's own fall, into an unyielding wedge-shaped space. Of the five columns, two on the right, and one on the left of the island were the largest, and the streams which formed them seemed each to exceed in size the falls of the Clyde at Stonebyres, when that river is in flood. This was the period of low water in the Leeambye, but, as far as I could guess, there was a flow of five or six hundred yards of water, which, at the edge of the fall, seemed at least three feet deep. I write in the hope that others more capable of judging distances than myself will visit this scene, and I state simply the impressions made on my mind at the time . . .

The fissure is said by the Makololo to be very much deeper farther to the eastward; there is one part at which the walls are so sloping, that people accustomed to it, can go down by descending in a sitting position. The Makololo on one occasion, pursuing some fugitive Batoka, saw them, unable to stop the impetus of their flight at the edge, literally dashed to pieces at the bottom. They beheld the stream like a 'white cord' at the bottom, and so far down (probably 300 feet) that they became giddy, and were fain to go away, holding on to the ground . . .

At three spots near these falls, one of them the island in the middle on which we were, three Batoka chiefs offered up prayers and sacrifices to the Barimo. They chose their places of prayer within the sound of the roar of the cataract, and in sight of the bright bows in the cloud. They must have looked upon the scene with awe. Fear may have induced the selection. The river itself is, to them, mysterious. The words of the canoe-song are:

The Leeambye! Nobody knows,
Whence it comes and whither it goes.

The play of colours of the double iris on the cloud, seen by them
elsewhere only as the rainbow, may have led them to the idea that
this was the abode of Deity. Some of the Makololo who went with
me near to Gonye, looked upon the same sign with awe. When seen
in the heavens it is named 'motse oa barimo' – the pestle of the
gods. Here they could approach the emblem, and see it stand steadily
above the blustering uproar below – a type of Him who sits supreme
– alone unchangeable, though ruling over all changing things. But
not aware of His true character, they had no admiration of the
beautiful and good in their bosoms. They did not imitate His benevolence, for they were a bloody imperious crew, and Sebituane
performed a noble service, in the expulsion from their fastnesses of
these cruel 'Lords of the Isles'.

Having feasted my eyes long on the beautiful sight, I returned to
my friends at Kalai, and, saying to Sekeletu that he had nothing else
worth showing in his country, his curiosity was excited to visit it the
next day . . . Sekeletu acknowledged to feeling a little nervous at
the probability of being sucked into the gulf before reaching the
island. His companions amused themselves by throwing stones down,
and wondered to see them diminishing in size, and even disappearing,
before they reached the water at the bottom.

I had another object in view in my return to the island. I observed
that it was covered with trees, the seeds of which had probably come
down with the stream from the distant north, and several of which
I had seen nowhere else; and every now and then the wind wafted
a little of the condensed vapour over it, and kept the soil in a state
of moisture, which caused a sward of grass, growing as green as on
an English lawn. I selected a spot – not too near the chasm, for there
the constant deposition of the moisture nourished numbers of polypi
of a mushroom shape and fleshy consistence – but somewhat back,
and made a little garden. I there planted about a hundred peach
and apricot stones, and a quantity of coffee-seeds. I had attempted
fruit-trees before, but, when left in charge of my Makololo friends,
they were always allowed to wither, after having vegetated, by
being forgotten. I bargained for a hedge with one of the Makololo,
and if he is faithful, I have great hopes of Mosioatunya's abilities as
a nurseryman. My only source of fear is the hippopotami, whose

footprints I saw on the island. When the garden was prepared, I cut my initials on a tree, and the date 1855. This was the only instance in which I indulged in this piece of vanity. The garden stands in front, and were there no hippopotami, I have no doubt but this will be the parent of all the gardens, which may yet be in this new country. We then went up to Kalai again.

* * *

MARY KINGSLEY (1862–1900)

from *Travels in West Africa*

The earlier part of the day we were steadily going uphill, here and there making a small descent, and then up again, until we came on to what was apparently a long ridge, for on either side of us we could look down into deep, dark, ravine-like valleys. Twice or thrice we descended into these to cross them, finding at their bottom a small or large swamp with a river running through its midst. Those rivers all went to Lake Ayzingo.

We had to hurry because Kiva, who was the only one among us who had been to Efoua, said that unless we did we should not reach Efoua that night. I said, 'Why not stay for bush?' not having contracted any love for a night in a Fan town by the experience of M'fetta; moreover the Fans were not sure that after all the whole party of us might not spend the evening at Efoua, when we did get there, simmering in its cooking-pots.

Ngouta, I may remark, had no doubt on the subject at all, and regretted having left Mrs N. keenly, and the Andande store sincerely. But these Fans are a fine sporting tribe, and allowed they would risk it; besides, they were almost certain they had friends at Efoua; and, in addition, they showed me trees scratched in a way that was magnification of the condition of my own cat's pet table leg at home, demonstrating leopards in the vicinity. I kept going, as it was my only chance, because I found I stiffened if I sat down, and they always carefully told me the direction to go in when they sat down; with their superior pace they soon caught me up, and then passed me, leaving me and Ngouta and sometimes Singlet and Pagan behind,

we, in our turn, overtaking them, with this difference that they were
sitting down when we did so.

About five o'clock I was off ahead and noticed a path which I
had been told I should meet with, and, when met with, I must
follow. The path was slightly indistinct, but by keeping my eye on it
I could see it. Presently I came to a place where it went out, but
appeared again on the other side of a clump of underbush fairly
distinctly. I made a short cut for it and the next news was I was in
a heap, on a lot of spikes, some fifteen feet or so below ground level,
at the bottom of a bag-shaped game pit.

It is at these times you realize the blessing of a good thick skirt.
Had I paid heed to the advice of many people in England, who
ought to have known better, and did not do it themselves, and
adopted masculine garments, I should have been spiked to the bone,
and done for. Whereas, save for a good many bruises, here I was
with the fullness of my skirt tucked under me, sitting on nine ebony
spikes some twelve inches long, in comparative comfort, howling
lustily to be hauled out. The Duke came along first, and looked
down at me. I said, 'Get a bush-rope, and haul me out.' He grunted
and sat down on a log. The Passenger came next, and he looked
down. 'You kill?' says he. 'Not much,' say I; 'get a bush-rope and
haul me out.' 'No fit,' says he, and sat down on the log. Presently,
however, Kiva and Wiki came up, and Wiki went and selected the
one and only bush-rope suitable to haul an English lady, of my exact
complexion, age, and size, out of that one particular pit. They seemed
rare round there from the time he took; and I was just casting about
in my mind as to what method would be best to employ in getting
up the smooth, yellow, sandy-clay, incurved walls when he arrived
with it, and I was out in a twinkling, and very much ashamed of
myself, until Silence, who was then leading, disappeared through the
path before us with a despairing yell. Each man then pulled the skin
cover off his gun lock, carefully looked to see if things there were
all right and ready loosened his knife in its snake-skin sheath; and
then we set about hauling poor Silence out, binding him up where
necessary with cool green leaves; for he, not having a skirt, had got
a good deal frayed at the edges on those spikes. Then we closed up,
for the Fans said these pits were symptomatic of the immediate
neighbourhood of Efoua. We sounded our ground, as we went into
a thick plantain patch, through which we could see a great clearing
in the forest, and the low huts of a big town. We charged into it,

going right through the guard-house gateway, at one end, in single
file, as its narrowness obliged us, and into the street-shaped town,
and formed ourselves into as imposing a looking party as possible
in the centre of the street. The Efouerians regarded us with much
amazement, and the women and children cleared off into the huts,
and took stock of us through the door-holes. There were but few
men in the town, the majority, we subsequently learnt, being away
after elephants. But there were quite sufficient left to make a crowd
in a ring round us. Fortunately Wiki and Kiva's friends were present,
and we were soon in another world – fog, but not so bad a one as
that at M'fetta; indeed Efoua struck me, from the first, favourably;
it was, for one thing, much cleaner than most Fan towns I have
been in.

As a result of the confabulation, one of the chiefs had his house
cleared out for me. It consisted of two apartments almost bare of
everything save a pile of boxes, and a small fire on the floor, some
little bags hanging from the roof poles, and a general supply of
insects. The inner room contained nothing save a hard plank, raised
on four short pegs from the earth floor.

I shook hands with and thanked the chief, and directed that all
the loads should be placed inside the huts. I must admit my good
friend was a villainous-looking savage, but he behaved most hospit-
ably and kindly. From what I had heard of the Fan, I deemed it
advisable not to make any present to him at once, but to base my
claim on him on the right of an amicable stranger to hospitality.
When I had seen all the baggage stowed I went outside and sat at
the doorway on a rather rickety mushroom-shaped stool in the cool
evening air, waiting for my tea which I wanted bitterly. Pagan came
up as usual for tobacco to buy chop with; and after giving it to him,
I and the two chiefs, with Gray Shirt acting as interpreter, had a
long chat. Of course the first question was, Why was I there?

I told them I was on my way to the factory of H. and C. on the
Rembwé. They said they had heard of 'Ugumu', i.e. Messrs Hatton
and Cookson, but they did not trade direct with them, passing their
trade into towns nearer to the Rembwé, which were swindling bad
towns, they said; and they got the idea stuck in their heads that I
was a trader, a sort of bagman for the firm, and Gray Shirt could
not get this idea out, so off one of their majesties went and returned
with twenty-five balls of rubber, which I bought to promote good
feeling, subsequently dashing them to Wiki, who passed them in at

Ndorko when we got there. I also bought some elephant-hair neck-laces from one of the chiefs' wives, by exchanging my red silk tie with her for them, and one or two other things. I saw fish-hooks would not be of much value because Efoua was not near a big water of any sort; so I held fish-hooks and traded handkerchiefs and knives.

One old chief was exceedingly keen to do business, and I bought a meat spoon, a plantain spoon, and a gravy spoon off him; then he brought me a lot of rubbish I did not want, and I said so, and announced I had finished trade for that night. However the old gentleman was not to be put off, and after an unsuccessful attempt to sell me his cooking-pots, which were roughly made out of clay, he made energetic signs to me that if I would wait he had got something that he would dispose of which Gray Shirt said was 'good too much'. Off he went across the street, and disappeared into his hut, where he evidently had a thorough hunt for the precious article. One box after another was brought out to the light of a bush torch held by one of his wives, and there was a great confabulation between him and his family of the 'I'm sure you had it last,' 'You must have moved it,' 'Never touched the thing,' sort. At last it was found, and he brought it across the street to me most carefully. It was a bundle of bark cloth tied round something most carefully with tie tie. This being removed, disclosed a layer of rag, which was unwound from round a central article. Whatever can this be? thinks I; some rare and valuable object doubtless, let's hope connected with Fetish worship, and I anxiously watched its unpacking; in the end, however, it disclosed, to my disgust and rage, an old shilling razor. The way the old chief held it out, and the amount of dollars he asked for it, was enough to make any one believe that I was in such urgent need of the thing, that I was at his mercy regarding price. I waved it off with a haughty scorn, and then feeling smitten by the expression of agonized bewilderment on his face, I dashed him a belt that delighted him, and went inside and had tea to soothe my outraged feelings.

The chiefs made furious raids on the mob of spectators who pressed round the door, and stood with their eyes glued to every crack in the bark of which the hut was made. The next door neighbours on either side might have amassed a comfortable competence for their old age, by letting out seats for the circus. Every hole in the side walls had a human eye in it, and I heard new holes being bored in all directions; so I deeply fear the chief, my host, must have found his palace sadly draughty. I felt perfectly safe and content, however, although Ngouta suggested the charming idea that 'P'r'aps them M'fetta Fan done sell we.' The only grave question I had to face was whether I should take off my boots or not; they were wet through, from wading swamps, etc., and my feet were very sore; but on the other hand, if I took those boots off, I felt confident that I should not be able to get them on again next morning, so I decided to lef 'em.

As soon as all my men had come in, and established themselves in the inner room for the night, I curled up among the boxes, with my head on the tobacco sack, and dozed.

After about half an hour I heard a row in the street, and looking out – for I recognized his grace's voice taking a solo part followed by choruses – I found him in legal difficulties about a murder case. An *alibi* was proved for the time being; that is to say the prosecution could not bring up witnesses because of the elephant hunt; and I went in for another doze, and the town at last grew quiet. Waking up again I noticed the smell in the hut was violent, from being shut up I suppose, and it had an unmistakably organic origin. Knocking the ash end off the smouldering bush-light that lay burning on the floor, I investigated, and tracked it to those bags, so I took down the biggest one, and carefully noted exactly how the tie tie had been put round its mouth; for these things are important and often mean a lot. I then shook its contents out in my hat, for fear of losing anything of value. They were a human hand, three big toes, four eyes, two ears, and other portions of the human frame. The hand was fresh, the others only so so, and shrivelled.

*   *   *

KAREN BLIXEN (Isak Dinesen) (1885–1962)

'The Ngong Farm'

I had a farm in Africa, at the foot of the Ngong Hills. The Equator runs across these highlands, a hundred miles to the north, and the farm lay at an altitude of over six thousand feet. In the day-time you felt that you had got high up, near to the sun, but the early mornings and evenings were limpid and restful, and the nights were cold.

The geographical position, and the height of the land combined to create a landscape that had not its like in all the world. There was no fat on it and no luxuriance anywhere; it was Africa distilled up through six thousand feet, like the strong and refined essence of a continent. The colours were dry and burnt, like the colours in pottery. The trees had a light delicate foliage, the structure of which was different from that of the trees in Europe; it did not grow in bows or cupolas, but in horizontal layers, and the formation gave to the tall solitary trees a likeness to the palms, or a heroic and romantic air like fullrigged ships with their sails furled, and to the edge of a wood a strange appearance as if the whole wood were faintly vibrating. Upon the grass of the great plains the crooked bare old thorn-trees were scattered, and the grass was spiced like thyme and bog-myrtle; in some places the scent was so strong, that it smarted in the nostrils. All the flowers that you found on the plains, or upon the creepers and liana in the native forest, were diminutive like flowers of the downs – only just in the beginning of the long rains a number of big, massive heavy-scented lilies sprang out on the plains. The views were immensely wide. Everything that you saw made for greatness and freedom, and unequalled nobility.

The chief feature of the landscape, and of your life in it, was the air. Looking back on a sojourn in the African highlands, you are struck by your feeling of having lived for a time up in the air. The sky was rarely more than pale blue or violet, with a profusion of mighty, weightless, ever-changing clouds towering up and sailing on it, but it has a blue vigour in it, and at a short distance it painted the ranges of hills and the woods a fresh deep blue. In the middle of the day the air was alive over the land, like a flame burning; it scintillated, waved and shone like running water, mirrored and doubled all objects, and created great Fata Morgana. Up in this high air you breathed easily, drawing in a vital assurance and lightness of heart. In the highlands you woke up in the morning and thought: Here I am, where I ought to be.

NORTH AFRICA

Elias Canetti (1905–1994)

'The Unseen'

At twilight I went to the great square in the middle of the city, and
what I sought there were not its colour and bustle, those I was
familiar with, I sought a small, brown bundle on the ground consisting not even of a voice but of a single sound. This was a deep,
long-drawn-out, buzzing 'e-e-e-e-e-e-e-e'. It did not diminish, it did
not increase, it just went on and on; beneath all the thousands of
calls and cries in the square it was always audible. It was the most
unchanging sound in the Djema el Fna, remaining the same all
evening and from evening to evening.

While still a long way off I was already listening for it. A restlessness drove me there that I cannot satisfactorily explain. I would have
gone to the square in any case, there was so much there to attract
me; nor did I ever doubt I would find it each time, with all that
went with it. Only for this voice, reduced to a single sound, did I
feel something akin to fear. It was at the very edge of the living; the
life that engendered it consisted of nothing but that sound. Listening
greedily, anxiously, I invariably reached a point in my walk, in exactly
the same place, where I suddenly became aware of it like the buzzing
of an insect:

'E-e-e-e-e-e-e-e.'

I felt a mysterious calm spread through my body, and whereas
my steps had been hesitant and uncertain hitherto I now, all of a
sudden, made determinedly for the sound. I knew where it came
from. I knew the small, brown bundle on the ground, of which I
had never seen anything more than a piece of dark, coarse cloth.
I had never seen the mouth from which the 'e-e-e-e-e' issued; nor
the eye; nor the cheek; nor any part of the face. I could not have

said whether it was the face of a blind man or whether it could see. The brown, soiled cloth was pulled right down over the head like a hood, concealing everything. The creature – as it must have been – squatted on the ground, its back arched under the material. There was not much of the creature there, it seemed slight and feeble, that was all one could conjecture. I had no idea how tall it was because I had never seen it standing. What there was of it on the ground kept so low that one would have stumbled over it quite unsuspectingly, had the sound ever stopped. I never saw it come, I never saw it go; I do not know whether it was brought and put down there or whether it walked there by itself.

The place it had chosen was by no means sheltered. It was the most open part of the square and there was an incessant coming and going on all sides of the little brown heap. On busy evenings it disappeared completely behind people's legs, and although I knew exactly where it was and could always hear the voice I had difficulty in finding it. But then the people dispersed, and it was still in its place when all around it, far and wide, the square was empty. Then it lay there in the darkness like an old and very dirty garment that someone had wanted to get rid of and had surreptitiously dropped in the midst of all the people where no one would notice. Now, however, the people had dispersed and only the bundle lay there. I never waited until it got up or was fetched. I slunk away in the darkness with a choking feeling of helplessness and pride.

The helplessness was in regard to myself. I sensed that I would never do anything to discover the bundle's secret. I had a dread of its shape; and since I could give it no other I left it lying there on the ground. When I was getting close I took care not to bump into it, as if I might hurt or endanger it. It was there every evening, and every evening my heart stood still when I first distinguished the sound, and it stood still again when I caught sight of the bundle. How it got there and how it got away again were matters more sacred to me than my own movements. I never spied on it and I do not know where it disappeared to for the rest of the night and the following day. It was something apart, and perhaps it saw itself as such. I was sometimes tempted to touch the brown hood very lightly with one finger – the creature was bound to notice, and perhaps it had a second sound with which it would have responded. But this temptation always succumbed swiftly to my helplessness.

I have said that another feeling choked me as I slunk away:

pride. I was proud of the bundle because it was alive. What it thought to itself as it breathed down there, far below other people, I shall never know. The meaning of its call remained as obscure to me as its whole existence: but it was alive, and every day at the same time, there it was. I never saw it pick up the coins that people threw it; they did not throw many, there were never more than two or three coins lying there. Perhaps it had no arms with which to reach for the coins. Perhaps it had no tongue with which to form the 'l' of 'Allah' and to it the name of God was abbreviated to 'e-e-e-e-e'. But it was alive, and with a diligence and persistence that were unparalleled it uttered its one sound, uttered it hour after hour, until it was the only sound in the whole enormous square, the sound that outlived all others.

* * *

ISABELLE EBERHARDT (1877–1904)

'The Oblivion Seekers'

In this *ksar*, where the people have no place to meet but the public square or the earthen benches along the foot of the ramparts on the road to Bechar, here where there is not even a café, I have discovered a kif den.

It is in a partially ruined house behind the Mellah, a long hall lighted by a single eye in the ceiling of twisted and smoke-blackened beams. The walls are black, ribbed with lighter-coloured cracks that look like open wounds. The floor has been made by pounding the earth, but it is soft and dusty. Seldom swept, it is covered with pomegranate rinds and assorted refuse.

The place serves as a shelter for Moroccan vagabonds, for nomads, and for every sort of person of dubious intent and questionable appearance. The house seems to belong to no one; as at a disreputable hotel, you spend a few badly advised nights there and go on. It is a natural setting for picturesque and theatrical events, like the antechamber of the room where the crime was committed.

In one corner lies a clean reed mat, with some cushions from Fez in embroidered leather. On the mat, a large decorated chest which serves as a table. A rose-bush with little pale pink blooms, surrounded by a bouquet of garden herbs, all standing in water inside one of those wide earthen jars from the Tell. Further on, a copper kettle on a tripod, two or three teapots, a large basket of dried Indian hemp. The little group of kif-smokers requires no other decoration, no other *mise-en-scène*. They are people who like their pleasure.

On a rude perch of palm branches, a captive falcon, tied by one leg.

The strangers, the wanderers who haunt this retreat sometimes mix with the kif-smokers, notwithstanding the fact that the latter are a very closed little community into which entry is made difficult. But the smokers themselves are travellers who carry their dreams with them across the countries of Islam, worshippers of the hallucinating smoke. The men who happen to meet here at Kenadsa are among the most highly educated in the land.

Hadj Idriss, a tall thin Filali, deeply sunburned, with a sweet face that lights up from within, is one of these rootless ones without family or specific trade, so common in the Moslem world. For twenty-five years he has been wandering from city to city, working or begging, depending on the situation. He plays the *guinbri*, with its carved wooden neck and its two thick strings fastened to the shell of a tortoise. Hadj Idriss has a deep clear voice, ideal for singing the old Andaluz ballads, so full of tender melancholy.

Si Mohammed Behaouri, a Moroccan from Meknès, pale-complexioned and with caressing eyes, is a young poet wandering across Morocco and southern Algeria in search of native legends and literature. To keep alive, he composes and recites verse on the delights and horrors of love.

Another is from the Djebel Zerhoun, a doctor and witch-doctor, small dry, muscular, his skin tanned by the Sudanese sun under which he has journeyed for many years following caravans to and fro, from the coast of Senegal to Timbuctoo. All day long he keeps busy, slowly pouring out medicine and thumbing through old Moghrebi books of magic.

Chance brought them here to Kenadsa. Soon they will set out again, in different directions and on different trails, moving unconcernedly toward the fulfilment of their separate destinies. But it was community of taste that gathered them together in this smoky refuge, where they pass the slow hours of a life without cares.

At the end of the afternoon a slanting pink ray of light falls from the eye in the ceiling into the darkness of the room. The kif-smokers move in and form groups. Each wears a sprig of sweet basil in his turban. Squatting along the wall on the mat, they smoke their little pipes of baked red earth, filled with Indian hemp and powdered Moroccan tobacco.

Hadj Idriss stuffs the bowls and distributes them, after having carefully wiped the mouthpiece on his cheek as a gesture of politeness. When his own pipe is empty, he picks out the little red ball of ash and puts it into his mouth – he does not feel it burning him – then, once his pipe is refilled, he uses the still red-hot cinder to relight the little fire. For hours at a time he does not once let it go out. He has a keen and penetrating intelligence, softened by being constantly in a state of semi-exaltation; his dreams are nourished on the narcotic smoke.

The seekers of oblivion sing and clap their hands lazily; their dream-voices ring out late into the night, in the dim light of the mica-paned lantern. Then little by little the voices fall, grow muffled, the words are slower. Finally the smokers are quiet, and merely stare at the flowers in ecstasy. They are epicureans, voluptuaries; perhaps they are sages. Even in the darkest purlieu of Morocco's underworld such men can reach the magic horizon where they are free to build their dream-palaces of delight.

* * *

ALEXANDER WILLIAM KINGLAKE (1809–1891)

'Cairo and the Plague'

Cairo and Plague! During the whole time of my stay, the plague was so master of the city, and stared so plain in every street and every alley, that I can't now affect to dissociate the two ideas.

When, coming from the Desert, I rode through a village lying near to the city on the eastern side, there approached me with busy face and earnest gestures a personage in the Turkish dress. His long flowing beard gave him rather a majestic look, but his briskness of manner and his visible anxiety to accost me seemed strange in an oriental. The man, in fact, was French, or of French origin, and his object was to warn me of the plague, and prevent me from entering the city.

> *Arrêtez-vous, Monsieur: je vous en prie – arrêtez-vous; il ne faut pas entrer dans la ville; la Peste y règne partout.*
>
> *Oui, je sais, mais—*
>
> *Mais, Monsieur, je dis la Peste – la Peste; c'est de* LA PESTE *qu'il est question.*
>
> *Oui, je sais, mais—*
>
> *Mais, Monsieur, je dis encore* LA PESTE *–* LA PESTE. *Je vous conjure de ne pas entrer dans la ville – vous seriez dans une ville empestée.*
>
> *Ou, je sais, mais—*
>
> *Mais, Monsieur, je dois donc vous avertir tour bonnement que si vous entrez dans la ville, vous serez – enfin vous serez* COMPROMIS!
>
> *Ouis, je sais, mais—*

The Frenchman was at last convinced that it was vain to reason with a mere Englishman who could not understand what it was to be 'compromised'. I thanked him most sincerely for his kindly-meant warning. In hot countries it is very unusual indeed for a man to go out in the glare of the sun and give free advice to a stranger.

When I arrived at Cairo I summoned Osman Effendi, who was, as I knew, the owner of several houses, and would be able to provide me with apartments. He had no difficulty in doing this, for there was not one European traveller in Cairo besides myself. Poor Osman! he met me with a sorrowful countenance, for the fear of the plague sat heavily on his soul. He seemed as if he felt that he was doing wrong in lending me a resting-place, and he betrayed such a listlessness about temporal matters as one might look for in a man who believed that his days were numbered. He caught me, too, soon after my arrival, coming out from the public baths, and from that time forward he was sadly afraid of me, for upon the subject of contagion he held European opinions.

Osman's history is a curious one. He was a Scotchman born, and when very young, being then a drummer-boy, he landed in Egypt with Fraser's force. He was taken prisoner, and according to Mahometan custom, the alternative of death or the Koran was offered to him; he did not choose death, and therefore went through the ceremonies necessary for turning him into a good Mahometan. But what amused me most in his history was this – that very soon after having embraced Islam, he was obliged in practice to become curious and discriminating in his new faith – to make war upon Mahometan dissenters, and follow the orthodox standard of the Prophet in fierce campaigns against the Wahabees, the Unitarians of the Mussulman world. The Wahabees were crushed, and Osman, returning home in triumph from his holy wars, began to flourish in the world; he acquired property, and became 'effendi', or gentleman. At the time of my visit to Cairo he seemed to be much respected by his brother Mahometans, and gave pledge of his sincere alienation from Christianity by keeping a couple of wives. He affected the same sort of reserve in mentioning them as is generally shown by orientals. He invited me, indeed, to see his harem, but he made both his wives bundle out before I was admitted; he felt, as it seemed to me, that neither of them would bear criticism; and I think that this idea, rather than any motive of sincere jealousy, induced him to keep them out of sight. The rooms of the harem reminded me of an English nursery rather than a Mahometan paradise. One is apt to judge of a woman before one sees her by the air of elegance or coarseness with which she surrounds her home: I judged Osman's wives by this test, and condemned them both. But the strangest feature in Osman's character was his inextinguishable nationality. In vain they had brought him over the seas in early boyhood – in vain had he suffered captivity, conversion, circumcision – in vain they had passed him through fire in their Arabian campaigns – they could not cut away or burn out poor Osman's inborn love of all that was Scotch; in vain men called him Effendi – in vain he swept along in Eastern robes – in vain the rival wives adorned his harem; the joy of his heart still plainly lay in this, that he had three shelves of books, and that the books were thoroughbred Scotch – the Edinburgh this – the Edinburgh that – and, above all, I recollect he prided himself upon the 'Edinburgh Cabinet Library'.

The fear of the plague is its forerunner. It is likely enough that at the time of my seeing poor Osman the deadly taint was beginning to creep through his veins, but it was not till after I had left Cairo that he was visibly stricken. He died.

As soon as I had seen all that interested me in Cairo and its neighbourhood I wished to make my escape from a city that lay under the terrible curse of the plague, but Mysseri fell ill in consequence, I believe, of the hardships which he had been suffering in my service. After a while he recovered sufficiently to undertake a journey, but then there was some difficulty in procuring beasts of burthen, and it was not until the nineteenth day of my sojourn that I quitted the city.

During all this time the power of the plague was rapidly increasing. When I first arrived, it was said that the daily number of 'accidents' by plague, out of a population of about 200,000 did not exceed four or five hundred; but before I went away the deaths were reckoned at twelve hundred a day. I had no means of knowing whether the numbers (given out, as I believe they were, by officials) were at all correct, but I could not help knowing that from day to day the number of the dead was increasing. My quarters were in one of the chief thoroughfares of the city, and as the funerals in Cairo take place between daybreak and noon (a time during which I generally stayed in my rooms), I could form some opinion as to the briskness of the plague. I don't mean that I got up every morning with the sun. It was not so, but the funerals of most people in decent circumstances at Cairo are attended by singers and howlers, and the performances of these people woke me in the early morning, and prevented me from remaining in ignorance of what was going on in the street below.

These funerals were very simply conducted. The bier was a shallow wooden tray carried upon a light and weak wooden frame. The tray had in general no lid, but the body was more or less hidden from view by a shawl or scarf. The whole was borne upon the shoulders of men, and hurried forward at a great pace. Two or three singers generally preceded the bier; the howlers (these are paid for their vocal labours) followed after; and last of all came such of the dead man's friends and relations as could keep up with such a rapid procession; these, especially the women, would get terribly blown, and would struggle back into the rear; many were fairly 'beaten off'. I never observed any appearance of mourning in the mourners; the pace was too severe for any solemn affectation of grief.

When first I arrived at Cairo the funerals that daily passed under my windows were many, but still there were frequent and long intervals without a single howl. Every day, however (except one, when I fancied that I observed a diminution of funerals) these intervals became less frequent and shorter, and at last the passing of the howlers from morn to noon was almost incessant. I believe that about one half of the whole people was carried off by this visitation. The orientals, however, have more quiet fortitude than Europeans under afflictions of this sort, and they never allow the plague to interfere with their religious usages. I rode one day round the great burial-ground. The tombs are strewed over a great expanse among the vast mountains of rubbish (the accumulations of many centuries) which surround the city. The ground, unlike the Turkish 'cities of the dead', which are made so beautiful by their dark cypresses, has nothing to sweeten melancholy – nothing to mitigate the hatefulness of death. Carnivorous beasts and birds possess the place by night, and now in the fair morning it was all alive with fresh comers – alive with dead. Yet at this very time when the plague was raging so furiously, and on this very ground which resounded so mournfully with the howls of arriving funerals, preparations were going on for the religious festival called the Kourban Bairam. Tents were pitched, and *swings hung for the amusement of children* – a ghastly holiday! but the Mahometans take a pride, and a just pride, in following their ancient customs undisturbed by the shadow of death.

I did not hear whilst I was at Cairo that any prayer for a remission of the plague had been offered up in the mosques. I believe that, however frightful the ravages of the disease may be, the Mahometans refrain from approaching Heaven with their complaints until the plague has endured for a long space, and then at last they pray God – not that the plague may cease, but that it may go to another city!

A good Mussulman seems to take pride in repudiating the European notion that the will of God can be eluded by shunning the touch of a sleeve. When I went to see the Pyramids of Sakkara, I was the guest of a noble old fellow – an Osmanlee (how sweet it was to hear his soft rolling language, after suffering as I had suffered of late from the shrieking tongue of the Arabs!). This man was aware of the European ideas about contagion, and his first care therefore was to assure me that not a single instance of plague had occurred in his village; he then inquired as to the progress of the plague at Cairo. I had but a bad account to give. Up to this time my host had carefully refrained from touching me, out of respect to the European theory of contagion; but as soon as it was made plain that he, and not I, would be the person endangered by contact, he gently laid his hand upon my arm in order to make me feel sure that the circumstance of my coming from an infected city did not occasion him the least uneasiness. In that touch there was true hospitality.

Very different is the faith and the practice of the Europeans, or rather I mean of the Europeans settled in the East, and commonly called Levantines. When I came to the end of my journey over the Desert I had been so long alone that the prospect of speaking to somebody at Cairo seemed almost a new excitement. I felt a sort of consciousness that I had a little of the wild beast about me, but I was quite in the humour to be charmingly tame and to be quite engaging in my manners, if I should have an opportunity of holding communion with any of the human race whilst at Cairo. I knew no one in the place, and had no letters of introduction, but I carried letters of credit; and it often happens in places remote from England that those 'advices' operate as a sort of introduction, and obtain for the bearer (if disposed to receive them) such ordinary civilities as it may be in the power of the banker to offer.

Very soon after my arrival I found out the abode of the Levantine to whom my credentials were addressed. At his door several persons (all Arabs) were hanging about and keeping guard. It was not till after some delay and the interchange of some communications with those in the interior of the citadel that I was admitted. At length, however, I was conducted through the court, and up a flight of stairs, and finally into the apartment where business was transacted. The room was divided by a good substantial fence of iron bars, and behind these defences the banker had his station. The truth was that from fear of the plague he had adopted the course usually taken by European residents, and had shut himself up 'in strict quarantine' – that is to say, that he had, as he hoped, cut himself off from all communication with infecting substances. The Europeans long resident in the East without any, or with scarcely any exception, are firmly convinced that the plague is propagated by contact, and by contact only – that if they can but avoid the touch of an infecting substance, they are safe, and that if they cannot, they die. This belief induces them to adopt the contrivance of putting themselves in that stage of siege which they call 'quarantine'. It is a part of their faith that metals and hempen ropes, and also, I fancy, one or two other substances, will not carry the infection: and they likewise believe that the germ of pestilence lying in an infected substance may be destroyed by submersion in water, or by the action of smoke. They therefore guard the doors of their houses with the utmost care against intrusion, and condemn themselves, with all the members of their family, including European servants, to a strict imprisonment within the walls of their dwelling. Their native attendants are not allowed to enter at all, but they make the necessary purchases of provisions: these are hauled up through one of the windows by means of a rope, and are afterwards soaked in water.

I knew nothing of these mysteries, and was not therefore prepared for the sort of reception I met with. I advanced to the iron fence, and putting my letter between the bars, politely proffered it to Mr Banker. Mr Banker received me with a sad and dejected look, and not 'with open arms', or with any arms at all, but with – a pair of tongs! I placed my letters between the iron fingers: these instantly picked it up as if it were a viper, and conveyed it away to be scorched and purified by fire and smoke. I was disgusted at this reception, and that the idea that anything of mine could carry infection to the poor wretch who stood on the other side of the bars – pale and trembling, and already meet for death. I looked with something of the Mahome-tan's feeling upon these little contrivances for eluding fate: and in this instance at least they were vain: a little while and the poor moneychanger who had strived to guard the days of his life (as though they were coins) with bolts and bars of iron – he was seized by the plague, and he died . . .

*

Better fate was mine. By some happy perverseness (occasioned perhaps by my disgust at the notion of being received with a pair of tongs) I took it into my pleasant head that all the European notions about contagion were thoroughly unfounded – that the plague might be providential or 'epidemic' (as they phrase it), but was not con-tagious, and that I could not be killed by the touch of a woman's sleeve, nor yet by her blessed breath. I therefore determined that the plague should not alter my habits and amusements in any one respect. Though I came to this resolve from impulse, I think that I took the course which was in effect the most prudent, for the cheerfulness of spirits which I was thus enabled to retain discouraged the yellow-winged angel, and prevented him from taking a shot at me. I however so far respected the opinion of the Europeans that I avoided touching when I could do so without privation or incon-venience. This endeavour furnished me with a sort of amusement as I passed through the streets. The usual mode of moving from place to place in the city of Cairo is upon donkeys; of these great numbers are always in readiness, with donkey-boys attached. I had two who constantly (until one of them died of the plague) waited at my door upon the chance of being wanted. I found this way of moving about exceedingly pleasant, and never attempted any other. I had only to mount my beast, and tell my donkey-boy the point for which I was bound, and instantly I began to glide on at a capital pace. The streets of Cairo are not paved in any way, but strewed with a dry sandy soil so deadening to sound, that the footfall of my donkey could scarcely be heard. There is no *trottoir*, and as you ride through the streets you mingle with the people on foot: those who are in your away, upon being warned by the shouts of the donkey-boy, move very slightly aside so as to leave you a narrow lane for your passage. Through this you move at a gallop, gliding on delightfully in the very midst of crowds without being inconvenienced or stopped for a moment; it seems to you that it is not the donkey but the donkey-boy who wafts you along with his shouts through pleasant groups, and air that comes thick with the fragrance of burial spice. 'Eh! Sheik – Eh! Bint, reggalek, shumalek, etc., etc. – O old man, O virgin, get out of the way on the right. O virgin, O old man, get out of the way on the left – this Englishman comes, he comes, he comes!' The narrow alley which these shouts cleared for my passage made it possible, though difficult, to go on for a long way without touching a single person, and my endeavours to avoid such contact were a sort of game for me in my loneliness. If I got through a street without being touched, I won; if I was touched, I lost – lost a deuce of a stake according to the theory of the Europeans; but that I deemed to be all nonsense – I only lost that game, and would certainly win the next . . .

*

Although the plague was now spreading quick and terrible havoc around [me], I did not see very plainly any corresponding change in the looks of the streets until the seventh day after my arrival: I then first observed that the city was *silenced*. There were no outward signs of despair nor of violent terror, but many of the voices that had swelled the busy hum of men were already hushed in death, and the survivors, so used to scream and screech in their earnestness whenever they bought or sold, now showed an unwonted indifference about the affairs of this world: it was less worth while for men to haggle and haggle, and crack the sky with noisy bargains, when the Great Commander was there who could 'pay all their debts with the roll of his drum'.

At this time I was informed that of 25,000 people at Alexandria,

12,000 had died already; the Destroyer had come rather later to Cairo, but there was nothing of weariness in his strides. The deaths came faster than ever they befell in the plague of London: but the calmness of orientals under such visitations, and their habit of using biers for interment instead of burying coffins along with the bodies, rendered it practicable to dispose of the dead in the usual way, without shocking the people by any unaccustomed spectacle of horror. There was no tumbling of bodies into carts as in the plague of Florence and the plague of London; every man, according to his station, was properly buried, and that in the accustomed way, except that he went to his grave at a pace more than usually rapid.

The funerals pouring through the streets were not the only public evidence of deaths. In Cairo this custom prevails: At the instant of a man's death (if his property is sufficient to justify the expense) professional howlers are employed. I believe that these persons are brought near to the dying man when his end appears to be approaching, and the moment that life is gone they lift up their voices and send forth a loud wail from the chamber of death. Thus I knew when my near neighbours died: sometimes the howls were near, sometimes more distant. Once I was awakened in the night by the wail of death in the next house, and another time by a like howl from the house opposite; and there were two or three minutes, I recollect, during which the howl seemed to be actually *running* along the street.

I happened to be rather teased at this time by a sore throat, and I thought it would be well to get it cured if I could before I again started on my travels. I therefore inquired for a Frank doctor, and was informed that the only one then at Cairo was a Bolognese refugee, a very young practitioner, and so poor that he had not been able to take flight as the other medical men had done. At such a time as this it was out of the question to *send* for a European physician; a person thus summoned would be sure to suppose that the patient was ill of the plague and would decline to come. I therefore rode to the young doctor's residence, ascended a flight or two of stairs, and knocked at his door. No one came immediately, but after some little delay the medico himself opened the door and admitted me. I of course made him understand that I had come to consult him, but before entering upon my throat grievance, I accepted a chair, and exchanged a sentence or two of commonplace conversation. Now the natural commonplace of the city at this season

was of a gloomy sort – '*Come va la peste?*' (how goes the plague?),
and this was precisely the question I put. A deep sigh, and the words,
'*Sette cento per giorno, signor*' (seven hundred a day), pronounced in a
tone of the deepest sadness and dejection, were the answer I received.
The day was not oppressively hot, yet I saw that the doctor was
perspiring profusely, and even the outside surface of the thick shawl
dressing-gown in which he had wrapped himself appeared to be
moist. He was a handsome, pleasant-looking young fellow, but the
deep melancholy of his tone did not tempt me to prolong the conversation, and without further delay I requested that my throat might
be looked at. The medico held my chin in the usual way, and
examined my throat; he then wrote me a prescription, and almost
immediately afterwards I bade him farewell, but as he conducted me
towards the door, I observed an expression of strange and unhappy
watchfulness in his rolling eyes. It was not the next day, but the next
day but one, if I rightly remember, that I sent to request another
interview with my doctor. In due time Dthemetri, my messenger,
returned, looking sadly aghast. He had '*met* the medico', for so he
phrased it, 'coming out from his house – in a bier!'

It was of course plain that when the poor Bolognese stood looking
down my throat and almost mingling his breath with mine he was
already stricken of the plague. I suppose that his violent sweat must
have been owing to some medicine administered by himself in the
faint hope of a cure. The peculiar rolling of his eyes which I had
remarked is, I believe, to experienced observers, a pretty sure test of
the plague. A Russian acquaintance of mine, speaking from the
information of men who had made the Turkish campaigns of 1828
and 1829, told me that by this sign the officers of Sabalkansky's force
were able to make out the plague-stricken soldiers with a good deal
of certainty.

It so happened that most of the people with whom I had anything
to do during my stay in Cairo were seized with plague; and all these
died. Since I had been for a long time *en route* before I reached
Egypt, and was about to start again for another long journey over
the Desert, there were of course many little matters touching my
wardrobe and my travelling equipments which required to be
attended to whilst I remained in the city. It happened so many times
that Dthemetri's orders in respect to these matters were frustrated
by the deaths of the tradespeople and others whom he employed,
that at last I became quite accustomed to the peculiar manner of the

man when he prepared to announce a new death to me. The poor fellow naturally supposed that I should feel some uneasiness at hearing of the 'accidents' continually happening to persons employed by me, and he therefore communicated their deaths as though they were the deaths of friends; he would cast down his eyes, and look like a man abashed, and then gently and with a mournful gesture allow the words 'Morto, signor', to come through his lips. I don't know how many of such instances occurred, but they were several; and besides these (as I told you before), my banker, my doctor, my landlord, and my magician, all died of the plague. A lad who acted as a helper in the house I occupied lost a brother and a sister within a few hours. Out of my two established donkey-boys one died. I did not hear of any instance in which a plague-stricken patient had recovered.

Going out one morning, I met unexpectedly the scorching breath of the Khamseen wind, and fearing that I should faint under the infliction, I returned to my rooms. Reflecting, however, that I might have to encounter this wind in the Desert, where there would be no possibility of avoiding it, I thought it would be better to brave it once more in the city, and to try whether I could really bear it or not. I therefore mounted my ass, and rode to old Cairo and along the gardens by the banks of the Nile. The wind was hot to the touch, as though it came from a furnace; it blew strongly, but yet with such perfect steadiness that the trees bending under its force remained fixed in the same curves without perceptibly waving; the whole sky was obscured by a veil of yellowish grey that shut out the face of the sun. The streets were utterly silent, being indeed almost entirely deserted; and not without cause, for the scorching blast, whilst it fevers the blood, closes up the pores of the skin, and is terribly distressing therefore to every animal that encounters it. I returned to my rooms dreadfully ill. My head ached with a burning pain, and my pulse bounded quick and fitfully, but perhaps (as in the instance of the poor Levantine whose death I was mentioning) the fear and excitement I felt in trying my own wrist may have made my blood flutter the faster.

It is a thoroughly well-believed theory that, during the continuance of the plague, you can't be ill of any other febrile malady; an unpleasant privilege that! For ill I was, and ill of fever, and I anxiously wished that the ailment might turn out to be anything rather than plague. I had some right to surmise that my illness might have been merely the effect of hot wind; and this notion was encouraged by the elasticity of my spirits, and by a strong forefeeling that much of my destined life in this world was yet to come, and yet to be fulfilled. That was my instinctive belief; but when I carefully weighed the probabilities on the one side and on the other, I could not help seeing that the strength of argument was all against me. There was a strong antecedent likelihood in *favour* of my being struck by the same blow as the rest of the people who had been dying around me. Besides, it occurred to me that, after all, the universal opinion of the Europeans upon a medical question, such as that of contagion, might probably be correct; and *if it were*, I was so thoroughly 'compromised', especially by the touch of and breath of the dying medico, that I had no right to expect any other fate than that which now seemed to have overtaken me. Balancing, then, as well as I could, all the considerations suggested by hope and fear, I slowly and reluctantly came to the conclusion that, according to all merely reasonable probability, the plague had come upon me.

You might suppose that this conviction would have induced me to write a few farewell lines to those who were dearest, and that having done that, I should have turned my thoughts towards the world to come. Such, however, was not the case; I believe that the prospect of death often brings with it strong anxieties about matters of comparatively trivial import, and certainly with me the whole energy of the mind was directed towards the one petty object of concealing my illness until the latest possible moment – until the delirious stage. I did not believe that either Mysseri or Dthemetri, who had served me so faithfully in all trials, would have deserted me (as most Europeans are wont to do) when they knew that I was stricken by plague; but I shrank from the idea of putting them to this test, and I dreaded the consternation which the knowledge of my illness would be sure to occasion.

I was very ill indeed at the moment when my dinner was served, and my soul sickened at the sight of the food, but I had luckily the habit of dispensing with the attendance of servants during my meal, and as soon as I was left alone, I made a melancholy calculation of the quantity of food I should have eaten if I had been in my usual health, and filled my plates accordingly, and gave myself salt, and so on, as though I were going to dine; I then transferred the viands to a piece of the omnipresent *Times* newspaper, and hid them away in a cupboard, for it was not yet night, and I dared not to throw the food into the street until darkness came. I did not at all relish this process of fictitious dining, but at length the cloth was removed, and I gladly reclined on my divan (I would not lie down) with the *Arabian Nights* in my hand.

I had a feeling that tea would be a capital thing for me, but I would not order it until the usual hour. When at last the time came, I drank deep draughts from the fragrant cup. The effect was almost instantaneous. A plenteous sweat burst through my skin, and watered my clothes through and through. I kept myself thickly covered. The hot tormenting weight which had been loading my brain was slowly heaved away. The fever was extinguished. I felt a new buoyancy of spirits, and an unusual activity of mind. I went into my bed under a load of thick covering, and when the morning came and I asked myself how I was, I answered, 'Perfectly well' . . .

*

At length the great difficulty I had had in procuring beasts for my departure was overcome, and now, too, I was to have the new excitement of travelling on dromedaries. With two of these beasts, and three camels, I gladly wound my way from out of the pest-stricken city. As I passed through the streets, I observed a grave elder stretching forth his arms, and lifting up his voice in a speech which seemed to have some reference to me. Requiring an interpretation, I found that the man had said, 'The Pasha seeks camels, and he finds them not; the Englishman says, "Let camels be brought," and behold! there they are.'

I no sooner breathed the free wholesome air of the Desert, than I felt that a great burthen, which I had been scarcely conscious of bearing, was lifted away from my mind. For nearly three weeks I had lived under peril of death: the peril ceased, and not till then did I know how much alarm and anxiety I had really been suffering.

* * *

GUSTAVE FLAUBERT (1821–1880)

'Flaubert to Louis Bouilhet'

On board our cange, *12 leagues beyond Assuan, 13 March 1850*

In six or seven hours we are going to pass the Tropic of that well-known personage Cancer. It is thirty degrees in the shade at this moment, we are barefoot and clad in nothing but shirts, and I am writing to you on my divan, to the sound of the *darabukehs* of our sailors, who are singing and clapping their hands. The sun is beating down mercilessly on the awning over our deck. The Nile is as flat as a river of steel. On its banks are clusters of tall palms. The sky is blue as blue. *O pauvre vieux! pauvre vieux de mon cœur!*

Ah! But if you expect a proper letter you are mistaken. I warn you seriously that my intelligence has greatly diminished. This worries me: *I am not joking* – I feel very empty, very flat, very sterile. What am I to do once back in the old lodgings? Publish or not publish? The *Saint Anthony* business dealt me a heavy blow, I don't mind telling you. I have tried in vain to do something with my oriental tale, and for a day or two I played with the story of Mykerinos in Herodotus (the king who slept with his daughter). But it all came to nothing. By way of work, every day I read the *Odyssey* in Greek. Since we have been on the Nile I have done four books; we are coming home by way of Greece, so it may be of use to me. The first days on board I began to write a little; but I was not long, thank God, in realizing the ineptitude of such behaviour; just now it is best for me to be all eyes. We live, therefore, in the grossest idleness, stretched out all day on our divans watching everything that goes by: camels, herds of oxen from the Sennaar, boats floating down to Cairo laden with negresses and elephants' tusks. We are now, my dear sir, in a land where women go naked – one might say with the poet 'naked as the hand', for by way of costume they wear only rings. I have lain with Nubian girls whose necklaces of gold piastres hung down to their thighs and whose black stomachs were encircled by coloured beads – they feel cold when you rub your own stomach against them. And their dancing! *Sacré nom de Dieu!!!* But let us proceed in proper order.

From Cairo to Benisuef, nothing very interesting.

At a place called Gebel el-Teir we had an amusing sight. On the top of a hill overlooking the Nile there is a Coptic monastery, whose monks have the habit, as soon as they see a boatload of tourists, of running down, throwing themselves in the water, and swimming out to ask for alms. Everyone who passes is assailed by them. You see these fellows, totally naked, rushing down their perpendicular cliffs and swimming towards you as fast as they can, shouting: 'Baksheesh, baksheesh, cawadja christiani!' And since there are many caves in the cliff at this particular spot, echo repeats 'Cawadja, cawadja!' loud as a cannon. Vultures and eagles were flying overhead, the boat was darting through the water, its two great sails very full. At that moment one of our sailors, the clown of the crew, began to dance a naked, lascivious dance that consisted of an attempt to bugger himself. To drive off the Christians he showed them his prick and his arse pretending to piss and shit on their heads (they were clinging to the sides of the *cange*). The other sailors shouted insults at them, repeating the names of Allah and Mohammed. Some hit them with sticks, others with ropes; Joseph rapped their knuckles with his kitchen tongs. It was a *tutti* of cudgelings, pricks, bare arses, yells and laughter. As soon as they were given money they put it in their mouths and returned home via the route they had come. If they weren't greeted with a good beating, the boats would be assailed by such hordes of them that there would be danger of capsizing.

In another place it's not men who call on you, but birds. At Sheik Sa'id there is a tomb-chapel built in honour of a Moslem saint where birds go of their own accord and drop food that is given to them – this food is then offered to poor travellers – You and I, *who have read Voltaire*, don't believe this. But everyone is so backward here! You so seldom hear anyone singing the songs of Béranger! 'What, sir, the benefits of civilization are not being introduced into this country? Where are your railway networks? What is the state of elementary education? Etc.' – so that as you sail past this chapel all the birds flock around the boat and land on the rigging – you throw them bits of bread, they wheel about, pick it up from the water, and fly off.

At Kena I did something suitable, which I trust will win your approval: we had landed to buy supplies and were walking peacefully

and dreamily in the bazaars, inhaling the odour of sandalwood that
floated about us, when suddenly, at a turn in the street, we found
ourselves in the whores' quarter. Picture to yourself, my friend, five
or six curving streets lined with hovels about four feet high, built of
dried grey mud. In the doorways, women standing or sitting on
straw mats. The negresses had dresses of sky-blue; others were in
yellow, in white, in red – loose garments fluttering in the hot wind.
Odours of spices. On their bare breasts long necklaces of gold piastres,
so that when they move they rattle like carts. They call after you in
drawling voices: 'Cawadja, cawadja,' their white teeth gleaming
between their red or black lips, their metallic eyes rolling like wheels.
I walked through those streets and walked through them again,
giving *baksheesh* to all the women, letting them call me and catch
hold of me; they took me around the waist and tried to pull me into
their houses – think of all that, with the sun blazing down on it.
Well, I abstained. (Young Du Camp did not follow my example.) I
abstained deliberately, in order to preserve the sweet sadness of the
scene and engrave it deeply in my memory. In this way I went away
dazzled, and have remained so. There is nothing more beautiful than
these women calling you. If I had gone with any of them, a second
picture would have been superimposed on the first and dimmed its
splendour.

　　I haven't always made such sacrifices on the altar of art. At Esna
in one day I came five times and sucked three. I say it straight out
and without circumlocution, and let me add that I enjoyed it. Kuchuk
Hanem is a famous courtesan. When we reached her house she was
waiting for us; her confidante had come that morning to the *cange*
escorted by a tame sheep all spotted with yellow henna and with a
black velvet muzzle on its nose, that followed her like a dog – it was
quite a sight. She had just left her bath. She was wearing a large
tarboosh.

*

That night we returned to Kuchuk Hanem's: there were four women
dancers and singers – *almehs*. (The word *almeh* means 'learned
woman', 'blue-stocking', or 'whore' – which proves, Monsieur, that
in all countries women of letters . . .!!!) When it was time to leave I
didn't leave . . . I sucked her furiously – her body was covered with
sweat – she was tired after dancing – she was cold – I covered her

with my pelisse, and she fell asleep with her fingers in mine. As for me, I scarcely shut my eyes. Watching that beautiful creature asleep (she snored, her head against my arm: I had slipped my forefinger under her necklace), my night was one long, infinitely intense reverie – that was why I stayed. I thought of my nights in Paris brothels – a whole series of old memories came back – and I thought of her, of her dance, of her voice as she sang songs that for me were without meaning and even without distinguishable words. That continued all night. At three o'clock I got up to piss in the street – the stars were shining. The sky was clear and immensely distant. She awoke, went to get a pot of charcoal and for an hour crouched beside it warming herself, then she came back to bed and fell asleep again. As for the *coups*, they were good – the third especially was ferocious, and the last tender – we told each other many sweet things – toward the end there was something sad and loving in the way we embraced.

In my absorption in all those things, *mon pauvre vieux*, you never ceased to be present. The thought of you was like a constant vesicant, inflaming my mind and making its juices flow by adding to the stimulation. I was sorry (the word is weak) that you were not there – I enjoyed it all for myself and for you – the excitement was for both of us, and you came in for a good share, you may be sure.

Just now we have stopped for lack of wind – the flies are stinging my face. Young Du Camp has gone off to take a picture. He is doing quite well; I think we'll have a nice album. As regards vice, he is calming down; it seems to us that I am inheriting his qualities, for I am growing lewd. Such is my profound conviction. When the brain sinks the prick rises. That isn't to say that I haven't collected a few metaphors. I have had a few stirrings. But how to make use of them, and when?

* * *

SENWOSRET I (ca. 1959–1914 BC)

'Letter to Sinuhe'

Horus, living in birth; the Two Ladies, living in birth; the King of Upper and Lower Egypt, Kheperkare; the Son of Re, Senwosret I, may he live forever and ever. Royal decree to the retainer Sinuhe:

Now this decree of the king is brought to you to inform you that it was through your own heart's decision that you travelled around foreign countries, leaving Kedem for Retenu, and that one country kept handing you over to the next country. What have you done for action to be taken against you? You did not blaspheme so that your speech should be reproved, nor did you speak out against the counsel of the magistrates so that your utterances should be opposed. This notion, it took over your senses. It was not in my mind against you. This heaven of yours (the queen) that is in the palace still endures and prospers today as in her former state in the kingship of the land, and her children are in the palace apartments. You shall accumulate riches that they give you and shall live off their bounty.

Return to Egypt and visit the Residence in which you grew up. You shall kiss the ground at the Great Double Portals and join with the courtiers, for today it is that you have started growing old and lost virility. Ponder the day of burial and the passing into a blessed state.

A night will be appointed for you with balsam oils and bandages from the arms of Tayet. A funeral procession will be made for you on the day of interment, with the mummy case being of gold and its head of lapis lazuli, with the sky above you as you lie on the funeral sledge, and with oxen hauling you as chanters precede you. The dance of the Muu will be performed for you at the entrance of your tomb. The menu of offerings will be invoked for you, and sacrifice will be made at your offering slab, your (tomb's) pillars being constructed of limestone amid those of the royal children.

You shall not die abroad! Asiatics shall not inter you! You shall not be placed in a sheep's skin when your grave enclosure is made. All this is too much for one who has roamed the earth. Be concerned for your corpse and come back!

Sinuhe to Senwosret I

Copy of the acknowledgment of this decree:

It is the palace servant Sinuhe who says: In very good peace! This flight which I, your humble servant, undertook without comprehension is understood by your *Ka*, O Perfect God, Lord of the Two Lands, beloved of Re and favoured of Montu, lord of the Theban nome, and also Amon, lord of the Thrones of the Two Lands, Sobek-Re, lord of Sumenu, Horus, Hathor, Atum and his ennead, Sopdu-Neferbau-Semseru, the eastern Horus, the Lady of Imet — may she enfold your head, the magistrates that are upon the flood-waters, Min-Horus residing in desert lands, Wereret, lady of Punt, Nut, Haroeris-Re, and all gods of Egypt and the Islands of the Sea. May they give life and dominion to your nose and endue you with their bounty. May they give you everlastingness without end and eternity without bounds. May fear of you be bruited abroad in lowland and highlands, for you have subdued what the solar disk encircles. Such is the prayer of this your humble servant on behalf of his lord, who has preserved him from the West . . .

*

This flight, which I, your humble servant, undertook, I did not anticipate. It was not in my mind. I did not devise it. I do not know who removed me from my place. It was after the manner of a dream, as when a Delta man sees himself in Elephantine or a marsh-man in Nubia. I did not become afraid, nor was I pursued. I did not hear a word of censure, nor was my name heard in the mouth of a herald. But it was those shudderings of my body as my legs kept scurrying and my heart kept impelling me, for the god who ordained this flight kept drawing me on.

I am not overly(?) presumptuous. Should a man be afraid to know his homeland when Re has instilled respect for you throughout the land and dread of you in every foreign country? Whether I am at the Residence or in this place, it is you who overspreads this horizon. The sun rises at your pleasure, while water is in the river to be drunk as you desire, and air is in the sky to be breathed as you bid. I, your humble servant, shall bequeath to my brood that I, your humble servant, have begotten in this place.

I, your humble servant, have been sent for. Your Majesty can do as he pleases! People live by the breath that you give. May Re, Horus, and Hathor love this august nose of yours, O you whom Montu, lord of the Theban nome, wishes to live forever.

ARABIA

RICHARD F. BURTON (1821–1890)

'On Seeing the Ka'aba in Mecca'

There at last it lay, the bourn of my long and weary pilgrimage, realizing the plans and hopes of many and many a year. The mirage medium of Fancy invested the huge catafalque and its gloomy pall with peculiar charms. There were no giant fragments of hoar antiquity as in Egypt, no remains of graceful and harmonious beauty as in Greece and Italy, no barbaric gorgeousness as in the buildings of India; yet the view was strange, unique, and how few have looked upon the celebrated shrine! I may truly say that, of all the worshippers who clung weeping to the curtain, or who pressed their beating hearts to the stone, none felt for the moment a deeper emotion than did the Haji from the far north. It was as if the poetical legends of the Arab spoke truth, and that the waving wings of angels, not the sweet breeze of morning, were agitating and swelling the black covering of the shrine. But, to confess humbling truth, theirs was the high feeling of religious enthusiasm, mine was the ecstasy of gratified pride.

* * *

TIM MACKINTOSH-SMITH (1961–)

'On Language'

The rain beat down. Horns rasped against the door: a sheep trying
to get in. I didn't blame it – spring was late in the Isle of Harris and
it was cosy inside, all peat smoke and roll-ups. An easterly gale was
whistling across the Sound from Skye and flinging sackfuls of hail at
the tin roof of the croft house. The noise was deafening.

You have to be somewhere quiet like Harris in the early stages of
learning Arabic, somewhere you can walk around unheard, muttering
strange, strangulated syllables, limbering up minute and never-used
muscles of tongue and glottis. I got up to make tea. *'Hhha'!'* I said
to the matches when I found them; *'Ghghgha'!'* when they refused to
light. "'I mouthed to the hooded crow on the fence outside the
window; that innocent-looking sign represented the trickiest letter
of all, 'a guttural stop pronounced with constriction of the larynx',
my grammar said. The hoodie croaked back and flapped off to peck
out lambs' eyes.

The fire let out a rich belch of smoke. I threw on another sod of
peat and drew up a chair. Cowan's *Modern Literary Arabic* lay open
at 'The Dual' (not content with mere singulars and plurals, Arabic
also has a form for pairs): 'The two beautiful queens', it said, 'are
ignorant.' The odds against ever uttering the sentence were high:
grammars, like theatre, call for a suspension of disbelief. Under
Cowan was an Arabic reader produced for British officers in the
Palestine Mandate. At the bottom of the pile, as yet untouched, was
a dictionary. I reached for it and looked at the title page. The
dictionary had been compiled for the use of students and published
Ad Majorem Dei Gloriam by the Catholic Press, Beirut, in 1915. As
I turned its foxed pages, I broke through the wall of words into a
wilderness of idea. It was another world, a surreal lexical landscape
whose inhabitants lived in a state of relentless metamorphosis.

Over there was a *zabab*, 'a messenger' or possibly 'a huge deaf
rat', while in the distance grazed a *na'amah*, 'an ostrich', although
it might have been 'a signpost', 'a pavilion on a mountain' or even
'a membrane of the brain'. Nearer to hand someone was *maljan*,

'sucking his she-camels out of avarice'; he'd be in for a shock if he had *istanwaq* them, 'mistaken male camels for she-camels'. He could just be suffering from *sada*, 'thirst', also 'a voice', 'an echo', 'a corpse', 'a brain' or 'an owl'. Maybe his well was *makul*, 'holding little water and much slime'. He was in a bad mood so I passed on quickly, worried that he might *tarqa* me, 'strike me upon the clavicle'.

In Dictionary Land you could come across a *malit*, 'a featherless arrow' or 'a hairless abortive foetus'. That, at least, showed a clear semantic link. So did *firash*, 'a mat/wife', and *siffarah*, 'an anus/whistle/fife'. But other entries defied rational explanation, seeming no more than the word-associations of a hopeless headcase: you could take your *qutrub*, your 'puppy/demon/restless insect/melancholia', for a walk; *qarurah* could be 'the apple of one's eye', also 'a urinal'. With a single verb, *nakha'*, you could both 'slay someone' and 'bear them sincere friendship'; with another, *istawsham*, you could 'look for a tattooist'; and if you were a calligrapher, you could be adept at *yayyaya*, 'forming a beautiful letter *ya'* – perhaps thus: ﻴ. On the culinary side, you might be *'akra'*, 'fond of trotters' or 'thin in the shank', while with the verb *karrash* you could 'contract your face' or 'prepare a haggis'; the latter could be accompanied by a helping of *wahisah*, 'a dish made of locusts and grease', and washed down by *adasiyah*, an 'aromatized soup of lentils' or 'bat-dung used as a medicine'. *Alkhan* doubled for 'a rotten walnut' and 'a stinking uncircumcised person'. The sounds of Dictionary Land included *inqad*, 'the squeaking of eagles/ the noise of fingers being cracked/ the smacking of lips to call goats' or even 'the noise made by truffles being extracted'. The truffles might be of a species called *faswat al-dab'*, also the name for a kind of poppy and, rendered literally, 'the noiseless flatulence of a male hyena'.

*

Time and again in the years that followed, some verbal curiosity or weirdness of phrase would sidetrack me out of the corridors of the Oxford Oriental Institute and back into Dictionary Land.

'I didn't get the drift of lines 66–7. Could you, er . . .?'

' "Verily I have seen upon your mandibles the belly- and tail-fat of a lizard./ Your words reveal the buttocks of your meanings." '

'I'm sorry?'

' *"Your words reveal the buttocks of your meanings."* '

'Oh.'

They taught us abstruse and arcane mysteries, how to compound the base elements of syntax into glittering and highly wrought prose. We were apprentices in a linguistic alchemy. And, like alchemy, Arabic seemed to be half science and two-thirds magic. The Arabs themselves are spellbound by their language. Look at the effect on them of the Qur'an: the Word – divinely beautiful, terrifying, tear-inducing, spine-tingling, mesmerizing, inimitable – was sufficient in itself. It did not need to become flesh. But Qur'anic Arabic is only one manifestation of the language. You can be preacher, poet, raconteur and fishwife in a single sentence. You can, with the Arabic of official reports, say next to nothing in a great many words and with enormous elegance. You can compose a work of literature on the two lateral extremities of the wrist-bone. You can even be cured of certain ailments by procuring a magic chit, infusing the ink out of it, and drinking the water: word-power at its most literal. They taught us all this, but they didn't teach us how to speak it. After two years of Arabic I couldn't even have asked the way to the lavatory.

*　*　*

WILFRED THESIGER (1910–)

from *Arabian Sands*

I knew that I had made my last journey in the Empty Quarter and that a phase in my life was ended. Here in the desert I had found all that I asked; I knew that I should never find it again. But it was not only this personal sorrow that distressed me. I realized that the Bedu with whom I had lived and travelled, and in whose company I had found contentment, were doomed. Some people maintain that they will be better off when they have exchanged the hardship and poverty of the desert for the security of a materialistic world. This I do not believe. I shall always remember how often I was humbled by those illiterate herdsmen who possessed, in so much greater measure than I, generosity and courage, endurance, patience, and lighthearted gallantry. Among no other people have I ever felt the same sense of personal inferiority.

On the last evening, as bin Kabina and bin Ghabaisha were tying up the few things they had bought, Codrai said, looking at the two small bundles, 'It is rather pathetic that this is all they have.' I understood what he meant; I had often felt the same. Yet I knew that for them the danger lay, not in the hardship of their lives, but in the boredom and frustration they would feel when they renounced it. The tragedy was that the choice would not be theirs; economic forces beyond their control would eventually drive them into the towns to hang about street-corners as 'unskilled labour'.

The lorry arrived after breakfast. We embraced for the last time. I said, 'Go in peace,' and they answered together, 'Remain in the safe keeping of God, Umbarak.' Then they scrambled up on to a pile of petrol drums beside a Palestinian refugee in oil-stained dungarees. A few minutes later they were out of sight round a corner. I was glad when Codrai took me to the aerodrome at Sharja. As the plane climbed over the town and swung out above the sea I knew how it felt to go into exile.

* * *

T. E. Lawrence (1888–1935)

Introduction to *Travels in Arabia Deserta* by C. M. Doughty

We export two chief kinds of Englishmen, who in foreign parts divide themselves into two opposed classes. Some feel deeply the influence of the native people, and try to adjust themselves to its atmosphere and spirit. To fit themselves modestly into the picture they suppress all in them that would be discordant with local habits and colours. They imitate the native as far as possible, and so avoid friction in their daily life. However, they cannot avoid the consequences of imitation, a hollow, worthless thing. They are like the people but not of the people, and their half-perceptible differences give them a sham influence often greater than their merit. They urge the people among whom they live into strange, unnatural courses by imitating them so well that they are imitated back again. The other class of Englishmen is the larger class. In the same circumstance of exile they reinforce their character by memories of the life they have left. In reaction against their foreign surroundings they take refuge in the England that was theirs. They assert their aloofness, their immunity, the more vividly for their loneliness and weakness. They impress the peoples among whom they live by reaction, by giving them an ensample of the complete Englishman, the foreigner intact.

Doughty is a great member of the second, the cleaner class. He says that he was never oriental, though the sun made him an Arab; and much of his value lies in the distinction. His seeing is altogether English: yet at the same time his externals, his manners, his dress, and his speech were Arabic, and nomad Arab, of the desert. The desert inhibits considered judgments; its bareness and openness make its habitants frank. Men in it speak out their minds suddenly and unreservedly. Words in the desert are clear-cut. Doughty felt this contagion of truthfulness sharply (few travel-journals show a greater sensibility to climate and geography than this), and among the tribes he delivered himself like them. Even in the villages he maintained an untimely and uncompromising bluntness, in a firm protest against the glozing politic speech of the town-Arabs. His own origin was from the settled country of England, and this preference for the nomad might seem strange; but in practice the Englishman, and especially the Englishman of family, finds the tribes more to his taste than the villages, and Doughty everywhere is the outspoken Bedouin. His 'stiffness to maintain a just opinion against the half-reason of the world' was often unwise – but always respectable, and the Arabs respected him for it even where they resented it most.

Very climatic, too, are his sudden changes of tone and judgment. The desert is a place of passing sensation, of cash-payment of opinion. Men do not hold their minds in suspense for days, to arrive at a just and balanced average of thought. They say good at once when it is good, and bad at once when it is bad. Doughty has mirrored this also for us in himself. One paragraph will have a harsh judgment; the next is warm kindness. His record ebbs and flows with his experience, and by reading not a part of the book but all of it you obtain a many-sided sympathetic vision, in the round, of his companions of these stormy and eventful years.

*

The realism of the book is complete. Doughty tries to tell the full and exact truth of all that he saw. If there is a bias it will be against the Arabs, for he liked them so much; he was so impressed by the strange attraction, isolation and independence of this people that he took pleasure in bringing out their virtues by a careful expression of their faults. 'If one live any time with the Arab he will have all his life after a feeling of the desert.' He had experienced it himself, the test of nomadism, that most deeply biting of all social disciplines, and for our sakes he strained all the more to paint it in its true colours, as a life too hard, too empty, too denying for all but the strongest and most determined men. Nothing is more powerful and real than this record of all his daily accidents and obstacles, and the feelings that came to him on the way. His picture of the Semites, sitting to the eyes in a cloaca, but with their brows touching Heaven, sums up contradictions of their thought which quicken our curiosity at our first meeting with them.

To try and solve their riddle many of us have gone far into their society, and seen the clear hardness of their belief, a limitation almost mathematical, which repels us by its unsympathetic form. Semites have no half-tones in their register of vision. They are a people of primary colours, especially of black and white, who see the world always in line. They are a certain people, despising doubt, our modern crown of thorns. They do not understand our metaphysical difficulties, our self-questionings. They know only truth and untruth, belief and unbelief, without our hesitating retinue of finer shades.

Semites are black and white not only in vision, but in their inner furnishing; black and white not merely in clarity, but in apposition. Their thoughts live easiest among extremes. They inhabit superlatives by choice. Sometimes the great inconsistents seem to possess them jointly. They exclude compromise, and pursue the logic of their ideas to its absurd ends, without seeing incongruity in their opposed conclusions. They oscillate with cool head and tranquil judgment from asymptote to asymptote, so imperturbably that they would seem hardly conscious of their giddy flight.

They are a limited narrow-minded people whose inert intellects lie incuriously fallow. Their imaginations are keen but not creative. There is so little Arab art today in Asia that they can nearly be said to have no art, though their rulers have been liberal patrons and have encouraged their neighbours' talents in architecture, ceramic and handicraft. They show no longing for great industry, no organizations of mind or body anywhere. They invent no systems of philosophy or mythologies. They are the least morbid of peoples, who take the gift of life unquestioning, as an axiom. To them it is a thing inevitable, entailed on man, a usufruct, beyond our control. Suicide is a thing nearly impossible and death no grief.

They are a people of spasms, of upheavals, of ideas, the race of the individual genius. Their movements are the more shocking by contrast with the quietude of every day, their great men greater by contrast with the humanity of their mass. Their convictions are by instinct, their activities intuitional. Their largest manufacture is of creeds. They are monopolists of revealed religions, finding always an antagonism of body and spirit, and laying their stress on the spirit. Their profound reaction against matter leads them to preach barrenness, renunciation, poverty: and this atmosphere stifles the minds of the desert pitilessly. They are always looking out towards those things in which mankind has had no lot or part.

The Bedouin has been born and brought up in the desert, and has embraced this barrenness too harsh for volunteers with all his soul, for the reason, felt but inarticulate, that there he finds himself indubitably free. He loses all natural ties, all comforting superfluities or complications, to achieve that personal liberty which haunts starvation and death. He sees no virtue in poverty herself; he enjoys the little vices and luxuries – coffee, fresh water, women – which he can still afford. In his life he has air and winds, sun and light, open spaces and great emptiness. There is no human effort, no fecundity in Nature; just heaven above and unspotted earth beneath, and the only refuge and rhythm of their being is in God. This single God is to the Arab not anthropomorphic, not tangible or moral or ethical, not concerned particularly with the world or with him. He alone is great, and yet there is a homeliness, an every-day-ness of this Arab God who rules their eating, their fighting and their lusting; and is their commonest thought, and companion, in a way impossible to those whose God is tediously veiled from them by the decorum of formal worship. They feel no incongruity in bringing God into their weaknesses and appetites. He is the commonest of their words.

This creed of the desert is an inheritance. The Arab does not value it extremely. He has never been either evangelist or proselyte. He arrives at this intense condensation of himself in God by shutting his eyes to the world, and to all the complex possibilities latent in him which only wealth and temptation could bring out. He attains a sure trust and a powerful trust, but of how narrow a field! His sterile experience perverts his human kindness to the image of the waste in which he hides. Accordingly he hurts himself, not merely to be free, but to please himself. There follows a self-delight in pain, a cruelty which is more to him than goods. The desert Arab finds no joy like the joy of voluntarily holding back. He finds luxury in abnegation, renunciation, self-restraint. He lives his own life in a hard selfishness. His desert is made a spiritual ice-house, in which is preserved intact but unimproved for all ages an idea of the unity of God.

*

Doughty went among these people dispassionately, looked at their life, and wrote it down word for word. By being always Arab in manner and European in mind he maintained a perfect judgment, while bearing towards them a full sympathy which persuaded them to show him their inmost ideas. When his trial of two years was over he carried away in his note-book (so far as the art of writing can express the art of living) the soul of the desert, the complete existence of a remarkable and self-contained community, shut away from the currents of the world in the unchanging desert, working out their days in an environment utterly foreign to us. The economic reason for their existence is the demand for camels, which can be best bred on the thorns and plants of these healthy uplands. The desert is incapable of other development, but admirably suited to this. Their camel-breeding makes the Bedouins nomads. The camels live only on the pasture of the desert, and as it is scanty a great herd will soon exhaust any one district. Then they with their masters must move to another, and so they circulate month by month in a course determined by the vegetation sprung up wherever the inter-mittent winter rains have this season fallen heaviest.

The social organization of the desert is in tribes, partly because of original family-feeling, partly because the instinct of self-preservation compels large masses of men to hold together for mutual support. By belonging to a recognized tribe each man feels that he has a strong body of nominal kinsmen, to support him if he is injured; and equally to bear the burden and to discharge his wrong-doing, when he is the guilty party. This collective responsibility makes men careful not to offend; and makes punishment very easy. The offender is shut out from the system, and becomes an exile till he has made his peace again with the public opinion of his tribesmen.

Each tribe has its district in the desert. The extent and nature of these tribal districts are determined by the economic laws of camel-breeding. Each holds a fair chance of pasture all the year round in every normal year, and each holds enough drinking water to suffice all its households every year; but the poverty of the country forces an internal subdivision of itself upon the tribe. The water-sources are usually single wells (often very scanty wells), and the pasturages small scattered patches in sheltered valleys or oases among the rocks. They could not accommodate at one time or place all the tribe, which therefore breaks into clans, and lives always as clans, wandering each apart on its own cycle within the orbit of the tribal whole.

The society is illiterate, so each clan keeps small enough to enable all its adults to meet frequently, and discuss all common business verbally. Such general intercourse, and their open life beside one another in tents makes the desert a place altogether without privacy. Man lives candidly with man. It is a society in perpetual movement, an equality of voice and opportunity for every male. The daily hearth or sheikh's coffee-gathering is their education, a university for every man grown enough to walk and speak.

It is also their news-office, their tribunal, their political expression, and their government. They bring and expose there in public every day all their ideas, their experiences, their opinions, and they sharpen one another, so that the desert society is always alive, instructed to a high moral level, and tolerant of new ideas. Common rumour makes them as unchanging as the desert in which they live; but more often they show themselves singularly receptive, very open to useful innovations. Their few vested interests make it simple for them to change their ways; but even so it is astonishing to find how whole-heartedly they adopt an invention fitted to their life. Coffee, gunpowder, Manchester cotton are all new things, and yet appear so native that without them one can hardly imagine their desert life.

Consequently, one would expect a book such as *Arabia Deserta*, written forty years ago, to be inaccurate today in such little respects, and had Doughty's work been solely scientific, dependent on the expression rather than the spirit of things, its day might have passed. Happily the beauty of the telling, its truth to life, the rich gallery of characters and landscapes in it, will remain for all time, and will keep it peerless, as the indispensable foundation of all true under-standing of the desert. And in these forty years the material changes have not been enough to make them really worth detailed record.

The inscriptions at Medain Salih have been studied since his day by the Dominican fathers from Jerusalem, and some little points added to his store. The great stone at Teima which lay in the *haddaj*, was looked for by later travellers, and at last purchased and carried off to Europe. Doughty's collections of these primitive Arab scripts have been surpassed; but he holds the enduring credit of their discovery. His map, and some of his geographical information have been added to, and brought into relation with later information. People with cameras have wandered up and down the Aueyrid *harrat* in which he spent weeks, and of which he wrote so vivid a description. We know their outside face exactly, from photographs; but to read Doughty is to know what they make one feel. Crossley and Rolls-Royce cars have made a road of some of that Wadi Humth, whose importance he first made clear to Europe. Aeroplanes have quartered the hills in which he found such painful going. Unfortunately those in cars and aeroplanes are not able to write intimate books about the country over which they pass.

Another change in Arabia has come from the Hejaz Railway, which in 1909 was opened from Damascus to Medina, and at once put an end to the great army which used to perform the pilgrimage by road. The Emir el Haj and his people now go by train, and the annual pageant of the camel-caravan is dead. The pilgrim road, of whose hundreds of worn tracks Doughty gave us such a picture, is now gone dull for lack of all those feet to polish it, and the *kellas* and cisterns from which he drank on the march to Medain Salih are falling into ruin, except so far as they serve the need of some guardhouse on the railway.

The Rashid dynasty in Hail has pursued as bloody a course since his day as before it. Saud, the last Emir, was murdered in 1920, and the sole survivor of the family is an infant, whose precarious minority is being made the play of the ambition of one and another of the great chiefs of the Shammar tribe. On the other hand, the Wahabi dynasty of Riath, which seemed in its decline has suddenly revived in this generation, thanks to the courage and energy of Abd el-Aziz, the present Emir. He has subdued all Nejd with his arms, has revived the Wahabi sect in new stringency, and bids fair to subject all the inner deserts of the peninsula to his belief. The Emir's younger son was lately in the Deputation he sent to this country, under the conduct of Mr H. St J. Philby, C.I.E., sometime British Resident at er-Riath, during the Great War. Whilst in England they visited Mr Doughty.

The Sherifate of Mecca, in whose humanity Doughty reposed at Taif at the end of his adventures, made a bid for the intellectual leadership of the Arabs in 1916 by rebelling against Turkey on the principle of nationality. The Western Arabs, among whom Doughty's ways had so long fallen, took a chivalrous part in the war as the allies of Great Britain and with our help. The Sherif's four sons put themselves at the head of the townsmen and tribesmen of the Hejaz, and gave the British officers assisting them the freedom of the desert. All the old names were in our ranks. There were Harb, Juheyma, and Billi, whom Doughty mentioned. His old hosts, the Abu Shamah Moahîb, joined us, and did gallantly. Ferhan, Motlog's son, brought with him the Allayda, and with the other Fejr they took Teyma and Kheybar from their Turkish garrisons, and handed them over to King Hussein.

Later the Shammar joined us, and volunteers came from Kasim, from Aneyza, Boreyda and Russ to help the common war upon the Turks. We took Medain Salih and El Ally, and further north Tebuk and Maan, the Beni Sakhr country, and all the pilgrim road up to Damascus, making in arms the return journey of that by which Doughty had begun his wanderings. *Arabia Deserta*, which had been a joy to read, as a great record of adventure and travel (perhaps the greatest in our language), and the great picture-book of nomad life, became a military text-book, and helped to guide us to victory in the East. The Arabs who had allowed Doughty to wander in their forbidden provinces were making a good investment for their sons and grandsons.

In this great experience of war the focus of motive in the desert changed, and a political revolution came to the Arabs. In Doughty's day, as his book shows, there were Moslems and Christians, as main divisions of the people. Yesterday the distinction faded; there were only those on the side of the Allies, and those with the Central Powers. The Western Arabs, in these forty years, had learned enough of the ideas of Europe to accept nationality as a basis for action. They accepted it so thoroughly that they went into battle against their Caliph, the Sultan of Turkey, to win their right to national freedom. Religion, which had been the motive and character of the desert, yielded to politics, and Mecca, which had been a City of worship, became the temporal capital of a new state. The hostility which had been directed against Christians became directed against the foreigner who presumed to interfere in the domestic affairs of Arabic-speaking provinces.

*

However, this note grows too long. Those just men who begin at the beginning of books are being delayed by me from reading Doughty, and so I am making worse my presumption in putting my name near what I believe to be one of the great prose works of our literature. It is a book which begins powerfully, written in a style which has apparently neither father nor son, so closely wrought, so tense, so just in its words and phrases, that it demands a hard reader. It seems not to have been written easily; but in a few of its pages you learn more of the Arabs than in all that others have written, and the further you go the closer the style seems to cling to the subject, and the more natural it becomes to your taste.

The history of the march of the caravan down the pilgrim road, the picture of Zeyd's tent, the description of Ibn Rashid's court at Hail, the negroid village in Kheybar, the urbane life at Aneyza, the long march across the desert of Western Nejd to Mecca, each seems better than the one before till there comes the very climax of the book near Taif, and after this excitement a gentle closing chapter of the road down to Jidda, to the hospitality of Mohammed Nasif's house, and the British Consulate.

To have accomplished such a journey would have been achievement enough for the ordinary man. Mr Doughty was not content till he had made the book justify the journey as much as the journey justified the book, and in the double power, to go and to write, he will not soon find his rival.

ISRAEL

Joanna Greenfield (1965–)

'Hyena'

Spotted hyenas are the sharks of the savanna, superpredators and astounding recyclers of garbage. They hunt in large, giggling groups, running alongside their prey and eating chunks of its flesh until it slows down through loss of blood, or shock, or sheer hopelessness, and then the hyenas grab for the stomach and pull the animal to a halt with its own entrails or let it stumble into the loops and whorls of its own body. They eat the prey whole and cough back, like owls, the indigestible parts, such as hair and hooves.

Hyenas in the wild can roam dozens of miles a day. They leave their young in small dens and trot or lope across the savanna, head down or held high and rear tucked under, until they've found a hare or a pregnant gazelle or a nicely rotted piece of flesh. But when the herds begin to migrate the hyenas leave their dens to follow them, and, passing over hills, through rifts and acacia stands, and along dry riverbeds, they reach the open plains of the Serengeti, where wildebeest beyond count mill and groan in clouds of dust.

I once saw a family of hyenas playing on an elephant skull. They rolled on their backs, biting gently at each other's legs. Two cubs squeezed under and then out of the elephant's mandible. A female turned on her side, paws in the air, and broke off a piece of the skull as if eating a biscuit in bed. Hyenas almost never kill humans – only now and then taking a piece from the cheek of a sleeping man, and that probably because some villagers used to put out their dead for hyenas, flies, and any vultures in the area. As the man jumps up – perhaps he is a messenger between villages or someone searching for a bride – the hyena instantly, peaceably, retreats.

*

Africa is like no other place on earth, and there is no better place to watch animals. They roam sun-dazed on the savanna by the million, sniffing up the scent of dried grass, swishing their tails, eyes often half closed. Sometimes they ignore human beings, sometimes they stare, but always there is something to look at: impalas dancing together in a mock fight, giraffes slow-swinging across the horizon. In the distance, vervet monkeys hop through branches. An ostrich runs with tail rampant, all the while flapping its wings in agitation, like a maiden aunt caught in a shower. A baboon nurses its toe. A lion quietly chuffs to itself.

I had wanted to go to Africa since my childhood, in Connecticut. Before I was born, my eyes lost their attachment to each other, the instinctive knowledge of how to swivel together, how to analyze data in tandem. The vision of one eye is only slightly cloudy, but it withdraws from cooperation with the other. My eyes do not work like two halves of a whole, and I have no perception of depth, so human faces blend into their background and are unreadable. The unreadable is frightening. When I was a child, friendly voices could dig deep and sharp without warning: without depth perception, there is no warning. I had to learn about emotions, which are subtle and often masked, from animals, who signal theirs so much more clearly, with mane and tail and the position of the body. Human beings were a hazard.

There was only one thing that my eyes took in with ease. As the school bus crossed the marshes on a small cement bridge, we could see down the river to the horizon, and up the river toward a bend of trees. In the swamp that ran alongside it grew cattails and rushes, as naturally gold as they were tall. They were semi-translucent. Each blade glowed separately in the morning sun as if lit within. Together in their bending, high-feathered swamp, they bowed under the weightlessness of light. Sometimes there was mist rising from the water, and altogether it was the only masterpiece I ever saw in my suburban town. I don't know why I needed to see those rushes so badly, or how I knew Africa would be the same, but it was.

*

I had never wanted to work anywhere except in Africa, but after I graduated from college a wildlife-reserve director from Israel told me that he needed someone to set up a breeding site for endangered animals and I decided to go. When I got there, I was told that the project had been postponed and was asked if I'd mind taking a job as a volunteer at another reserve, cleaning enclosures. The reserve was dedicated to Biblical animals, many of them predators from the Israeli wild – hyenas, wolves, foxes, and one unmated leopard – attackers of kibbutz livestock. It was something to do, with animals, so I trudged off every day in the hundred-and-fourteen-degree heat with half a sandwich and a water canteen. I was being groomed for the job I'd initially been offered, but for the moment I sifted maggots for the lizards and snakes, and cleaned the fox, cat, hyena, wolf, and leopard corrals.

As the days got hotter, my fellow-workers and I carried gallon jugs of water in our wheelbarrows, poured it over our heads, and drank the rest until our stomachs were too full for food. It became a steady rhythm: sift dung, pour, drink, sift. We worked in pairs among the larger animals for safety, but toward the end of the month I was allowed to feed a young hyena and clean his cage. Efa had been taken from his parents as a cub because his mother rejected him. Also, he was a cross between a North African and an Israeli striped hyena, and nobody wanted him to confuse the gene pool further by mating. He was a beautiful animal. A mane trickled down sloped shoulders like a froth of leftover baby hair; he looked strangely helpless, as if weighed down by the tangled strands, and his back rounded to a dispirited slump. Even though he had a hyena's posture, he was like a German shepherd, a little dirty, but graceful, and so strong he didn't seem to have any muscles. His stripes twisted a bit at the ends and shimmered over the coat like feathers at rest. With his bat face and massed shoulders, he would have been at home in the sky, poised in a great leap, or swooping for prey. But here he was given aged meat, and he often left even that to rot before he ate it.

He had been, they said, an adorable cub, crying 'Maaaaaa!' to Shlomi, the gentlest of the workers and the one who reared him, and he followed Shlomi everywhere. Then he grew too big to run loose, and he started biting at people, so they put him in a corral – a square of desert surrounded by an electrified fence with a large water basin perched in the center.

Efa was bored and lonely. He flipped the basin over every day, attacking it as if it were prey. When we fed him in the morning, there was nowhere to put his water. He knocked over everything, so we had no choice: we had to put him in a holding cage outside his corral while we built a concrete pool that he couldn't move. This was worse. Locked in a cage, he rebelled. He refused to eat, and every box we gave him for shade was torn to pieces. After a few days, I walked by and saw him standing defiant in the cage, his shade box in splinters and his water overturned again. '*Maaaaaaaa! Mmaaaaa!*' he croaked at me. I made a note to return and water him when I'd finished with the others.

I stopped to talk to the leopard, who was in heat. This was my first chance to get near her; when she was not hormonally sedated, she lunged at passersby, swatting her claws through the chicken wire.

'You're so beautiful.'

She purred, and rubbed against the mesh. The men said you could stroke her like a house cat when she was in these moods. I wanted to touch her, a leopard from the oases of Israel's last deserts, but I stayed away, in case she changed her mind, and squatted out of reach to talk to her. I didn't want to force her to defend herself.

*

It might have been the attention I gave the leopard, but Efa was in a frenzy of '*Mmmaaaaaaaa*'s when I returned to his cage. He crouched like a baby, begging for something. I filled a water tray and unlatched the door that opened into a corridor running between the cage and the corral, then I closed it. If only I'd just squirted the hose into the cage, but instead I unlatched the cage door and bent over to put the dish down, talking to him. The mind, I found, is strange. It shut off during the attack, while my body continued to act, without thought or even sight. I don't remember him sinking his teeth into my arm, though I heard a little grating noise as his teeth chewed into the bone.

Everything was black and slow and exploding in my stomach. Vision returned gradually, like an ancient black-and-white television pulling dots and flashes to the center for a picture. I saw at a remove the hyena inside my right arm, and my other arm banging him on the head. My body, in the absence of a mind, had decided that this was the best thing to do. And scream. Scream in a thin angry hysteria that didn't sound like me. Where was everyone? My mind was so calm and remote that I frightened myself, but my stomach twisted. I hit harder, remembering the others he'd nipped. He'd always let go.

Efa blinked and surged back, jerking me forward. I stumbled out of my sandals into the sand, thinking, with fresh anxiety, I'll burn my feet. I tried to kick him between the legs, but it was awkward, and he was pulling me down by the arm, down and back into the cage. When I came back from Africa the first time, I took a class in self-defense so I'd feel safer with all the soldiers, guerrilla warriors, and policemen when I returned. I remembered the move I'd vowed to use on any attacker: a stab and grab at the jugular, to snap it inside the skin. But the hyena has callused skin on its throat, thick and rough, like eczema. I lost hope and felt the slowness of this death to be the worst insult. Hyenas don't kill fast, and I could end up in the sand watching my entrails get pulled through a cut in my stomach and eaten like spaghetti, with tugs and jerks. I started to get mad, an unfamiliar feeling creeping in to add an acid burn to the chill of my stomach. Another removal from myself. I never let myself get mad. I want peace. I tried to pinch his nostrils so he'd let go of my arm to breathe, but he shook his head, pulling me deeper into the cage.

I think it was then that he took out the first piece from my arm and swallowed it without breathing, because a terror of movement settled in me at that moment and lasted for months. He moved up the arm, and all the time those black, blank eyes evaluated me, like a shark's, calm and almost friendly. By this time, my right arm was a mangled mess of flesh, pushed-out globs of fat, and flashes of bone two inches long, but my slow TV mind, watching, saw it as whole, just trapped in the hyena's mouth, in a tug-of-war like the one I used to play with my dogs – only it was my arm now instead of a sock. It didn't hurt. It never did.

The hyena looked up at me with those indescribable eyes and surged back again, nearly pulling me onto his face. I remembered self-defense class and the first lesson: 'Poke the cockroach in the eyes.' All the women had squealed, except me. 'Ooooh, I could *never* do that.' Ha, I'd thought. Anyone who wants to kill me has no right to live. I'd poke him in the eyes.

*

I looked at those eyes with my fingers poised to jab. It was for my family and my friends that I stuck my fingers in his eyes. I just wanted to stop watching myself get eaten, either be dead and at peace or be gone, but other lives were connected to mine. I'm not sure if I did more than touch them gently before he let go and whipped past me to cower against the door to the outside, the Negev desert.

Events like this teach you yourself. We all think we know what we would do, hero or coward, strong or weak. I expected strength, and the memory of my tin-whistle scream curdles my blood, but I am proud of the stupid thing I did next. He cowered and whimpered and essentially apologized, still with those blank unmoving eyes, and I stood still for a second. My arm felt light and shrunken, as if half of it were gone, but I didn't look. From the corridor, I had a choice of two doors: the one through which I'd entered, leading back to the desert, and the one opening onto the corral. I didn't think I could bend over him and unlatch the door to the desert. He'd just reach up and clamp onto my stomach. And I didn't want to open the door to the corral, or he'd drag me in and be able to attack the men if they ever came to help me. My body, still in control, made the good hand grab the bad elbow, and I beat him with my own arm, as if I had ripped it free to use as a club. 'No!' I shouted. 'No, no!' *Lo lo lo*, in Hebrew. I might even have said 'Bad boy,' but I hope not. It was the beating that damaged my hand permanently. I must have hit him hard enough to crush a ligament, because there is a lump on my hand to this day, five years later, but he didn't even blink. He came around behind me and grabbed my right leg, and again there was no pain – just the feeling that he and I were playing tug-of-war with my body – but I was afraid to pull too hard on the leg. He pulled the leg up, stretching me out in a line from the door, where I clung with the good hand to the mesh, like a dancer at the barre. It felt almost good, as if the whole thing were nearer to being over. In three moves I didn't feel, he took out most of the calf.

I opened the door to the desert and he ran out, with a quick shove that staggered me. I couldn't move the right leg, just crutched myself along on it into the Negev. He waited for me. The cold in my stomach was stabbing my breath away. The hyena and I were bonded now. Even if someone did come to help, there was still something left to finish between us. I was marked – his. I saw, in color, that he was going to knock me over, and I thought, in black-and-white, No, don't, you'll hurt my leg, I should keep it still.

A workman stood by a shed uphill, leaning on a tool in the sand. He watched me walk toward the office, with the hyena ahead and looking back at me. He was the only spectator I noticed, though I was told later, in the hospital, that some tourists, there to see the animals, were screaming for help, and three – or was it five? – soldiers had had their machine guns aimed at us throughout the whole thing. Israeli soldiers carry their arms everywhere when they're in uniform; but they must have been afraid to shoot. I don't know. Stories get told afterward. I didn't see anyone except the workman, looking on impassively, and the leopard, pacing inside her fence, roaring a little, with the peace of her heat gone as suddenly as it had appeared.

*

As I walked, the black-and-white faded, and color washed back in. I saw the blood for the first time. It was in my hair, had soaked into my clothes all the way to the skin, and was drying in a trickle from arm and legs. Each step left a cold puddle of blood around the right foot. I held up the arm and fumbled for the pressure point. The hyena trotted ahead of me as if he were afraid to be alone in the desert but was all right with me. Every now and then, he looked back as if thinking about finishing me off – once again a predator, calm and competent, silver, and splashed with blood. But then men ran up shouting, and I stopped, and snapped, sorry even then for sounding like a bitch, 'Get Efa and bring around the van.'

Shlomi ran up and grabbed my good left arm, hustling me forward. Not so fast, I wanted to say, but I didn't. Every step felt more wrong, and I dragged back against moving until he almost shoved me forward.

In the van, blood sloshed around my feet and I tried to find the pressure point of the groin but gave up. I held up the arm instead, and pretended I knew what I was doing. Shlomi stopped to open the reserve gate, and then again to close it. As he got back in, I lost feeling in my right leg.

We drove for what seemed like a long time, then turned into a kibbutz and roared past lines of women planting pineapples, past a cement yard, and then he was running me into a clinic past gasping women. And I wanted to apologize. I never cut in line. Shlomi pulled me forward while I stiffened up. Damn it, I want to be carried, I've done enough by myself, I remember thinking. But I made it to the examining table and Shlomi yelled for a doctor in Hebrew. A woman came in and told him there was no doctor – only nurses. They stopped telling me what was happening. Hands shaking, she yanked me forward and stuck my arm under a faucet. Hey. She turned on the water and it fell onto the bone and a minor nerve, full force.

That was a sensation I wish I couldn't remember. No pain, but a tremendous feeling of wrongness. My insides were out.

She tried to get my leg into the sink, pulling at the ankle, and the shrivelled arm twitched in the air for balance. I tensed, so she couldn't; I wished later that I'd let her, because it was weeks before the dried blood and dirt peeled off. She told me to get on a stretcher, and then she poured hydrogen peroxide into the trenches in my leg. It foamed with a roar that spat froth in the air. That felt wrong, too. Shlomi grabbed the sink for support. I told him it didn't hurt. He wasn't listening. I was starting to feel better. Someone was making the decisions.

'Don't worry, Shlomi. I never wanted to dance ballet.'

'No, I don't know, the leg is very bad.'

Like all Israelis, he could make a statement of fact sound like an accusation. I knew it was bad, I just didn't see the need to dwell on it when I was so very surprised to be alive. The nurse picked up a towel and started wiping off the blood and dirt with brisk, scratchy strokes, and I cramped in the stomach again, worrying about infection. And what were we waiting for? We waited awhile, and then she gave me anti-shock injections.

'I'm not in shock,' I said, and meant it. I thought I was thinking more clearly than she was. Shlomi told me that we were waiting for an ambulance. He was gray, with sick, inturned eyes, the way I must have looked while the attack was happening. But I was over it, and he was just beginning. He and the nurse did not share my pleasure. In fact, they seemed taken aback at my jokes, so I stopped talking.

*

I had a new terror, but it was peaceful compared with the other, so I lay back. Fly home, microsurgery, I can spare the leg if something has to go, but I have to have the hand for graduate school. Helicopters, international flights, nerve damage.

The ambulance came. The nurse and Shlomi looked as bloodless as I felt. They pushed me around, telling me to get onto the gurney, and I tried to make them let go so I could just roll onto it instead of jumping down from the table. They did, and wheeled me out in state through a crowd of horrified kibbutzniks. They showed no excitement over it; pain is too real to Israelis.

*

I am sure Efa crawled out to greet me with no intention to kill. He had cried to me like an infant in distress, hunched over and rounded. His ruff lay flat and soft and his tail hung down. He attacked me, I think, in a moment of thirst-induced delirium and loneliness. If he had wanted to eat or to attack, he could have taken my arm in a snap: one sharp jab and jerk, and the wrist would have been gone before I even noticed. If he had wanted to kill me, he could have leaped for my stomach as soon as he had pulled me down by the arm.

Cheetahs often catch hold of their prey's nose and run alongside it. As the victim stumbles and falls, or staggers, or tries to run, the cheetah holds tight, closing mouth and nostrils in one stapled hold, or – with larger prey – bitting into the throat to cut off air. Leopards like to leap down from trees for a quick crack of the back. Lions improvise. Each has its own specialty. Some leap up from behind, like a terrestrial leopard; some try a daring front leap, risking hooves and horns to bite into neck or face.

Hyenas are far more efficient. They catch hold of flesh, not with small nips and throwing of weight but by smoothly and quickly transferring chunks of it from prey to throat. Food slips instantly from toothhold to stomach. Like human infants nursing, they seem to swallow without pausing for breath, as if food and air travelled in separate channels. They are the only predators adapted to eating bone. Their dung is white with it.

I heard a story of a young boy in Nairobi who was watching over a herd of goats and fell asleep leaning on his stick. A hyena appeared and opened the boy's stomach with one quick rip. For the hyena it might have been play, this trying on of assault. But he won, as he was bound to do. I was told that someone took the boy to a doctor and he died a while later. He could have lived; we don't need all our intestines, and the hyena had probably left enough behind. But maybe they didn't have the right antibiotics or sterile dressings. I would have liked to ask him what he saw in the hyena's eyes.

*

In the ambulance, the driver chatted for a bit, then said, 'Don't close your eyes. If you feel faint, tell me and I'll stop right away.'

To do what, watch me? I didn't tell him that I'd been exhausted for months – I'd got parasites in Africa – and always shut my eyes when I had the chance. I closed them now, and he asked me questions with an anxiety that warmed my heart. I love to be taken care of. It was good to be strapped down and bandaged, all decisions out of my hands after the hard ones, the life-and-death ones. It was also, I learned, a good thing to have the wounds hidden. Once they were open to the air, my stomach clenched with pain that made life temporarily not worth living. The arm, I finally noticed, was curled up on itself, like paper shrivelling inward in a fire, but heavy instead of too light.

We arrived at the hospital with a screech and a yank and a curse. The doors were stuck, but the driver pushed, and ran me in. Then he left with a wave of farewell. I waited and waited. A doctor came in and plowed my arm in search of a vein with blood, going deep under the muscle, to attach a saline drip. My nails were white, like things soaked in formaldehyde, and I was freezing. Bled white, I was. Nothing left to fill a test tube.

I asked the doctor to talk with the reserve's veterinarian before he did anything. Hyena bites are violently infectious. The animals' mouths are full of bacteria from rotten meat. He shrugged. But when Shlomi told him to wait for the vet he did. The vet told him to clean the holes out and leave them open for now, because the infection could kill me.

'The infection will probably take the leg anyway,' the doctor told me. 'The chances are fifty-fifty that we'll have to amputate.'

I looked down once at the leg before they began cutting out the dirtier shreds of flesh and paring the whole surface of the wound. The holes were impossibly wide, more than twice the size of the hyena's face. I know now that skin and muscle are stretched over bone like canvas over a canoe. One thinks of skin as irrevocably bonded to flesh, and all as one entity. But skin is attached to flesh only with the lightest of bonds, and, once it has been ripped, the body gives way naturally, pulling the flesh back to its scaffolding of bone. The invisible woman, I thought, as the chill took me; I can see right through my leg.

I couldn't see all of it because of my bad eyesight, and the leg was still covered with blood-stuck sand, but it was strange the way the leg went down normally, then cut in to the bone, along the bone, and then out again to a normal ankle, except for a small gash on the side with fat poking out. I couldn't yet see the other hole. It was lower down, starting halfway past the one I could see, and continuing around the back of the leg to the other side, so almost the whole leg was girdled around. I still don't know how blood got to that stranded wall of flesh.

The doctor worked on the leg for an hour, clipping pieces of flesh out of the wounds with little scissor snips, as if my leg were a piece of cloth that he was carefully tailoring with dull tools. I asked for a larger dose of anesthetic, not because I felt any pain – I never felt any, really – but because I could feel the scissors scissoring away the flesh and I couldn't breathe. Between bouts of cutting, I kept joking, happy it was over, or might be over, and people crowded into the room to watch. No sterilization? Who cares? I was alive. They pumped saline into me so fast that my arm swelled and I had to go to the bathroom. For the first time, I realized how my life had changed. There is, after all, no simple dichotomy: intact and alive versus torn and dead.

They sent some of the people out and stuck a bedpan under the sheet. With one wrist locked to the IV and the other paralyzed, I couldn't wipe. Warrior to newborn babe in an hour. Someone brought me my sandals. They were dirty and covered with dried blood, like small dead animals.

*

I had expected the hyena bite in Africa, not in Israel. I had expected the price I paid for Africa to be high. The need that had driven me since I was eight years old had made me willing to risk anything, even death, to be in Africa watching animals. Anyone who works with animals expects to get hurt. You are a guest in their life – any intrusion is a threat to them. It is their separateness that makes them worthy of respect.

After the hospital, I went back to America for physical therapy and treatment of the parasites, which burned a path in my stomach for the next six months. Before I left, people from the reserve asked me to stand near Efa's cage. They wanted to know if his animosity was specific to me. He looked at me, again with those friendly blank eyes, and then rose up against the wire with a crash so loud that I thought he was breaking through. For one second, I saw his face coming toward me, mouth open, and I hopped back. They told me they were going to send him to a zoo where the keepers wouldn't have to go into the cage, but I heard later that a veterinarian came and put Efa to sleep. ('Forever asleep,' the workers said.)

MONGOLIA, CHINA, TIBET

MILDRED CABLE (1878–1952) AND
FRANCESCA FRENCH (1871–1960)

from *The Gobi Desert*

An aerial view of the Desert of Gobi on a midsummer day would show a burning arid waste of dunes interspersed with monotonous rolling expanses of gravel and crossed by occasional ridges of high mountains whose foothills dwindle to low rocky mounds. The whole plain is shadeless and exposed to scorching heat under a pitiless sun. All living creatures seek shelter from its fierce rays and the roads are deserted, for the reverberation of heat makes travel almost impossible.

By night it is quite otherwise, and as darkness falls the desert quickens into life. Scorching heat gives way to a sudden chill which rises from the ground and strikes the traveller with a cold impact which makes him lift his head to catch the warmer upper stratum of the air as a relief from that too palpable cold. Soon that layer too will be permeated by the chill, and he will wrap a sheepskin coat around him in an endeavour to keep warm.

At this hour the observer would see caravans emerge from all the oasis inns and move slowly in various directions. Long trains of two hundred camels, roped together in strings of twelve, stretch out in thin lines over the narrow tracks; caravans of large carts, each laden with a thousand pounds of merchandise, follow one another across the plain; these join up for safety and keep within hailing distance of each other. Pedestrians carrying their own baggage balanced over the shoulder from the two ends of a pole come from many places and look like swinging dots as they move briskly at first, but later settle down to the inevitable pace of Gobi travel.

Half-way through the night all these travellers are seen to halt. This is the moment when caravans moving in opposite directions meet and greet each other. Carters recognize friends from other towns, but there is no more talk between them than is necessary for the passing of needed warnings. Camel-drivers on their immensely long journeys are alert for all unusual sights or sounds, and often carry letters to be handed to those whom they may meet at some halting-place. Pedestrians lay down their loads, rest aching shoulders and drink from their water-bottles, squatting lightly on their heels for a while before they make the second half of the stage. All these men speak but little and there is no easy chat on a desert night journey, nor is loud conversation ever heard; desert talk is always spare, subdued and unhurried, for the spaces teach men to be sharers of their dignity, and to scorn noise and tattle as only suited to the vulgarity of towns. Moreover, in the still air voices carry dangerously well, and silence becomes a cautionary instinct.

The sand deadens the sound of wheels, and camels' soft padded feet move quietly between the dunes. The camp watch-dogs might give a sharp sound by day, but at night they follow at the camels' heels or leap on to the back of one beast and lie there until the halt is called, when they jump down to take on duty. The sonorous, monotonous camel-bell has no sharp clang, but only a deep dull boom, and the rhythmic dip of the camels' neck keeps it in perfect measure. This bell is such a part of desert quiet that it breaks silence without disturbing it. When the great carts draw up for the mid-stage halt, a heavy smell of opium often comes from the pipe of some smoker hidden behind the curtains who lies there listless while the drivers exchange their greeting and then move on again.

Not only humans but innumerable small animals and insects come from their hiding-places as soon as darkness falls. All through the hours of heat they have slept in the tunnelled world which they have burrowed for themselves a few feet underground, and of which the openings are on the sheltered side of many a tiny sand-mound, blown up round the foot of a tuft of camel-thorn or of a low bush of scrub. All through the night the little live things move ceaselessly, silently and invisibly over the sand, and only by chance does a traveller become aware of their presence; after sunrise, however, he sees the sand patterned with all kinds of beautiful markings left by small rodents, beetles, centipedes and other insects which scuttle back to their sleeping-quarters with the first ray of sunshine.

Near the oases an observer might see slinking forms of wolves prowling vigilantly lest a goat or a child should wander from the shelter of the houses, and when some tired beast lags behind the caravan the dark forms gather from all sides to snatch a share of the spoil. Other sinister forms sometimes crouch behind rocks or in gullies – evil men waiting for lonely pedestrians or for some cart which has ventured unattached over the desert waste. The robbers hide themselves at those points on the route where caravans going north must pass just after sunset and where others, travelling south, come in shortly before daylight, for during the grey, twilight hours they will be unnoticed among the elusive shadows.

In the dry desert air the sky becomes a beautiful background for the brilliant stars which hang clear, showing themselves as shining orbs and never creating the illusion of lights twinkling through holes in a curtain, as is the case in dull and murky climes. The Milky Way is not the whitish haze seen in Western skies, but like a phosphorescent shower of myriad spots of light. Night travellers are great stargazers, and look out over an uninterrupted line of horizon to skies which are always cloudless. The clearness and watchfulness of each planet suggests a personal and friendly interest toward the wayfarer, and Venus has served as beacon to many a caravan crossing doubtful stages.

Of starlight in the desert, Lawrence of Arabia writes: 'The brilliant stars cast about us a false light, not illumination, but rather a transparency of air, lengthening slightly the shadow below each stone and making a diffused greyness of the ground.'[1] Desert men, accustomed all their lives to that most subtle of all light diffusions, walk freely, even on rough ground, with no other illuminant. The moon, also, is more self-revealing than in heavier atmospheres, and never pretends to be merely a silver sickle or a cradle swinging in the void. She shows her full-orbed sphere, hanging in space, with a varying portion of brilliance outlining her darkened luminosity. With the rising of the moon the desert takes on its most captivating appearance, and through the long hours while she travels from one side of the horizon to the other she has her own way with human imagination, softening all the austere outlines and investing the barest formations with subtle charm. She is a mistress of magic and with one touch can turn the wilderness into a dream world.

1. *The Seven Pillars of Wisdom*, by T. E. Lawrence.

Over these vast plains old ruined towns, surrounded with more or less decrepit battlemented walls, are scattered. The caravan track enters an enclosure at the place where a city gate used to stand, and leaves it at a gap in the opposite wall where another gate once stood. Inside the enclosed space are ruined walls, and the remains of houses long since destroyed. No one can build them up and use them again, for water has withdrawn itself from these cities of the dead and the old well openings are choked to the brim with sand and eroded matter. The main streets are often quite distinguishable, and even crooked lanes are sometimes recognizable. Silent progress by moonlight through such an ancient ruin vividly stirs the imagination and suggests that these old ruins may well be the haunt, not only of wild beasts, as they certainly are, but also of the ghostly habitants.

Not least remarkable of the Gobi night effects is the dancing magnetic light, which bewilders the inexperienced with its suggestion of men and camps in a region which is wholly deserted. The light flickers on the horizon, appearing and disappearing suddenly and unaccountably; one moment it is there, but a second later it has vanished, and when the traveller decides that it must be an illusion it is back again and yet again. Should he throw off his coat, or a driver touch a mule with his whip, the flash comes quite close, and the garment or the mule's back is streaked with light, and anyone holding a piece of silk, or touching a fur coat, may feel an electric shock. The Mongol poetically speaks of all these magnetic lights as 'the Rosary of Heaven', because, through the long hours of darkness, the fires flash and shine like falling beads.

During silent stages when nothing is heard but the soft grind of wheels on loose sand, sound becomes subtly rhythmic and the rhythms resolve themselves into music, harmonizing according to the perception of the listener. The muleteer probably hears nothing but a monotonous grating measure, while the more imaginative traveller listens to the rise and swell of mighty cadences, broad melodies and spacious harmonies.

With the rising sun the aerial observer could watch all the caravans reaching their respective destinations at the end of their night's journey. The camels kneel among the sands to have their loads removed, and wide-open doors of oasis inns wait to receive the tired wayfarers who, throughout the night, have covered another thirty-mile stage of the desert road. By divergent ways they come, meeting at the welcome *serai*, and disappear into the darkness and quiet of inn cells to pass the day in sleep . . .

*

The desert atmosphere has a special quality which makes every object in the landscape stand out stereoscopically and with amazing clearness. One traveller very accurately observes: 'The air is so clear that there is no perspective,' and others have remarked on the surprise which they experienced when, sighting a caravan which they thought was close at hand, they have found that hours passed before it reached them. Trees, walls and landmarks which appear to be but a mile distant are, in fact, half a day's journey away.

This atmospheric peculiarity has its counterpart in the human intercourse of the desert, and in the personal incidents of each traveller's journey. In other surroundings many contacts and happenings might seem too trivial to be remembered, but in the desert the detachment of life from all normal intercourse imparts a sense of gravity to every rencontre, and each touch with human beings is fraught with a significance lacking in the too hurried intercourse of ordinary everyday life.

On the desert track there is no such thing as a casual meeting, for even wayside contacts instantly become significant, and the spot where the meeting took place is for ever associated in the mind of each with that incident. The details of each Gobi journey are recalled as a series of pictures which associate every stage of the road with men and women who were met there, and with unforgettable scenes in which each took part. Just as in a desert landscape the detail of the only cultivated patch on a sandy hillside will stand apart from its grey setting with a brilliance which is like enamel, so these incidents stand out unforgettably against a background which is free from the blurs, the confusion and the turmoil of a preoccupied life. There is nothing hurried in the occasion, but space for such conversation as forms a permanent link between two individuals who will never meet again. Each, in sharing some experience of life with the other, has stripped himself of the trammels of conventionality and the make-believes of artificiality. In such conditions men instinctively speak soberly, never idly nor merely in order to pass the time, but with a sense of living in a world of reality where nothing is trivial. Great journeys do not merely consist in passing over vast spaces, but owe their greatness far more to the human intercourse and knowledge of fellow-men which they involve. It is this which makes them memorable.

Sometimes the *rencontre* leaves an indelible impression, clear, precise and full of meaning, like a picture composed by a master-hand. One morning at sunrise I walked on a high overhanging bank which skirted an oasis stream. I was out of earshot of the small camp noises, and silence prevailed such as only the desert knows, but the stillness was suddenly broken by a low murmur which seemed to be that of a human voice and appeared to come from beneath the very ground on which I stood. I looked around but could see nothing, so made a wide circuit to reach a place from which I could see what lay under the overhanging bank. When I did so, I looked for a moment on a scene which will ever remain in my memory.

Under the bank there was a low grotto, and in its centre a living, bubbling spring. The face of the small pool was tremulous with air-bubbles which rose and broke perpetually on its surface. By the pool there crouched a lama in red cap and maroon travel-coat. With hollowed palms he lifted the cool water and scattered it on the ground, paying homage to the great life-sustaining element. Utterly unconscious of being watched, he performed each minute gesture of the ritual, and I heard the rise and fall of his clear, sonorous mountaineer's voice reciting the liturgies of dawn.

At other times the encounter may take the form of talk with an unseen person. Midway on a tedious Gobi night stage we heard the faint clang of a distant bell which warned us that some other traveller was moving toward us. We could see nothing, but the sound came slowly nearer, and in time one large covered cart, drawn by five mules, loomed from the darkness. The carters exchanged a word, and I called out in Chinese: 'Where do you come from?' 'From Urumchi,' was the answer. There was a movement in the cart and a woman's voice spoke, saying, 'Who is there?' The tone showed me that she was not Chinese and I went over to speak to her. 'My guest is a Russian,' her carter told me, and when I spoke in Chinese she ventured on a few halting sentences, but when one of us addressed her in French she instantly responded fluently in that language.

The carters sat on their heels and smoked their pipes, exchanging news of the road. The mules stood at ease and rested. I never saw the woman's face, nor did I even ask her name, but under the veil of darkness which enabled us to remain unidentified we talked with great intimacy. She told us of her flight from Russia with husband and child at the time of the Revolution, of their journey across Siberia to Turkestan, of losing all they possessed and of their terrible poverty. When her husband had the chance of a job in Uliassutai they went to that remote place and lived there for some years. She went on to speak of her husband, of his hasty temper and of his impatient handling of the Chinese. 'I hate those people, I can never forgive them,' she exclaimed. It was evident that this was a woman who had known embittering sorrow and must be met with no easy, comfortable words, but with strong, courageous sympathy. Encouraged by the response, she poured out a tragic story. 'The Chinese are so revengeful,' she said, 'and never forget an injury. My husband was too outspoken and he made one of them lose face. The man said little, but watched his chance to pay him back. He did it through our only child. He was a lovely boy. One day he came in from play and I saw that he was not well. He seemed to be so limp and sleepy that I took him into my arms and nursed him. Then I put him to bed and he was quiet, only unnaturally sleepy. I could not understand it for I had never seen such an illness before, and, of course, there was no doctor in the place. When it was too late I realized to my horror that he was dying of opium poisoning. There was nothing that I could do to save him, and soon he lay dead. That was the work of a Chinese who had been employed by my husband, and that was his repayment for my husband's anger. Soon after this my husband also died, and now I am on my way to Tientsin or to Shanghai. I have no money, but I shall find some kind of work there. My parents gave me the best education that could be had in Russia. I can teach French, German or Russian. I shall surely find something to do, but if all else fails I will do housework.'

I saluted the courageous spirit with which this woman faced life, and a future that might terrify anyone. She was undaunted, and there was nothing of defeatism in her heart. The carters moved. 'Tsou, tsou!' (On, on!) they called, 'we must get on.' 'Tsou, tsou!' we responded, knowing that a long stretch lay ahead, but there was still one message to be handed over to this woman which, if she received it, would release her from the torment of hatred which was like a canker in her heart, embittering every part of her existence, a word which might speed her on her lonely way with a sense of care, love and protection. Only a few sentences could be exchanged, but they were vital, as every word spoken in such circumstances must be, and

I handed her a New Testament in the Russian language, a book which told of One Who alone could make everything new for her and would be her ultimate defence. This book she took with her into the unknown . . .

*

The still days when dust-demons walk abroad are good for caravans on the march, but sooner or later the time comes when the camels, alert as a barometer to atmospheric changes, show signs of uneasiness and become restive. The driver knows the indications and scans the horizon for signs of the coming storm, then moves among his animals, tightening ropes and securing packs. Before long there is a distant roar, and a cloud like rolling smoke with a livid edge advances and invades the sky, blotting out sun and daylight; then suddenly the sandstorm breaks on the caravan. No progress is possible and human beings shelter behind a barrage of kneeling camels from the flying stones and choking sand. When such a blinding storm is in progress there is no indication by which to find the way, and the only safe course is to stay still until it has exhausted itself by the surcharge of its own violence. It is a stirring of earth's surface which blots out the light of day, robs the atmosphere of its purity, blurs the outline of tracks and landmarks and takes all sense of direction from men, making them helpless to use even their natural powers of orientation. It cannot be overcome by resistance, and those who dissipate energy in fighting it will inevitably be exhausted by its fury. The camel-driver is too wise to waste strength in fight and, following the instinct of the camel that kneels in order to offer less resistance, he learns to shelter till the terrible blast passes over. Such a storm will not last many hours, and as soon as it has spent itself the sun reappears in a serene sky, the violently disturbed sand and stones sink to their own place, and the caravan can continue its journey.

Had I been without an experienced guide I should certainly have been deceived when I first heard that strange illusory voice calling for help, of which so many travellers have spoken.

'Halt,' I said, 'there is someone calling!'

'There is no one calling,' said the *bash*, 'and there is no reason to halt.'

'Cannot you hear?' I persisted. 'Someone is calling from among the dunes.'

'Never listen to those voices,' he replied. 'It is not a man's cry, and those who follow it may never come back to the caravan. We must push on.' He urged the beasts forward and refused to listen. As he trudged ahead he spoke again: 'Those voices are heard all over Gobi, but are worse in the Desert of Lob. One night when I was travelling there I got separated from my caravan. I heard a shout and the sound of camel-bells which I tried to overtake for hours. Then the moon rose and I saw there were no recent tracks of camels, so I halted, and turned back, but something held me and the voice still called. At last, with a great effort I retraced my steps to where I could see the tracks of our camels leading off in another direction. It was a strange experience, but as soon as I was on the right road those devilish voices ceased, and by midday I caught up with the caravan once more. They nearly had me that time, as they have had many others.'

'What then,' I asked, 'are those strange voices which I heard?'

'The people of Lob call them *Azghun*,' he replied, 'and say that it is a *kwei* which lives among the sand-hillocks and sometimes takes the form of a black eagle. If travellers listen, it leads them away to waterless places where they perish.'

Dust-demons, phantom voices with their insistence, always trying to turn travellers out of the way – it sounded so fantastic that at first I was inclined to dismiss it all with an incredulous smile, but something in the subconscious arrested me, and I repeated aloud those words: 'When an evil spirit has left a man it roams about in the desert, seeking rest.' I had to acknowledge that they were spoken by the only One Who really knows, so I thought on those words and kept silence.

It seemed as though the pastime of those demons was to make sport of the few lonely human beings who ventured into the desert, by encircling them with every manner of deception.

By night, lights which were like flames from a camp-fire played on the horizon, but no one has ever located them or come any nearer by following them. Watching my two companions walking ahead of the caravan one day, I was amazed to see four people where I had believed there were only two. My eyes saw something which my reason refused to accept. I overtook them and there were but two: I dropped back, and again there were four. Thus do the refractions of desert light shake confidence in the powers of discernment and call for a new standard of discrimination in which things seen with mortal eye are not to be relied upon, whereas the things which are relied on may be contrary to the evidence of the senses.

Mirage is the desert traveller's constant companion and his perpetual torment. As soon as the sun is high above the horizon, the sand begins to glitter like water and appears to move like wavelets, while the clumps of camel-thorn look like tall bushes or stunted trees, and seem to be set by the edge of a lake. All through the day this illusion persists, and not until near sunset does the mirage vanish, the sand cease to glitter, and the landscape show itself for what it really is, a dull grey surface. Even the old traveller must never reckon himself free from the snare of illusion. On one occasion we were to spend a night in a Qazaq tent, but it was autumn, and the coarse desert-grass grew rank and hid the encampment. In the late afternoon the carter gave the cry: 'Dao-liao!' (We have arrived), and sure enough, there were the tents, the herds and the pasturing flocks. A man hurried on to prospect, and we urged our tired beasts to further effort. In an hour's time the tents, herds and pastures, though still there, were no nearer, and when darkness fell the voice of our man was heard shouting: 'We are lost! I cannot find any yurts. We must stay here till morning.' In the straight clear light of dawn we saw the plain in its true aspect; there were no tents, no cattle and no water in sight. Not till the following sunset did we reach the encampment.

How terrible if in this realm of illusion where that which seemed real was not true, and where true things appeared false, I were left to find my way without a guide. Never could I hope to disentangle the web of deception, and free both mind and sense from its impalpable net. In the desert I learnt to detect some of the illusions which constantly surround me on the greater journey of life, and to depend for direction on the wisdom of Him Who is my unerring guide.

*

Without water the desert is nothing but a grave, and is useless either as a dwelling-place or even as a high-road for the living. If the traveller's food is poor he will go hungry, if his road is long he will be weary, if his lot is hard he will be lonely, but to all these things he can become inured. No one, however, can be inured to thirst. When the craving for water assails a man he will forget all else in his frantic search for it, knowing that life itself depends on finding it, and that failing it he will soon be the victim of delirium, madness and death.

When a traveller first starts out to cross the desert he is inclined to take water for granted, and though the old innkeepers warn everyone to carry it, he may refuse to listen and prefer taking a risk to being burdened with a water-bottle, but once that man has experienced the torture of thirst his outlook is changed, and nothing will induce him to start upon any stage without a supply.

As the long hours pass, the burning sun seems to sap the moisture through every pore of the skin, until thirst is not only felt in the dry throat and cracked lips, but throughout the body, and as the days of rationed water go by, the whole system, tormented by a craving which becomes more and more, urgent, calls out for the sight, the smell and the feeling of moisture. Sometimes the sunset hour brings a caravan to a lonely spot where a water-hole should be found but is hard to detect. All members of the caravan dismount and hunt for the small depression, perhaps marked only by a stone. It is so easy to miss, and once darkness has fallen it would be impossible to locate it. Then a shout is heard, 'Water, water!' and all run to the spot to quench their desperate thirst.

The mirage has been a decoy to many thirsty men. I myself, when I first saw a lovely lake with trees standing on its farther bank in mid-Gobi, urged the drivers to push on and reach it quickly, but the *bash* only smiled and spoke indulgently, as one might speak to an ignorant child: 'That's not water,' he said, 'that's glitter sand – dry water.' That lake was but a mirage, and the farther we went the farther it receded, tantalizing our thirst with its falsity.

I was caught by another deception to which weary wayfarers are subject, and this time it was not 'glitter sand' but the brackish water of the salt desert. The sparkle of the limpid spring was irresistible, but when I ran toward it, certain this time of the water's reality, the same gruff voice cautioned me: 'Drink as little of that water as you can,' it said. This time I cared for none of his warnings, for I had found real water and would enjoy it to the full. I soon learnt that the *bash* knew better than I, for the more I took of this water, the more parched I became. It was brackish – neither salt nor sweet. Not salt as sea-water which drives to madness, nor sweet like spring-water which heals and refreshes, but brackish, leaving thirst for ever unquenched. I drank my fill, and came again, but I was thirsty still.

This experience made me wary of all desert waters, and when I came to the oasis of Ever-Flowing-Stream, though the water looked so tempting and so cool in the little grotto under the shady trees, I was shy of it, for other water had looked cool and tempting too. I tasted it cautiously, but here there was no deception and it was a stream of sweet, satisfying quality. This was *karez* water and came direct from the eternal snows of the distant mountains. Through a deep underground channel it had crossed the torrid plain, and when it emerged at the place where I stood it was as sweet, as cool and as pure as when it left the foot of the glacier, nor would the stream run dry so long as the snow-clad hills remained and the channel was kept unchoked.

Occasionally I heard a desert spring spoken of as 'living water', and when I saw one I understood the expression. Its vitalized energy was so irrepressible that from the depths of the water-hole it pushed upward and broke on the surface in shimmering bubbles. Those who draw from such a living spring always speak of it reverently and as of something akin to the divine. The pilgrim prays there at break of day, the Buddhist erects a shrine in its vicinity, the Moslem goes to it for water of purification, and when I stood and looked into the moving depths I better understood the question asked of Christ, 'Where do you get living water?' and the answer He gave: 'The water I give becomes a spring, welling up to eternal life.'

It is water which marks the stage, and only where there is water are there human habitations. The people who live there may be terribly poor, but though poverty-stricken and sordid, their houses are homes and their hamlets are oases because water, which is an essential of life, is accessible to them. These men of the water-holes had another supreme need beyond that of bread and water, for man does not live by these alone, and though I could not bring to them life's normal amenities yet I was there to offer each one that living water for which his spirit craved.

I sat for long hours in my sand-chair by the Crescent Lake and reflected on the teaching of those desert experiences, the illusive mirage, the tormenting bitter water, the sweet water of the *karez* channel and the invigorating water of the living spring. Then slowly the lovely lake at my feet recaptured my attention, seeming to say, 'Now consider what lies before your eyes.' So I dismissed all thought of desert rigours and yielded myself to the charm of the moment.

The whole scene, from the brilliant glazed-tiled roofs, the light loggia, the golden sand, the silver trees, the fringe of green sedge,

and the delicate hues of wheeling pigeons, was reflected in the still
water as sharply as in a mirror. An acolyte came to the water's edge,
stooped, filled a bucket with lake water and turned back toward the
temple. The scene had an unreal quality which held me motionless
as though a movement on my part might shatter the spell and
disperse its beauty like a dream. Overhead the great dunes towered
threateningly. 'Why,' I asked, 'why was this lake not long since buried
by these encroaching sands? Why does its fragile beauty last when
the whole configuration of the landscape is changed by obliterating
sand-storms? Towns and villages have vanished in a wilderness of
death and desiccation, yet this lake remains and no one has ever seen
its water margin low. What is the secret of its permanence and of
the unseen source from which it draws such plentiful supplies that
drought has no effect on it?'

At that moment I saw one of my comrades walking over the
crest of the hill, ploughing a deep furrow in the sands as she went.
From the summit she slid down the face of the dune, and as she did
so I heard the sands sing, then she walked to the guest-house and
passed through the door, leaving the whole line of her path, from
the top of the hill to the lip of the lake, profoundly disturbed. The
sands which, before, had not shown one wrinkle were now furrowed
with deep ridges, but, as I watched, I saw their surface slowly but
surely smoothed out again till, gradually, every mark was obliterated.
The ceaseless winds of God were at work and, as always, they blew
off the lake and upward toward the crest of the hill. By some mystery
of orientation the lake was so placed that every breath which stirred
the encircling sand-mounds blew upward and lifted the drift away
from the water. I picked up a handful of sand and threw it downward, but the breeze caught it and blew it back in my face. This,
then, was the secret of this exquisite lake's permanence – its exposure
to the upward-wafting winds of God, and its deep unfailing source
of supply.

'Do you understand this picture of one who has attained what
you seek and reached the goal of your desire?' something within me
said. 'In the midst of threatening danger this lake lifts its face heaven-
ward, reflecting as in a mirror the glory of the sky. It is not withdrawn
from the terrible sand which constantly threatens to engulf it, its
position is always perilous and it lives dangerously, but every time
the sand threatens, the winds of God are there to protect it, and no
harm touches it. This is why its peace, its purity and its serenity can

never be destroyed. Surely the parable is clear – it is the pure in
heart who see God.'

The sight of a red-robed lama walking in my direction called me
back to the immediate, and I rose, greeting him, then sat down and
talked with him, first of his long pilgrimage and later of the search
for God which urged him to such an arduous undertaking. Walking
back together toward the guest-house we met the guardian of the
temple, who appeared strangely agitated. 'Look,' he said, 'did you
ever see anything like that?' He pointed to a curious triple halo in
the sky. The three rims of light spread a diffused radiance, and we
all stood and watched the strange atmospheric effect. 'This is a
terrible omen,' said the priest, 'a sign of awful happenings, and of
trouble coming such as the world has never known. Alas, alas for
this world!' Too profoundly disturbed to say more, the old man
turned off to the temple shrine to burn incense and seek to pacify
the anger of the gods.

Next morning the lama, carrying his little bundle, passed on his
way toward Tibet. With my companions I walked once more round
the lovely lake, gazing till every detail of its beauty was impressed
on my memory. Then we said goodbye to the priest, walked to the
foot of the great sand-hills, stood there for a moment and gave one
last backward look, then waved a long farewell to the lovely lake,
and rode away.

* * *

GORE VIDAL (1925–)

'Mongolia!'

In August, Moscow's weather is like that of Edinburgh; the cool wind
has begun to smell of snow while the dark blue sky is marred
with school-of-Tiepolo clouds. Last August the rowan trees were
overloaded with clusters of red berries. 'Rowan-berries in August
mean a hard winter,' said the literary critic as he showed me the
view from the Kremlin terrace. 'But after the hard winter,' I said,
sententious as Mao, 'there will come the spring.' He nodded. 'How
true!' As we pondered the insignificance of what neither had said, a

baker's dozen of ornithologists loped into view. Moscow was acting as host to a world ornithological congress. To a man, ornithologists are tall, slender, and bearded so that they can stand motionless for hours, imitating kindly trees, as they watch for birds. Since they are staying at our group's hotel, we have dubbed them the tweet-tweets.

The critic asked, 'Have you read *Gorky Park?'* I said that I had not because I have made it a rule only to read novels by Nobel Prize winners. That way one will never read a bad book. I told him the plot of Pearl Buck's *This Proud Heart.* He told me the plot of *Gorky Park.* 'It's a really good bad book,' he said. 'You know, everyone's making such heavy weather about it here, I can't think why. It's wonderfully silly. An American gunman loose in Moscow!' He chuckled. 'It's so surrealist.' I said that they should publish it as an example of American surrealism, with a learned commentary explaining the jokes.

As we chatted, two Russian soldiers walked by us. One was in uniform; the other wore blue jeans and a T-shirt emblazoned with the words 'The United States Military Academy, West Point'. The literary critic smiled. 'Could an American soldier wear a Kremlin T-shirt?' I explained to him, patiently, I hope, the difference between the free and the unfree worlds. Abashed, he changed the subject to, where was I going next? When I said, 'Ulan Bator,' he laughed. When I wanted to know what was so funny, he said, 'I thought you said you were going to Ulan Bator.' When I told him that that was exactly where I was going, to the capital of the Mongolian People's Republic (sometimes known as Outer Mongolia), he looked very grave indeed. 'It is said', he whispered so that the ubiquitous KGB would not overhear us, 'that the British and French embassies have a spy at the airport and that anyone who looks promising is approached – oh, very furtively – and asked if he plays bridge. You did not hear this from me,' he added.

At midnight the plane leaves Moscow for Ulan Bator, with stops at Omsk and Irkutsk (in Siberia). The trip takes ten hours; there is a five-hour time difference between Moscow and Ulan Bator (UB to us fans). Moscow Aeroflot planes have a tendency to be on time, but the ceilings are too low for claustrophobes, and there is a curious smell of sour cream throughout the aircraft. Contrary to legend, the stewardesses are agreeable, at least on the Siberia run.

Our party included an English-born, Nairobi-based representative of the United Nations Environment Programme – White Hunter, his name. A representative of the World Wildlife Fund International who turned out to be a closet tweet-tweet – and was so named. And the photographer, Snaps. We were accompanied by the youthful Boris Petrovich, who has taught himself American English through the study of cassettes of what appears to have been every American film ever made. We had all met at the Rossya Hotel in Moscow. According to the Russians, it is the largest hotel in the world. Whether or not this is true, the Rossya's charm is not unlike that of New York's Attica. In the Soviet Union the foreigner is seldom without a low-level anxiety, which can, suddenly, develop into wall-climbing paranoia. *Where are the visas?* To which the inevitable Russian answer, 'No problem,' is ominous indeed.

Now our little group was being hurtled through the Siberian skies to a part of Outer Mongolia where no white – or, for that matter, black – Westerner had ever been before, or as one of our men at the American Embassy put it: 'You will be the first American ever to set foot in that part of the Gobi Desert.' I asked for my instructions. After all, those of us who believe in freedom must never not be busy. When I suggested that I might destabilize the Mongolian government while I was there, one of our men was slightly rattled. 'Actually,' he said, 'no American has ever been there because there isn't anything there.' My fierce patriotism was seriously tried by this insouciance. 'Then why', I asked, 'am I going?' He said he hadn't a clue. Why was I going?

It all came back to me on the night flight to Ulan Bator. The World Wildlife Fund has taken to sending writers around the world to record places where the ecology is out of joint. My task was a bit the reverse. I was to report on the national park that the Mongolian government is creating in the Gobi in order to keep pristine the environment so that flora and fauna can proliferate in a perfect balance with the environment.

As I stared out the porthole window at my own reflection (or was it Graham Greene's? The vodka bottle seemed familiar), my mind was awhirl with the intense briefings that I had been subjected to. For instance, is the People's Republic of Mongolia part of the Soviet Union? No. It is an independent socialist nation, grateful for the 'disinterested' aid that it gets from the other socialist nations. When did it come into being? Sixty years ago, when the Chinese were ejected and their puppet, the Living Buddha, was shorn of his powers and the twenty-eight-year-old Damdiny Sükh, known as

Ulan Bator (Red Hero in Mongolian), took charge of the state, with disinterested Soviet aid. Meanwhile, back at the Kremlin, Vladimir Ilyich Ulyanov Lenin was not entirely thrilled. Classic Marxism requires that a state evolve from feudalism to monarchy to capitalism and then to communism. As of 1920, whatever had been going on in Mongolia for two millennia, it was not capitalism. The people were nomadic. Every now and then, in an offhand way, they'd conquer the world. Genghis Khan ruled from the Danube to the Pacific Ocean, and some 1,200 years ago, according to one account, Mongol tribes crossed from Asia to North America via the Bering Strait, making the Western Hemisphere a sort of Mongol colony. Lenin knitted his brow and came up with the following concept: 'With the aid of the proletariat of the advanced countries, backward countries can go over to the Soviet system and, through certain stages of development, to communism, without having to pass through the capitalist stage.' So it came to pass. In sixty years an illiterate population has become totally literate, life expectancies have increased, industries and mining have taken the place of the old nomadic way of life, and there is a boom in population. 'Sixty per cent of the population', said Boris Petrovich, 'is under sixteen years of age.' Tweet-tweet looked grim. 'So much the worse for them,' he said. Boris Petrovich said, 'But, gosh, they need people here. Why, they've only got one and a half million people to one and a half million square kilometres. That's not enough people to feed themselves with.' As the environmental aspect was carefully explained to Boris Petrovich, his eyes lost their usual keenness. 'Should I', he asked me, changing the subject, 'buy Lauren Bacall's book?'

Jet lag and culture shock greeted us at the airport, where blue asters had broken through the landing strip. But no one was asked to play bridge, because we were whisked aboard an Air Mongolia plane and flown five more hours to the provincial capital of Gobi Altai, the southwestern province of Mongolia. At the foot of the Altai range of mountains is the town of Altai. Here we spent the night in a two-storey hotel on the main street, whose streetlamps did not turn on. Opposite the hotel is the police station. At the end of the street is a new hospital of raw cement.

We were given dinner by the deputy chairman of the province, the Soviet director of the park, and the deputy minister of forestry (under whose jurisdiction is the near-treeless Gobi), as well as two ministerial officials assigned to the United Nations Environment

Programme. Toasts were drunk as dishes of mutton came and went. Money is no longer flowing from the UN, White Hunter pointed out. The Reagan administration is cutting back. The Soviet Union is making a fair contribution to the fund, but – such is the Soviet sense of fun – the money is in unconvertible rubles. This means that the Soviet contribution can be spent only in the Soviet sphere. Hence, the Gobi park.

Although Mongolia smells of mutton fat, the Mongols smell not at all, even though the Russians go on about the great trouble they have getting them to bathe. Men and women are equally handsome: tall, narrow-waisted, with strong white teeth. Some wear the national tunic with sash and boots; others wear the international uniform of blue jeans. 'Why', I asked one of our Mongolian colleagues, 'are there no bald men here?' He was startled by the question. 'The old men shave their heads,' he said, as if this was an answer. Even so, there are no bald men to be seen anywhere. Our group came to the conclusion that over the millennia bald babies were exposed at birth.

As the evening ended, I had a sense of what the English call *déjà vu*. I had been in this company before. But where? It came to me: in my grandfather's state of Oklahoma, on one of the Indian reservations. Physically, the Mongolians are dead ringers for the Cherokees, whose nation my grandfather represented as an attorney in an effort to get some money for the land that the American government had stolen from them. All in all, the Russians are doing rather better by their Mongols than we are doing by ours.

I proposed a toast to Kublai Khan, 'China's great Mongol emperor, who opened up a peaceful discourse between East and West'. The Mongols at table were amused. The Russians less so. 'You know,' said one of the ministerials, 'we are making a number of movies about Mongolian history.' I did not ask if any of these films would deal with the 250-year Mongol occupation of Russia. The Russians still complain of their suffering during the Mongol occupation. 'Now', said the ministerial, 'we are making a movie about American Indians.' When I asked what the theme was, I got a vague answer. 'Oh, the . . . connections. You'll see.'

The next day there was rain in the Gobi. Something unheard of, we were told. In fact, there had been a flood a few days before, and many people were said to have been drowned. Due to bad weather, the plane would not take us to the encampment. So we set out on a grey afternoon in jeeps and Land Rovers. There is no road, only a more or less agreed-upon trail.

*

As we left Altai, we saw a bit of the town that Snaps and I had not been allowed to see earlier that morning, when we had set out to record the Real Life of the Mongols, who live in what the Russians call *yurtas* and the owners call *gers*: round tents, ingeniously made of felt, with a removable flap across the top to let out smoke. In winter the fire is lit in the morning for cooking; then it goes out until sundown, when it is lit again for the evening meal. Apparently the *yurtas* retain warmth in winter and are cool in summer. At Altai, every hundred or so *yurtas* are surrounded by wooden fences, 'to hold back the drifts of snow in winter,' said a Russian, or 'to keep them in their particular collective,' said a cynical non-Russian. Whatever, the wooden fences have curious binary devices on them: 'king's ring and queen's ring,' I was told by a Mongol – and no more.

Every time Snaps and I were close to penetrating one of the enclosures, a policeman would indicate that we should go back to the hotel. Meanwhile, the children would gather around until Snaps snapped; then they would shriek *nyet* and scamper off, only to return a moment later with many giggles. The older people quite liked being photographed, particularly the men on their ponies, whose faces – the ponies' – are out of prehistory, pendulous-lipped and sly of slanted eye. In costume, women wear boots; not in costume, they wear high heels as they stride over the dusty gravelled plain, simulating the camel's gait.

The Gobi Desert by Mildred Cable with Francesca French is an invaluable look at central Asia in the twenties and thirties by two lady missionaries who travelled the trade routes, taught the Word, practised medicine. 'The Mongol's home is his tent, and his nomadic life is the expression of a compelling instinct. A house is intolerable to him, and even the restricting sense of an enclosing city wall is unbearable.' One wonders what today's Mongols think, cooped up in their enclosures. 'They hate the new housing,' said one official. 'They put their animals and belongings in the apartment houses, and then they stay in their *yurtas*.' Others told me that, in general, the people are content, acclimatized to this bad century. 'The Mongol lives in and for the present, and looks neither backward toward his ancestors nor forward to his descendants.'

'Snaps, one word is worth a thousand pictures,' I said. 'Which word?' he asked. 'That would be telling,' I told him. But now comes the time when I must come to Snaps's aid and through the living word transmit to the reader's eye the wonder that is Mongolia when the monsoons are almost done with and the heat has dropped after July's 113 degrees Fahrenheit, when lizards cook in the Gobi.

*

We are in a jeep, lurching over rough terrain. The driver is young, wears a denim jacket, grins as he crashes over boulders. Picture now a grey streaked sky. In the distance a dun-coloured mountain range, smooth and rounded the way old earth is. We are not yet in the Gobi proper. There is water. Herds of yaks and camels cross the horizon. But once past this watered plain, the Gobi Desert begins – only it is not a proper desert. Sand is the exception, not the rule. Black and brown gravel is strewn across the plain. Occasional white salt slicks vary the monotony. All sorts of shy plants grow after a rain or near one of the rare springs. Actually, there is water under a lot of the Gobi, in some places only a few feet beneath the surface. For those who missed out on the journeys to the moon, the Gobi is the next-best thing.

'The word Gobi', authority tells us (*Géographie Universelle*, P. Vidal de la Blache et L. Gallois), 'is not the proper name of a geographical area, but a common expression used by Mongols to designate a definite order of geographical features. These are wide, shallow basins in which the smooth rocky bottom is filled with sand, pebbles, or, more often, with gravel.' *L'autre* Vidal tells us that, properly speaking, the Gobi covers a distance of 3,600 miles, 'from the Pamirs to the confines of Manchuria'. But in Mongolian Gobi, together with that part of the Gobi inside China to our south and west, is the Gobi's heart, once crossed by the old silk route that connected the Middle Kingdom with the West.

We arrive in darkness at Tsogt, a small town on whose edge is the fenced-in administrative centre of the park. We slept in spacious *yurtas*, worthy of the great Khan. In the dining *yurta* a feast of mutton had been prepared. We were joined by several Russian specialists connected with the park. One was a zoologist, given to wearing green camouflage outfits with a most rakish hat. Another had spent a winter in New York City, where 'every square metre costs one million dollars'.

Next day, at second or third light, we were shown a fuzzy film of all the fauna that the park contained, from wild Bactrian camels to wild bears to the celebrated snow leopard and, of course, the ubiquitous goat. But once the Gobi is entered, there are few herds to be seen, and only the occasional tweet, usually a kite or a variety of low-flying brown-and-white jay. As befits a World Wildlife Funder, Tweet-tweet was becoming unnaturally excited. Snaps, too, was in his heaven. Bliss to be in Gobi, almost.

After the film we boarded a plane that I had last flown in in 1935, and flew south across the Gobi, which I had last seen in the pages of the old *Life* magazine, *circa* 1935, as portrayed by Margaret Bourke-White. Time kept warping until I noticed that Snaps was furtively vomiting into his camera case; others were also queasy. When I suggested that air be admitted to the cabin, I was greeted with 1935 stares of disbelief. So we returned to base. We were then loaded into jeeps and crossed a low mountain range to the park itself.

On a high hill with dark mountains behind, the Gobi stretches as far as anyone could wish, its flatness broken by the odd mountain, set islandlike in the surrounding gravel. I got out of the jeep to commune with the silence. The driver started to pluck at small dark-green clumps of what turned out to be chives. We ate chives and looked at the view, and I proceeded to exercise the historical imagination and conjured up Genghis Khan on that famous day when he set his standard of nine yak tails high atop Gupta, and the Golden Horde began its conquest of Europe. 'Hey' – I heard the American-ized voice of Boris Petrovich – 'did any of you guys see *The Little Foxes* with Elizabeth Taylor?' A chorus of noes did not faze him. 'Well, why not?' It was Tweet-tweet who answered him. 'If you have gone to the theatre seriously all your life,' he said sternly, 'there are plays that you know in advance that you will not be caught dead at.' But Tweet-tweet had not reckoned with the Russian sense of fair play. 'How can you say that when you wouldn't even go *see* her in the play? I mean, so she was crucified by the reviewers . . .' Thus, put in our place, we descended into Gobi. Thoughts of Taylor's fleshy splendour had restored Genghis to wraithdom and dispersed the Horde.

We stopped at an oasis, a bright strip of ragged green in the dark shining gravel. Water bubbles up from the earth and makes a deep narrow stream down a low hill to a fenced-in place where a Mongol grows vegetables for the camp. The water is cool and pure, and the

Mongols with us stare at it for a time and smile; then they lie down on their bellies and drink deeply. We all do. In fact, it is hard to get enough water in Gobi. Is this psychological or physiological? The Mongol gardener showed me his plantation. 'The melons don't grow very large,' he apologized, holding up a golf ball of a melon. 'It is Gobi, you see.' I tried to explain to him that if he were to weed his patch, the vegetables would grow larger, but in that lunar landscape I suspect that the weeds are as much a delight to him as the melons.

As we lurched across the desert to the Yendiger Mountains, we passed an empty village where nomads used to winter. Whether or not they are still allowed in the park is a moot point. No straight answer was available. We were told that certain sections of the park are furrowed off – literally, a furrow is ploughed and, except for the park rangers, no human being may cross the furrow unless he wants to be detained for poaching. Are there many poachers? A few . . .

At the deserted village, each jeep took a different route toward the dark mountains in the distance. *En route*, the jeep that I was travelling in broke down four times. Long after the others had arrived at camp, our group was comfortably seated on a malachite-green rock, sipping whisky from the bottle and watching the sun pull itself together for a Gobi Special Sunset, never to be forgotten. Tweet-tweet said that in the Galapagos Islands Tom Stoppard had worked out a numeric scale with which to measure the tasteless horror of each successive night's overwrought sunset. But I defended our Gobi Special. For once, Mother Nature was the soul of discreet good taste. Particularly the northern sky, where clouds like so many plumes of Navarre had been dipped in the most subtle shade of Du Barry grey, while the pale orange of the southern sky did not cloy. True, there was a *pink* afterglow in the east. But then perfection has never been Mother Nature's ideal.

The jeep functional, we drove between dark brown rocks along the bottom of what looked to be an ancient riverbed until we came to a turn in the ravine, and there was the campsite. In a row: one *yurta*, a dozen pup tents, a truck that contained a generator. 'This is the first electricity ever to shine in this part of Gobi,' said the Soviet director. As the Mongol lads strung electric lines from tent to tent, Snaps, with narrowed eyes and camera poised, waited. 'You never know', he whispered, 'when you'll get a shot of electrified Mongol. *Tremendous* market for that, actually.'

We were told that close to camp there is a famous watering hole where, at sundown, the snow leopard lies down, as it were, with the wild ass. But we had missed sundown. Nevertheless, ever game, our party walked halfway to the hole before settling among rocks on the ridge to fortify ourselves with alien spirits against the black desert night that had fallen with a crash about us. As we drank, we were joined by a large friendly goat. Overhead, the stars (so much more satisfactory than the ones beneath our feet) shone dully: rain clouds were interfering with the Gobi's usual surefire light show. I found the Dipper; it was in the wrong place. There was a sharp difference of agreement on the position of Orion's Belt. Shooting stars made me think, comfortably, of war. I showed Boris Petrovich what looked to be one of the Great Republic's newest satellites. 'Keeping watch over the Soviet Union,' I said. 'Unless', he said, 'it is one of our missiles on its way to Washington. But, seriously,' he added, 'don't you agree that Elizabeth Taylor was a first-rate *movie* actress? You know, like Susan Hayward.'

First light seized us from our pup tents, where we had slept upon the desert floor, inhaling the dust of millennia. As I prepared for a new day of adventure, sinuses aflame, there was a terrible cry, then a sob, a gasp – silence. Our friend of the evening before, the goat, was now to be our dinner.

We checked out the watering hole, which turned out to be a muddy place in the rocks; there were no signs of beasts. Again we were on the move, this time southeasterly toward the Mount Mother system. The heat was intense. We glimpsed a wild ass, wildly running up ahead of us. Some gazelles skittered in the distance. The country-side was almost always horizontal but never pleasingly flat. To drive over such terrain is like riding a Wild West bronco. As we penetrated deeper into the preserve, vegetation ceased. What thornwood there was no longer contained greenery. Thornwood – with camel and goat dung – provides the nomads with their fuel. We were told that poachers are more apt to steal the wood in the preserve than the animals.

Suddenly, all of our jeeps converged on the same spot, close to the steep dark-red Khatan Khairkhan, an island of rock rising from a dry sea. The drivers gathered around a circle of white sand some six feet in diameter. Three spurts of icy water bubbled at the circle's centre. Again, the happy smiles. Mongols stare at water rather the way northerners stare at fires. Then each of us tried the water. It

tasted like Badoit. Camel and wild-ass dung in the immediate vicinity
testified to its excellent, even curative, mineral qualities.

Halfway up the red mountain, we made camp at the mouth of
a ravine lined with huge, smooth red rocks. Glacial? Remains of a
sea that had long since gone away? No geologist was at hand to tell
us, but in the heights above the ravine were the Seven Cauldrons of
Khatan Khairkhan, where, amongst saxaul groves and elm trees, the
waters have made seven rock basins, in which Tweet-tweet and White
Hunter disported themselves while Snaps recorded the splendours of
nature. The author, winded halfway up, returned to camp and read
Mme de La Fayette's *La Princesse de Clèves*.

That night our friend the goat was served in the famous Mongolian hot pot. Red-hot rocks are dropped into metal pots containing
whatever animal has been sacrificed to man's need. The result is
baked to a tee. As usual, I ate tomatoes, cucumbers, and bread. We
drank to the Golden Horde, now divided in three parts: Outer
Mongolia, which is autonomous, thanks to the 'disinterested' Soviet
Union's presence; Inner Mongolia, which is part of China and filling
up with highly interested Chinese; and Siberia, which contains a large
Mongolian population. Since functioning monasteries are not allowed
in China or Siberia, practising Buddhists come to Ulan Bator, where
there are a large school, a lamasery, and the Living Buddha. This
particular avatar is not the result of the usual search for the exact
incarnation practised in ancient times. He was simply selected to
carry on.

Even rarer than a functioning lamasery in Mongolia is Przhevalski's horse. These horses exist in zoos around the world, but whether
or not they are still to be found in Gobi is a subject of much
discussion. Some think that there are a few in the Chinese part of
the Gobi; some think that they are extinct there. In any case, the
Great Gobi National Park plans to reintroduce – from the zoos –
Przhevalski's horse to its original habitat. We drank to the Przhevalski
horse. We drank to the plane that was to pick us up the next morning
when we returned to base. 'Will it really be there?' I asked. 'No
problem.'

At dawn we lurched across the desert beneath a lowering sky. At
Tsogt there was no plane. 'No problem.' We would drive four or
five hours to Altai. Along the way we saw the marks that our tyres
had made on the way down. 'In Gobi, tracks may last fifty years,'
one of the Russians said.

At the Altai airport low-level anxiety went swiftly to high: the plane for Ulan Bator might not take off. Bad weather. The deputy minister of forestry made a ministerial scene, and the plane left on time. There was not a cloud on the route. We arrived at dusk. The road from the airport to the city passes beneath not one but two huge painted arches. From the second arch, Ulan Bator in its plain circled by mountains looks very large indeed. Four hundred thousand people live and have their being beneath a comforting industrial smog. As well as the usual fenced-off *yurtas*, there are high-rise apartment houses, an opera house, a movie palace, functioning street-lamps, and rather more neon than one sees in, say, Rome. Although our mood was gala as we settled in at the Ulan Bator Hotel, low-level anxiety never ceased entirely to hum. Would the visas for the Soviet Union be ready in time? Had the plane reservations for Moscow and the West been confirmed? Would we get back, the passports that we had surrendered upon arrival?

*

The next day, our questions all answered with 'No problem,' we saw the sights of Ulan Bator. A museum with a room devoted to odd-shaped dinosaur eggs, not to mention the skeletons of the dinosaurs that had laid them. Every public place was crowded. A convention of Mongol experts was in town; there was also a delegation of Buddhists, paying their respects to the Living Buddha, who would be, his secretary told me, too busy with the faithful to receive us that day. Undaunted, Snaps and I made our way to the Buddhist enclosure, where we found several temples packed with aged priests and youthful acolytes with shaved heads. As the priests read aloud from strips of paper on which are printed Sanskrit and Tibetan texts, their voices blend together like so many bees in a hive while incense makes blue the air and bells tinkle at odd intervals to punctuate the still-living texts. In a golden robe, the Living Buddha sat on a dais. As the faithful circled him in an unending stream, he maintained a costive frown. Outside, aged costumed Mongols of both sexes sat about the enclosure, at a millennium's remove from cement block and Aeroflot.

The United Kingdom's man in Ulan Bator, James Paterson, received us at the British Embassy. Outside, a suspicious policeman stands guard with a walkie-talkie, keeping close watch not only on the ambassador and his visitors but on the various Mongols who paused in front of the embassy to look at the colour photographs, under glass, of the wedding of the Prince and Princess of Wales. The Mongols would study the pictures carefully and then, suddenly, smile beatifically. How very like, I could practically hear them say to themselves, our own imperial family – the Khans of yesteryear!

Paterson is tall and tweedy with a charming wife (in central Asia all of us write like the late Somerset Maugham). 'I am allowed to jog,' he said. 'But permission must be got to make trips.' Since he knew that I was asking myself the one question that visitors to UB ask themselves whenever they meet a non-Communist ambassador (there are four, from Britain, France, Canada, and India) – What on earth did you *do* to be sent here?' – he brought up the subject and laughed, I think, merrily. He was raised in China; he was fascinated by the Mongol world – unlike the French ambassador who, according to diplomats in Moscow, used to go about Ulan Bator muttering, 'I am here because they fear me at the Quai d'Orsay.' When I asked Paterson where the French ambassador was, I was told, 'He is no longer here.' Tact, like holly at Christmas, festooned the modest sitting room, where a much-fingered month-old *Economist* rested on the coffee table.

A reception was given us by the minister of forestry. He is a heavyset man with grey hair and a face much like that of the old drawings of Kublai Khan. He hoped that we had enjoyed the visit to the park. He hoped that there would be more money from the United Nations, but if there should be no more, he quite understood. White Hunter found this a bit ominous, as he favours further UN funding of the park. Tourism was discussed: a new guest complex would be built at Tsogt. The plans look handsome. Room for only eighteen people – plainly, a serious place for visiting scientists. Elsewhere, hunters are catered for.

Tweet-tweet spoke eloquently of the Wildlife Fund's work around the world. 'Under its president, Prince Philip,' he intoned. The Mongol translator stopped. 'Who?' Tweet-tweet repeated the name, adding, 'The husband of our queen.' The translator could not have been more gracious. 'The husband of *whose* queen?' he asked. Tweet-tweet went on to say that if it were not for the politicians, there would be world peace and cooperation, and the environment would be saved. I noticed that the minister's highly scrutable Oriental face, so unlike our veiled Occidental ones, was registering dismay. I interrupted. 'As one politician to another,' I said, 'even though I have just lost an election, having polled only a half-million votes' – roughly a third of the population of Mongolia, I thought, in a sudden frenzy of demophilia – 'I am as peace-loving as, I am sure, His Excellency is.' I got a wink from the minister, and after dinner a powerful pinch of snuff. Even in Mongolia, we pols must stick together in a world made dangerous for us by well-meaning Tweet-tweets.

The next day all was in order; there was indeed no problem. The ten-hour trip took place in daylight. As we stretched our legs in Omsk, White Hunter noticed a handsome blonde girl beyond the airport railings. He turned to Boris Petrovich. 'What are the girls like here?' Boris Petrovich shook his head. 'Well, I was only here once, when I was on the junior basketball team. We played everywhere.' White Hunter said, 'You mean you didn't make out?' Boris Petrovich looked shocked. 'Well, gosh, I was only sixteen.' I told him that in the United States many males at sixteen have not only passed their sexual peak but are burned-out cases. Boris Petrovich's eyes glittered. 'I'll bet there are some movies on that,' he said. 'You know, that soft-porn stuff on cassettes.'

Before our party separated at the Moscow airport, we agreed that the Great Gobi National Park was a serious affair and not a front for Soviet missiles or, worse, a hunters' paradise with Gobi bears and snow leopards as the lure. Snaps was thrilled with the Buddhist pictures; less thrilled with the Gobi, 'of an ugliness not to be reproduced'; pleased with the pictures of the people, though we had failed to penetrate a single *yurta*. White Hunter had hopes that the United Nations would raise enough money to keep the park going. Tweet-tweet was satisfied that wildlife was being tended to. Meanwhile, Boris Petrovich darted between the two groups – one headed for London, one for Rome.

As I was leaving the reception area, he made a small speech about the necessity of good Soviet-American relations, the importance of world peace, the necessity of cooperation on environmental matters. Then he lowered his voice. 'I have a question to ask you.' He looked about to see if we were being overheard. Thus, I thought to myself, Philby was recruited. Swiftly, I made my decision. If I were to sell out the free world, I must be well paid. I would want a dacha on the Baltic, near Riga. I would want . . . 'How tall', asked Boris Petrovich, 'is Paul Newman, really?'

* * *

NYOSHUL KHENPO RINPOCHE (1932–)

'Enlightened Vagabond'

I lived in India for twenty-five years by myself, without accumulating anything, just one old man alone, sometimes walking around in red Tibetan-style lama clothes, sometimes in old orange or yellow *sadhu* robes or simple wraps. Sometimes I gave Dharma talks inside monasteries. I also stayed sometimes with sadhus in Rishikesh and Haridwar, along the Ganges, in ashrams, huts, lean-tos, under trees, wherever the descent of dusk found me. So many different dream-like experiences! Sometimes I was exalted and quite comfortable, more often I was bereft and poverty-stricken. Yet the inexhaustible wealth of inner truth and peace that is the Dharma always sustained me well. Sometimes I gave empowerments to great assemblies of people, including dozens of tulkus and lamas, where they put a golden initiation vase in my hand and I placed it on the heads of thousands of monks. At other times I was utterly poor, living hand-to-mouth on the streets in Calcutta, wandering around with my hand out begging for pennies. So many unexpected ups and downs, who can describe them? Life is like that, full of unexpected twists and turns – illusory, impermanent, ungovernable, and unstable. And in the end, we all die. What a spectacle!

So many different experiences, memories, and reflections – some good and some bad – just like different kinds of dreams. One night in 1959 I was with about seventy people who were escaping together from Tibet, and a few thousand Chinese soldiers were in the surrounding mountains, searching for fugitives in the darkness. The soldiers suddenly opened fire, and machine gun bullets and tracers flew everywhere. Of the seventy in my party, only five could be found alive the next day. I don't know what happened to the rest. Our small band of five continued on foot through the high Himalayan passes to India, following in the footsteps of the Dalai Lama, seeking refuge in Assam, Bhutan, Darjeeling, and Kalimpong – wherever food, shelter, and political asylum were to be found.

I then lived in the lowlands as a refugee for years, in exile from the Land of Snows, huddled with others in crowded refugee camps and steamy trains, collecting alms in hot and dusty Indian streets. Some years later I unexpectedly found myself riding across vast oceans in jet airplanes, and coasting up and down the length of giant needle-shaped skyscrapers in boxcar-like air-conditioned elevators in the great capitals of the modern world, sleeping in both grand hotels and on the rugs and couches of modern living rooms, eating in restaurants and outdoors on sunny patios, being served like a king.

In the early seventies, I seemed to have a stroke and almost died. Some think I was poisoned in a restaurant in Kalimpong. My nervous system was traumatized; I was a complete invalid for several years. Before that, I had given vast and profound teachings and cycles of empowerments to many people, including monks, lamas, tulkus, and laypersons, all over the Himalayan region. Afterwards, I could not see very well, I was lame, my hands shook, and I was expected to die. During that difficult time I was cared for in Kangyur Rinpoche's monastery in Darjeeling. Kangyur Rinpoche and his family graciously cared for me. I always think of them with profound gratitude and respect. Lama Sonam Tobgyal from Riwoché Gompa was my faithful attendant for six years during that period, in India and later in Europe.

The grand yogi-master of Bhutan, Lopon Sonam Zangpo, suggested to me that if I would take a wife and undertake longevity practices my health would improve. (I had been a monk until this time.) The old and venerable yogi, who was the father of Trinley Norbu Rinpoche's late wife, arranged for me to marry Damcho Zangmo, who proved to be a perfectly suitable long-life consort and wife. We have been together since then . . .

*

Isn't life like a movie or a dream, like a series of dreams within a vast, dream-like mirage? How to possibly remember all the different scenes that inevitably transpired from the time that I was an illiterate little scamp in Kham until now, when I am a talkative old vagabond with white hair, glasses, and wrinkles? What a surprise! Old and bent already. What a spectacle! A dim-sighted aged Tibetan tourist peering around at foreign lands. *Emaho*! Marvellous! Wonderful!

* * *

INDIA

V. S. NAIPAUL (1932–)

'The Village of the Dubes'

The Emergency was over. And so was my year. The short winter was fading fast; it was no longer pleasant to sit out in the sun; the dust would not now be laid until the monsoon. One journey remained, and for this I had lost taste. India had not worked its magic on me. It remained the land of my childhood, an area of darkness; like the Himalayan passes, it was closing up again, as fast as I withdrew from it, into a land of myth; it seemed to exist in just the timelessness which I had imagined as a child, into which, for all that I walked on Indian earth, I knew I could not penetrate.

In a year I had not learned acceptance. I had learned my separateness from India, and was content to be a colonial, without a past, without ancestors. Duty alone had brought me to this town in eastern Uttar Pradesh, not even graced by a ruin, celebrated only for its connexions with the Buddha and its backwardness. And it was duty that, after a few days of indecision, idleness and reading, was taking me along this country road, infested with peasants indifferent to wheeled vehicles, to the village which my mother's father had left as an indentured labourer more than sixty years before.

When you drive through parts of western and central India you wonder about the teeming millions; settlements are so few, and the brown land looks so unfruitful and abandoned. Here wonder was of another sort. The land was flat. The sky was high blue and utterly without drama; below it everything was diminished. Wherever you looked there was a village, low, dust-blurred, part of the earth and barely rising out of it. Every tiny turbulence of dust betrayed a peasant; and the land was nowhere still.

At a junction we took on a volunteer guide and turned off on to an embankment of pure dust. It was lined with tall old trees. Below them my grandfather had doubtless walked at the start of his journey. In spite of myself I was held. For us this land had ceased to exist. Now it was so ordinary. I did not really want to see more. I was afraid of what I might find, and I had witnesses. Not that one, not that, cried the guide, excited both by my mission and the unexpected jeep ride, as village after village died in our dust. Presently he pointed: there on our right, was the village of the Dubes.

It was set far back from the embankment. It exceeded anything I had expected. A large mango grove gave it a pastoral aspect, and two spires showed white and clean against the dark green foliage. I knew about those spires and was glad to see them. My grandfather had sought to re-establish the family he had left behind in India. He had recovered their land; he had given money for the building of a temple. No temple had been built, only three shrines. Poverty, fecklessness, we had thought in Trinidad. But now, from the road, how reassuring those spires were!

We got out of the jeep and made our way over the crumbling earth. The tall, branching mango trees shaded an artificial pond, and the floor of the grove was spotted with blurred sunshine. A boy came out. His thin body was naked save for his dhoti and sacred thread. He looked at me suspiciously – our party was large and ferociously official – but when the IAS officer who was with me explained who I was, the boy attempted first to embrace me and then to touch my feet. I disengaged myself and he led us through the village, talking of the complicated relationship that bound him to my grandfather and to me. He knew all about my grandfather. To this village that old adventure remained important: my grandfather had gone far beyond the sea and had made *barra paisa*, much money.

A year before I might have been appalled by what I was seeing. But my eye had changed. This village looked unusually prosperous; it was even picturesque. Many of the houses were of brick, some raised off the earth, some with carved wooden doors and tiled roofs. The lanes were paved and clean; there was a concrete cattle-trough. 'Brahmin village, brahmin village,' the IAS man whispered. The women were unveiled and attractive, their saris white and plain. They regarded us frankly, and in their features I could recognize those of the women of my family. 'Brahmin women,' the IAS man whispered. 'Very fearless.'

It was a village of Dubes and Tiwaris, all brahmins, all more or less related. A man, clad in loincloth and sacred thread, was bathing, standing and pouring water over himself with a brass jar. How elegant his posture, how fine his slender body! How, in the midst of populousness and dereliction, had such beauty been preserved? They were brahmins; they rented land for less than those who could afford less. But the region, as the *Gazeteer* said, 'abounds in brahmins'; they formed twelve to fifteen per cent of the Hindu population. Perhaps this was why, though they were all related in the village, there appeared to be no communal living. We left the brick houses behind and, to my disappointment, stopped in front of a small thatched hut. Here resided Ramachandra, the present head of my grandfather's branch of the Dubes.

He was away. Oh, exclaimed the men and boys who had joined us, why did he have to choose this day? But the shrines, they would show me the shrines. They would show me how well they had been kept; they would show me my grandfather's name carved on the shrines. They unlocked the grilled doors and showed me the images, freshly washed, freshly dressed, marked with fresh sandalwood paste, the morning's offerings of flowers not yet faded. My mind leapt years, my sense of distance and time was shaken: before me were the very replicas of the images in the prayer-room of my grandfather's house.

An old woman was crying.

'Which son? Which one?'

And it was seconds before I realized that the old woman's words were in English.

'Jussodra!' the men said, and opened a way for her. She was on her haunches and in this posture was advancing towards me, weeping, screeching out words in English and Hindi. Her pale face was cracked like drying mud; her grey eyes were dim.

'Jussodra will tell you all about your grandfather,' the men said.

Jussodra had also been to Trinidad; she knew my grandfather. We were both led from the shrine to the hut. I was made to sit on a blanket on a string bed; and Jussodra, squatting at my feet, recited my grandfather's genealogy and recounted his adventures, weeping while the IAS officer translated. For thirty-six years Jussodra had lived in this village, and in that time she had polished her story into a fluent Indian *khisa* or fairytale. It could not have been unknown, but everyone was solemn and attentive.

When he was a young man (Jussodra said) my grandfather left

this village to go to Banaras to study, as brahmins had immemorially done. But my grandfather was poor, his family poor, and times were hard; there might even have been a famine. One day my grandfather met a man who told him of a country far away called Trinidad. There were Indians in Trinidad, labourers; they needed pundits and teachers. The wages were good, land was cheap and a free passage could be arranged. The man who spoke to my grandfather knew what he was talking about. He was an *arkatia*, a recruiter; when times were good he might be stoned out of a village, but now people were willing to listen to his stories. So my grandfather indentured himself for five years and went to Trinidad. He was not, of course, made a teacher; he worked in the sugar factory. He was given a room, he was given food; and in addition he received twelve annas, fourteen pence, a day. It was a lot of money, and even today it was a good wage in this part of India, twice as much as the government paid for relief work in distress areas. My grandfather added to this by doing his pundit's work in the evenings. Banaras-trained pundits were rare in Trinidad and my grandfather was in demand. Even the sahib at the factory respected him, and one day the sahib said, 'You are a pundit. Can you help me? I want a son.' 'All right,' my grandfather said. 'I'll see that you get a son.' And when the sahib's wife gave birth to a son, the sahib was so pleased he said to my grandfather, 'You see these thirty *bighas* of land? All the canes there are yours.' My grandfather had the canes cut and sold them for two thousand rupees, and with this he went into business. Success attracted success. A well-to-do man, long settled in Trinidad, came to my grandfather one day and said, 'I've been keeping my eye on you for some time. I can see that you are going to go far. Now I have a daughter and would like her to be married to you. I will give you three acres of land.' My grandfather was not interested. Then the man said, 'I will give you a buggy. You can hire out the buggy and make a little extra money.' So my grandfather married. He prospered. He built two houses. Soon he was wealthy enough to come back to this village and redeem twenty-five acres of his family's land. Then he went back to Trinidad. But he was a restless man. He decided to make another trip to India. 'Come back quick,' his family said to him. (Jussodra spoke these words in English: 'buggy' had also been in English.) But my grandfather didn't see Trinidad again. On the train from Calcutta he fell ill, and he wrote to his family: 'The sun is setting.'

Her story finished, Jussodra wept and wept, and no one moved.

'What do I do?' I asked the IAS officer. 'She is very old. Will I offend her if I offer her some money?'

'It will be most welcome,' he said. 'Give her some money and tell her to arrange a *kattha*, a reading of the scriptures.'

I did so.

Photographs were then brought out, as old to me and as forgotten as the images; and it was again disturbing to my sense of place and time to handle them, to see, in the middle of a vast land where I was anchored to no familiar points and could so easily be lost, the purple stamp of the Trinidad photographer – his address, so clearly pictured – still bright against the fading sepia figure, in my reawakened memory forever faded, belonging to imagination and never to reality like this.

I had come to them reluctantly. I had expected little, and I had been afraid. The ugliness was all mine.

Someone else wanted to see me. It was Ramachandra's wife and she was waiting in one of the inner rooms. I went in. A white-clad figure was bowed before me; she seized my feet, in all their Veldt-schoen, and began to weep. She wept and would not let go.

'What do I do now?' I asked the IAS officer.

'Nothing. Soon someone will come in and tell her that this is no way to receive a relation, that she should be offering him food instead. It is the form.'

So it happened.

But food. Though they had overwhelmed me, my colonial prudence remained. It had prevented me emptying my pocket into Jussodra's sad, wrinkled hands. Now it reminded me of the Commissioner's advice: 'Once it's cooked, you can risk it. But never touch the water.' He, however, was of the country. So: no food, I said. I was not very well and had been put on a diet.

'Water,' Ramachandra's wife said. 'At least have water.'

The IAS officer said, 'You see that field? It is a field of peas. Ask for some of those.'

We ate a pod of peas each. I promised to come back again; the boys and men walked with us to the jeep; and I drove back along a road that had been robbed of all its terror.

*

In the hotel in the town that evening I wrote a letter. The day had provided such an unlikely adventure. It distorted time; again and again I came back, with wonder, to my presence in that town, in that hotel, at that hour. There had been those images, those photographs, those scraps of Trinidad English in that Indian village. The letter did not exhaust my exaltation. The act of writing released not isolated memories but a whole forgotten mood. The letter finished, I went to sleep. Then there was a song, a duet, at first part of memory, it seemed, part of that recaptured mood. But I was not dreaming; I was lucid. The music was real.

> Tumhin ne mujhko prem sikhaya,
> Soté hué hirdaya ko jagaya.
> Tumhin ho roop singar balam.[1]

It was morning. The song came from a shop across the road. It was a song of the late thirties. I had ceased to hear it years before, and until this moment I had forgotten it. I did not even know the meaning of all the words; but then I never had. It was pure mood, and in that moment between waking and sleeping it had recreated a morning in another world, a recreation of this, which continued. And walking that day in the bazaar, I saw the harmoniums, one of which had lain broken and unused, part of the irrecoverable past, in my grandmother's house, the drums, the printing-blocks, the brass vessels. Again and again I had that sense of dissolving time, that alarming but exhilarating sense of wonder at my physical self.

At the barber shop, where I stopped for a shave and begged in vain for hot water, exaltation died. I became again an impatient traveller. The sun was high; the faint morning chill had been burnt away.

I returned to the hotel and found a beggar outside my door.

'Kya chahiye?' I asked, in my poor Hindi. 'What do you want?'

He looked up. His head was shaved, except for the top-knot; his face was skeletal; his eyes blazed. My impatience momentarily turned to alarm. Monk, I thought, monk; I had been reading *Karamazov*.

---

1. You gave my love meaning.
   You awoke my sleeping heart.
   My beauty is you, my lover,
       my jewels are you.
   The translation is by my friend Aley Hasan of the BBC Indian Section.

'I am Ramachandra Dube,' he said. 'I did not see you yesterday.'

I had expected someone less ingratiating, less of a physical wreck. His effort at a smile did not make his expression warmer. Spittle, white and viscous, gathered at the corners of his mouth.

There were some IAS cadets in the hotel. Three of them came to act as interpreters.

'I have spent all day looking for you,' Ramachandra said.

'Tell him I thank him,' I said. 'But there was really no need. I told them at the village I was coming back. Ask him, though, how he found me. I left no address.'

He had walked for some miles; then he had taken a train to the town; then he had gone around the secretariat, asking for the IAS officer who had taken out a man from Trinidad.

While the cadets translated, Ramachandra smiled. His face, I now saw, was not the face of a monk but of someone grossly undernourished; his eyes were bright with illness; he was painfully thin. He was carrying a large white sack. This he now humped with difficulty on to my table.

'I have brought you some rice from your grandfather's land,' he said. 'I have also brought you *parsad*, offerings, from your grandfather's shrine.'

'What do I do?' I asked the cadets. 'I don't want thirty pounds of rice.'

'He doesn't want you to take it all. You just take a few grains. Take the *parsad*, though.'

I took a few grains of the poor rice, and took the *parsad*, grubby little grey beads of hard sugar, and placed them on the table.

'I have been looking for you all day,' Ramachandra said.

'I know.'

'I walked, then I took a train, then I walked around the town and asked for you.'

'It was good of you to take all that trouble.'

'I want to see you. I want to have you in my poor hut and to give you a meal.'

'I am coming back to the village in a few days.'

'I have been looking for you all day.'

'I know.'

'I want to have you in my hut. I want to talk to you.'

'We will talk when I come to the village.'

'I want to see you there. I want to talk to you. I have important things to say to you.'

'We will talk when the time comes.'

'Good. Now I will leave you. I have been looking for you all day. I have things to say to you. I want to have you in my hut.'

'I can't keep this up,' I said to the IAS cadets. 'Tell him to go away. Thank him and so on, but tell him to go.'

One of the cadets passed on my message, involving and extending it with expressions of courtesy.

'Now I must leave you,' Ramachandra replied. 'I must get back to the village before dark.'

'Yes, I can see that you must get back before dark.'

'But how can I talk to you in the village?'

'I will bring an interpreter.'

'I want to have you in my poor hut. I have spent all day looking for you. In the village there are too many people. How can I talk to you in the village?'

'Why can't you talk to me in the village? Can't we really get him out?'

They eased him towards the door.

'I have brought you rice from your grandfather's land.'

'Thank you. It will get dark soon.'

'I want to talk to you when you come.'

'We will talk.'

The door was closed. The cadets went away. I lay down on the bed below the fan. Then I had a shower. I was towelling myself when I heard a scratching on the barred window.

It was Ramachandra, in the veranda, attempting a smile. I summoned no interpreters. I needed none to understand what he was saying.

'I cannot talk in the village. There are too many people.'

'We will talk in the village,' I said in English. 'Now go home. You travel too much.' By signs I persuaded him to edge away from the window. Quickly, then, I drew the curtains.

*

Some days passed before I decided to go back to the village. The journey began badly. There was some trouble about transport and it was not until the middle of the afternoon that we were able to leave. Our progress was slow. It was market day at the junction settlement and the road was dangerous with carts, now occupying the right-hand lane, now changing without warning to the left, their manoeuvres obscured by clouds of dust. Dust was thick and constant; it obliterated trees, fields, villages. There were traffic jams, the carts inextricably snarled, the drivers then as passive as their bullocks.

At the junction it was simple chaos. I breathed dust. There was dust in my hair, dust down my shirt, dust, nauseatingly, on my fingernails. We halted and waited for the traffic to clear. Then our driver disappeared, taking the ignition key. It was useless to look for him: that would only have meant groping about in the dust. We sat in the jeep and occasionally sounded the horn. Half an hour later the driver returned. His eyelashes, moustache and oiled hair were blond with dust, but his smile was wet and triumphant: he had managed to buy some vegetables. It was late afternoon when we got on to the embankment; and the sun was setting, converting the dust into clouds of pure gold, so that each person walked in a golden aura, when we arrived at the village. No terror attached to the land now, no surprise. I felt I knew it well. Yet some anxiety remained: the village held Ramachandra.

He was waiting for me. He was without the cloak he had worn to the hotel. He wore only a dhoti and sacred thread, and I could scarcely bear to look at his emaciated, brittle body. As soon as he saw me he held himself in an attitude of ecstatic awe: shaved shining head thrown back, eyes staring, foam-flecked mouth resolutely closed, both sticks of arms raised. We already had an audience, and he was demonstrating his possession of me. It was seconds before he relaxed.

'He says God has sent you to him,' my IAS friend said.

'We'll see.'

The IAS man converted this into a formal greeting.

'Would you like something to eat in his poor hut?'

'No.'

'You must at least have some water.'

'I am not thirsty.'

'You are rejecting his hospitality because he is a poor man.'

'He can take it that way.'

'A mouthful of food.'

'Tell him it is late. Tell him you have to investigate that embezzle-ment of the National Defence Fund you were telling me about.'

'He says God has sent you to him today.'

'I don't think I can keep this up much longer. Ask him what he wanted to see me about.'

'He says he won't tell you until you eat something in his poor hut.'

'Tell him good-bye.'

'He believes you might appreciate a little privacy.'

He led us through his hut into a small paved courtyard, where his wife, she who had held on to my Veldtschoen and wept, squatted in one corner, her head decorously covered, and made a pretence of scouring some brass vessels.

Ramachandra paced up and down. Then: wouldn't I eat?

The IAS man interpreted my silence.

It was really quite remarkable, Ramachandra said, that I had come to the village just at that time. He was, as it happened, in a little trouble. He was thinking of starting a little piece of litigation, but the litigation he had just concluded had cost him two hundred rupees and he was short of cash.

'But that solves his problems. He can simply forget the new litigation.'

'How can he forget it? This new litigation concerns you.'

'Me?'

'It is about your grandfather's land, the land that produced the rice he gave you. That is why God sent you here. Your grandfather's land is now only nineteen acres, and some of that will be lost if he can't get this new litigation started. If that happens, who will look after your grandfather's shrines?'

I urged Ramachandra to forget litigation and the shrines and to concentrate on the nineteen acres. That was a lot of land, nineteen acres more than I had, and he could get much help from the government. He knew, he knew, he said indulgently. But his body – he turned his long bony back to me, and the movement was not without pride – was wasted; he devoted himself to religious austerities; he spent four hours a day looking after the shrines. And there was this litigation he wanted to get started. Besides, what could be got out of nineteen acres?

Our discussion remained circular. The IAS man didn't help; he softened all my sharpness into courtesy. Outright refusal didn't release me: it only enabled Ramachandra to start afresh. Release would come only when I left. And this I at last did, suddenly, followed out to the grove by many men and all the boys of the village.

Ramachandra kept up with me, smiling, bidding me farewell, proclaiming his possession of me till the last. One man, clearly his rival, sturdier, handsomer, more dignified, presented me with a letter and withdrew; the ink on the envelope was still wet. A boy ran out to the jeep, tucking his shirt into his trousers, and asked for a lift into the town. While Ramachandra had been outlining his plans for litigation, while the letter was being written, this boy had hurriedly bathed, dressed and prepared his bundle; his clothes were fresh, his hair still wet. My visit had thrown the brahmins into a frenzy of activity. Too much had been assumed; I felt overwhelmed; I wished to extricate myself at once.

'Shall we take him on?' the IAS man asked, nodding towards the boy.

'No, let the idler walk.'

We drove off. I did not wave. The headlamps of the jeep shot two separate beams into the day's slowly settling dust which, made turbulent again by our passage, blotted out the scattered lights of the village.

So it ended, in futility and impatience, a gratuitous act of cruelty, self-reproach and flight.

★   ★   ★

PIER PAOLO PASOLINI (1922–1975)

from *Scent of India*

It is almost midnight. At the Taj Mahal the atmosphere is one of a market closing. The big hotel, one of the most famous in the world, is riddled from one side to the other by corridors and high saloons (like seeing the inside of an enormous musical instrument), peopled only by 'boys' clothed in white, and by porters in festive turbans waiting for dubious taxis to pass. It is not the moment, it is really not the moment to go to bed, in those rooms as big as dormitories, full of furniture of the miserable, retarded twentieth century, with ventilators which seem like helicopters.

These are the first hours of my presence in India, and I don't know how to calm the thirsty beast trapped within me as in a cage.

I persuade Moravia to make at least a short stroll outside the hotel, and to breathe a little of the air of our first Indian night.

So we go out through the secondary exit on to the narrow sea promenade that runs behind the hotel. The sea is calm, giving no sign of its presence. Along the little embankment which contains it there are some cars parked and, near to them, are those fabulous beings without roots, without consciousness, full of ambiguous and disturbing meaning, but endowed with powerful fascination, who are the first Indians with experiences, experiences which desire to be exclusive, like mine.

They are all beggars, or the kind of people who live at the edges of a big hotel, experts in its functional and secret life: they wear a white rag which covers their thighs, another rag on their shoulders and, some of them, another rag around the head: they are almost all black-skinned, like negroes, some very black.

There is a group of them under the porticoes of the Taj Mahal, towards the sea, youngsters and boys: one of them is mutilated, with 'corroded' limbs, and is stretched out wrapped in his rags as if he were in front of a church instead of a hotel. The others wait, silent, ready.

I don't yet understand what their duty or their hope is. I look at them sideways on, chattering with Moravia, who was here twenty-four years ago and knows the world well enough not to be in the painful state I find myself.

On the sea there is no light, no sound: here we are almost at the point of a long peninsula, a horn of the bay which forms the port of Bombay: the port is in the distance. Under the little wall there are only some ships, bare and empty. At a few metres distance, against the sea and the summer heavens, rises up the Gateway of India.

It is a kind of triumphal arch, with four gothic portals, of a quite severe *liberty* style: its mass imposes itself on the edge of the Indian Ocean as if visibly joining it with the interior land, which, at that point, forms a round square with some gloomy gardens and constructions, all large, floral and a little dissipated like the Taj Mahal itself. It is earthy and artificial in colour, standing amidst the scattered immobile lamps in the peace of deep summer.

Again at the edges of this large symbolic gateway, there are other figures from the European prints of the 17th century: little Indians, their thighs enveloped in a white drape and, above faces as dead as the night, the circle of a narrow turban of rags. Only that, when seen close up, these rags are lurid with a miserable, natural dirt, very prosaic in comparison to the figurative suggestions of an epoch at which they, in every other sense, have come to a halt. They are still young beggars, or survivors, tarrying by night in the places which by day are probably the centre of their activities. They look askance at us, I and Moravia, letting us go: their inexpressive eye cannot see in us anything promising. On the contrary, they almost close in on themselves as we walk tiredly along the little chestnut-coloured parapet . . .

*

In front of the hotel with the porticoes a whole group of them is bunched on the ground in the dust: limbs, rags and shadows get mixed together. Seeing me pass, two or three get up and follow behind me, as if waiting. Then I stop and smile at them, uncertain.

A black one, thin, with a delicate Aryan face and an enormous pile of black hair, greets me, then approaches me barefoot, his rags around him, one between his legs, one on his shoulders; behind him appears another, glossy black this one, with a big negroid mouth on which the down of adolescence is shadowed. Yet when he smiles, there flames behind his black face an immaculate candour: a flash within, a wind, a blaze that removes the black layer from the white layer which is his inner smile.

The first one is called Sundar, the second one Sardar. One is Muslim, the other Hindu. Sundar comes from Hyderabad, where he has his family: he is seeking his fortune in Bombay like a Calabrian boy might come to Rome: in a city where he knows no one, doesn't have a house, must arrange a bed just as it happens, and eat when he can. He coughs, from a small bird-like thorax: – perhaps he is consumptive. The Muslim religion gives to his sweet, delicate face a certain air of timid shrewdness, whereas the other one, Sardar, is all sweetness and devotion: Hindu to the bone.

He comes from far Andhra, the region of Madras: he also is without a family, without a house, without anything.

The others, their friends, have remained behind in the shadow of the hotel's secondary door. But now I see them move, in silence. They hunch around a large paper bag which they open on the dusty pavement.

I ask Sardar and Sundar what they are doing. They are eating the *pudding*, the left-overs of hotel suppers. They eat in silence like dogs, but without fighting, with the reasonableness and sweetness of the Hindu.

Sardar and Sundar look at them along with me, wearing a smile as if to say that they also act like that and, if I hadn't been there, they also would be eating those scraps at this very moment. Instead we go to have a walk in the neighbourhood.

The streets are deserted by now, lost in their dusty, dry, dirty silence. They have something about them which is grandiose as well as miserable. This is the central, modern part of the city, but with the corrosion of the stones, the shutters, and the woodwork is like an ancient village.

Almost all of the dilapidated houses have a little portico in front of them: and here . . . I stand face to face with one of the most impressive facts about India.

All the porticoes, *all* the pavements spill over with sleepers. They are stretched out on the earth, against the columns, against the walls, against the doorposts. Their rags envelop them entirely, smeared with filth. Their sleep is so deep that they seem like the dead, wrapped in torn, fetid shrouds.

They are made up of youngsters, boys, old men, and women with children. They sleep rolled up or stretched out, in their hundreds. Some of them are still awake, especially the boys: they pause to turn round or to speak quietly, seated at the door of a closed shop, or on the steps of a house. Someone stretches out at that moment and turns round in his sheet, covering his head. The whole street is full of their silence: and their sleep is similar to death. Yet to a death which, in its turn, is as gentle as sleep.

Sardar and Sundar look at them with the same smile with which they were watching their friends devour the remains of the *pudding*: they also will sleep like this soon.

They accompany me towards the Taj Mahal . . . Just look at the Gateway of India against the sea. The song has ceased: the two boys that were singing must now be sleeping on the bare pavement, in their rags. Already I have learnt something from their song. A horrendous poverty.

Sardar and Sundar politely take their leave of me, a smile of solar brilliance within their gloomy faces. They don't expect me to give them some rupees: therefore they take them full of joyful surprise.

Sardar grips my hand and kisses it, saying to me: 'You are a good sir.'

I leave them, touched in my heart like an idiot. Something has already begun.

*   *   *

PAUL BOWLES (1910–1999)

'Notes Mailed at Nagercoil'

Cape Comorin

I have been here in this hotel now for a week. At no time during the night or day has the temperature been low enough for comfort; it fluctuates between 95 and 105 degrees, and most of the time there is absolutely no breeze, which is astonishing for the seaside. Each bedroom and public room has the regulation large electric fan in its ceiling, but there is no electricity; we are obliged to use oil lamps for lighting. Today at lunchtime a large Cadillac of the latest model drove up to the front door. In the back were three little men wearing nothing but the flimsy dhotis they had draped around their loins. One of them handed a bunch of keys to the chauffeur, who then got out and came into the hotel. Near the front door is the switch box. He opened it, turned on the current with one of the keys, and throughout the hotel the fans began to whir. Then the three little men got out and went into the dining room where they had their lunch. I ate quickly, so as to get upstairs and lie naked on my bed under the fan. It was an unforgettable fifteen minutes. Then the fan stopped, and I heard the visitors driving away. The hotel manager told me later that they were government employees of the State of Travancore, and that only they had a key to the switch box.

Last night I awoke and opened my eyes. There was no moon; it was still dark, but the light of a star was shining into my face through the open window, from a point high above the Arabian Sea. I sat up, and gazed at it. The light it cast seemed as bright as that of the moon in northern countries; coming through the window, it made its rectangle on the opposite wall, broken by the shadow of my silhouetted head. I held up my hand and moved the fingers, and their shadow too was definite. There were no other stars visible in that part of the sky; this one blinded them all. It was about an hour before daybreak, which comes shortly after six, and there was not a breath of air. On such still nights the waves breaking on the nearby shore sound like great, deep explosions going on at some distant place. There is the boom, which can be felt as well as heard, and which ends with a sharp rattle and hiss, then a long period of complete silence, and finally, when it seems that there will be no more sound, another sudden boom. The crows begin to scream and chatter while the darkness is still complete.

The town, like the others here in the extreme south, gives the impression of being made of dust. Dust and cow-dung lie in the streets, and the huge crows hop ahead of you as you walk along. When a gust of hot wind wanders in from the sandy wastes beyond the town, the brown fans of the palmyra trees swish and bang against each other; they sound like giant sheets of heavy wrapping paper. The small black men walk quickly, the diamonds in their earlobes flashing. Because of their jewels and the gold thread woven into their dhotis, they all look not merely prosperous, but fantastically wealthy. When the women have diamonds, they are likely to wear them in a hole pierced through the wall of one nostril.

The first time I ever saw India I entered it through Dhanushkodi. An analogous procedure in America would be for a foreigner to get his first glimpse of the United States by crossing the Mexican border illegally and coming out into a remote Arizona village. It was God-forsaken, uncomfortable, and a little frightening. Since then I have landed as a bona fide visitor should, in the impressively large and unbeautiful metropolis of Bombay. But I am glad that my first trip did not bring me in contact with any cities. It is better to go to the villages of a strange land before trying to understand its towns, above all in a complex place like India. Now, after travelling some eight thousand miles around the country, I know approximately as little as I did on my first arrival. However, I've seen a lot of people and places, and at least I have a somewhat more detailed and precise idea of my ignorance than I did in the beginning.

If you have not taken the precaution of reserving a room in advance, you risk having considerable difficulty in finding one when you land in Bombay. There are very few hotels, and the two or three comfortable ones are always full. I hate being committed to a reservation because the element of adventure is thereby destroyed. The only place I was able to get into when I first arrived, therefore, was something less than a first-class establishment. It was all right during the day and the early hours of the evening. At night, however, every square foot of floor space in the dark corridors was occupied by sleepers who had arrived late and brought their own mats with them; the hotel was able in this way to shelter several hundred extra guests each night. Having their hands and feet kicked and trodden on was apparently a familiar enough experience to them for them never to make any audible objection when the inevitable happened.

Here in Cape Comorin, on the other hand, there are many rooms and they are vast, and at the moment I am the only one staying in the hotel.

It was raining. I was on a bus going from Alleppey to Trivandrum, on my way down here. There were two little Indian nuns on the seat in front of mine. I wondered how they stood the heat in their heavy robes. Sitting near the driver was a man with a thick, fierce moustache who distinguished himself from the other passengers by the fact that in addition to his dhoti he also wore a European shirt; its scalloped tail hung down nearly to his knees. With him he had a voluminous collection of magazines and newpapers in both Tamil and English, and even from where I sat I could not help noticing that all this reading matter had been printed in the Soviet Union.

At a certain moment, near one of the myriad villages that lie smothered in the depths of the palm forests there, the motor suddenly ceased to function, and the bus came to a stop. The driver, not exchanging a single glance with his passengers, let his head fall forward and remain resting on the steering wheel in a posture of despair. Expectantly the people waited a little while, and then they began to get down. One of the first out of the bus was the man with the moustache. He said a hearty goodbye to the occupants in general, although he had not been conversing with any of them, and started up the road carrying his umbrella, but not his armful of printed matter. Then I realized that at some point during the past hour, not foreseeing the failure of the motor and the mass departure which it entailed, he had left a paper or magazine on each empty seat – exactly as our American comrades used to do on subway trains three decades ago.

Almost at the moment I made this discovery, the two nuns had risen and were hurriedly collecting the 'literature'. They climbed down and ran along the road after the man, calling out in English: 'Sir, your papers!' He turned, and they handed them to him. Without saying a word, but with an expression of fury on his face, he took the bundle and continued. But it was impossible to tell from the faces of the two nuns when they returned to gather up their belongings whether or not they were conscious of what they had done.

A few minutes later everyone had left the bus and walked to the village – everyone, that is, but the driver and me. I had too much luggage. Then I spoke to him.

'What's the matter with the bus?'

He shrugged his shoulders.

'How am I going to get to Trivandrum?'

He did not know that, either.

'Couldn't you look into the motor?' I pursued. 'It sounded like the fan belt. Maybe you could repair it.'

This roused him sufficiently from his apathy to make him turn and look at me.

'We have People's Government here in Travancore,' he said. 'Not allowed touching motor.'

'But who *is* going to repair it, then?'

'Tonight making telephone call to Trivandrum. Making report. Tomorrow or other day they sending inspector to examine.'

'And then what?'

'Then inspector making report. Then sending repair crew.'

'I see.'

'People's Government,' he said again, by way of helping me to understand. 'Not like other government.'

'No,' I said.

As if to make his meaning clearer, he indicated the seat where the man with the large moustache had sat. 'That gentleman Communist.'

'Oh, really?' (At least, it was all in the open, and the driver was under no misapprehension as to what the term 'People's Government' meant.)

'Very powerful man. Member of Parliament from Travancore.'

'Is he a good man, though? Do the people like him?'

'Oh, yes, sir. Powerful man.'

'But is he *good*?' I insisted.

He laughed, doubtless at my ingenuousness. 'Powerful man all rascals,' he said.

Just before nightfall a local bus came along, and with the help of several villagers I transferred my luggage to it and continued on my way.

Most of the impressively heavy Communist vote is cast by the Hindus. The Moslems are generally in less dire economic straits, it is true, but in any case, by virtue of their strict religious views, they do not take kindly to any sort of ideological change. (A convert from Islam is unthinkable; apostasy is virtually non-existent.) If even Christianity has retained too much of its pagan décor to be acceptable to the puritanical Moslem mind, one can imagine the loathing inspired in them by the endless proliferations of Hindu religious art with its gods, demons, metamorphoses and avatars. The two religious systems are antipodal. Fortunately the constant association with the mild and tolerant Hindus has made the Moslems of India far more understanding and tractable than their brothers in Islamic countries further west; there is much less actual friction than one might be led to expect.

During breakfast one morning at the Connemara Hotel in Madras the Moslem head waiter told me a story. He was travelling in the Province of Orissa, where in a certain town there was a Hindu temple which was noted for having five hundred cobras on its premises. He decided he would like to see these famous reptiles. When he had got to the town he hired a carriage and went to the temple. At the door he was met by a priest who offered to show him around. And since the Moslem looked prosperous, the priest suggested a donation of five rupees, to be paid in advance.

'Why so much?' asked the visitor.

'To buy eggs for the cobras. You know, we have five hundred of them.'

The Moslem gave him the money on condition that the priest let him see the snakes. For an hour his guide dallied in the many courtyards and galleries, pointing out bas-reliefs, idols, pillars and bells. Finally the Moslem reminded him of their understanding.

'Cobras? Ah, yes. But they are dangerous. Perhaps you would rather see them another day?'

This behaviour on the priest's part had delighted him, he recalled, for it had reinforced his suspicions.

'Not at all,' he said. 'I want to see them now.'

Reluctantly the priest led him into a small alcove behind a large stone Krishna, and pointed into a very dark corner.

'Is this the place?' the visitor asked.

'This is the place.'

'But where are the snakes?'

In a tiny enclosure were two sad old cobras, 'almost dead from hunger', he assured me. But when his eyes had grown used to the dimness he saw that there were hundreds of eggshells scattered around the floor outside the pen.

'You eat a lot of eggs,' he told the priest.

The priest merely said: 'Here. Take back your five rupees. But if you are asked about our cobras, please be so kind as to say that you saw five hundred of them here in our temple. Is that all right?'

The episode was meant to illustrate the head waiter's thesis, which was that the Hindus are abject in the practice of their religion; this is the opinion held by the Moslems. On the other hand, it must be remembered that the Hindu considers Islam an incomplete doctrine, far from satisfying. He finds its austerity singularly comfortless, and deplores its lack of mystico-philosophical content, an element in which his own creed is so rich.

I was invited to lunch at one of the cinema studios in the suburbs north of Bombay. We ate our curry outdoors; our hostess was the star of the film then in production. She spoke only Marathi; her husband, who was directing the picture, spoke excellent English. During the course of the meal he told how, as a Hindu, he had been forced to leave his job, his home, his car and his bank account in Karachi at the time of partition, when Pakistan came into existence, and emigrate empty-handed to India, where he managed to remake his life. Another visitor to the studio, an Egyptian, was intensely interested in his story. Presently he interrupted to say: 'It is unjust, of course.'

'Yes,' smiled our host.

'What retaliatory measures does your govenment plan to take against the Moslems left here in India?'

'None whatever, as far as I know.'

The Egyptian was genuinely indignant. 'But why not?' he demanded. 'It is only right that you apply the same principle. You have plenty of Moslems here still to take action against. And I say that, even though I am a Moslem.'

The film director looked at him closely. 'You say that *because* you are a Moslem,' he told him. 'But we cannot put ourselves on that level.'

The conversation ended on this not entirely friendly note. A moment later packets of betel were passed around. I promptly broke a tooth, withdrew from the company and went some distance away into the garden. While I, in the interests of science, was examining the mouthful of partially chewed betel leaves and areca nut, trying to find the pieces of bicuspid, the Egyptian came up to me, his face a study in scorn.

'They are afraid of the Moslems. That's the real reason,' he whispered. Whether he was right or wrong I was neither qualified nor momentarily disposed to say, but it was a classical exposition of the two opposing moral viewpoints – two concepts of behaviour which cannot quickly be reconciled.

Obviously it is a gigantic task to make a nation out of a place like India, what with Hindus, Parsees, Jainists, Jews, Catholics and Protestants, some of whom may speak the arbitrarily imposed national idiom of Hindi, but most of whom are more likely to know Gujarati, Marathi, Bengali, Urdu, Telugu, Tamil, Malayalam or some other tongue instead. One wonders whether any sort of unifying project can ever be undertaken, or, indeed, whether it is even desirable.

When you come to the border between two provinces you often find bars across the road, and you are obliged to undergo a thorough inspection of your luggage. As in the United States, there is a strict control of the passage of liquor between wet and dry districts, but that is not the extent of the examination.

Sample of conversation at the border on the Mercara–Cannanore highway:

'What is in there?' (Customs officer.)

'Clothing.' (Bowles.)

'And in that?'

'Clothing.'

'And in all those?'

'Clothing.'

'Open all, please.'

After eighteen suitcases have been gone through carefully: 'My God, man! Close them all. I could charge duty for all of these goods, but you will never be able to do business with these things here anyway. The Moslem men are too clever.'

'But I'm not intending to sell my clothes.'

'Shut the luggage. It is duty-free, I tell you.'

A professor from Raniket in North India arrived at the hotel here the other day, and we spent a good part of the night sitting on the window seat in my room that overlooks the sea, talking about what one always talks about here: India. Among the many questions I put to him was one concerning the reason why so many of the Hindu temples in South India prohibit entry to non-Hindus, and why they have military guards at the entrances. I imagined I knew the answer in advance: fear of Moslem disturbances. Not at all, he said. The principal purpose was to keep out certain Christian missionaries. I expressed disbelief.

'Of course,' he insisted. 'They come and jeer during our rituals, ridicule our sacred images.'

'But even if they were stupid enough to want to do such things,' I objected, 'their sense of decorum would keep them from behaving like that.'

He merely laughed. 'Obviously you don't know them.'

The post office here is a small stifling room over a shop, and it is full of boys seated on straw mats. The postmaster, a tiny old man who wears large diamond earrings and gold-rimmed spectacles, and is always naked to the waist, is also a professor; he interrupts his academic work to sell an occasional stamp. At first contact his English sounds fluent enough, but soon one discovers that it is not adapted to conversation, and that one can scarcely talk to him. Since the boys are listening, he must pretend to be omniscient, therefore he answers promptly with more or less whatever phrase comes into his head.

Yesterday I went to post a letter by airmail to Tangier. 'Tanjore,' he said, adjusting his spectacles. 'That will be four annas.' (Tanjore is in South India, near Trichinopoly.) I explained that I hoped my letter would be going to Tangier, Morocco.

'Yes, yes,' he said impatiently. 'There are many Tanjores.' He opened the book of postal regulations and read aloud from it, quite at random, for (although it may be difficult to believe) exactly six minutes. I stood still, fascinated, and let him go on. Finally he looked up and said: 'There is no mention of Tangier. No airplanes go to that place.'

'Well, how much would it be to send it by sea mail?' (I thought we could then calculate the surcharge for air mail, but I had mis-judged my man.)

'Yes,' he replied evenly. 'That is a good method, too.'

I decided to keep the letter and post it in the nearby town of Nagercoil another day. In a little while I shall have several to add to it, and I count on being able to send them all together when I go. Before I left the post office I hazarded the remark that the weather was extremely hot. In that airless attic at noon it was a wild understatement. But it did not please the postmaster at all. Deliberately he removed his glasses and pointed the stems at me.

'Here we have the perfect climate,' he told me. 'Neither too cold nor too cool.'

'That is true,' I said. 'Thank you.'

In the past few years there have been visible quantitative changes in the life, all in the one direction of Europeanization. This is in the smaller towns; the cities of course have long since been Westernized. The temples which before were lighted by bare electric bulbs and coconut oil lamps now have fluorescent tubes glimmering in their ceilings. Crimson, green, and amber floodlights are used to illumine bathing tanks, deities, the gateways of temples. The public-address system is the bane of the ear these days, even in the temples. And it is impossible to attend a concert or a dance recital without discovering several loudspeakers in operation, whose noise completely destroys the quality of the music. A mile before you arrive at the cinema of a small town you can hear the raucous blaring of the amplifier they have set up at its entrance.

This year in South India there are fewer men with bare torsos, dhotis and sandals: more shirts, trousers and shoes. There is at the same time a slow shutting-down of services which to the Western tourist make all the difference between pleasure and discomfort in travelling, such as the restaurants in the stations (there being no dining-cars on the trains) and the showers in the first-class compartments. A few years ago they worked; now they have been sealed off. You can choke on the dust and soot of your compartment, or drown in your own sweat now, for all the railway cares.

At one point I was held for forty-eight hours in a concentration camp run by the Ceylon government on Indian soil. (The euphemism for this one was 'screening camp'.) I was told that I was under suspicion of being an 'international spy'. My astonishment and indignation were regarded as almost convincing in their sincerity, thus proof of my guilt.

'But who am I supposed to be spying *for*?' I asked piteously.

The director shrugged. 'Spying for international,' he said.

More than the insects or the howling of pariah dogs outside the rolls of barbed wire, what bothered me was the fact that in the centre of the camp, which at that time housed some twenty thousand people, there was a loudspeaker in a high tower which during every moment of the day roared forth Indian film music. Fortunately it was silenced at ten o'clock each evening. I got out of the hell-hole by making such violent trouble that I was dragged before the camp doctor, who decided that I was dangerously unbalanced. The idea in letting me go was that I would be detained further along, and the responsibility would fall on other shoulders. 'They will hold him at Talaimannar,' I heard the doctor say. 'The poor fellow is quite mad.'

Here and there, in places like the bar of the Hotel Metropole at Mysore, or at the North Coorg Club of Mercara, one may still come across vestiges of the old colonial life; ghosts in the form of incredibly sunburned Englishmen in jodhpurs and boots discussing their hunting luck and prowess. But these visions are exceedingly rare in a land that wants to forget their existence.

The younger generation in India is intent on forgetting a good many things, including some that it might do better to remember. There would seem to be no good reason for getting rid of their country's most ancient heritage, the religion of Hinduism, or of its most recent acquisition, the tradition of independence. This latter, at least insofar as the illiterate masses are concerned, is inseparable not only from the religious state of mind which made political victory possible, but also from the legend which, growing up around the figure of Gandhi, has elevated him in their minds to the status of a god.

The young, politically minded intellectuals find this not at all to their liking; in their articles and addresses they have returned again and again to the attack against Gandhi as a 'betrayer' of the Indian people. That they are motivated by hatred is obvious. But what do they hate?

For one thing, subconsciously they cannot accept their own inability to go on having religious beliefs. Then, belonging to the group without faith, they are thereby forced to hate the past, particularly the atavisms which are made apparent by the workings of the human mind with its irrationality, its subjective involvement in exterior phenomena. The floods of poisonous words they pour forth are directed primarily at the adolescents: it is an age group which is often likely to find demagoguery more attractive than common sense.

There are at least a few of these enlightened adolescents in every town; the ones here in Cape Comorin were horrified when, by a stratagem, I led them to the home of a man of their own village named Subramaniam, who claims that his brother is under a spell. (They had not imagined, they told me later, that an American would believe such nonsense.) According to Subramaniam, his brother was a painter who had been made art-director of a major film studio in Madras. To substantiate his story he brought out a sheaf of very professional sketches for film sets.

'Then my brother had angry words with a jealous man in the studio,' said Subramaniam, 'and the man put a charm on him. His mind is gone. But at the end of the year it will return.' The brother presently appeared in the courtyard; he was a vacant-eyed man with a beard, and he had a voluminous turkish towel draped over his head and shoulders. He walked past us and disappeared through a doorway.

'A spirit doctor is treating him . . .' The modern young men shifted their feet miserably; it was unbearable that an American should be witnessing such shameful revelations, and that they should be coming from one in their midst.

But these youths who found it so necessary to ridicule poor Subramaniam failed to understand why I laughed when, the conversation changing to the subject of cows, I watched their collective expression swiftly change to one of respect bordering on beatitude. For cow-worship is one facet of popular Hinduism which has not yet been totally superseded by twentieth-century faithlessness. True, it has taken on new forms of ritual. Mass cow worship is often practised now in vast modern concrete stadiums, with prizes being distributed to the owners of the finest bovine specimens, but the religious aspect of the celebration is still evident. The cows are decorated with garlands and jewellery, fed bananas and sugar-cane by people who have waited in line for hours to be granted that rare privilege, and when the satiated animals can eat no more they simply lie down or wander about, while hundreds of young girls perform sacred dances in their honour.

In India, where the cow wishes to go, she goes. She may be lying in the temple, where she may decide to get up, to go and lie instead in the middle of the street. If she is annoyed by the proximity of the traffic streaming past her, she may lumber to her feet again and continue down the street to the railway station, where, should she feel like reclining in front of the ticket window, no one will disturb her. On the highways she seems to know that the drivers of trucks and buses will spot her a mile away and slow down almost to a stop before they get to her, and that therefore she need not move out from under the shade of the particular banyan tree she has chosen for her rest. Her superior position in the world is agreed upon by common consent.

The most satisfying exposition I have seen of the average Hindu's feeling about this exalted beast is a little essay composed by a candidate for a post in one of the public services, entitled simply: 'The Cow'. The fact that it was submitted in order to show the aspirant's mastery of the English language, while touching, is of secondary importance.

THE COW

The cow is one wonderful animal, also he is quadruped and because he is female he gives milk – but he will do so only when he has got child. He is same like God, sacred to Hindu and useful to man. But he has got four legs together. Two are foreward and two are afterwards.

His whole body can be utilized for use. More so the milk. What it cannot do? Various ghee, butter, cream, curds, whey, kova and the condensed milk and so forth. Also, he is useful to cobbler, watermans and mankind generally.

His motion is slow only. That is because he is of amplitudinous species, and also his other motion is much useful to trees, plants as well as making fires. This is done by making flat cakes in hand and drying in the sun.

He is the only animal that extricates his feedings after eating. Then afterwards he eats by his teeth whom are situated in the inside of his mouth. He is incessantly grazing in the meadows.

His only attacking and defending weapons are his horns, especially when he has got child. This is done by bowing his head whereby he causes the weapons to be parallel to ground of earth and instantly proceeds with great velocity forwards.

He has got tail also, but not like other similar animals. It has hairs on the end of the other side. This is done to frighten away the flies which alight on his whole body and chastises him unceasingly, whereupon he gives hit with it.

The palms of his feet are so soft unto the touch, so that the grasses he eats would not get crushed. At night he reposes by going down on the ground and then he shuts his eyes like his relative the horse which does not do so. This is the cow.

The moths and night insects flutter about my single oil lamp. Occasionally, at the top of its chimney, one of them goes up in a swift, bright flame. On the concrete floor in a fairly well-defined ring around the bottom of my chair are the drops of sweat that have rolled off my body during the past two hours. The doors into both the bedroom and the bathroom are shut; I work each night in the dressing-room between them, because fewer insects are attracted here. But the air is nearly unbreathable with the stale smoke of cigarettes and bathi sticks burned to discourage the entry of winged creatures. Today's paper announced an outbreak of bubonic plague in Bellary. I keep thinking about it, and I wonder if the almost certain eventual victory over such diseases will prove to have been worth its price: the extinction of the beliefs and rituals which gave a satisfactory meaning to the period of consciousness that goes between birth and death. I doubt it. Security is a false god; begin making sacrifices to it and you are lost.

*   *   *

IBN BATTUTA (1304–1377)

'Delhi depopulated by the excesses of Sultan Tughlag, c. 1340'

One of the gravest charges against the sultan is that of compelling the inhabitants of Delhi to leave the town. The reason for this was that they used to write missives reviling and insulting him, seal them and inscribe them, 'By the hand of the Master of the World, none but he may read this.' They then threw them into the audience-hall at night, and when the sultan broke the seal he found them full of insults and abuse. He decided to lay Delhi in ruins, and having bought from all the inhabitants their houses and dwellings and paid them the price of them, he commanded them to move to Dawlat Ábád. They refused, and his herald was sent to proclaim that no person should remain in the city after three nights. The majority complied with the order, but some of them hid in the houses. The sultan ordered a search to be made for any persons remaining in the town, and his slaves found two men in the streets, one a cripple and the other blind. They were brought before him and he gave orders

that the cripple should be flung from a mangonel and the blind
man dragged from Delhi to Dawlat Ábád, a distance of forty days'
journey [700 miles]. He fell to pieces on the road and all of him that
reached Dawlat Ábád was his leg. When the sultan did this, every
person left the town, abandoning furniture and possessions, and the
city remained utterly deserted. A person in whom I have confidence
told me that the sultan mounted one night to the roof of his palace
and looked out over Delhi, where there was neither fire nor smoke
nor lamp, and said 'Now my mind is tranquil and my wrath
appeased.' Afterwards he wrote to the inhabitants of the other cities
commanding them to move to Delhi to repopulate it. The result was
only to ruin their cities and leave Delhi still unpopulated, because of
its immensity, for it is one of the greatest cities in the world. It was
in this state that we found it on our arrival, empty and unpopulated,
save for a few inhabitants.

*   *   *

PANKAJ MISHRA (1969–)

from Butter Chicken In Ludhiana: Travels in Small Town India

I wanted to find out the reasons behind Mr Sharma's profuse hospitality. I had been given a large guest-room, furnished in the most
expensive – and needless to say, hideous – style with silk bedspreads
and curtains, bulbous suede sofas, wall-to-wall carpet, colour TV and
a small fridge – quite like a honeymoon suite I had once seen in a
new hotel in Mussoorie.

Then, the dinner that evening was a very large and elaborate
affair; it certainly wasn't what anyone ate every day. I was undoubtedly the guest of honour at the table – if such things are determined
by the number of questions one is asked while eating one's food.

Mr Sharma's younger daughter, Neha, was the first to enter the
dining room, giggling over something, followed by another girl,
whose name was Roli and who, Mrs Sharma whisperingly informed
me, was a friend of Neha from Delhi in addition to being – and here
a bit of awe entered her voice – the daughter of a very rich and very
famous industrialist. Both stared at me blankly as they took their

seats at the dining table, and then continued scrutinizing my face with the same unblinking gaze.

Neha, Roli . . . How does one describe them? There is a sameness about spoilt upper-middle-class maidenhood that frustrates conventional description. Words fail one utterly. Indeed, words seem an offence against a thing so heartbreakingly simple. One has to fall back upon enumerating the eclectic furniture of their minds and souls. Not a satisfactory solution by any means, but naming individually the ingredients is what one will eventually do, faced with the onerous task of describing two tubs of Processed Amul Cheese.

So, here goes: Nancy Drew, MTV, Barbara Cartland, Mills & Boon, Cliff Richard, *Santa Barbara*, Agatha Christie, *Stardust*, Shah Rukh Khan, *The Bold and the Beautiful*, Sanjay Dutt, *Femina*, Pooja Bhatt, *Khubsoorat*, Milind Soman, Sushmita Sen, Tom Cruise, Richard Gere, Julia Roberts, Sharon Stone, Bryan Adams, Michael Bolton, Danny McGill . . .

Mr Sharma's eldest daughter, Kavita, was the next to enter the dining room, wearing jeans and a light-grey pullover, a look of frank appraisal on her oval face as I stood up and Mrs Sharma introduced me incorrectly as a writer writing a book on Ambala.

It was her photo I had seen in the living room. But it wasn't easy to tell. The photo had misled; it was possible it had been worked over in the developing room – as photographers do for marriageable, but unattractive, young women. Certainly, Kavita had the withered jaded sulkiness of women who have been made to wait far too long for marriage. Her hair, in defiance of current trends, was long and straight. She wore no make-up except some barely discernible white lipstick.

Like Neha and Roli before her, she continued to look unsmilingly at me well after she sat down, and their collective gaze was beginning to make me feel very awkward. Luckily, Mr Sharma, who had somehow managed to lift himself up from the living-room divan and into the dining room, chose that moment to say:

'*Ab to suna hai ki kitaab-vitaab likhne mein bhi bahut paisa hai*, I have heard there's a lot of money to be made in writing books.'

Before I could say something, Mrs Sharma spoke up: 'Yes, Mrs Bindra was saying today, she must have heard this from her son, Amarjit, he's very fond of reading and all, she was telling how this writer . . . what's his name . . . became a *crorepati* with just one book . . .'

'Vikram Seth?' Kavita prompted.

'Yes . . . yes . . . some Seth,' Mrs Sharma added.

'It's a bad book,' declared Kavita.

The words were out of my mouth before I realized it. 'Have you read it?' I asked.

'No,' she replied slightly awkwardly, 'I haven't read it, I just heard it was bad.'

I almost asked: 'From whom?' But it would have meant taking the matter too far.

There was only one person left to come, and that was Dharam Kumar who now appeared in the dining room, still as nervous as the first time I had seen him.

It was his thick mop of hair that now caught my eye. The hair was simply too long. It was arranged in a style – overlapping the ears, parted almost down the middle – popularized by Amitabh Bachchan in the late seventies and which, though still sported by him in the few pictures of him I saw here and there, was now clearly dated. It made Dharam Kumar resemble those young, paan-chewing rakes swaggering around the main streets of the small towns one passed through in a thick cloud of dust on your way to a bigger destination, instinctively pitying the place for its hopeless backwardness, its stagnant air, its dejected appearance, its dilapidated cinemas showing last year's flops.

Neha went over to the TV set in the corner and switched it on. Our evening's entertainment was to be *The Bold and the Beautiful*, which was about to begin when Dharam Kumar came in. He stood uncertainly for some time after everyone took their usual seats; and then slid into the chair facing mine.

Immediately, Neha spoke up:

'Not here. Not here. You'll block the TV.'

He stood up abruptly and knocked his knees against one of the table legs.

The assorted steel bowls and tureens and jugs and glasses and plates trembled for a second; their glinting reflections in each other's polished surfaces shifted, and then were still again.

Mrs Sharma remained frozen for more than a second in her position, dipping a ladle into one of the bowls. Nothing was spilt: I quickly ascertained that and then turned to Dharam Kumar who stood there half-bent, pain and embarrassment alternating wildly on his face.

'Are you hurt?' I asked.

'No, no . . . just a little . . . injury,' he mumbled.

Mrs Sharma said: 'Come and sit beside me, Dharam.'

Neha and Kavita gaped with open mouths as he half-hobbled, half-walked across to Mrs Sharma's side. I saw something flicker in Kavita's eyes: a sudden interest, a quickening of womanly curiosity, prompted as though by a new awareness of the handsomeness of the man before her.

It disappeared the next moment, the smug crevices reappeared around her mouth as Dharam Kumar eased himself into his chair and, simultaneously, the first scene of that evening's entertainment began on the blazing television set in the corner.

The omnivorousness of the sexual instinct: it was the high-powered engine which dragged the lumbering plot of *The Bold and the Beautiful* from day to day, week after week. Today was no different. Ridge has been furtively having sex with his sister-in-law, Caroline. Her husband comes to know of it, shoots Ridge in a fit of rage, and then promptly loses all memory of the incident. Meanwhile, Ridge's fiancée, Brooke, has got wind of his relationship with Caroline: this, the story until today in one of the infinite sub-plots of that much-loved – by India's English-knowing sophisticates – soap.

Mrs Sharma scooped out a ladleful of aromatic *dal* and poured it into the bowl on my plate, her gold bangles clanking, as she repeatedly jerked the ladle free of all possibility of spillage and then dipped it again into the steaming bowl. As she brought it up over the bowl again, I spoke out: '*Bas, bas*, Enough, enough.'

Mrs Sharma smiled, very much at this moment the proud patron of my gastronomic pleasures, and said:

'Why *bas*? You are a growing boy. You should eat a lot.'

I do not remember what I said, but I did see Neha turn her head back from Ridge's depravities to exchange a brief grin with Kavita.

Mr Sharma – who did not seem to have much interest in degenerate Los Angeles plutocrats – asked me:

'*Aapko apni kitaab ke liye kitna paisa mila hai*, How much money have you got for your book?'

I espied Kavita looking at me from the corner of her eye. She looked sceptical. Her expression said: How much money after all can somebody writing a book on Ambala make?

I said: 'That depends on how many copies the book sells.'

'No,' Mr Sharma said, 'thad is the royalty. How much advance did you get?'

It was clear Mr Sharma knew much more than he let on about the book trade.

I told him.

Mr Sharma's face fell. He looked absolutely crushed. I saw plain pity on Kavita's face. Dharam Kumar, who had been listening to our conversation in the absence of anything better to do, looked slightly confused. Only Mrs Sharma kept her countenance intact and managed to ask: 'How did this . . . what's his name . . . Vikram Sethi earn so much money?'

Luckily, *The Bold and the Beautiful* chose just this moment to dissolve into its signature tune, oddly interposed always after the first five unheralded minutes; and there now appeared on the screen in swift succession shots of an overflowing *décolletage* adorned with a diamond necklace, bare thighs emerging out of a high-cut swimsuit, busy-looking executives set against skyscrapers, fashion models posing as extravagantly theatrical mummies – all this meant to extinguish any doubts, if existing, about *The Bold and the Beautiful* as the truest portrait of the world's maddeningly infinite and unattainable sexiness. Presently, offering a less-charged titillation, some familiar locally made ads for soft-drinks came on – trendily dressed teenagers prancing around in wet clothes – and all eyes turned to me in expectation of my answer.

'Well,' I said, 'he's a big writer, it's a big book.'

Mr Sharma, overcoming his disappointment at last, asked me: 'How much number of books you write before earning thad much money?'

It would have been too much of a task to explain that it was not a matter of numbers but . . .

So I said: 'At least ten books.'

Mr Sharma seemed to ponder this.

He began, '*Chalo, maan liya aapne ek saal mein ek kitaab likhi*, Let's assume you write one book every year . . .' and then stopped to ponder a little more.

I waited.

'Bud see!' he cried. 'One book every year. Thad means after ten years, you'll be a *crorepati*!'

He looked pleased with his calculations. 'Very good!' he chirped. 'Thad is better than doing business. Very good! Very good!'

Looking slightly pleased herself, Mrs Sharma asked: 'How many books there are on Ambala?'

This was the moment to make it clear I was not writing a whole book on Ambala. But I let it pass, and said: 'Not many. Have you heard of Kipling?'

I saw Kavita at the far end of the table nod her head vigorously in assent. Mrs Sharma looked like she was remembering hard: her schooldays, probably . . . snake . . . a mongoose . . . Rikki Tikki . . . Tavi?

In *The Bold and the Beautiful*, Brooke had reached a kind of temporary reconciliation with Ridge. In other words, this was where the scriptwriter had chosen to insert the sex scene for the day. The tension was building up; both Ridge and Brooke were edging closer to each other. A couple of whispers, and then they were in each other's arms with Ridge saying:

'I want you now, Brooke.'

A moist-eyed Brooke replied: 'You can have me, Ridge,' and crushed her lips against Ridge's.

I was looking at Neha who had gone perfectly still. Only her eyes widened slightly in expectation; her mouth was open, her throat presumably dry, her face strangely effulgent with the erotic curiosity of virginal adolescence.

Mrs Sharma finally gave up and asked: 'No. Who's he?'

I told her. I had been reading Angus Wilson's *The Strange Ride of Rudyard Kipling*. The book was still fresh in my mind. And so I told Mrs Sharma about *Kim*; I told her about the *Jungle Books*; I told her about *Plain Tales from the Hills*; and I took my time telling her.

There was only one way to forestall further questioning, and that was to keep talking yourself. Mrs Sharma looked a bit unsettled by this sudden outpouring of perfectly useless information. Kavita nodded her head a few times during my account. It was when I was about to go into the details of Kipling's troubled sojourn in America that Mr Sharma, who had been strangely quiet until now, finally interrupted me, saying:

'*Yeh saale Angrezon ne Hindustan ke upar kitaben likhkar khoob paisa kamaya*, These bloody Englishmen made a lot of money out of writing books on India.'

Mr Sharma, Mrs Sharma, Kavita were still looking at me; another avalanche of queries seemed headed my way. In desperation, I turned to Dharam Kumar, and asked:

'Which school did you go to in Meerut?'

It wasn't a purely idle question. I knew Meerut slightly; I had plans to go there soon; and then I wanted to know more about Dharam Kumar.

The limelight turned on him. Dharam Kumar blinked, swallowed, and cleared his throat in rapid succession. I saw Neha and Kavita exchange scornful looks that said: 'Oh there he goes again, the stupid yokel from Meerut.'

It was becoming rapidly clear to me that Dharam Kumar was an unwanted member of the Sharma family, cast in the role of a poor parasite on his rich relatives. Kavita and Neha in particular had an intense dislike for their cousin. His rustic gawkiness shamed and embarrassed them in front of friends like the ineffably glamorous Roli. It was imperative to separate themselves from him, to disentangle their identities from his; and one of the ways was to pour scorn and contempt on him.

Aware of their hostile scrutiny, he balked at first, almost ashamed to reply to my question – which I now regretted asking. Neha, meanwhile, got up with a great flourish, said 'Excuse Me' in her most haughty convent-school manner, and left the table. Roli followed suit.

Their departure seemed to give Dharam Kumar the courage he had been lacking. He waited until they had disappeared, and then replied in a curiously sibilant tone: 'St Joseph's Cross School.'

St Joseph's Cross School?

Even the name sounded dubious. I couldn't recall a school with that name in Meerut. It was probably very recent, cleverly exploitative of the Indian regard, not entirely misplaced, for Christian schools and English-medium education. Scores of such schools, more than half of them fraudulent, had come up all over small-town India, some with incomplete buildings that frequently collapsed and left in their stead a turbid dust of recriminations and denials hanging over buried bodies.

What was the school like? Brief images flashed before my mind's eye: some primly devout nuns leading an all-school choir of secretly mocking heathen teachers and students in prayer every morning on an unpaved open courtyard in front of a rectangular naked-brick building. Shabbily dressed, grossly underpaid teachers slumped on wicker armchairs in a staff room darkened by gloom and resentment. A gaggle of noisily rebellious students, the sons of middle-level shopkeepers, sure of their paternal inheritance, and so indifferent to continuously falling marks and the not infrequent canings in the principal's office for using a Hindi swear-word.

I began to wonder where Dharam Kumar had figured in all this. But I had been thinking too long, and not doing enough talking. Mr Sharma and Mrs Sharma used the opportunity to assail me with a fresh set of questions, this time about my career plans.

I explained as best as I could that I had none at the moment. They weren't satisfied: I was too old to be not thinking about the future, they said. Surely, I must have thought of something to do.

I invented a few probable careers: writing, journalism, advertising . . . Finally, I made the time-honoured excuse of having to use the bathroom urgently. Dinner was already over. Mrs Sharma deputed Dharam Kumar to show me the nearest bathroom.

I had got up from my chair and was moving towards the corridor where Dharam Kumar stood when I first heard Neha's voice. She was saying something while still in her room and it was too unclear for me to hear. And then I saw her come out into the corridor and towards where I, and Dharam Kumar a few paces ahead, were standing, her face distorted with anger, hysterically shouting:

'WHO HAS BEEN USING MY CAMAY SOAP?!! DOES ANYONE IN THIS HOUSE CARE THAT I BUY IT FROM MY POCKET MONEY?!! DOES ANYONE CARE?!!'

I heard Mrs Sharma say in her oddly melodious sing-song:

'Neha, stop shouting.'

This only aggravated her more.

'Stop shouting! Stop shouting!' she mimicked. 'Do you people care at all about me?!! Do you ever think about my needs?!!'

For a dreadful second I thought I had mistakenly used Neha's bathroom and washed a few skins off her precious Camay soap. But then I saw Dharam Kumar's face turn pale; and in that appalling moment of his guilt, I knew I was safe.

Also, it was at him that Neha was staring with wildly inflamed eyes, her entire torso heaving with the large deep breaths she took. Despite the rage that bloated her features, she looked curiously expectant, as if before a sneeze, waiting perhaps for that encouraging prod – some further provocation from Dharam Kumar – which would make her expel the rest of her bile.

This went on for a painful eternity before Mrs Sharma bustled in from the dining room to where Neha stood and putting her arm around her started whispering something in her ear.

I stole a glimpse at Dharam Kumar. He stood there immobilized, aware of his guilt, but too fearful to say anything.

It was only after Mrs Sharma had led Neha away to her bedroom to pacify her there in seclusion, that he said:

'*Mujhe maafi maangni chaiye Neha didi se. Mein aaj raaste mein saabun kharidna bhool gaya tha*, I should ask Neha didi to forgive me. I forgot to buy soap today on my way back from the office.'

'*Kyon bhool gaya tha re?* Why did you forget?' barked Mr Sharma. '*Jaanta hai kitna mahnga saabun hai yeh*, Do you know how expensive this soap is?'

*

I left Ambala the next morning much to the surprise and dismay of the Sharmas. Mr Sharma said he had arranged a day-long car trip through the town for me. Mrs Sharma said she was planning to take the entire family out for dinner at Ambala's best restaurant. Kavita said nothing, but seemed to suggest she wouldn't have minded discussing Kipling with me over tea.

I lied and said I had to reach Delhi before 3 p.m. in order to send an important document abroad.

Mr Sharma promptly offered to send it from Ambala, but I was ready for that. Oh no, the document is in Delhi, I lied again.

Finally, after many more cajolings, the Sharmas let go. They looked almost angry in their disappointment as I left; and, while being driven to the railway station by the same lunatic speedster who had received me, I had this time a much stronger suspicion that getting me into the car with him was an elaborate ruse to have me murdered. There was certainly a good reason this time.

Or perhaps, I thought at the station, Mr Sharma had merely instructed him to terrify me to the point of derangement.

Whatever it was, Mr Sharma, I was to learn later from Mr Khanna in Delhi, had ample cause to be displeased with me. According to what Mr Khanna said, from the moment he came to know about me, he had seen in me a prospective husband for his daughter, Kavita. With that intent, he had mercilessly stalked Mr Khanna while I was in Simla, plying him on the phone with queries about my family he was in no way equipped to answer. Mr Khanna had tried to warn me, but was unable to reach me in Simla.

Suddenly, I had a logical explanation for Mr Sharma's over-generous hospitality, the car at the station, the plush guest-room, the multi-course dinner. Suddenly, it all became clear to me with the result that I began to feel much better about leaving Ambala as abruptly as I did. I had been feeling somewhat guilty about that. Now I knew I was right to follow my instinct that night, the very urgent impulse that came over me after dinner, the impulse to leave as soon as possible, to put behind me the unpleasantness I had witnessed. I had got out in time, and no amount of self-congratulation seemed enough for that.

*   *   *

VICTOR JACQUEMONT (1801–1832)

from *Letters from India*

Between the Beas and the Sutlej, in Captain Wade's camp, October 19

I spent a week at Amritsar with the excellent M. Allard. On the second day after my arrival I had an audience of Ranjit Singh, with nobody else present. Only guess what he offered me . . . The viceroyalty of Kashmir! I laughed heartily at him and his offer, which was doubtless nothing but a trap laid in order to find out what I thought. I liked him even more than when I passed through Lahore, no doubt because of the fuss he made of me. I found that I had changed my name at the Sikh court, and that from having been 'Jakmon Sahib Bahadur' I had become *Aflatun al zaman*[1] quite currently to everybody. Captain Wade arrived at Amritsar three days after I did, with two other officers whom I also know. He had come from the Governor-General to meet Ranjit Singh and escort him across his territories to the spot where the interview between the two potentates is to take place, at Rupar on the left bank of the Sutlej. I was very pleased to see him again. This was the season of the Feast of the Dasehra, at which I saw Asia in all its picturesque pageantry. Wade invited me to join him and since then I have shared in all the

1. *The Plato of the Universe.*

privileges enjoyed by the members of the English Commission. On the eve of the Feast the King paid me the polite attention of allowing me to see the famous Holy Tank of Amritsar, in the middle of which stands the Golden Temple where the *Granth*, or sacred book of the Sikhs, is kept. The fanaticism and madness of the Akalis, or warrior monks, with whom this holy place is always crowded would threaten almost certain danger to any European who was to visit it, unless he had a powerful guard; but this I did not lack. I rode to the temple with a strong escort of Sikh cavalry, on an elephant which pushed the terrible Akalis aside to right and left, though without hurting any of them, and the temple was occupied by a regiment of Sikh infantry. Within its precincts I visited an old man famous for his reputed sanctity. He was waiting for me, and by the King's orders the governor of the city, an old man who is equally respected, awaited me there too and conducted me into the temple. He took me by the hand and led me everywhere like that. Had he let go of it the Akalis would no doubt have played me some nasty trick; but arm in arm with the aged Dessa Singh, I was sacred. The temple at nightfall, when it was already illuminated by lamps, was a perfect image of Pandemonium. I humbly offered the *Granth* a *naza* of three hundred rupees out of those which the King had sent me as a present the day before, and received in return rather a paltry *khilat*. The Dasehra is a Hindu festival, the greatest of them all. The Sikhs celebrate it with even more noise and brilliance than their Hindu ancestors and brethren do. It is the day on which Ranjit reviews his whole army. In my capacity as a temporary diplomat I went and sat with Wade near the King in a magnificent tent erected on a platform in the middle of the plain of Amritsar. All the noblemen of the Sikh court came to do homage to the King, after which the army filed past before us. It was very like the armies described by the historians and poets of antiquity. This time the reality enormously surpassed my expectation.

On the following day (that is, the day before yesterday) the King broke camp at daybreak and left with Captain Wade. I could not part with M. Allard in time to join the royal procession on the road, and did not reach Wade's tent till evening. From this point onwards I shall not leave him again, for fear of getting lost in the appalling *mêlée* before which the King appears to be in flight, though it is really following him against his wish.

Yesterday morning *Aflatun al zaman* rode along on an elephant

side by side with Ranjit Singh, discoursing with him like an oracle.
Since there was not the smallest growing plant to be gathered on
the scorched and sandy plains which we were crossing, I did not
regret my inability to stop when the fancy seized me. Today, however,
I imagined I had caught sight of one, so without the least cer-
emony I made my elephant kneel and got down to have a closer
look at a plant, which, on seeing it better, I recognized and left alone.
Everybody else came to a halt with me. You see that *aflatuns* have
great privileges!

Hateli [Hatteli] in the mountains between the Beas and Sutlej, October 28

On the evening of the 21st, at Hoshiarpur [Ouchiarpoor], I took a
final leave of my beloved Ranjit Singh. During the morning's march,
as I rode along by his side on my horse, we talked of my proposed
visit to Mandi, which I am now carrying out, and he had the candour
– not a common virtue of his – to confess that the petty Rajah of
Mandi is the most recalcitrant of his Rajput hill vassals. He is always
obliged to send an army of from eight to ten thousand men every
spring to collect his paltry tribute of a hundred thousand rupees.
However, he held out a hope that with a little adroitness, his firmans
to the Rajah, and the assistance of an old Sikh officer, a confidential
man of his whom he had added to my escort, I should succeed in
my enterprise. Our last interview was long and extremely amiable.
Ranjit made the greatest fuss of me. He took my hands and pressed
them several times, on receiving my richest broadsides of flattery,
into which I introduced a little feeling without deliberate effort. I
was embarrassed to find from his neglect of the English officer in
command of Wade's escort, who was calling upon him with me,
that his attentions were all for me; but the English are so awkward
with Asiatics, and so unsociable, that I was not surprised. They have
no reply to make but 'yes' and 'no'; and Ranjit likes to be amused.
I did not part with the King till it was black dark, leaving him all
my best wishes for fame and prosperity in this world and the next –
if it exists – and taking away with me a magnificent *khilat* in exchange
for these golden words. On returning to my tent I found that the
King had sent me a further present of five hundred rupees. I then
supped with Wade for the last time, and he gave me a firman from

his own hand for the Rajah of Mandi, who will, I hope, pay attention to it, for he is near the English frontier.

I can assure you, it took all my love of rocks to make me leave the pleasantness and safety which I found in his company and plunge back again into the mountains all alone. I expected to meet with some difficulties, and there has been no lack of them. As early as my third day's march I had to go through the Papal States of the Punjab, a small mountainous district belonging to and inhabited by a centenarian, the spiritual head of the Sikhs, who not long ago, in a fit of rage with his eldest son – an ambitious young fellow of eighty – rose to his feet and without a word of warning chopped off his head with a single blow of his sabre. Out of policy Ranjit lavishes every mark of respect upon this terrible old man. I had reckoned to appease this Cerberus by throwing him a sop in the shape of a hundred rupees or so; but I was obliged to go round his fortress without being allowed to enter it, for fear I might contaminate it. And while I was camping a few leagues further on, near the last village before his frontier, orders were brought me to evacuate His Holiness's territory as quickly as possible. Since his heralds were some fearsome Akalis, carrying long matchlocks with the matches already lighted, I did not wait to be told a second time. So I went on and took up my quarters in a valley separated from that one by a small mountain range. There I thought I was in friendly territory, for I was quite near one of Ranjit's son Sher Singh's fortresses. But on the following morning, as I was about to mount my horse and continue on my way, my old Sikh officer, Kaja Singh, showed me with some embarrassment a band of about twenty ruffians posted opposite my camp with their guns on their shoulders, blocking my way. My horsemen proposed to ride them down and spit them on the end of their lances, a foolish suggestion which I rejected with a shrug of the shoulders. Instead of this I wrapped myself in my magnificent dressing-gown of white flowered Kashmir stuff, settled myself comfortably in my armchair, and prepared to smoke my cigar and drink my drop of brandy as a preservative against the fever prevalent in these mountains. In this comfortable position I conducted diplomatic negotiations with my enemies. Eight months ago this adventure would have made me most uncomfortable, but I was used to such ways by now, and saw perfectly well that it was nothing but one of the most ordinary commonplaces of Punjabi manners. One day, when we are sitting at our fireside, I will tell you the details of these negotiations; suffice it to say for the present that, after much parleying with my two officers, the enemy leader decided to approach me. I complimented him on his vigilance and ordered him to summon all his men, who received the same praise; then, to their great surprise and astonishment, I mounted my white horse with a majestic and patronizing air and lightly waved them farewell. They responded with a most respectful salaam, stammering some excuses (I do not yet know why), and stood watching my departure, as bewildered as a flock of geese, while my baggage went by in front of them. After this I advanced for three days like a conqueror, and arrived here. But at this point I had to stop and open negotiations with the Rajah of Mandi, who will, I think, reply to my diplomatic communication this evening. His capital is fifteen leagues away and it is there I have had to send Ranjit and Wade's firmans, besides the one which I have had the impudence to write him on my own account. Only fourteen leagues from here is Bilaspur. Having learnt of my approach – by what means I do not know – the Rajah of Bilaspur sent me an officer of his wretched little court with twenty soldiers. His vizier will receive me six leagues from his capital, on this side of the Sutlej; so that if I fail at Mandi, which would be most regrettable from the geological point of view, I shall at least have a good line of retreat straight towards Bilaspur. I confess that I shall be glad to cross the Sutlej again. Not that I should not be willing and ready to begin this year's campaign all over again, even with my present knowledge of the certain difficulties and possible dangers of travel on this side of the river. But if one of my friends wished to repeat it, I confess that at times I should feel some anxiety until he returned to the bosom of the English possessions. Is this courage or presumption on my part? I do not know; but I think I can distinguish a touch of superstition in my sense of security. I have confidence in my own adroitness in getting out of a tight place, and trust my good star not to lead me into many very bad ones; but I should not have the same confidence in the luck and presence of mind of another person of whom I was fond. After all, what I have just done (for all danger is over now) only one man has attempted before, M. Moorcroft; and he never came back – some say as the result of fever, others of poison. But I learnt for certain in Kashmir that he died miserably of sabre and gunshot wounds, together with one of his companions.

I have certainly exhausted all my chances of Indian adventure in the Punjab and the hills, and I am glad of it. For one who is travelling light, adventures may be a most interesting distraction; but for a poor devil in my profession, who has plenty of work to do, they are a most inconvenient accessory.

I feel a most pleasing sense of satisfaction as I look back upon the ground I have already covered with so much success and good fortune. I have fulfilled half my task, and that the one presenting most difficulties in the shape of human obstacles. With the exception of the first summer, which I spent in the steam-bath of Calcutta, I have had no cause for anything but pleasant surprise at the climate of the places where I have dwelt since, thanks to travelling in the plains during the winter and the hills during the summer. From this point onwards this will no longer be the case. I shall have to be prepared to sweat frightfully during the coming summer in Bombay, after which, as I approach Cape Comorin, the winter will hardly be perceptible. But I feel that my constitution has grown tougher in the Himalayas and will only droop gradually under the enervating influence of the damp heat of Malabar. I shall be prudent. I shall buy twenty francs worth of shade a month in the shape of a very large parasol, which I shall have made for me in Delhi and which will be held over my head constantly by a servant walking or running beside my horse. I shall buy another big double tent, so that I always find one of that sort ready pitched every day when I dismount. And if I am still sweltering, in order to refresh myself mentally, at least, I shall think of the scenes of ice and snow on the lofty summits of the Himalayas. Adieu.

* * *

Claude Levi-Strauss (1908–)

'The Kyong'

In September 1950, I happened to find myself in a Mogh village in the Chittagong hill tracts; for several days I had been watching the women take food every morning to the priests in the temple; during the siesta period, I could hear the beating of the gong which regulated the rhythm of the prayers and childish voices intoning the

Burmese alphabet. The *kyong* stood just outside the village at the top of a little wooded hillock like those that Tibetan painters love to depict in the backgrounds of their pictures. At the foot of the hill was the *jédi*, that is the pagoda: in such a poor village it was no more than a circular, earth construction, rising in seven concentric tiers, and set in a square enclosure surrounded by bamboo fencing. We had taken off our shoes to climb the hillock, and the fine, damp clay felt soft under our bare feet. On either side of the slope, we could see pineapple plants which had been torn out the day before by the villagers, who were shocked that their priests should take the liberty of growing fruit when their needs were provided for by the lay population. The top of the hill had the appearance of a little square, surrounded on three sides by open-sided straw shelters containing enormous bamboo objects, covered with multicoloured paper-like kites, and which were used as decorations for processions. On the fourth side stood the temple, which was built on stilts, like the village huts to which it was very similar, except that it was bigger and had a square-shaped structure with a thatched roof rising above the principal building. After the climb through the mud, the prescribed ablutions seemed quite natural and devoid of any religious significance. We went into the temple. The only light, apart from the rays filtering in through the thatch walls, came from the lantern formed by the central structure just above the altar, which was hung with standards made of rags or rush-matting. Fifty or so brass statuettes were piled up on the altar, at the side of which hung a gong: on the walls were a few pious coloured lithographs and a stag's skull. The floor, which was made of thick bamboo canes split lengthwise and plaited, had been polished by the constant rubbing of bare feet and was springier than a carpet. A peaceful barn-like atmosphere pervaded the place and there was a smell of hay in the air. The simple and spacious room which was like a hollowed-out haystack, the courteous behaviour of the two priests standing next to their beds with straw-mattresses, the touching care with which they had brought together or made the instruments of worship – all these things helped to bring me closer than I had ever been before to my idea of what a shrine should be like. 'You need not do what I am doing,' my companion said to me as he prostrated himself on the ground four times before the altar, and I followed his advice. However, I did so less through self-consciousness than discretion: he knew that I did not share his beliefs, and I would have been afraid of debasing the ritual gestures by letting him think I considered them as mere conventions: but, for once, I would have felt no embarrassment in performing them. Between this form of religion and myself, there was no likelihood of misunderstanding. It was not a question of bowing down in front of idols or of adoring a supposed supernatural order, but only of paying homage to the decisive wisdom that a thinker, or the society which created his legend, had evolved twenty-five centuries before and to which my civilization could contribute only by confirming it.

What else, indeed, have I learned from the masters who taught me, the philosophers I have read, the societies I have visited and even from that science which is the pride of the West, apart from a few scraps of wisdom which, when laid end to end, coincide with the meditation of the Sage at the foot of the tree? Every effort to understand destroys the object studied in favour of another object of a different nature; this second object requires from us a new effort which destroys it in favour of a third, and so on and so forth until we reach the one lasting presence, the point at which the distinction between meaning and the absence of meaning disappears: the same point from which we began. It is 2,500 years since men first discovered and formulated these truths. In the interval, we have found nothing new, except – as we have tried in turn all possible ways out of the dilemma – so many additional proofs of the conclusion that we would have liked to avoid.

This is not to say that I am not also aware of the dangers of overhasty resignation. This great religion of non-knowledge is not based on our inability to understand. It bears witness to that ability and raises us to a pitch at which we can discover the truth in the form of a mutual exclusiveness of being and knowledge. Through an additional act of boldness it reduces the metaphysical problem to one of human behaviour – a distinction it shares only with Marxism. Its schism occurred on the sociological level, the fundamental difference between the Great and the Little Ways being the question of whether the salvation of a single individual depends, or does not depend, on the salvation of humanity as a whole.

However, the historical solutions offered by Buddhist morality face us with two chilling alternatives: anyone who gives an affirmative reply to the question shuts himself up in a monastery: anyone who replies in the negative can achieve easy satisfaction in the practice of egotistical virtue.

Yet injustice, poverty and suffering exist; they supply a mediatory term between the two alternatives. We are not alone, and it does not depend on us whether we remain deaf and blind to mankind, or believe exclusively in the humanity within ourselves. Buddhism can remain coherent while agreeing to respond to appeals from outside. It may even be that, over a vast area of the world, it has found the link that was missing from the chain. If the last phase of the dialectic leading to illumination is legitimate, then all the others which preceded and resembled it are legitimate too. The complete denial of meaning is the end point in a succession of stages each one of which leads from a lesser to a greater meaning. The final step, which cannot be achieved without the others, validates them all retroactively. In its own way and on its own level, each one corresponds to a truth. Between the Marxist critique, which frees man from his initial bondage – by teaching him that the apparent meaning of his condition evaporates as soon as he agrees to see things in a wider context – and the Buddhist critique which completes his liberation, there is neither opposition nor contradiction. Each is doing the same thing as the other, but on a different level. The transition from one extreme to the other is guaranteed by all the advances in knowledge that man has accomplished in the last two thousand years, thanks to an unbroken movement of thought going from East to West, and then from West to East – perhaps for no other reason than to confirm its origin. As beliefs and superstitions dissolve when one thinks in terms of the real relationships between men, ethics gives way to history, fluid forms are replaced by structures and creation by nothingness. It is enough to fold the initial process back upon itself to discover its symmetry; its parts are superimposable one upon the other: the completed stages do not destroy the validity of those that went before; they confirm it.

As he moves about within his mental and historical framework, man takes along with him all the positions he has already occupied, and all those he will occupy. He is everywhere at one and the same time; he is a crowd surging forward abreast, and constantly recapitulating the whole series of previous stages. For we live in several worlds, each truer than the one it encloses, and itself false in relation to the one which encompasses it. Some are known to us through action; some are lived through in thought; but the seeming contradiction resulting from their coexistence is solved in the obligation we feel to grant a meaning to the nearest and to deny any to those furthest away; whereas the truth lies in a progressive dilating of the meaning, but in reverse order, up to the point at which it explodes.

This being so, as an anthropologist, I am no longer the only one to suffer from a contradiction affecting humanity as a whole and containing its own inherent cause. The contradiction remains only when I isolate the extremes: what is the use of action, if the thought guiding it leads to the discovery of the absence of meaning? But this discovery is not immediately accessible: I have to arrive at it by thought, and I cannot do so in one go. Whether there are twelve stages, as in the Boddhi, or whether they are more or less numerous, they all exist together, and in order to reach this conclusion, I am constantly called upon to live through situations each one of which demands something of me: I have a duty to men, just as I have a duty to knowledge. History, politics, the economic and social world, the physical world and even the sky surround me with concentric circles, from which I cannot escape in thought without ceding a fragment of my person to each one of them. Like a pebble striking water and making rings on the surface as it cuts through, in order to reach the bottom I too must take the plunge.

The world began without man and will end without him. The institutions, morals and customs that I shall have spent my life noting down and trying to understand are the transient efflorescence of a creation in relation to which they have no meaning, except perhaps that of allowing mankind to play its part in creation. But far from this part according man an independent position, or his endeavours – even if doomed to failure – being opposed to universal decline, he himself appears as perhaps the most effective agent working towards the disintegration of the original order of things and hurrying on powerfully organized matter towards ever greater inertia, an inertia which one day will be final. From the time when he first began to breathe and eat, up to the invention of atomic and thermonuclear devices, by way of the discovery of fire – and except when he has been engaged in self-reproduction – what else has man done except blithely break down billions of structures and reduce them to a state in which they are no longer capable of integration? No doubt he has built towns and cultivated the land; yet, on reflection, urbanization and agriculture are themselves instruments intended to create inertia, at a rate and in a proportion infinitely higher than the amount of organization they involve. As for the creations of the human mind, their significance only exists in relation to it, and they will merge into the general chaos, as soon as the human mind has disappeared. Thus it is that civilization, taken as a whole, can be described as an extraordinarily complex mechanism, which we might be tempted to see as offering an opportunity of survival for the human world, if its function were not to produce what physicists call entropy, that is inertia. Every verbal exchange, every line printed, establishes communication between people, thus creating an evenness of level, where before there was an information gap and consequently a greater degree of organization. Anthropology could with advantage be changed into 'entropology', as the name of the discipline concerned with the study of the highest manifestations of this process of disintegration.

Yet I exist. Not, of course, as an individual, since in this respect, I am merely the stake – a stake perpetually at risk – in the struggle between another society, made up of several thousand million nerve cells lodged in the ant-hill of my skull, and my body, which serves as its robot. Neither psychology nor metaphysics nor art can provide me with a refuge. They are myths, now open to internal investigation by a new kind of sociology which will emerge one day and will deal no more gently with them than traditional sociology does. The self is not only hateful: there is no place for it between *us* and *nothing*. And if, in the last resort, I opt for *us*, even though it is no more than a semblance, the reason is that, unless I destroy myself – an act which would obliterate the conditions of the option – I have only one possible choice between this semblance and nothing. I only have to choose for the choice itself to signify my unreserved acceptance of the human condition; in thus freeing myself from an intellectual pride, the futility of which I can gauge by the futility of its object, I also agree to subordinate its claims to the objective demands of the emancipation of the many, to whom the possibility of such a choice is still denied.

Just as the individual is not alone in the group, nor any one society alone among the others, so man is not alone in the universe. When the spectrum or rainbow of human cultures has finally sunk into the void created by our frenzy; as long as we continue to exist and there is a world, that tenuous arch linking us to the inaccessible will still remain, to show us the opposite course to that leading to enslavement; man may be unable to follow it, but its contemplation affords him the only privilege of which he can make himself worthy;

that of arresting the process, of controlling the impulse which forces him to block up the cracks in the wall of necessity one by one and to complete his work at the same time as he shuts himself up within his prison; this is a privilege coveted by every society, whatever its beliefs, its political system or its level of civilization; a privilege to which it attaches its leisure, its pleasure, its peace of mind and its freedom; the possibility, vital for life, of *unhitching*, which consists – Oh! fond farewell to savages and explorations! – in grasping, during the brief intervals in which our species can bring itself to interrupt its hive-like activity, the essence of what it was and continues to be, below the threshold of thought and over and above society: in the contemplation of a mineral more beautiful than all our creations; in the scent that can be smelt at the heart of a lily and is more imbued with learning than all our books; or in the brief glance, heavy with patience, serenity and mutual forgiveness, that through some involuntary understanding, one can sometimes exchange with a cat.

EPILOGUE

NASA

STS-84

Report #01

Thursday, May 15, 1997, 5 a.m. CDT

The Space Shuttle Atlantis lifted off precisely on schedule at 3:08 a.m. CDT today after a smooth and uneventful countdown. The ascent phase was completely normal, as were the early phases of on-orbit operations. Forty-five minutes after launch, the vehicle's Orbital Maneuvering System engines were fired to circularize Atlantis' orbit at 185 statute miles. Payload bay door opening followed shortly thereafter.

At the time of launch, the Russian space station, Mir, was approximately 11,500 miles west of Australia. It was approximately one hour after launch that the Russian control center was able to advise the Mir crew of the successful launch of Atlantis. Jerry Linenger, the U.S. astronaut member of the Mir crew, responded to the news with the exclamation, 'That's great!'

NASA Johnson Space Center Mission Status Reports and other information are available automatically by sending an Internet electronic mail message to jscnews-request@listserver.jsc.nasa.gov. In the body of the message (not the subject line) users should type 'subscribe' or 'unsubscribe' (no quotes). This will add or remove the email address that sent the subscribe message to the news release distribution list. The system will reply with a confirmation via email of each subscription. Once you have subscribed you will receive future news releases via email.

Permissions Acknowledgements

Robyn Davidson and Picador wish to thank the following for permission to use copyright material:

Edmund Wilson – 'Notes on London at the End of the War' from *Europe Without Baedeker* by Edmund Wilson, © 1966 Edmund Wilson. Renewed © 1994 by Helen Miranda Wilson. Reprinted by permission of Farrar, Straus and Giroux LLC.

Heinrich Heine – 'London'; excerpt from *Poetry of Heinrich Heine*, selected and edited with an introduction by Frederic Ewe. © 1969 Citadel Press, an imprint of Kensington Publishing Corp. All rights reserved. Reprinted by arrangement with Citadel Press and Kensington Publishing Corp.

Walter Benjamin – 'Marseilles', excerpt from *Denkbilder Gesamelte Schriften Vol IV* I pp. 359–364. © Suhrkamp Verlag Frankfurt am Main 1972 and Harvard Univ Press.

Elizabeth David – Introduction to *Mediterranean Food*. Reprinted with the kind permission of Jill Norman.

John Cowper Powys – from *Autobiography* published by John Lane, Bodley Head. Reprinted with permission of Sinclair-Stevenson.

Hector Berlioz – from 'Memoirs', excerpt from *The Memoirs of Hector Berlioz* by Hector Berlioz, translated by Rachel and Eleanor Holmes. © 1932 by Alfred A. Knopf Inc and renewed 1960 by Vera Newman. Reprinted by permission of Alfred A. Knopf, a division of Random House Inc.

V. S. Pritchett – from *The Spanish Temper*. © V. S. Pritchett 1954. Reprinted by permission of Peters Fraser & Dunlop Group on behalf of the Estate of Sir Victor Sawdon Pritchett.

Ernest Hemingway – 'Bullfighting', excerpt from *Death in the Afternoon*

Bruce Chatwin – 'Nadezhda Mandelstam: A Visit', excerpt from *What Am I Doing Here?* by Bruce Chatwin, published by Jonathan Cape. Reprinted with permission of The Random House Group Limited.

Gontran de Poncins – *Kabloona: Among the Inuit*, translated by Lewis Galantiere © Graywolf Rediscovery Series.

Simone de Beauvoir – 'Harlem', excerpt from *America Day by Day* by Simone de Beauvoir. Reprinted by permission of Victor Gollancz Ltd.

Martin Luther King, Jr. – from 'A Letter from Birmingham Jail', excerpt from *Why We Can't Wait* by Martin Luther King, Jr. Reprinted with permission of Laurence Pollinger Limited and the Estate of Martin Luther King, Jr.

Tobias Wolff – from *This Boy's Life: A Memoir* © 1988 Bloomsbury Publishers Ltd.

John Cage – from *Silence*. © 1939, 1944, 1949, 1952, 1955, 1957, 1958, 1959, 1961 John Cage. Reprinted with permission of Wesleyan University Press.

Hunter S. Thompson – from *Fear and Loathing in Las Vegas* © 1971. Reprinted by permission of Flamingo, an imprint of HarperCollins Publishers.

Margaret Fountaine – from *Butterflies and Late Loves: The Further Travels and Adventures of a Victorian Lady*. © 1986 W. F. Cater.

Esteban Montejo – 'Life in the Forest' from *The Autobiography of a Runaway Slave* by Esteban Montejo as told to and edited by Miguel Barnet © 1968 Bodley Head.

Derek Walcott – 'The Antilles: Fragments of Epic Memory', © 1992 by The Nobel Foundation. Published by Farrar, Straus and Giroux, LLC. Reprinted by kind permission of the author.

Elizabeth Bishop – 'A Trip to Vigia', excerpt from *The Collected Prose* by Elizabeth Bishop. © 1984 by Alice Helen Methfessel. Reprinted by permission of Farrar, Straus and Giroux LLC.

Apsley Cherry-Garrard – from *The Worst Journey in the World*. Reprinted by kind permission of Angela Mathias.

Molly Nungarrayi – 'How We Fled When I Was A Girl', excerpt from

Warlpiri Women's Voices: Our Lives Our History compiled and edited by Petronella Vaarzon-Morel, published by IAD Press (1995).

Matsuo Basho – 'The Narrow Road to the Deep North', excerpt from *The Narrow Road to the Deep North and Other Travel Sketches* by Matsuo Basho, translated by Nobuyuki Yuasa (Penguin Classics, 1966). © Nobuyuki Yuasa 1966. Reprinted with permission of Penguin Books Limited.

Doris Lessing – 'The Bush', excerpt from *African Laughter* by Doris Lessing, published by HarperCollins Publishers. Reprinted with permission of the publishers.

Karen Blixen – 'The Ngong Farm', excerpt from *Out of Africa* by Karen Blixen (Isak Dinesen). © 1937 Reprinted by kind permission of Jonathan Cape, an imprint of Randon House UK Ltd.

Elias Canetti – 'The Unseen', excerpt from *The Voices of Marrakesh* by Elias Canetti, published by Marion Boyars Publishers Limited, London 1978. Reprinted with permission of the publishers.

Gustave Flaubert – 'Flaubert to Louis Bouilhet' from The Letters of Gustave Flaubert 1857–1880. Translation copyright © 1982 Francis Steegmuller. Reproduced by permission of Macmillan Publishers Ltd.

Tim Mackintosh-Smith – 'On Language', excerpt from *Yemen* by Tim Mackintosh-Smith, published by John Murray (Publishers) Limited. Reprinted with permission.

Wilfred Thesiger – from *Arabian Sands* © Wilfred Thesiger. Reprinted by permission of Curtis Brown on behalf of Wilfred Thesiger.

Joanna Greenfield – 'Hyena'. Taken from the *New Yorker*. Reprinted by kind permission of the author and of ICM Agency.

Mildred Cable and Francesca French – from *The Gobi Desert*, published by Hodder & Stoughton. Reprinted with permission of the publishers.

Gore Vidal – 'Mongolia!', excerpt from *Armageddon: Essays* by Gore Vidal, published by Andre Deutsch, 1987. © Gore Vidal 1987. Reprinted with permission of Curtis Brown on behalf of Gore Vidal.

Nyoshul Khenpo Rinpoche – 'Enlightened Vagabond', excerpt from *Natural Great Perfection: Dzogchen Teachings and Vajra Songs* by Nyoshul Khenpo and Lama Surya Das, published by Snow Lion Publications. Reprinted with permission of the publishers.

V. S. Naipaul – 'The Village of the Dubes', excerpt from *An Area of Darkness* by V. S. Naipaul (Penguin Books 1968). © V. S. Naipaul 1968. Reprinted with permission of Penguin Books Limited.

Pier Paolo Pasolini – from *Scent of India*. Translation © 1984, The Olive Press. Reprinted with permission of Impact Books (1998) Limited.

Pankaj Mishra – from *Butter Chicken in Ludhiana: Travels in Small Town India* by Pankaj Mishra, published by Penguin India 1995. Reprinted by permission of the author.

Claude Levi-Strauss – 'The Kyong', excerpt from *Tristes Tropiques* by Claude Levi-Strauss, published by Jonathan Cape. Reprinted with permission of The Random House Group Limited.

Every effort has been made to trace the copyright holders for this anthology but if any have been inadvertently overlooked the publishers will be pleased to make the necessary arrangement at the first opportunity.